# Malicious Cryptography

# Malicious Cryptography

## Exposing Cryptovirology

Adam Young

Moti Yung

**WILEY**

Wiley Publishing, Inc.

Executive Publisher: Robert Ipsen
Executive Editor: Carol A. Long
Developmental Editor: Eileen Bien Calabro
Editorial Manager: Kathryn A. Malm
Production Manager: Fred Bernardi

This book is printed on acid-free paper.

Published by Wiley Publishing, Inc., Indianapolis, Indiana
Published simultaneously in Canada

For general information on our other products and services please contact our Customer Care Department within the United States at (800) 762-2974, outside the United States at (317) 572-3993 or fax (317) 572-4002.

Wiley also publishes its books in a variety of electronic formats. Some content that appears in print may not be available in electronic books.

ISBN: 0-7645-4975-8

Printed in the United States of America

10 9 8 7 6 5 4 3 2 1

*Dedicated to Elisa (A. Y.)*
*and to Maya (M. Y.)*

# Contents

Foreword                                                                   xiii

Acknowledgments                                                             xix

Introduction                                                               xxi

1  Through Hacker's Eyes                                                      1

2  Cryptovirology                                                           33

3  Tools for Security and Insecurity                                        51
   3.1  Sources of Entropy . . . . . . . . . . . . . . . . . . . . .        53
   3.2  Entropy Extraction via Hashing . . . . . . . . . . . . . .          54
   3.3  Unbiasing a Biased Coin . . . . . . . . . . . . . . . . . .         57
        3.3.1  Von Neumann's Coin Flipping Algorithm . . . . .             57
        3.3.2  Iterating Neumann's Algorithm . . . . . . . . . .           59
        3.3.3  Heuristic Bias Matching . . . . . . . . . . . . . .         60
   3.4  Combining Weak Sources of Entropy . . . . . . . . . . .            62
   3.5  Pseudorandom Number Generators . . . . . . . . . . . . .           66
        3.5.1  Heuristic Pseudorandom Number Generation . . . .            66
        3.5.2  PRNGs Based on Reduction Arguments . . . . . .              67
   3.6  Uniform Sampling . . . . . . . . . . . . . . . . . . . . . .        68
   3.7  Random Permutation Generation . . . . . . . . . . . . . .          71
        3.7.1  Shuffling Cards by Repeated Sampling . . . . . . .          71
        3.7.2  Shuffling Cards Using Trotter-Johnson . . . . . . .         73
   3.8  Sound Approach to Random Number Generation and Use                 76
   3.9  RNGs Are the Beating Heart of System Security . . . . . .          77
   3.10 Cryptovirology Benefits from General Advances . . . . . .          78
        3.10.1  Strong Crypto Yields Strong Cryptoviruses . . . . .        78
        3.10.2  Mix Networks and Cryptovirus Extortion . . . . . .         80

    3.11  Anonymizing Program Propagation . . . . . . . .  85

**4  The Two Faces of Anonymity**                                           **89**
    4.1  Anonymity in a Digital Age . . . . . . . . . . . . . .  89
        4.1.1  From Free Elections to the Unabomber . . . . . . .  90
        4.1.2  Electronic Money and Anonymous Payments . . . .  90
        4.1.3  Anonymous Assassination Lotteries . . . . . . . . .  92
        4.1.4  Kidnapping and Perfect Crimes . . . . . . . . . .  93
        4.1.5  Conducting Criminal Operations with Mixes . . . .  94
    4.2  Deniable Password Snatching . . . . . . . . . . . . .  97
        4.2.1  Password Snatching and Security by Obscurity . . .  97
        4.2.2  Solving the Problem Using Cryptovirology . . . .  98
        4.2.3  Zero-Knowledge Proofs to the Rescue . . . . . . .  100
        4.2.4  Improving the Attack Using ElGamal . . . . . . .  101

**5  Cryptocounters**                                                       **103**
    5.1  Overview of Cryptocounters . . . . . . . . . . . . .  104
    5.2  Implementing Cryptocounters . . . . . . . . . . . .  105
        5.2.1  A Simple Counter Based on ElGamal . . . . . . .  105
        5.2.2  Drawback to the ElGamal Solution . . . . . . .  106
        5.2.3  Cryptocounter Based on Squaring . . . . . . . .  107
        5.2.4  The Paillier Encryption Algorithm . . . . . . . .  108
        5.2.5  A Simple Counter Based on Paillier . . . . . . . .  111
    5.3  Other Approaches to Cryptocounters . . . . . . . . . .  111

**6  Computationally Secure Information Stealing**                          **113**
    6.1  Using Viruses to Steal Information . . . . . . . . . . .  114
    6.2  Private Information Retrieval . . . . . . . . . . . . .  115
        6.2.1  PIR Based on the Phi-Hiding Problem . . . . . . .  117
        6.2.2  Security of the Phi-Hiding PIR . . . . . . . . . .  120
        6.2.3  Application of the Phi-Hiding Technique . . . . . .  122
    6.3  A Variant of the Phi-Hiding Scheme . . . . . . . . . .  122
    6.4  Tagged Private Information Retrieval . . . . . . . . . .  126
    6.5  Secure Information Stealing Malware . . . . . . . . . .  131
    6.6  Deniable Password Snatching Based on Phi-Hiding . . . .  132
        6.6.1  Improved Password-Snatching Algorithm . . . . . .  133
        6.6.2  Questionable Encryptions . . . . . . . . . . . .  134
        6.6.3  Deniable Encryptions . . . . . . . . . . . . . . .  139
    6.7  Malware Loaders . . . . . . . . . . . . . . . . . .  140
    6.8  Cryptographic Computing . . . . . . . . . . . . . .  141

**7   Non-Zero Sum Games and Survivable Malware            147**
   7.1   Survivable Malware . . . . . . . . . . . . . . . . . . . .   148
   7.2   Elements of Game Theory . . . . . . . . . . . . . . .   150
   7.3   Attacking a Brokerage Firm . . . . . . . . . . . . . .   151
      7.3.1   Assumptions for the Attack . . . . . . . . .   152
      7.3.2   The Distributed Cryptoviral Attack . . . . . . .   153
      7.3.3   Security of the Attack . . . . . . . . . . . .   158
      7.3.4   Utility of the Attack . . . . . . . . . . . . .   159
   7.4   Other Two-Player Game Attacks . . . . . . . . . . .   161
      7.4.1   Key Search via Facehuggers . . . . . . . . .   161
      7.4.2   Catalyzing Conflict Among Hosts . . . . . .   167
   7.5   Future Possibilities . . . . . . . . . . . . . . . . . .   167

**8   Coping with Malicious Software                        171**
   8.1   Undecidability of Virus Detection . . . . . . . . . .   171
   8.2   Virus Identification and Obfuscation  . . . . . . . . .   172
      8.2.1   Virus String Matching . . . . . . . . . . . .   173
      8.2.2   Polymorphic Viruses . . . . . . . . . . . . .   176
   8.3   Heuristic Virus Detection . . . . . . . . . . . . . . .   182
      8.3.1   Detecting Code Abnormalities . . . . . . . .   182
      8.3.2   Detecting Abnormal Program Behavior . . . . . .   183
      8.3.3   Detecting Cryptographic Code . . . . . . . . .   191
   8.4   Change Detection . . . . . . . . . . . . . . . . . . .   197
      8.4.1   Integrity Self-Checks . . . . . . . . . . . .   197
      8.4.2   Program Inoculation . . . . . . . . . . . . .   198
      8.4.3   Kernel Based Signature Verification . . . . . . .   199

**9   The Nature of Trojan Horses                           201**
   9.1   Text Editor Trojan Horse  . . . . . . . . . . . . . .   202
   9.2   Salami Slicing Attacks . . . . . . . . . . . . . . . .   202
   9.3   Thompson's Password Snatcher . . . . . . . . . . . .   203
   9.4   The Subtle Nature of Trojan Horses . . . . . . . . . .   206
      9.4.1   Bugs May In Fact Be Trojans . . . . . . . .   208
      9.4.2   RNG Biasing Trojan Horse . . . . . . . . . .   208

**10  Subliminal Channels                                   211**
   10.1  Brief History of Subliminal Channels . . . . . . . . .   212
   10.2  The Difference Between a Subliminal and a Covert Channel  214
   10.3  The Prisoner's Problem of Gustavus Simmons . . . . . . .   215
   10.4  Subliminal Channels New and Old  . . . . . . . . . .   216

    10.4.1  The Legendre Channel of Gus Simmons . . . . . . 217
    10.4.2  The Oracle Channel . . . . . . . . . . . . . . 220
    10.4.3  Subliminal Card Marking . . . . . . . . . . . 222
    10.4.4  The Newton Channel . . . . . . . . . . . . . . 223
    10.4.5  Subliminal Channel in Composites . . . . . . . 224
  10.5  The Impact of Subliminal Channels on Key Escrow . . . . 226

**11  SETUP Attack on Factoring Based Key Generation            229**
  11.1  Honest Composite Key Generation . . . . . . . . . . . . 231
  11.2  Weak Backdoor Attacks on Composite Key Generation . . 232
    11.2.1  Using a Fixed Prime . . . . . . . . . . . . . 233
    11.2.2  Using a Pseudorandom Function . . . . . . . . 234
    11.2.3  Using a Pseudorandom Generator . . . . . . . . 236
  11.3  Probabilistic Bias Removal Method . . . . . . . . . . . 239
  11.4  Secretly Embedded Trapdoors . . . . . . . . . . . . . . 241
  11.5  Key Generation SETUP Attack . . . . . . . . . . . . . 244
  11.6  Security of the SETUP Attack . . . . . . . . . . . . . . 249
    11.6.1  Indistinguishability of Outputs . . . . . . . . 249
    11.6.2  Confidentiality of Outputs . . . . . . . . . . . 252
  11.7  Detecting the Attack in Code Reviews . . . . . . . . . . 256
  11.8  Countering the SETUP Attack . . . . . . . . . . . . . . 259
  11.9  Thinking Outside the Box . . . . . . . . . . . . . . . . 261
  11.10 The Isaac Newton Institute Lecture . . . . . . . . . . . 262

**12  SETUP Attacks on Discrete-Log Cryptosystems              265**
  12.1  The Discrete-Log SETUP Primitive . . . . . . . . . . . 266
  12.2  Diffie-Hellman SETUP Attack . . . . . . . . . . . . . . 268
  12.3  Security of the Diffie-Hellman SETUP Attack . . . . . . 270
    12.3.1  Indistinguishability of Outputs . . . . . . . . 270
    12.3.2  Confidentiality of Outputs . . . . . . . . . . . 271
  12.4  Intuition Behind the Attack . . . . . . . . . . . . . . . 275
  12.5  Kleptogram Attack Methodology . . . . . . . . . . . . . 276
  12.6  PKCS SETUP Attacks . . . . . . . . . . . . . . . . . . 277
    12.6.1  ElGamal PKCS SETUP Attack . . . . . . . . . 277
    12.6.2  Cramer-Shoup PKCS SETUP Attack . . . . . . 279
  12.7  SETUP Attacks on Digital Signature Algorithms . . . . . 280
    12.7.1  SETUP in the ElGamal Signature Algorithm . . . . 281
    12.7.2  SETUP in the Pointcheval-Stern Algorithm . . . . 282
    12.7.3  SETUP in DSA . . . . . . . . . . . . . . . . . 283

       12.7.4  SETUP in the Schnorr Signature Algorithm . . . . 284
12.8  Rogue Use of DSA for Encryption . . . . . . . . . . . . 285
12.9  Other Work in Kleptography . . . . . . . . . . . . . . 286
12.10 Should You Trust Your Smart Card? . . . . . . . . . . 288

## Appendix A: Computer Virus Basics                                          295
A.1  Origins of Malicious Software . . . . . . . . . . . . 295
A.2  Trojans, Viruses, and Worms: What Is the Difference? . . 297
A.3  A Simple DOS COM Infector . . . . . . . . . . . . . . 299
A.4  Viruses Don't Have to Gain Control Before the Host . . . 303

## Appendix B: Notation and Other Background Information   307
B.1  Notation Used Throughout the Book . . . . . . . . . 307
B.2  Basic Facts from Number Theory and Algorithmics . . . . 309
B.3  Intractability: Malware's Biggest Ally . . . . . . . . . 312
       B.3.1  The Factoring Problem . . . . . . . . . . . . 313
       B.3.2  The $e^{th}$ Roots Problem . . . . . . . . . . . . 314
       B.3.3  The Composite Residuosity Problem . . . . . . . 314
       B.3.4  The Decision Composite Residuosity Problem . . . 315
       B.3.5  The Quadratic Residuosity Problem . . . . . . . 315
       B.3.6  The Phi-Hiding Problem . . . . . . . . . . . 315
       B.3.7  The Phi-Sampling Problem . . . . . . . . . . . 317
       B.3.8  The Discrete Logarithm Problem . . . . . . . . 318
       B.3.9  The Computational Diffie-Hellman Problem . . . . 318
       B.3.10 The Decision Diffie-Hellman Problem . . . . . . 318
B.4  Random Oracles and Functions . . . . . . . . . . . . 319

## Appendix C: Public Key Cryptography in a Nutshell        321
C.1  Overview of Cryptography . . . . . . . . . . . . . . 321
       C.1.1  Classical Cryptography . . . . . . . . . . . . 322
       C.1.2  The Diffie-Hellman Key Exchange . . . . . . . 324
       C.1.3  Public Key Cryptography . . . . . . . . . . . 325
       C.1.4  Attacks on Cryptosystems . . . . . . . . . . . 326
       C.1.5  The Rabin Encryption Algorithm . . . . . . . . 330
       C.1.6  The Rabin Signature Algorithm . . . . . . . . 331
       C.1.7  The RSA Encryption Algorithm . . . . . . . . 332
       C.1.8  The RSA Signature Algorithm . . . . . . . . . 334
       C.1.9  The Goldwasser-Micali Algorithm . . . . . . . 335
       C.1.10 Public Key Infrastructures . . . . . . . . . . . 336
C.2  Discrete-Log Based Cryptosystems . . . . . . . . . . 337

C.2.1  The ElGamal Encryption Algorithm . . . . . . . . 338
C.2.2  Security of ElGamal . . . . . . . . . . . . . . . . 338
C.2.3  The Cramer-Shoup Encryption Algorithm . . . . . 340
C.2.4  The ElGamal Signature Algorithm . . . . . . . . 342
C.2.5  The Pointcheval-Stern Signature Algorithm . . . . 343
C.2.6  The Schnorr Signature Algorithm . . . . . . . . . 344
C.2.7  The Digital Signature Algorithm (DSA) . . . . . . 345

Glossary                                                        347

References                                                      357

Index                                                           387

# Foreword

Terms such as cryptovirology, malware, kleptogram, or kleptography may be unfamiliar to the reader, but the basic concepts associated with them certainly are familiar. Everyone knows—often from sad experience—about viruses, Trojan horses, and worms and many have had a password "harvested" by a piece of software planted surreptitiously on their computer while browsing the Net. The realization that a public key could be placed in a virus so that part of its payload would be to perform a one-way operation on the host computer that could only be undone using the private key held by the virus' author was the discovery from which *Malicious Cryptography* sprang. Rather than describe these notions here, intriguing as they are, I'll only try to set the stage for the authors' lucid description of these and other related notions.

Superficially, information security, or information integrity, doesn't appear to be much different from other functions concerned with preserving the quality of information while in storage or during transmission. Error detecting and correcting codes, for example, are intended to ensure that the information that a receiver receives is the same as that sent by the transmitter. Authentication codes, or authentication in general, are also intended to ensure that information can neither be modified nor substituted without detection, thus allowing a receiver to be confident that what he receives is what was sent and that it came from the purported transmitter. These sound remarkably alike in function, but they are fundamentally different in ways that are at the heart of *Malicious Cryptography*. The greatest service this Foreword can render is to give the reader a crisp, clear understanding of the nature of this difference in order to set the stage for the book that follows.

Most system functions can be quantitatively specified and tested to verify that the specifications are met. If a piece of electronic equipment is supposed to operate within a specified range of a parameter (such as voltage, acceleration, temperature, shock, vibration, and so forth), then

it is a straightforward matter to devise tests to verify that it does. Closer
in spirit to information security and integrity than physical environmen-
tal specifications would be a specification of a communication system's
immunity to noise or bit errors. One might specify the minimum data
bandwidth for a given signal to noise (SN) ratio or the allowable bit error
rate. Again it is a straightforward matter to devise tests that verify the
data bandwidth or the bit error rate for a signal possessing the specified
signal to noise ratio. Error detecting and correcting codes may be tailored
to the expected statistical nature of the noise, Fire codes for burst errors
or Grey codes for an angular position reading device, etc. But the verification that the system is meeting specifications remains straightforward
and quantitative.

Security is fundamentally different from any other system parameter,
however. One of the largest alarm and vault manufacturers in the U.S.
discovered this in a costly example a few years ago. Vaults and safes
are routinely certified for the time documents will survive undamaged in
a fire—itself specified by temperature and type (oil, structural, electrical, etc.). They had developed a new composite material that was very
resistant to cutting, drilling, burning, etc. Extensive tests had been conducted with cutting tools of all sorts including oxyhydrogen burning bars,
drilling with mechanical drills and hypervelocity air-abrasive drills, etc.
Based on these results, they guaranteed their safes and vaults made of
the new material would provide a specified minimum time for penetra-
tion. What they had overlooked was that linear cutting charges (shaped
charges) that were widely used in the oil industry for cutting oil well cas-
ings and in the demolition business for slicing building supports to bring
down buildings could be used to cut out a panel from the side of a safe
or vault in milliseconds instead of requiring hours. This long aside is very
germane to this Foreword. The safe and vault company had measured the
resistance of their product to the attacks they anticipated would be used
against them. The robbers used an entirely unexpected means to open the
vault—and the company paid dearly for their oversight. *Malicious Cryptography* is almost entirely about doing things in completely unexpected
ways in information integrity protocols.

Going back to the example with which we started, the fundamental
difference between error detecting and correcting codes and authentication, both of which function to ensure the integrity of information, is that
the first is pitted against nature and the other against a human adversary.
Nature may be hostile, the signal to noise ratio may be large, the signal

may drop out for extended periods of time, other signals may randomly mask the desired signal, but nature is neither intelligent nor adaptive. A human opponent is both. He may also be interactive, probing to gain information to allow him to refine and adapt his attacks. As those of us in the information security business like to say, there is no standard attacker and no standard attack. This is in contrast with all other specifications where standard environments, no matter how hostile or unpredictable, are the norm.

What the authors of *Malicious Cryptography* have done very successfully is to capture the essence of how security can be subverted in this non-standard environment. On several occasions, they refer to game theory without actually invoking the formalism of game theory—emphasizing instead the game-like setting in which security is the value of the ongoing competition between a system designer and its attackers.

There have been many books on hacking, software subversion, network security, etc., which consist mainly of descriptions of successful attacks— some exceedingly clever and many very devious in their execution. These are similar in style and feeling to Modern Chess Openings (MCO) that every chess player knows, studies, and on which he depends. There are of course many possible lines of play in chess, but the several hundred openings that have stood the test of time and repeated tournament play make up the MCO. Roughly the first twenty moves or so of these openings, with promising variations, have been so thoroughly analyzed and understood that it is rare indeed for an opening not in the MCO to be successful in match play. A similar situation is true for the end game—not that the endings are so cataloged and restricted, but rather that the game has simplified to where almost a counting-like analysis reveals the outcome to a knowledgeable player. Masters will resign a game as lost at a point where a less experienced player may not even be able to see who has the advantage. As most books on hacking recount one clever attack after another, MCO recounts one opening after another with an ! or !! in the annotation to flag a particularly brilliant move. I almost expect to find an exclamation mark in the margin of most books on software subversion when the deception on which a particular protocol failure turns is revealed.

The middle game in chess, though, must be guided by general principles since the number of lines of play—the attack, counter attack—between two masters is virtually unlimited. So it is with information security protocols and cryptosystems. The possibilities are virtually unlimited so general principles must guide both the system designer and the counter designer; the attacker seeking to exploit hidden weaknesses in the design; the designer seeking to prevent such attacks or failing that, to detect them when they occur. *Malicious Cryptography* pioneers in motivating and clearly enunciating some of these principles.

Cryptography, authentication, digital signatures, and indeed, virtually every digital information security function depend for their security on pieces of information known only to a select company of authorized insiders and unknown to outsiders. Following the usual convention in cryptography we will refer to this privileged information as the key although in many situations the only thing in common with the usual notion of a cryptographic key is that it is secret from all but a designated select few. It may well be that no individual knows the key but that a specified set of them have the joint capability to either recover it (shared secret schemes) or to jointly execute a function that in all probability no outsider or any proper subset of them can do (shared capability schemes). It is almost always the case that this secret piece of information is supposed to be chosen randomly—from a specified range of values and with a specified probability distribution, generally the uniform distribution. The assumption is that this insures that an unauthorized user will have no better chance of discerning the secret key than the probability the same key will be drawn in an independent drawing of a new value under the same conditions. It is also generally assumed that only the person choosing the random number knows it. In fact he may share it with someone else at the time it is drawn, or they may have chosen the number in advance of the supposed drawing. In the most extreme case it may be dictated by some other participant and not chosen by the person supposed to be choosing it all. Every one of these surreptitious variants has been the basis for serious subversions of information integrity and security protocols. One of the central themes in *Malicious Cryptography* is the mischief that is possible if these conditions are not met; in other words, if the "random" value is not random in the sense supposed.

Since security or integrity is directly measured by the probability the secret key can be discovered (computed) by unauthorized cabals of attackers, the information content of the key (roughly speaking, the size of the random number) must be great enough that it is computationally infeasible to simply try all possible values—known as a brute force key space search. But this means that it is then computationally infeasible for a monitor to tell whether the random values produced were actually randomly chosen as supposed or not. This is at the heart of subliminal channels, for example. The subliminal transmitter and receiver share in secret information about the bias imposed on the selection of the session keys which enables them to communicate covertly in the overt communications while it remains computationally infeasible (impossible?) for a monitor to detect a bias in the session key selection process, and hence impossible for him to detect either the presence or use of a subliminal channel.

The dilemma is that if the key is large enough to be secure, it is also large enough to make it impossible to detect a bias in the selection process. It therefore becomes possible to hide information in the keys, to communicate other keys subliminally, to make it computationally feasible for designated receivers to perform a key space search while a full search remains computationally infeasible for outsiders to do, to subvert information integrity protocols from within, etc. The list of possible deceptions is virtually unlimited and the authors of *Malicious Cryptography* have exploited many of these in innovative ways.

In information integrity protocols nothing can be taken for granted, i.e., nothing can be assumed that cannot be enforced. If the protocol calls for a number to be chosen from a specified range using a particular probability distribution, then the assumption must be that it isn't unless the other parties to the protocol can force it to be in a secondary protocol. Otherwise you must assume it could be chosen from a restricted range or chosen using a different probability distribution, or that it was chosen earlier and shared with persons assumed not to know it, or that it isn't being selected at random at all by the person supposed to be choosing it, or that it is dictated to him by another party not even considered in the protocol. Several of the subversions described in *Malicious Cryptography* depend on this ability to undetectably hide information in keys. The point germane to this Foreword, though, is that it is the general principle that is vital for both the designer and the counter-designer to keep in mind. There are interactive protocols to insure that the objectives of randomness are met. Those protocols are not the subject of *Malicious Cryptography*, but made all the more important because of the weaknesses exposed in it.

There are other examples, though, in which no means is known to enforce the desired outcome. Several protocols call for a public modulus to be the product of two secret primes chosen so as to make it computationally infeasible to factor the modulus—usually only a function of the size of the factors although in some protocols the factors must satisfy some number theoretic side condition such as belonging to a particular residue class, etc. It is possible to work a variety of mischiefs if a modulus that is the product of more than two prime factors can be passed off as the product of only two. In particular, a subliminal channel becomes possible with the desirable feature that while the subliminal receiver can receive subliminal messages sent by the transmitter he cannot falsely attribute a forged message to the transmitter. It is only polynomially difficult to distinguish between primes and composite numbers. But so far as is known it is just as hard to tell if a composite number has three or more factors as it is to factor the number itself! In the absence of an interactive protocol to ensure that a modulus has two and only two prime factors, deceptions that depend on the existence of three or more factors remain a possibility. Deceptions of this sort do not appear in *Malicious Cryptography* and are mentioned here only to illustrate that not all general principles for deception have solutions available to the designer at the moment.

*Malicious Cryptography* is a remarkable book; remarkable for what it attempts and remarkable for what it achieves. The realization that cryptography can be exploited to achieve malicious ends as easily as it can to achieve beneficial ones is a novel and valuable insight—to both designers and counter-designers of information security and integrity protocols.


Gus Simmons

September, 2003

# Acknowledgments

We have so many people to thank that it is difficult to figure out where to begin. It has been said that ideas cannot be created in a vacuum and in this we believe wholeheartedly. *Malicious Cryptography* is the product of interactions and collaborations that span over a decade. In truth we have family, friends, teachers, coworkers, researchers, students, anonymous referees, journalists,[1] science-fiction authors, movie writers, artists, and musicians[2] to acknowledge. Without such support, enthusiasm, artistic creativity, teachers, and listeners, this book would not have been possible.

First and foremost we thank Columbia University, our mutual alma mater. It was at Columbia that our research began, and it was at Columbia where we met a great number of brilliant people from whom we learned, and with whom we worked and shared ideas. We thank Zvi Galil, Dean of the School of Engineering and Applied Science, who served as faculty advisor to us both. We thank Jonathan Gross and Andrew Kosoresow, both of whom served on Adam's PhD committee. Andrew was a great and dedicated educator, and we mourn his untimely passing. We thank Matt Franklin and Stuart Haber, both of whom graduated from Columbia. Matt and Stuart have served as collaborators to us both as well as lecturers in graduate courses taken by Adam. On numerous occasions Adam flew into Matt Franklin's office, wide-eyed and somewhat insane looking, for the sole purpose of scrawling a brand new attack on his blackboard just to see how he would react. Adam also thanks Matt Blaze for teaching an inspiring course on computer security in 1995 and for fostering great interest in cryptography among his students. Moti extends his gratitude to

---

[1] John Markoff, Steven Levy, Katie Hafner, and Bruce Sterling among others.

[2] Adam thanks Nine-Inch-Nails, Sonic Mayhem, White Zombie, Looking Glass Studios (System Shock 2 Soundtrack), Devo, and Danzig for setting the mood for the beginning of the book.

all of his coauthors and everyone he has worked with over the years, since it is through scientific work and the exchange of ideas that one develops as a researcher.

We thank Markus Jakobsson from RSA Data Security. Moti mentored Markus throughout his dissertation defense preparation and Markus in turn served on Adam's PhD committee. Markus reviewed this text and has sponsored annual lectures on Cryptovirology at NYU. We thank Yiannis Tsiounis, another student that Moti assisted, for sharing ideas and for reviewing this book. We thank our colleague Yair Frankel for sponsoring an invited lecture on kleptography for the Information Surety Group at Sandia National Labs. We thank Michael Reiter for supporting Adam while at Lucent Technologies in the Secure Systems Research Division, and for hosting a lecture on subliminal channels and kleptography.

Adam thanks Matthew Hastings from Los Alamos National Laboratory. Over the course of four years at Yale, Matt and Adam jointly experimented with self-replicating code in a safe and controlled environment. Many of the discoveries and open problems that were found gave impetus to investigating advanced malicious software attacks. Adam also thanks Mark Reed from the Yale University Department of Electrical Engineering. Mark served as Adam's undergraduate faculty advisor and provided support for his career both inside and outside of the classroom.

Adam thanks Cigital Labs and in particular Jeff Voas, Jeff Payne, Gary McGraw, and Matt Schmid for encouraging this work. We thank Christoph C. Michael, senior research scientist at Cigital Labs, for engaging conversations, contributing artwork, and for lending an ear to a never-ending stream of clandestine malware rhetoric. We also thank Alexander Antonov and Paul DesRivières from the Cigital Secure Software Group for reviewing the manuscript line by line and Mike Copenhafer, Bruce Potter, Mike Firetti, Viren Shah, Frank Hill, Coleman Baker, and Chris Ren from Cigital for helpful reviews and discussions.

From Wiley we thank Carol Long,[3] Eileen Calabro, Fred Bernardi, Robert Ipsen, and Kathryn Malm. Carol and her team produced this book in remarkably short order with the utmost degree of professionalism.

Special thanks goes to Dmitriy Pozdnyakov, Michael Makarius, Leo C. Petroski, and H. Robert Feinberg for helpful feedback and overall support of this work. Finally Adam would like to thank his wife, Elisa Young, for being. Without her this book would cease to have meaning.

---

[3]Or *cryptolady*, as she is known at Wiley.

# Introduction

This book is a compendium of malicious software and hardware attacks geared towards subverting computer systems. The attacks are not of the sort that exploit software bugs, design flaws, and so forth. The business of bypassing security measures is outside the scope of this work. Rather, we present a series of cryptographic methods for defiling computer systems once internal access is acquired.

Some of the attacks are more technical than others, involving recent advances in the field of cryptology. As a result this book is likely to be received in a variety of different ways. To hackers it may serve as a vade mecum. To security professionals it may serve as a long overdue warning. To science fiction buffs it may serve as a good read, and to intelligence agencies it may serve as a challenge to our First Amendment rights.

Chapter 1 is a motivational chapter that portrays the world through the eyes of a hacker. It reveals the very fabric of a hacker's existence and due to its illicit nature we mention the standard disclaimer that reads, "do not try this at home." To perform any of the acts described therein is to risk violating the Computer Fraud and Abuse Act of 1986, among others. Hackers face *scientific* problems when trying to infiltrate computer systems. It was by experiencing these problems first hand that many of these attacks were discovered.

A great number of people share a close kinship with our digital brethren and to hackers it is no different. But whereas to writers it is through text, to artists it is through images, and to musicians it is through music, to hackers it is through the very language that computers speak when speaking with each other, the language of *binary*. To speak in binary and hear every word they say is to be one with the machine and that feeling can be hopelessly and utterly addictive.

To the uncorrupt of spirit the need to join with the machine can be controlled to a degree. This need is illustrated in Chapter 1 over the course of three short stories. They are written in second person singular and as such force the reader to play the role of the subduer. It is the reader that steals passwords using a Trojan horse program. It is the reader that spends years developing an insidious computer virus, and it is the reader that takes over the local area network of a small company. Yet everywhere in the storyline the privacy and integrity of other people's data is respected. It portrays the pursuit of knowledge and the thrill of the hunt, not the kill.

As Lord Acton once said, "power corrupts; absolute power corrupts absolutely." This could not be truer with respect to hacking. For this reason we urge readers not to abuse the ideas presented in this book. If our efforts coax so much as a single hacker to embrace the greater mathematical challenges facing system security, then our writing will not have been for naught, for such a hacker is likely to seek recognition in the form of conference papers in lieu of news reports.

Given the clandestine nature of the algorithms and protocols that are presented, it is important to emphasize the nature of secure systems research. Cryptanalysis exists to help make cryptosystems more secure. *The goal of cryptanalysis is not to undo the honorable work of others, but to find vulnerabilities and fix them.* Many a cryptographer has suffered the disheartening realization that his or her cipher has been broken. Lucky are those who discover this themselves, but many are they who learn the hard way when another researcher publishes the discovery in an academic forum. Cryptanalysis is the mathematician's version of hacking: it is both devil's advocate and antithesis of cryptography. History has proven the need for cryptanalysis and hence the need to find weaknesses in cryptosystems and publish them. It may be reasoned that the need for cryptanalysis extends directly to the need to investigate attacks on modern computer systems. This, we argue, is the realm of cryptovirology and in this treatise we take a first step in this direction.

In the public eye, the word *cryptography* is virtually synonymous with *security*. It is a means to an end, a way to send e-mail privately and purchase items securely on-line. If nothing else this book will challenge that view. In the chapters that follow it is shown how modern cryptographic paradigms and tools including semantic security, reduction arguments, polynomial indistinguishability, random oracles, one-way functions, Feistel ciphers, entropy extractors, pseudorandom number generators, etc., can in fact be used to *degrade system security*.

It is shown how to devise a cryptovirus to usurp data from a host machine without revealing that which is sought, even if the virus is observed at every turn. It is shown how to design a password-snatching cryptotrojan that makes it virtually impossible to identify the author when the encrypted passwords are retrieved. Furthermore, it is intractable to determine if the cryptotrojan is encrypting anything at all even when it is under constant surveillance.

Still other cryptotrojans are described that attack industry-standard cryptosystems. By design, these Trojans give the attacker covert access to the private keys of users and are extremely robust against reverse engineering. When implemented in tamper-resistant devices these transgressions cannot be detected by anyone save the attacker. Such Trojans are ideal for governments that wish to obtain covert access to the encrypted communications of their citizens. These Trojans show how to apply cryptography within cryptography itself to undermine the very trust that cryptosystems were designed to provide. In so doing we will expose the dark side of cryptography and thereby reveal its true dual-edged nature.

Several of the attacks have known countermeasures, some of which are ideal and others that are merely heuristic in nature. These defenses are described in detail to give the book a more balanced presentation to the community at large. It is our belief that these malicious software attacks should be exposed so that security analysts will recognize them in the event that they appear in fielded computer systems. Doing so has the potential of minimizing the malicious software learning curve that practitioners might otherwise face.

In all likelihood the attacks that are described in this book constitute the tip of the iceberg in terms of what is possible. Offensive information warfare is an area of research that is scarcely funded by the U.S. government, for obvious reasons. However, the notion of malicious software as well as cryptography is by no means new to the federal government, and so one would expect that there has been more classified research in this area than unclassified research. This book is our earnest attempt to expose the open research in this area, since corporations, governments, and individuals have a right to know about that which threatens the integrity of their computing machinery.

Some readers will inevitably object to the nature of this book. To this end we remark that these attacks exist, they are real, and that it is perilous to sweep them under the rug. We believe that they will surface sooner or later. It is our hope that this book will encourage the study of cryptography as a whole and at the same time reveal some of the more serious threats that computer systems face, both *from within* and from without.

A. Y.

M. Y.

October, 2003

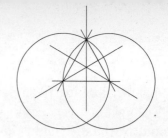

# Chapter 1

# Through Hacker's Eyes

There is no way to describe the feeling of approaching a computer system to download the data that your Trojan horse has been collecting for days. Your heart begins to race. You look over your shoulder out of instinct and start to have major second thoughts about proceeding. The computer terminal is unoccupied and sits directly in front of you.

Questions plague your thoughts: How many people are capable of finding the cleverly hidden Trojan? More importantly, does anyone *in this room* know it is there? You ease yourself down into the chair. Glancing to your right you see a student stare at his calculator with a perplexed look on his face. To your left a girl is laughing on her cell phone. If you could shrink yourself into nothing and crawl through the cracks in the machine you would gladly do so. But you are physical and there is nothing you can do about that now. The coast is clear. You reach for your floppy and insert it into the drive. Sheens of sweat glaze over your palms. Why? Because after all, you are returning to the scene of a crime.

*Your crime.*

Deep down, you rationalize your actions. There is no blood involved, no money is being stolen, and in the end no real harm is being done... or is there? The floppy drive begins to spin. In moments it will be over. In moments all of the login/password pairs will be on the disk and you will be hightailing it to your next class. Perspiration breaks out on your forehead but is easily dismissed with a waft of your hand. You navigate to the floppy drive and double-click on the game of Tetris. There is time for one quick game. The first block is 1 by 5, your favorite. If only they'd come down like that one after the other you'd have the game in the bag by laying them out horizontally. But it never works out that way. The law of probabilities won't allow it. A book hits the ground and you jump.

A lanky-looking freshman picks it up. The title—*Differential Equations: Theory and Applications*. Smart guy. Most students are only studying multivariable calculus in their first year. Words begin to echo in the back of your mind: *there has to be a better way, there has to be a better way....* An odd, misshapen block comes into view. You hate those. They make you lose Tetris every time. A whirring noise emanates from the drive and this time you know it is writing to the floppy. One more minute and your doctored up version of Tetris will have downloaded all of the passwords to the disk. Who'd ever guess this version of Tetris packed such a punch?

A four-sided cube comes down and you ease it over to the left-hand side of the screen. You love those shapes too. On the surface you are just playing a game. Your mouse button clicks and space bar presses are as innocuous as they come. But the real game you are playing is not so easy to see, and at times it feels like Russian roulette. Your thoughts wander to your password-snatching Trojan. The possibility that it was found and that silent sysadmin alarms are sounding *in a nearby room* is very, very real.

Something's wrong.

Something's not right; you can feel it in the air. The drive should have stopped spinning by now. Your heart goes still. Looking up, you catch a glimpse of a man you didn't notice before. He makes eye contact with you. Fighting the urge to flee, you quickly look back at your screen. You missed placing two blocks. You will not make high score. Your mind begins conjuring swear words without biblical precedent...it has *never* taken this long before.

The floppy drive finally stops whirring. You quit out of Tetris, eject the floppy, and reboot the machine. You leave the computer cluster and enter the hallway half expecting to be halted by university officials. But none are there. You think yourself silly. You think that there was no way it could have been found. But the reality is that you know all too well how to write a background process capable of catching you in the act and that is what makes you scared. Stepping outside the building, you breathe a sigh of relief in the midday sun. You made it this time, but maybe you were just lucky. Maybe it wasn't in the cards just yet. Like a junkie to drugs, you are drawn to these machines. They speak to you the way they speak to no one else. You put in your time. You paid your dues, and yet for some reason your vision is still shrouded in darkness. There is something they are not telling you. Perhaps it is something they don't even know. It is a question that nags at you like no other, and you sense that the answer lies hidden somewhere within the deepest recesses of your soul, somewhere out of sight and just beyond your grasp. *There has to be a better way.*

Shortly before sundown that same day...

The dull roar of thunder reverberates somewhere far off in the distance as menacing storm clouds roil in from the west. They exhibit all the signs of a true nor'easter and threaten to engulf the entire city of New Haven. You swear you just felt a drop of rain hit your left shoulder. Reaching down, you feel for the disk at your side. The floppy is still there, its presence reassured at the touch of a thumb. The data it contains is dear to you, and you'll be damned if you're gonna let a little $H_2O$ seep through your denim pocket and claim your catch of the day. So you decide to pick up the pace a bit.

The path you follow winds in and around, gently sloping downward as you go, eventually leading to a clearing that overlooks a stand of maples. The trees are enormous and have stood here for ages. At their center lies a lone apple tree. It is dwarfed by the older trees and is helplessly sheltered under a canopy of leaves. Having sensed your unexpected approach, a nearby squirrel dashes for the safety of a nearby tree. Before reaching the trunk, it fumbles over an apple and sends it rolling along the ground. The fruits around you give off a racy odor, a telltale reminder of the approaching change of season.

Had it not been for the disk, you would chance a brief pause underneath the eaves to contemplate greater things. Physics lectures always left you spellbound regarding the mysteries of the world. It was the dream of being struck in the head by a falling apple that guided you to this school in the first place, a dream that you summarily dismissed upon meeting your brilliant roommate. He is a National Merit scholar and received 1580 out of a possible 1600 on his SATs. The deduction was in the verbal section, and you always attributed it to his difficulty in comprehending the human condition. On many levels he is more machine than man, yet his inference engine is second to none. Physics is his second language and he speaks it fluently. You abandoned the idea of majoring in physics since the thought of taking the same classes as he was too much to bear, and since he had an uncanny ability to make you feel stupid without even trying. Answers to scientific problems just came *naturally* to him. Your hacking obsession combined with a thoroughly tenderized ego would do little to help you finish school.

A gust of wind billows through the trees. The limbs creak and sway in response, causing rain droplets to roll off their leaves. The water splashes onto your face and exposed arms, causing you to start. You realize that you had zoned out completely and had lost all track of time. Your eyes had stared off into space, fixated on some solitary trees, and subconsciously absorbed the surrounding scenery. You shrug in spite of yourself. No use in crying over spilled milk. Your true path has yet to be determined and there is no reason to worry about it now.

You shift the weight of your backpack to your other shoulder and leave the small wooded area behind. As always the students took Prospect Street back to Old Campus while you ventured along an overgrown yet shorter route, preferring to take the road less traveled. *Hypotenuse* action your roommate called it. Over time you discerned the shortest route between the Sloane Physics Lab and your dorm and it took you through more than one private yard, not to mention a vast cemetery. It saved you an innumerable number of backaches to be sure. Take aside any science student and you will hear the same tale of woe. The cumbersome textbooks are murderous to haul and the university couldn't place the science buildings at a more remote location if it tried.

The Payne Whitney Gymnasium looms ahead, shadowed by the black storm cover above. Were it not for the parked cars and street signs, the darkness could easily lead one to mistake it for a castle. Gulls from the nearby seashore circle above the parapets that line the rooftop. Some dive and soar, some pick up speed, and still others hover in place in blatant defiance of the wind. Nightfall descended prematurely on the city, and what had been just a few droplets of rain minutes before has turned into a veritable deluge. A small pack of students run through the stone archway at the base of the gym with newspapers outstretched overhead. The brunt of the storm is upon you and rainwater quickly seeps into every quarter. You break into a sprint down Tower Parkway in a last-ditch effort to keep your data dry.

The torrential rain pummels your body in sheets as you approach the backdoor of Morse College. You pass quietly into the building under cover of dusk and enter the underground labyrinth of steam tunnels and storage rooms. The humdrum of washers and dryers from a nearby laundry room fills your ears. You take a brief moment to wring what water you can from your clothing. After regaining your composure, you head down the narrow hallway and pass alongside the laundry room. It is empty and devoid of movement, save for a loose ball of lint circling beneath a ventilation shaft.

You continue along the corridor towards the small staircase at its end, leaving a puddle of water with each passing step. A steam release valve hisses as you pass it by, only to be replaced by the distant clamor of trays and dishes. The student body has assembled in the Morse cafeteria for the high-quality food service afforded by the university. It is the early part of dinner hour and the thought of eating couldn't be further from your mind.

You fish the keys out of your pocket as you gain the steps to your floor. If your roommate is in he'll probably give you a hard time about tracking water inside, and rightfully so. You open the door and swing it wide, revealing the darkened room beyond. He's out, probably studying in the science library as usual. You pass through his room and into yours, opting to leave the lights out for fear of ruining the picturesque atmosphere. With the toil of the long trek behind, you ease your backpack to the ground and rest at the foot of your bed. You suspect that he'll be gone for the better part of the evening.

It is nights like these that you live for.

A momentary flash of lightning illuminates every darkened corner of the room. You are not alone. A woman stares at you from across your bed. Her eyes are as cold as ice and she has daggers at her sides, drawn at the ready. *Li* could lunge at you at any moment. It is perhaps one of H. R. Giger's most beautiful yet grotesque works of art ever, and you purchased the poster for twenty dollars at The Forbidden Planet in Manhattan.[1]

Is she man or machine? Does she need blood or electricity to survive? Perhaps she needs a bit of both. No one really knows of course, no one except H. R. Giger himself. But the purpose of the metal sheaths is clear. They were carefully designed to extract every last drop of blood for her consumption. Her face is paradoxical: it is clearly frozen in a state of suspended animation, yet her eyes are seeing and behind them she is actively calculating. Li has all the makings of perfection: the memory capacity and precision of a supercomputer, the ability to reason as humans do and perform *modus ponens*, yet exist free of fear and pain and want, with the life expectancy of a *machine*. There is a definite eeriness about her, for her eyelids are at half mast and she gives off the impression of total boredom, as if it is out of curiosity alone that she permits you to gaze upon her before taking your life.

After a time you get up and seat yourself at your computer, feeling

---

[1]The mesmerizing 56" × 80" original is entitled "Li II" and hangs in the Swiss Art Museum (see http://www.giger.com).

her eyes penetrate deep into the back of your head as you do so. She has watched all of your feeble attempts at becoming one with the machine.

The disk is soaking wet. You pull it out and lay it down next to your keyboard. The writing on the label is smeared beyond recognition. A blow dryer simply will not do, and neither will a tissue since it can leave nasty scratches if sand gets in the way. It will require surgery to salvage it on such short order. You remove the sliding metal door causing a small metal spring to fly out and fall to the ground. The door is warped irreparably, but you will not be needing it again. The two plastic halves separate easily and you gingerly extract the silicon disk from its casing. It has water droplets all over it. They are not too big, but it's a good thing you didn't insert the disk into your drive. You take a dry towel from the bathroom and lay it out on the desk, carefully placing the thin silicon platter on top of it. The water will evaporate soon enough.

You draw your attention to your computer. The power is still off and the pen that you positioned carefully atop the keyboard has not moved. The upper end rests squarely between the "5" and "6" keys and the ball-point end lies between the "c" and "v" keys. Had it not been aligned as such there would have been hell to pay, and the inquisition would have commenced with your roommate. You remove the pen and flip on the power switch. The desktop appears. The background art reads "Night City" haphazardly spray painted along a worn and weathered wall set beneath a neon sky. The steel rods from the reinforced concrete stand rusted and jagged along the top, making for rough passage should anyone try to reach the ruined building beyond. You dubbed the machine Night City in honor of the cyberpunk role-playing game that bears the same name.[2]

The protagonists in the cyberpunk genre are a truly admirable lot. They are high-tech lowlifes that challenge authority at every given opportunity, blend in with the crowd, and make commercial programmers look like toddlers playing with tinker toys. The *sprawl* is their home, a megalopolis formed from the eventual unification of Boston, New York, and Philadelphia. The cyberpunks live on the fringes of society and form a counterculture unto themselves. They know not of greed. They know not of rapacity, and they know not of hegemony. However, these things are not alien to them since they are contended with on a regular basis. They are technologists absolute and embrace mankind's tendency to both make its own problems and later overcome them: deplete the ozone then sell sun block; pollute the air then sell gas masks; trash this planet then

---

[2]See [27, 229].

move on to the next. It is in science and technology that they *believe*. Like renegade cowboys out of the Wild West, they serve their own needs in the largely lawless and uncontrollable digital realm. Yet they frequently perform valuable services for the common good, and play a crucial role in keeping the powers that be in check, thus preserving the freedoms that we take for granted. In the end their heroic acts are seldom if ever rewarded, let alone recognized. Such is the divine tragedy of the good hacker. *When the megacorporations of the world and their puppet governments wrest control of our lives completely, when they see and hear and record every move we make, when they tell us how we should think and how we should act and what we should buy, who else will there be to turn to?*

The terminate-and-stay-resident programs load one after another, creating a line of icons along the bottom of the screen. After the last one loads you reach around the left side of the machine and press the hardware debugging switch. Time to go manual. You type in a command to view the two bytes located at address 0x05DE1940. It contains 0x007E, just as it should. It read 0x007D when you left, implying that you are the only one who booted the machine since you went to class this morning. Your computer is running a number of custom-made Trojan horses, and this is the result of one of them. Every time the machine boots the Trojan increments the counter by one.

On one occasion you rebooted the machine and found that the value had been incremented by two. After a prompt interrogation of your roommate you learned that he had turned on your machine to see if you had some software he needed. When he was finished he turned the machine back off. Paranoia perhaps? Well, call it what you will. You regard it as a simple matter of dotting your i's and crossing your t's. Anyone who walks more than 10 feet inside *Night City* will set off one alarm or another. There are those who would search your machine, if not for your list of pilfered passwords, then for evidence regarding your other extracurricular activities. *Trojans help solve this problem too.* Any such person would only find ciphertexts and a machine so riddled with custom-made Trojans as to lead one to wonder why you hadn't written the operating system from the ground up in the first place.

There was no need to admonish your roommate for using your computer. You trusted him more than anyone else in the world with its contents. He had won your respect on the first day of school due to his raw intellect alone. There seemed to be no question he could not answer, no system of equations he could not solve. This applied to everything, from using Maxwell's equations to describe an electrical phenomena to figuring out how computer viruses worked. This had its downsides of course, since there is nothing more frustrating than knowing that whenever you got stuck on a homework problem, the oracle in the adjacent room could produce the answer in a matter of seconds.

The stage has been set. Soon the disk will be dry and you will be able to read its contents. You lean back in your chair and throw your hands behind your head. Ruminations of the previous lecture take over your thoughts. It was a class on the history of physics, and was taught by Professor Klein. He is one of the world's foremost authorities on the subject, and what adds greatly to his lectures is the fact that he even looks like Albert Einstein, although you'd be hard-pressed to get another classmate to admit it openly.

His lecture centered on Neils Bohr, the 1922 winner of the Nobel Prize in physics. It was awarded for his successful investigations on the structure of atoms and the radiation emanating from them. However, as Professor Klein explained, his contributions to mankind far exceeded his status as a Nobel laureate. He was arguably deserving of a peace prize as well for his heroic efforts at saving Jews from Nazi tyranny. Under threat of complete Nazi dictatorship, Bohr held science conferences to bring foreigners to his research institute. Behind the scenes these conferences were really job fairs in which Bohr assisted Jewish scientists to find sponsorship abroad. It was a time in which you were not permitted to leave the country without a foreign employer to work under.

One of the most interesting aspects of the lecture was what Bohr did when the Nazis took to the streets of Copenhagen. Bohr had been entrusted with the Nobel prizes of Max von Laue and James Franck who had remained in Germany. Their medals were successfully smuggled out of Germany at a time in which such exportations were considered to be capital crimes. The Nazis gathered any and all valuables to feed their war machine. The Nobel prizes remained at Bohr's institute for safekeeping, and as Professor Klein explained, Bohr began to worry considerably that the Nazis might take over the lab and find the medals. The recipient's names were engraved on them, and this would not have bode well for Laue and Franck had they fallen into enemy hands.

The thought of burying them was immediately ruled out for fear that they would be unearthed. George de Hevesy, a Nobel prize winner in chemistry, suggested that the medals be dissolved using a powerful acidic solution. They proceeded to precipitate the gold from acid and stored the medals in two separate unmarked jars. The Nazis ended up searching the lab and left the two jars containing the liquefied Nobel prizes alone. The jars were promptly sent to the royal mint in Stockholm to be recast as soon as the war was over [170]. It was a fascinating lecture and it was clear that this was a scientist's solution to a scientific problem.

You found any and all techniques that can be used to outsmart others fascinating, especially when it involved outsmarting evil tyranny. But how can this idea be extrapolated from the physical realm to the digital realm? You glance at the floppy drying next to you. How can we hide the Tetris Trojan from prying eyes? The way to do so is not clear at all. In the next instant a thought occurred to you. The salient aspect of the Bohr-Hevesy approach was that the gold was effectively melted to assume the same liquid form as the acid. The acid and gold were then intertwined at the atomic level, leading to an apparently worthless liquid. A separate process could later extract all of the $Au$ atoms. This process could be repeated ad infinitum. How can a virus be seamlessly integrated into its host? One certainly cannot dissolve an assembly language virus. After all, this is the digital realm we are dealing with.

Given a high-level programming language $J$ that can be decompiled, the solution is simple. Suppose that the host is written in $J$ and suppose that the virus is written in $J$ as well. The virus exists in compiled binary form, but totes around its $J$ source code as well as a compiler and decompiler if needed. When the virus decides to infect a host, it decompiles the host. It then inserts its own viral source code into the host source code. The resulting infected source code is then compiled and saved, replacing the old program in the process. The virus ipso facto adheres to all of the compiler conventions of its host.[3] Depending on what compilers are available, the virus could be made to conform to the register and calling conventions of a gnu $J$ compiler, a Microsoft $J$ compiler, a Borland $J$ compiler, and so forth. This would make the virus more difficult to detect. Of course there is ample room for improvement. It would be nice to be able to infer and subsequently mimic the high-level language programming *style* of the host program. You glance over at the floppy lying next to you. It is finally dry. This research topic will have to wait for another rainy day.

What the disk needs now is a new home. You pull open the top drawer and pull out a previously dismantled floppy. It had been prepared for just

---

[3]One could argue that the decompilability of Java is a security weakness that does not exist in the C++ language, for example. A language that behaves akin to a cryptographic one-way function during compilation guards against this vulnerability.

such an occasion. You set about reassembling the disk in its new housing. Moments later it is ready. You insert it into the drive in eager anticipation. The resident operating system mounts the floppy without a hitch. The file system properties have to be adjusted on the password file since the file was designated as invisible. You copy it onto your hard drive and eject the disk. After double-clicking on the file you find that it has 143 login/password pairs.

Presto.

When left to their own devices people choose the funniest passwords imaginable. This holds especially true for college undergraduates:

Login: pc541
Password: JoeIsUg1y

Login: sr412
Password: Pee∅nMe

Login: ds912
Password: SnakeH∅ℓe

You double-click on your saved collection and enter the password that is needed to decrypt it. One second later the plaintext file opens up in a text editor. You copy and paste the newly obtained passwords to your master list. Your running total is now 655. Some of the passwords were obtained via your password-snatching Trojan; still others were obtained from brute-force dictionary attacks. The university system administrators were still making the mistake of letting the Unix *passwd* file be easily accessible.

It was a good catch given that your last visit to the Trojan was only a week before. However, the running total is not really 655. You earmarked several of these accounts as potential honeypots. The most suspicious of all is:

Login: Password
Password: Password

Every time a user logs into a university machine, the user is warned that any unauthorized use is a criminal act and a violation of U.S. law. These honeypots are a way of trapping rogue users since they are easily guessed and grant access to accounts that are under 24-hour surveillance. You surmise that at least 620 of the user accounts should be safe to play with.

Before calling it a day you run your coin-flipping program. You type in 655 and let it flip away, prepared to toss the coin again if it winds up on a honeypot. The result comes up 422. You cross-reference this with your master list and determine that it's probably not a honeypot account.

Login: edc42
Password: m4Tds∅1

Tomorrow you shall be edc42 for a while.

* * * * *

The night is young as you step out of the house. In the distance, the Transco Tower stands silhouetted against the skyline. Like a municipal sentry it watches as the denizens of the city slowly make their way onto the streets. You smile in spite of yourself, for on this night you have something very special planned and you doubt that anyone has a vantage point good enough to see that the sequence of zeros and ones on the disk at your side is just a little unusual, a tad bit out of place, and in fact upon closer inspection downright insidious in nature.

You hop on your bike and pedal away from your home. Well, your home away from home is more aptly put. It has been over a year since you last visited your father, and the last time you were in Houston this new creation was little more than an idea on the drawing board. The city takes on a new hue as the headlights and 7-11 signs shed their evening glow. With not a cloud in the sky and no chance of rain, a new feeling begins to grow deep inside. This is the night. She will be free. You hope your due diligence will keep her alive. She will travel to strange lands and traverse hostile environments and will rely almost exclusively on what you taught her to do.

Turning a street corner you head out onto Westheimer. The traffic lights spread out as far as the eye can see, turning from red to green to yellow and back again in steady cadence. A small copy shop appears on the right. Looking inside you see a customer at a computer and a cashier looking off into space. Two people. No bustle. Not a chance. The last thing you need is a proprietor looking over your shoulder watching your every move. You pedal down an access road and jump a curb. Some more distance is necessary. Every mile counts. You traveled halfway across the country with her in tow, and it was important that you see her off safely.

A small shopping center comes into view. It is surprisingly full of cars. You swing into the lot and see a Burger King, a movie theater, a restaurant or two, and nestled in the middle of it all, an enticing-looking copy shop. Chaining your bike to the nearest pole, you scope the place out. Video cameras are mounted fore and aft, a convex mirror hangs over the computer area, there is no *uniformed* guard, and there is no tape measure along the side of the front door. Half a dozen customers are in line, and the copyists are buzzing around like worker bees. Drawing your attention to the computer area you see three people seated at computers, and another hovering over a color laser printer. It looks promising. In fact, it looks as promising as can be. Those *machines* don't stand a chance. You get up and walk into the establishment, just another face in the crowd, another customer needing to print out documents. You pass into the computer area and not a single person pays you notice.

As you seat yourself in front of a computer you try to recall how many times you washed the dishes after eating at a restaurant. Zero. Why? It's very simple really. It's not your responsibility. You pay for the food. You pay for the service. Cleaning up after yourself is *not your responsibility*. How silly would you look if you got up after paying, walked into the kitchen, and said "here, let me help you with those plates" to the employees? They would look at you sideways. Leaving your virus on this *general-purpose* computing machine is no different than this. The fact that others lack the cranial capacity to *see the grime* is not your fault. If it spoke to them the way it speaks to you then they'd be aware of her presence. But the privileged are few in number.

A message on the screen informs you of the rate: *Ten cents per minute.* The blinking caret asks you for your name. It is waiting. You give it one stochastically chosen from among the most frequent names in America: John. This machine is no longer for hire. It is temporarily yours, to do with as you will provided that it remains functional enough for the next customer. But most importantly, it must remain an intact vehicle for making the corporation money. That is what really matters in America. It will be so, you say to yourself, as you pull out the disk. It will be so.

You glance at the floppy in your hand and question once again your insatiable need to spread digital diseases. *This is the wrong thing to do.* Yet there is no helping your compulsion. You are diseased, but there is solace in the fact that your disease stems from the morally ruined society you live in. Greed begets punishment.

From idea in the back of your head, to scribbles on a drawing board, to mnemonics in an ASCII file, and on through the assembler your creation has traveled. You trained her on every antiviral program you could get your hands on. She bypasses them all. You click on the control panel and notice that the machine is running a virus shield. The shield consists of operating system hooks to file system interrupts that analyze their callers for suspicious behavior. Not a problem. Your virus already knows the location of the native interrupts needed to avoid the patches altogether. She has all the needed ROM addresses stored in her internal circularly linked list. You wonder how long it will be until she forgets them in lieu of newer ones, ones that have yet to be chosen by the computer manufacturer. You wonder if she will even live long enough to see that day. She is so clever, you think to yourself as you insert the disk, and fastidious too. She will never get a byte fatter than she already is.

A guy sitting down at the machine next to you looks over his printout. You make out a pie graph on it that seems to reference budgetary plans. While he is busy there making money you get busy running your infected version of Tetris. You spent well over a year designing her, calculating her cold-hearted offensive and defensive mechanisms.

... and now it is time to *bring down the machine.*

Seconds later a u-shaped block comes down the screen. Bingo. No system crashes and no antiviral warnings. She is free. She moved into her new home in the boot sector. But she has yet to leave her burrow and survey her surroundings. Experience has shown that crashes are not uncommon in these copy shops, so you hit the restart button knowing full well that the accounting software will not lose a second of billing time. As you eject the disk you look to the right and notice that the line has gotten even longer. The guy next to you signs out and heads to the back of the line to pay.

The machine boots up without a hitch. You see your name John on the start screen and click on the button labeled continue. Everything seems to be going smoothly. You take the liberty of running some of the resident programs: Photoshop, Microsoft Word, Acrobat reader, and a few text editors to boot. They all put on a few pounds. But who's going to notice? Infecting these programs manually is a good measure against any futile attempt to remove the virus. She's flying high, having beaten the heuristic scanners to the punch. She rerouted the interrupts first this time and will never be on the defensive on this particular machine *ever again.*

The clock in the lower right-hand corner of the screen reads "00:12." *Twelve minutes.* That's only one dollar and twenty cents. It was worth it. You sign out and head to the back of the line. A lady at the front of the line is unhappy with her glossy printouts. They are sprawled out all over the counter and she is taking forever to resolve the issue. The people behind her are visibly agitated.

You contemplate the future of your creation. Will she survive? Your gut tells you that she will. She has to. She has so much going for her. But how will you know how she fares in her new world? She'll never write. She'll never call. If you're lucky you might even hap upon her some day. Even then she won't tell you anything. You won't know how many children she has, or how many children her children have, and so on.

The lady reaches for her purse and pulls out a checkbook. Unbelievable. And you thought it was the information age. She finally takes her bag of glossies and leaves, to the relief of all. The line moves silently forward.

The problem with your creation is that she is an open book. Anyone can read her and with any luck she'll be notorious enough that lots of people will. You could have trained her to tell you of her exploits, but it is not clear how this could have been done in such a way that she would tell you and you alone. Ideally you would like one of her offspring to tell you some of the names of the infected machines and the order in which they were infected. You contemplated using Intel CPU IDs and IP addresses as unique identifiers to record the path that she and her progeny takes. However, one obvious problem with this approach is that the data could easily take up too much space in the virus. The real problem is the sheer stupidity of it. You may as well hand the Feds a road map to your house and draw a target on your back since it would have the same effect. Even encrypting the path with 3DES and storing the key within the virus would do little to hide the path from trained eyes.

A less detailed approach would be to divulge only the number of infected machines instead of the names of the machines and the order in which they were infected. This could be accomplished by giving her two generation counters. The idea is simple. A counter $i$ would be included in the virus that would initially be set to a randomly chosen value $r$. Each time a virus has a child it increments $i$ in the child by 1. For example, if the first virus had 8 offspring then they would each contain $i = r + 1$. Each of their children would have $i = r + 2$ and so forth. Another counter $j$ would store the cumulative number of children that each forefather had.

The value $j$ would initially be set to a random value $s$. After the original virus had a child it would store $j = s + 1$ in itself and in the child. After the original virus had a second child it would store $j = s + 2$ in itself and in the child. The purpose of using the random values $r$ and $s$ is to throw off antiviral experts as much as possible, since you know these random initial conditions and they don't.

The idea was to try to obtain a future copy $\mathcal{V}$ of the virus. In it would be values for $i$ and $j$. The distance from $\mathcal{V}$ to the root of the family tree is $h = i - r$. The average number of children per forefather of $\mathcal{V}$ is $b = \frac{2(j-s)}{i-r}$. So, a very rough estimate[4] on the number of existing viruses is $(b^{h+1} - 1)/(b - 1)$ (see Figure 1.1). This is the number of vertices in a complete tree in which each parent has $b$ children. Although the accuracy of this mechanism is highly suspect,[5] it would nonetheless be fun to obtain these values later on. . . .

The person at the front of the line pays for some printouts and then motions towards the computer area. The cashier nods, says something unintelligible, and then points towards the computer you just left. The customer then walks over to it and sits down. For a moment you freeze. You didn't expect it to be used *while you were still there*. Suddenly the line seems way too long and your aggravation level rises a notch. It will be cool, you tell yourself. It's under control.

You thoroughly contemplated the pros and cons of including the counters while the virus was on the drawing board. The cons outweighed the pros. Like any viral outbreak the epicenter paints a strong picture of where and when the infections commenced. This was the reason you waited. This is the reason you are here in Houston. You shudder to think of the information you would give to antiviral analysts if you released it at school with the counters. The counter values would be low in the viral samples found on campus and the values would increase as the viruses moved further away, plus or minus the noise introduced by FTP transfers and the like. No, the decision not to include the counters was a good one. It would give the enemy even more information than it would give you.

The person in front of you pays the cashier and walks away. You approach the counter with cash in hand. The cashier pulls up some information on the computer and presses the screen once. A paper begins printing out. He hands the sheet to you. It reads your fake name, your

---

[4]This is the sum of terms where the terms form a geometric progression.

[5]An active adversary could change the counters without killing the virus, and so forth.

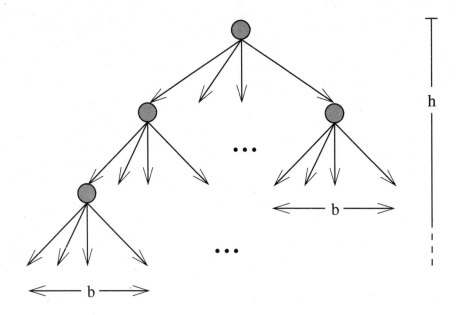

**Figure 1.1** Estimated number of viruses in the wild

alias du jour, John. He will get a good look at your face but there is no helping it. You pay the balance and take the receipt. As you head out the door you pause and glance back at the machine one more time. You silently bid her farewell, and pray that she will go forth and multiply.

While heading over to your bike, a familiar feeling comes over you in a wave. *There must be a better way*, you think to yourself. *There has to be a better way.*

Nine months later...

From within the darkened confines of your dorm room you sit and contemplate your creation for the thousandth time. Your drawing board is filled with pseudocode, directed graphs, and the names of pertinent operating system calls. Despite your efforts the battle you waged is not going as planned. Not at all. You push back on your easy chair, causing the padded leg rest to rise up to your legs. Throwing your hands behind your head, you stare at your war machine, split down the middle and dissected in gross detail to enable careful analysis. Your agent was sent off into the wild blue yonder with tools that now seem to be woefully inadequate, for not even a whisper of her exploits has found its way to your ears.

In many ways her design followed a tried-and-true methodology: she is a multipartite virus that, like several parasitic organisms, has three phases of existence (see Figure 1.2). She started out life in a deliberately infected executable. From there she migrated to the boot sector. While in the boot sector she copied herself into RAM. Finally, when in RAM she hunts down potential host applications and infects them, thus completing the lifecycle.

*She was a prototype and nothing more*, you think to yourself in a feeble attempt to dismiss her apparent shortcomings. A moment later, you feel ashamed for even thinking this. She's done nothing to warrant being belittled so. Perhaps separation anxiety was getting the best of you, for no matter how hard you tried you could not shake the feeling that part of you was missing.

You draw your attention to the top of the board and take note of the words "polymorphism engine no. 1." She has no routines to modify her own byte representation but they've been in the making for some time. After an entire week of bug hunting you finally figured out why your first polymorphic version kept crashing with a bus error. It turns out that the CPU uses an instruction look-ahead cache and was executing the ciphertext when you thought it was executing the decrypted code. Even the assembly level debugger led you to believe that the CPU was executing the decrypted code correctly. Silly computer manufacturers, they should know that a program often likes to change itself while it runs. The solution? Flush the cache. There are a variety of ways to do that.

For a moment you feel an extreme urge to erase everything related to polymorphism on the board. In all likelihood polymorphism would not help her spread, since in cleartext form she already bypasses every antiviral program on the market. Making her polymorphic now would be like teaching her to run before she could walk. Deep down you know she can walk. She should be all over the place by now and should've been found.

To ensure that she would spread rapidly, she was designed to handle *battleprogs* and memory resident antiviral programs. Battleprogs is the term you use to refer to applications that perform integrity checks on their own code. These battle programs are written with the foresight that one day they may become infected by a virus or Trojan horse. Once an application is compiled, it can have integrity checking code built into it by the developer. One way of doing so is by attaching a beneficial Trojan horse to the program. This program may be structurally similar to malicious Trojans but serves to verify the integrity of the host. To

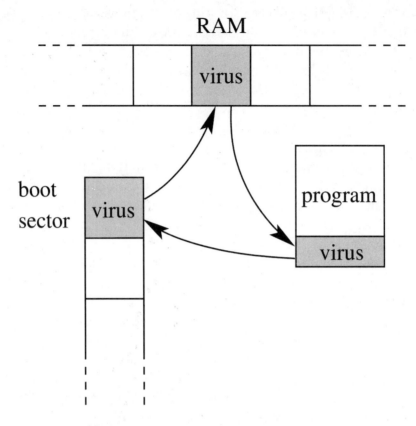

**Figure 1.2** 3-Phase multipartite virus

create this beneficial Trojan the developer first computes a checksum on
the compiled binary using a one-way function, for example. The input to
the one-way function can be the body of the host concatenated with the
integer representing the length of the host and the attached Trojan. The
file length may be found by making an appropriate file system call. The
resulting checksum is then stored within the beneficial Trojan.[6] When the
executable is run the Trojan gains control first. It then recomputes the
checksum and compares the result to the checksum that stored within the
Trojan. If they don't match then the Trojan assumes that the application
has been tampered with and refuses to send control to the executable. The

---

[6]A problem arises when trying to design a Trojan that computes the checksum of
the host concatenated with the Trojan itself. By storing the resulting hash value within
the Trojan, the hash value that is computed will differ from the stored hash. When a
typical hash function is used, there is little reason to suspect that a reasonable number
of iterations will cause the hash to converge on a fixed-point.

Trojan can also perform the checksum on the copy of the host that resides on the disk drive. The original executable along with the beneficial Trojan forms a battleprogram that acts as a whistleblower against unexpected changes.

Over time you encountered many battleprogs and taught her how to handle them. When she is in her memory resident form, she looks for currently running executables to infect. She only infects such programs immediately after they terminate. When she runs from within an executable, she infects the boot sector if it isn't already infected. Following that she *removes herself from the host executable in memory and on disk.* This way, when the host gets control, the host is in its pristine shrink-wrapped form. As a result, if it computes a checksum on itself then it will always match. It will match because the program is in fact no longer infected. You carefully measured the overhead of this approach, and it has proven to be unnoticeable to the naked eye. To implement generation counters on top of this, it would be necessary to have the counters only record the number of boot sector versions of the virus. This is necessary to avoid overinflating the counter values, since the virus copies itself to *and deletes itself from* executable programs.

The first rays of dawn pierce through the darkness of your dorm, passing over your head and onto the drawing board beyond. You get up and approach the window. The courtyard below is completely deserted. In a matter of hours dreary-eyed students will be bustling to class, and you will be a sleepless walking zombie among them.

You detest daybreak, for it is a pale reminder of yet another night spent working on your creation, another night *not* working on quantum mechanics or signal analysis homework. How you've managed to keep your GPA up given your hacking obsession is a mystery. No doubt part of it has to do with your electrical engineering study group. The four of you work on everything together, and when your collective minds are brought to bear on the written exercises, you usually fare quite well. The problem is, the Electrical Engineering department has compensated for such study groups by dishing out *impossible assignments.* Every problem set contains at least one problem that is so elusive that it leaves the entire group dumbfounded. Lately, your contributions to the problem-solving effort have been lacking, and it hasn't gone unnoticed. If you keep going at this rate one or two members of the group are certain to defect, thus bringing an end to your precious scholastic support network. It is expected that each person show up with at least two or three solutions to share,

even if they are the solutions to the easiest exercises. This at least provides
some measure of assurance that the answers are correct. Last night you
didn't open a single textbook. They are sitting at the foot of your bed,
ruefully neglected.

*. . . your sickness is getting the best of you.*

Besieged on all sides by feelings of guilt, you react in the only way you
know how. You pull the curtains over the window so that the night may
continue within. You head over to the drawing board and try to focus
on the task at hand. The assembly code at the bottom of the board has
recently been incorporated into the latest prototype and can therefore be
spared. You pick up the eraser and wipe it away. Workspace is always
necessary to solve problems. There is one thing that you know for sure
could be hindering her attempts to replicate. It is a problem that has
been a thorn in your side for over a year. You crack open a new can of
soda and sit back down in your chair.

When your virus encounters a new computer model that hit the market
after the virus was released and when the computer is running memory-
resident antiviral software, your virus can't get in. The problem is that
these programs patch critical operating system routines that your virus
needs to call in order to replicate. The patched code analyzes the caller for
suspicious features shared by many viruses, features that your virus has.
When found, the antiviral software alerts the user to the presence of the
virus. If the original operating system vectors are known, then the virus
can bypass the antiviral patches entirely. But, on new machines *these
vectors are not known.* Even though future operating system routines
are based on previous ones, the vectors cannot be safely guessed. The
computer manufacturer will inevitably debug, reorder, and add to the
existing operating system routines, thereby mucking with all of the offsets.

Furthermore, manually incorporating all of the needed proprietary
code into the virus and making calls directly to the IDE driver would make
her look like the circus fat lady. No, there is no way to solve this problem
adequately. But at least she knows her limitations. She *knows* when this
situation arises, and she *knows* not to act. If there's one thing that these
antiviral sentries lack it's the element of surprise, and she knows when
they're watching. Your fielded avatar is designed to learn these needed
interrupt addresses. If she chances upon an unguarded machine, she will
teach herself the needed vectors. She will remember them henceforth and

whence not in her circularly linked list of memory cells, only to be forgotten when the machine's era comes to pass.

You glance back at the newly created space on the drawing board and take a swig of the soda at your side. There might be a way, you think to yourself. But deep down your gut is telling you that this problem is different from the others. It doesn't *feel* the same. It is mired in operating system theory and specifics. On a more technical level there might be a solution, but it would most likely involve different assumptions regarding the internal workings of the operating system, and therefore assume a different underlying operating system altogether. In the end it would not help in constructing the real-world juggernaut you so desperately wanted to create.

You decide to put the problem on hold for the moment and head out to the local computer cluster. When you arrive you see two dreary-eyed students. One is engrossed in an AutoCAD program at the far end of the room and the other is waiting impatiently by the laser printer. He is clearly at the end of an all-nighter since he's in a robe and his hair is standing on end. You recall programming your creation once for three days straight. The last twelve hours were marked by hallucinations and tingling sensations and you didn't call it quits until you observed a stapler crawling towards you on your desk. Such has been the commitment you have made to her. You seat yourself at a terminal and log onto the network. The message of the day appears on the screen:

*"MOTD — A computer virus has been discovered at several colleges and universities along the west coast . . . The CERT coordination center has issued a warning and a virus definition has been made available. We are asking all students and faculty to perform updated virus scans as soon as possible. The virus is set to activate on. . . "*

Like visors on a horse your peripheral vision falls away until all you can see is the message. Blood accelerates through your veins and fear clenches your heart.

She has been found.

She has been found and not just at one place, but at several. You want to delete the message of the day. You want to erase it from every computer in the entire university. You want to delete the virus definition and take the advisory down from the CERT web site. It's all too real. You glance over your shoulder. The other two students are oblivious to your plight. Given the enormity of your discovery it seems hard to be believe that this could be so. Never before has the virus seemed as much like a disease as it did now, because unlike before, it cannot be stopped. It cannot be contained. It is out there and it will no longer heed your call.

It took a day to sink in, and yet another to stop worrying about SWAT teams and unmarked vans. Then a new feeling began to grow deep inside. There was no doubt about it now. She had been snatched up and spirited away to an antivirus lab. You envision her digital form lying bare on an operating table with her midsection sliced open, her insides succumbing to the machinations of skilled surgeons. With tools that bore and cut, she would be systematically dissected and learned. How utterly exposed and violated she must feel right now. Multitudes of her offspring were now destined to perish, for nothing of what she had would remain hidden. They will be caught dead in their tracks, quarantined, and ultimately destroyed. But she still has one major advantage; there is power in numbers. Her replication will be exponential and this alone will secure her a place in the digital food chain. She may even reign supreme, for a time, on the proving grounds that is *information warfare*.

Deep down you know that she will multiply while this operating system version, and possibly the next one remain on the market. You nostalgically recall a game of cat and mouse you played with her while she was growing up. She initiated the game, of course, and it lasted for weeks. For some reason the computer in your dorm began showing a slow but marked degradation in CPU performance. It wasn't anything that could be quantified at first. But something just didn't feel right. The machine's speech was sort of slurred. After a while the pause between sentences became unbearable and your suspicions codified into a hypothesis: You were the victim of a virus yourself. The thought was both embarrassing and at the same time exhilarating.

The more you thought about it the more sense it made, and so you downloaded all of the latest virus definitions. The number of infected programs on your machine came up nil after the virus scans. Hmmmm. Something else then, you thought to yourself. You decided to pull out the microscope and tweezers and analyze the assembler that you used to assemble your virus. Your mouth nearly dropped to the floor when you noticed not one but five viruses hitching a ride at the end of the binary. They were all earlier prototypes of your virus. Over time the assembly language alterations had affected her offsets, and she managed to slip past you as a result. She replicated right under your very nose and you of all people were none the wiser. She had truly become a thing of beauty.

As a result of her escapade, you revised your software development practice to include a stiff regimen of custom antivirus scans. It was a simple task to come up with virus definitions for your own creations to prevent this from happening again. It was ironic how useful the antiviral software turned out to be in the virus software development process.

Overall it was a valuable lesson she taught you. The day the cat-and-mouse game ended was the day in which she started showing her true colors. The machine ran at full speed and she spread with a virulence heretofore never seen. Her ability to slow the machine to a standstill without being noticed by trained eyes was testament to her readiness to leave the nest, and she did very well for herself in the end.

* * * * *

One sunny afternoon in a small office in midtown Manhattan three employees meet to discuss the progress of a software development project that is lagging behind schedule. It could have been virtually any software company in any city and the situation would be the same, only the names would change. . . .

A young, somewhat disheveled software developer shifts uncomfortably in his chair with a look of utter consternation on his face.

"So you want us to rewrite the entire system so that all of the commands are in ASCII," announced the programmer aposematically.

"That is correct, Brian," replied the man at the head of the table. "Something might go wrong with the client/server software and they may want to have a look at it. After all, it is theirs. They paid for it."

It was an asinine explanation for making such a major last-minute change to software that is already functional. There is no way in the world the client would find and read the obscure log file. The three of you are more likely to be hit by a meteor during this very meeting. Brian shoots a glance at you from across the table and you nod knowingly.

"But if the messages are in ASCII then they will be five times larger than necessary," you reply.

Rajeev casually glances at his Rolex, implying that he has better things to do than argue with his software developers. He folds his hands in front of him and considers carefully his response. You have only been at the company a short while and deserve a better answer than this. He turns to address you.

"I know this, of course. I have developed software in the past as well. What is important is that we have an intelligible audit log of our system. If something goes wrong we may have to ask them to send us the log file," said Rajeev in a matter-of-fact tone of voice.

His response this time was closer to the truth. Yet in the end there was no point in arguing with the managing director. The bottom line was that Rajeev cofounded the company, he won the contract, and you and Brian were here to fulfill the contract however he saw fit. Rajeev knew how to keep things running smoothly, despite the inevitable bumps in the road. The truth was that he wanted the commands for the protocol to be in ASCII for human resource reasons, not technical reasons. The companies' software development team was almost exclusively college interns. The average turnover rate for team members was only six to nine months. This was hardly enough time for a neophyte to learn the protocol and then extend it before leaving the company. By making the protocol messages ASCII instead of binary, the protocol could be learned, monitored, and debugged more easily.

"Okay, Rajeev," you concede. "I'll make the necessary adjustments and replace the enumeration constants by ASCII strings by close of business Monday."

The first two months on the job had been a crash course on software reality as opposed to software engineering as you knew it. The company cared more about your commenting style, indentation style, and variable and function naming style than anything else. It was as if everything you learned in school meant nothing, no research into using the best algorithms and no attention paid to running times. The only priority was to make the code readable, get it done on time, and try not to let it crash on the user.

Rajeev's cell phone rings and with a wave of his hand he brings the meeting to a close. You and Brian head back to your desks.

"Well, that went as expected," said Brian.

You nod in agreement. The company had a way of taking a brainless task and making it even more so. But for the time being it is looking as if you might actually have something to look forward to. Last night you put the finishing touches on your latest piece of software and rolled it out, so to speak. It now resides on every machine in the company, and is ready to do your bidding. Like a djinni from a bottle the program is prepared to grant your every wish, no questions asked, and without failure. Only this djinni gives out more than three wishes.

Your job had been to develop the client/server suite from scratch. The server ran in the background and processed requests made by remote clients over the local area network. You fulfilled your end of the bargain, but found the final product to be woefully inadequate for your personal needs. After all, the server had little if any power over the machine it ran on and was not amenable to being camouflaged in any way, shape, or form. So, you took the liberty to develop your own client/server suite. The key difference being that your server is a Trojan horse that resides deep within the heart of the operating system. It sends and receives packets at a subterranean layer of the network protocol stack that is high enough to facilitate rapid software development, yet low enough to keep the Trojan's activities from drawing unwanted attention.

With only two other developers in the room you decide that it's as good a time as any to test-drive your new client/server suite. You eagerly fire up your client program. Your senses are piqued and through the corner of your eye you take note of what Brian is doing next to you. He is an avid object oriented programmer and can run circles around you when it comes to writing anything in excess of 20,000 lines. You've got to play it cool this time, you think to yourself, cool as school. These are no run-of-the-mill computer users about you. These are young and alert programmers and unlike the people in marketing you're always a bit skittish about messing with them.

You click on a button and row upon row of computers appear on the screen. They are interconnected by a twisting array of wires and are undulating with a servo-electronic pulse that can only come from something truly living. Graphical user interfaces always add an extra panaché to rogue software and are reminiscent of the imaginings of many cyberpunk novelists. Brian is too close to your machine to be a guinea pig so you decide to prey on Adrian instead. You move the mouse pointer over his machine and click on it. His machine slowly rises above the rest. Adrian has his back to you and his face is buried in a book. It will be his undoing.

*Enter your command for this machine, oh great one:*

For a fleeting moment you experience a burst of euphoria and power, but then just as quickly as it came on you lapse back into the reality of your peon status at the firm. If nothing else you'll get your kicks. You click on the button labeled "hardware interrupt."

*and which flavor of interrupt will you prefer, oh great one?:*

1. *key strokes*

2. *N system beeps*

3. *N deletes*

4. *eject CD*

5. *system reboot in 120 seconds*

Cooing inwardly at your creation, you rub your hands together in eager anticipation. Your Trojan is about to test its wings. Glancing back over your shoulder, you see that Adrian's face is still buried in his book. It is unclear whether it's a trade book, a software manual, or one of those Japanese animés he's always reading. He is an exceptionally good programmer and to pull one over on him would be a major accomplishment. He's also a really great friend, but that is beside the point. You are currently engaged in an important military exercise and must not let yourself get sidetracked by unimportant details.

Knowing that Adrian may turn his attention back to his screen at any moment, you quickly decide to do option 1. He's currently editing the C source code to a massive program and you know that he wouldn't draw his attention away from his screen unless his program was syntactically correct. You also couldn't help but notice that his cursor was at the end of a statement in *main()*.

*A most excellent choice oh great one, and what string shall I conjure?:*

You enter the text,

```
for (;;);
```

and hit the carriage return. The characters "for(;;);" spring to life on Adrian's screen. You immediately quit out of the client program. Unable to contain yourself, you proceed in the only way you know how to avoid entering into hysterics. You pick up a book, open it to a random page, and bite down hard on your free hand. Pain was the only way to contain the laughter growing inside. The server worked like a charm.

Using the reflection in the corner of your screen, you perceive the events behind you as they unfold. Adrian hits a few keys on the keyboard, drops the book to his side, sits back in his chair, and waits. He waits as it saves. He waits impatiently as it compiles. He then waits some more as it links. As usual, this alone takes so long that he shifts his position to hunch over the keyboard. He rolls his fingertips on the table in rapid succession and waits some more as it runs. He waits, and waits, and waits.

"Come on then!" Adrian shouts at his screen.

Adrian finally stood up and threw his book against the wall, cursing wildly at his screen. The entire ordeal promptly drew the attention of Brian, who asked him what his problem was. Adrian replied using every four-letter word imaginable that his machine was busted. He even threatened to throw it out the window. Fearing that Adrian might be a bit too tightly wound on this particular occasion, you decided to lend some moral support. You put on your best poker face, spun around in your chair, and expressed your deepest concern for Adrian's predicament.

Like it or not, Adrian was forced to experience the *halting problem* firsthand. The act of doing so left him quite undone. When Adrian finally found the infinite loop in his source code, the infinite loop that materialized out of literally nowhere, he simply stared at his screen and was unable to utter a single word.

After regaining his composure, Adrian set about trying to determine what had happened. He downloaded and ran the latest antiviral software. He called the help desk to see if the desktop group did anything to his machine. Despite being poorly versed in Intel assembly language, he downloaded a disassembler and tried his hand at analyzing the boot sector. But it was to no avail. In the end he simply could not discern from whence the offending loop came. Being pressed for time, he eventually abandoned the hunt altogether.

In all it cost the company an hour or two of Adrian's time, but the reparations that it made to your job motivation were without bound. You simply could not wait to go to work from that day on. Your djinni was capable of much, much more. It dutifully awaited the arrival packets from your client and processed them in due course. The network packets came in two varieties: data and code. The data packets caused the server to execute predefined commands such as the emulation of keystrokes, and the code packets were executed by the server verbatim. Every so often a truly creative prank would occur to you and the code packets sated your need to perform it on someone's machine *immediately*.

Yet this particular training drill was but the first of many. Sometime later a similar opportunity manifested itself and you accepted the call to action. Howls and hooting emanated from the marketing division and like a predator to prey your ears perked up. . . .

You look over to Brian, your coworker and soon to be partner in crime.[7]

"It's bonehead again," he says to you with that annoyed look in his eyes that can only come from one employee who knows that another is currently getting away with murder.

With Rajeev out smoothing over a client, Eddie took the liberty to play Quake again, as usual.

Eddie is one of those people everyone can do without. There is nothing particularly notable about his skill set and it is not clear exactly what his job responsibilities are. He is simply *there*. If nothing else Eddie is a master of keeping himself busy. He manages to find things to do day in and day out. Sooner or later every new hire learns not to cross swords with him since he has friends in high places and can make your job miserable at the drop of a dime.

Brian gets up and heads over to the marketing division and you follow him. A crowd of people is standing around Eddie's desk. His speakers are blaring techno-industrial and the blue-green glow of the game is reflected in his eyes. Eddie is consumed by his game. Joining the crowd of onlookers, you notice that he is wielding his favorite weapon, a shoulder-mounted railgun that fires depleted Uranium shells. He rounds a corner to find a battle droid directly in front of him. Before it can react Eddie fires his gun. In a flash of light the weapon sends a shell down the hallway, leaving a spiral of smoke in its wake. It slams into the droid with a horrific puncturing sound. The droid was caught off guard and is sent reeling into the far wall. Its armor plating is badly damaged, but it manages to get up on all fours. It will take another shot to bring it down. Eddie is doing quite well and in a matter of minutes he will beat his high score. It just so happens to be the highest score in the entire company. It's not like he doesn't have enough time to hone his skills or anything.

Smiling inwardly, you excuse yourself to go to the bathroom. As you head over to pick up the key to the men's room, you contemplate your premeditated act. He has it coming to him, you think to yourself. The guy rubbed your rhubarb the wrong way during your first week on the job, and now it's payback time. You pick up the key and head back to

---

[7]In a manner of speaking, of course.

your desk. You load up your client program, enter a few commands, hit return, and then terminate the client: Two minutes and counting.

You head back out into the lobby and make sure to make eye contact with some of the people around Eddie's desk. It seems that while you were in the bathroom, Eddie's machine rebooted for reasons unknown. You had the pleasure of hearing every delicious detail about it from Brian, who was as perplexed as everyone else in the matter. For whatever reason the neurons in Eddie's brain never fired appropriately to make the connection that you were never around when the digital boogieman struck his machine. In his mind it was exactly this that exonerated you from his list of likely suspects.

On one occasion Eddie got so pissed he charged into the development room on a rampage to discover the identity of the digital boogieman. He was certain that one of the smart-mouthed developers was to blame. He did it at lunch hour, immediately following yet another attack on his system. He moved meticulously from screen to screen, hoping that somehow despite his complete programming incompetence, he might be able to glean some incriminating piece of evidence. Like a promising lab rat, Eddie eventually learned to save his games often, particularly when he was about to make high score.

But, being the self-appointed sysadmin for your company was not always so easy. On one occasion Adrian came close to finding your Trojan horse server. *Way too close.* In a last-ditch effort to conceal the presence of your malware, you laid out a series of explanations to divert his search efforts. It succeeded, and Adrian ended up analyzing benign sections of the operating system.

In all, the client/server suite performed very reliably, but this did not prevent the overall series of occurrences from drawing the attention of upper management. In a rather bizarre turn of events, you were asked to investigate the suspicious string of events at a team meeting. Your were the resident security expert and so Rajeev figured you were the man for the job. He would probably reimage everyone's machine before outsourcing the problem to another company. Rajeev liked to save money that way. The irony of the request hit home and so you decided that you'd better cool down a little. You thought about it but could not get yourself to take down any of the rogue servers. So, you decided to simply maintain a lower profile instead. You disciplined yourself not to reboot Eddie's machine for the heck of it, but rather only rebooted it when he was *asking for it*.

The game suddenly came to a grinding halt when one day you found

that you could no longer get to the desktop on Eddie's machine. Facing
the screen, you looked at it in amazement. It had nothing on it save for
a modal window that prompted you for a password. It seems that Eddie
was trying anything and everything to keep the boogieman off his machine.
Luckily Eddie's machine was free for you to use since your current task
involved software testing, and it was important that the final product be
compatible with Dell machines. Eddie had the misfortune of having the
only Dell in the company.

Without arousing any suspicion, you sat at his desk during lunch hour
and tried to break in. You tried everything you could think of but it
was to no avail. The machine was locked down. The floppy you held
and the Trojan it contained could not be executed, and you suffered an
infuriating defeat. Before leaving for the day, you took the liberty to
scour the shelves in marketing for the software that successfully thwarted
your attacks. Sure enough, the offending product was located not five feet
from Eddie's machine. It was a shrink-wrapped disk-locking program.
You plucked it off the shelf and read the back of the box.

*"with our patented technology... keeps unwanted intruders at bay, al-
lowing your data to remain safe from modification and prying eyes."*

Raising a brow, you conceded that you fell squarely into the category
of unwanted intruders. You placed the box back on the shelf and left work
seething with animosity.

That night you contemplated the day's events. Having never played
with a disk-locking program before, you were left to hypothesize how it
worked. While pondering how such a program could render your efforts
so ineffective you reached the stark conclusion that all attempts to break
in would be futile.

The following simple design would be good enough to thwart all of
your attacks. A small partition could be created on the hard drive next
to the resident operating system. The partition would be populated with
a small boot program that is capable of sending control to the resident
operating system. The file system or critical portions thereof could be
encrypted using a cipher like 3DES that uses Eddie's password as the
key. His key would therefore be needed to decrypt it and the key would
not be stored anywhere on the disk. Furthermore, a checksum $C$ could be
computed by running Eddie's password through a cryptographically strong
one-way hash function. The value $C$ would be stored internally in the new
partition. When the computer reboots, the partition program would get

control first. It would prompt you for the password, hash whatever you enter, and then compare the result to $\mathcal{C}$. If they matched, it would then decrypt the file system using the password you supplied. If they didn't match, then it would tell you that the password was incorrect. When implemented properly you could stare at every single bit on the hard disk and still have no clue what Eddie's password is. The method effectively cripples the underlying file system and only when it is uncrippled is it possible to install rogue software.

Whether or not this is the way Eddie's program actually worked was immaterial. It did not change the fact that *it could have been written this way.* So, there is no reason in theory that you should be able to get back on his machine. It was bad enough that a shrewd sysadmin could easily track your activities when you ran the client. This is the same problem that you faced when you accessed the password-snatching Trojan back at school. What this situation spelled out was much worse. It meant that in order to hack into Eddie's machine it was not enough to be the world's greatest hacker. You had to be the world's greatest cryptanalyst.

In the end Eddie's machine succumbed to a Trojan horse attack that commenced from a floppy inserted into his machine while he was present. He was the one who did the honors by double-clicking on the infected program, and so he was the one who let you back into his machine. From then on the servers paid particular attention to all keystrokes that the users entered into their machines and the lockout never occurred again.

However, the final victory did nothing to ease the mental repercussions that ensued. The initial failure was bitterly tangible and wore on your ego. The fact that someone like Eddie with no understanding of computer security whatsoever could simply install an intelligently written program and lock you out was disheartening to say the least. The disk-locking program accomplished its directive, *and accomplished it well.*

This was not the first time that you had been denied access to a machine. Everyone has seen password screens without knowing a valid password to enter. What this situation implied was quite different. Here you had the entire hard disk at your disposal along with the technical savvy needed to analyze it *and still* you could not get in. No other situation you had ever encountered illuminated the true power of cryptography more than this. Crypto was not merely being used to prove Eddie's identity or conceal his data from your prying eyes. In this situation, crypto was being used to keep you from *modifying* Eddie's data in any meaningful way. For hours you dwelled on the issue and in the end, accepted defeat.

Just how broad is this field that hampered your Trojan horse attack so? In what other ways can cryptography foil hacking attempts? In gaining an understanding of the cryptographic defense that foiled your attack, a Pandora's Box of possibilities was opened to you.

In those last few months on the job you infused your brethren with an inexplicable sense of hope in the workplace. It seemed that justice was in fact a thing of this world, and that the old saying "what goes around comes around" is true indeed. It's just that at your company, it seemed to come around a lot sooner for some reason. Being the good Samaritan that you are, you confided in Brian in your final week about the Ethernet client/server suite that you concocted. The torch was passed on to Brian to help make the company a more bearable place to work.

In the years that followed you heard through the grapevine that a database weenie joined the team. He had an affinity for music, and brought with him a CD collection that filled an entire wall. The tortured soul suffered from a mental condition that compelled him to listen to Kenny Rogers CDs over and over again. He quickly learned that the gods of the almighty CD-ROM did not share his taste in country-western, and they showed their wrath by ejecting his compact disks at every turn.

*...and so began the quest, born of questions unanswered, to confirm intuitions and discover yet newer possibilities, a quest that would lead to a mathematician buried beneath tome and scroll in an ivory tower to the south wherein these words were inscribed... uimibfdscjuiebuspfxfjtjtg!*

# Chapter 2

# Cryptovirology

*The digital realm is a truly magical one indeed. Where else can an object be conjured out of thin air, be teleported across vast distances, be duplicated in its exact form, be rendered invisible at the blink of an eye, and be cast back into oblivion?*

Professor Matt Blaze bounded from one end of the chalkboard to the other scrawling the words "multilevel security" as he went. When he finished he turned to face the class and waited patiently as the students distributed the handouts to each other. He rubbed his eyes under his glasses and then glanced at his cell phone, the same cell phone that Customs gave him such a hard time about when he went on a trip to the Caribbean. Apparently it was suspected as being a high-tech encryption device, an article considered to be munitions under ITAR regulations. The fact that customs was suspicious is not surprising given the nature of his research. If you were a cryptographer you'd recognize him on sight for his contributions to the field, and if you weren't you would be certain due to his outward appearance that he could dismantle and reassemble a computer system at a glance. He just had that intelligent, computer-savvy look about him.

When I received my copy I looked at it and couldn't wait to read it. In the center of the page was a mug shot of the infamous hacker Kevin Mitnick. It was a clip from the morning paper, and before diving into the theory of secure operating systems Matt took the time to discuss the truly historic events that were unfolding outside of the classroom. Tsutomu Shimomura was hot on the trail of Kevin Mitnick and Matt made a point of keeping us informed of the events as they occurred. Having already read *The Cuckoo's Egg* [294] and *Cyberpunk: Outlaws and Hackers on the*

*Computer Frontier* [127], I appreciated both the significance and difficulty involved in tracking such a notorious hacker. The combination of news discussions and spellbinding lectures captivated the class and created a general feeling that we were all a part of something larger than ourselves in that Fall '95 course on computer security.

Matt's enthusiasm towards computer security was contagious, and the topics on his syllabus were fascinating: multilevel security, public key cryptography, zero-knowledge protocols, just to name a few. He brought in several guest lecturers to add to his presentations. Among them were Jack Lacy and Joan Feigenbaum. Matt, Jack, and Joan were from AT&T, a baby Bell that descended from Ma Bell. In 1984 the federal government forced Ma Bell, then a solitary goliath in the telecom industry, to break up. To many the mere mention of Ma Bell still conjures up visions of old men pacing the corridors and ramparts of Bell Labs with staves in hand, contemplating technologies that would take decades to reach maturity.

Jack Lacy discussed the cryptographic library called *CryptoLib* that he helped to develop [166]. His lecture covered the library and the algorithms that it used. Only later did I learn how advanced the library was in comparison to the GNU projects' multiprecision library, GNUmp. To implement modular exponentiation, Cryptolib utilizes Karatsuba multiplication, Montgomery reduction, and vector addition chains. Also, in the case that the multiplicands are identical, a well-known squaring speed-up is utilized. At that time GNUmp did not incorporate all of these algorithms. The lecture covered many aspects of algorithmic number theory, and showed just how involved the programming can get when implementing cryptographic primitives.

Lacy went on to describe the random number generator used in CryptoLib called *truerand*. The truerand algorithm exploits the fact that most motherboards come equipped with two crystal timing devices. One crystal is used to generate the real-time clock signal and the other is used to generate the CPU clock signal. The CPU crystal operates at a much higher frequency than the clock crystal. Truerand pits these two oscillators against each other and extracts randomness based on their discrepancies.

Truerand operates as follows. Initially, a global Boolean flag $\mathcal{F}$ is set to false and a local variable $i$ is set to zero. Then, the address of a call-back function is passed as an argument to an operating system call that sets an alarm. The alarm is set to go off in one tick.[1] The call-back function sets $\mathcal{F}$ to true and then terminates. After the operating system call is made,

---

[1]A tick is typically $1/60^{\text{th}}$ of a second.

a while loop is entered in which $i$ is incremented by one in each iteration. The loop terminates only when $\mathcal{F}$ is set to true, which occurs when the call-back function is invoked by the operating system. The key to the operation of truerand is that it will not always take exactly one tick for the timer to go off, and hence the number of increments of $i$ is dictated by the number of CPU instructions executed within that time. In theory, the inconsistencies in the total number of CPU instructions executed until the alarm goes off will be reflected most in the least significant bits of $i$. In multitasking operating systems great care must be taken to verify that the counter gets incremented a sufficient number of times.

Joan Feigenbaum gave a lecture on zero-knowledge interactive proofs (ZKIP). A ZKIP is a protocol that allows a prover to convince a verifier of some fact without revealing why the fact is true to the verifier [118]. For example, there exists a ZKIP that allows a prover to prove that $n = pq$ is the product of two primes without revealing either prime $p$ or $q$ to the verifier. A zero-knowledge proof of knowledge is similar to a ZKIP, however, it also proves that the prover knows some fact, for example, the prime $p$ in $n = pq$. The fact that the prover *knows* this prime implies that the prover can write it down. There are numerous ways to utilize such protocols to make computer systems more secure. In the military, a fighter pilot needs to be able to identify an inbound warplane as being a friend-or-foe. This can be accomplished by assigning to each fighter pilot a unique composite $n$. Each pilot can be ordered to prove knowledge of the factorization of his or her own value $n$ when approaching another aircraft. ZKIPs are ideal friend-or-foe protocols since they reveal nothing to the enemy over the airways that would allow the enemy to impersonate friendly craft in the future.

In computer authentication systems, ZKIPs operate in much the same way. The user wants to be able to prove his or her identity to the computer system without revealing any information that would allow a hacker to impersonate the user at a later time. The zero-knowledge aspect of the proof implies that a password-snatching Trojan will be unable to collect information that will enable the Trojan horse author to impersonate the user. This holds true even if the Trojan observes every single log on that takes place. Due to the slow but sure introduction of smart card technology, the days in which users authenticate to sensitive systems using passwords are undoubtedly numbered.

Perhaps one of Matt's most interesting lectures was the one covering the elegant symmetric cipher called *TEA*. Whereas most ciphers are designed to be both fast and secure, the Tiny Encryption Algorithm [317] was specifically designed to be tiny as well. This has the benefit of taking up less disk space, less random access memory, and so on, since the algorithm itself is so small. Matt indicated in his lecture that anyone who could *break* TEA would have a result worthy of scientific publication. To prod his students into actually thinking about the problem he gave out an intriguing assignment. He asked us to figure out the TEA decryption algorithm given only the encryption algorithm.

The reason that breaking TEA is such a challenge is that it is a full-fledged 32-round Feistel cipher.[2]  So, the almighty gauntlet had been thrown down.  But, rather than beating my brain against a wall trying to investigate how to break TEA, I decided instead to investigate how to use TEA to attack computer systems. I marveled at and extolled its compactness and strength. It is ideal for incorporation into code that's not supposed to be there. When the lecture ended I headed out for a bite to eat with the revised challenge foremost in my mind.

My favorite haunt between classes was Amsterdam Pizza, located directly across from the Columbia University engineering building. There is a certain comfort to walking into an eatery, getting food, and sitting down without breathing a word. It is a courtesy extended only to true regulars. Smiling at the cashier, I took my slices and soda and sat down at a small table.

While looking past the line of people to the avenue beyond, I contemplated TEA. Never had I dreamed that such a strong cipher could be implemented in four lines of C code. The fact that it constituted a full-fledged Feistel cipher while being so compact was impressive indeed.  It seemed that there had to be some novel application of TEA to computer viruses. Most viruses use trivial encryption techniques such as repeated XOR encryption to hide their code. This form of encryption uses a randomly chosen key over and over to encipher the bulk of the virus, and is not secure since the key is reused.[3] It became apparent that TEA possesses the potential to make polymorphic viruses much harder to detect.

---

[2]Some security issues have been uncovered [153] and an improved version called XTEA has been proposed [318]. XTEA is given in Figure 2.1. A weakness in XTEA was addressed by the authors [319]. XTEA has been cryptanalyzed when reduced to 14 rounds [195].

[3]The Vernam cipher uses a One-time pad and is subject to known-plaintext attacks when some or all of the pad is reused.

```
/* XTEA
v gives the plaintext of 2 words
k gives the key of 4 words
N gives the number of cycles, 32 are recommended
if negative causes decoding, N must be the same as
     for coding
if zero causes no coding or decoding
assumes 32 bit "long" and same endian coding or
     decoding */

tean(long *v,long *k,long N)
{
unsigned long y = v[0],z = v[1],DELTA = 0x9e3779b9;
unsigned long limit,sum;

if (N > 0) /* the "if" code performs encryption */
   {
   limit = DELTA * N;
   sum = 0;
   while (sum != limit)
       y += (z << 4^z >> 5) + z^sum + k[sum&3],
       sum += DELTA,
       z += (y << 4^y >> 5) + y^sum + k[sum >> 11&3];
   }
else      /* the "else" code performs decryption */
   {      /* IT IS TRULY MINUSCULE */
   sum = DELTA * (-N);
   while (sum)
       z -= (y << 4^y >> 5) + y^sum + k[sum>>11&3],
       sum -= DELTA,
       y -= (z << 4^z >> 5) + z^sum + k[sum&3];
   }
v[0] = y;
v[1] = z;
return;
}
```

**Figure 2.1** Extended Tiny Encryption Algorithm

The tiny decryption algorithm could be used in the decryption header and the body of the virus could be encrypted using a strong Feistel cipher.

I then turned my attention from defensive applications to offensive applications of TEA. Having read about the One-half virus, I wondered if TEA could make virus attacks more devastating. The One-half virus uses encryption to render information on the hard disk inaccessible. The virus stores the decryption keys in the partition table on the infected machine. When the virus is in memory, it decrypts the data when it is accessed so that the user will not notice that the encryption occurred [123]. The novelty behind this attack is that it integrates the virus with its host to a certain degree. However, since the key can be extracted by specially designed software and the encrypted data can be decrypted, the attack is somewhat weak. Therefore, the attack really only contributes one more hurdle to the disinfection process.

It would be possible to modify the One-half virus so that it never decrypts the host information. The decryption algorithm could be removed from the One-half virus in an attempt to give the virus writer an exclusive advantage over the victim: since only the virus writer knows the decryption algorithm, only the virus writer can restore the data. However, this logic is flawed since, as illustrated by Matt's homework assignment, it is often possible to derive the decryption algorithm from the encryption algorithm alone.

Alternatively, a virus could be designed to encrypt the data using TEA and then throw away the key as a means of destroying the data. But a much stronger attack is to simply delete the data. It was apparent that the compactness of TEA would not improve the attack carried out by the One-half virus.

The One-half virus is a perfect illustration of the Achilles heel of viruses. The vulnerability of viruses lies in the fact that they are inherently scrutable once found. Using the model of computation known as a *Turing machine*, a virus can be viewed as a state-transition table and a starting state. When an antiviral analyst gets a hold of a virus, the analyst learns the table and starting state and therefore learns the operations that the virus is programmed to perform.

It was at this point in time that the improvement to the One-half virus became clear.[4] The attack carried out by the One-half virus is repairable

---

[4]It was one of those situations in which you know things are happening around you but you are zoned out completely. I happened to be watching livery cabs speed uptown but was scarcely aware of it.

for the simple reason that the view of the virus writer and the view of the antiviral analyst are *symmetric* (see Figure 2.2).

It was the word *symmetric* that triggered the realization. The key needed to be removed from the antiviral analyst's view but not from the virus writer's view. This would make the views *asymmetric*. Matt had recently given a lecture on asymmetric cryptography, also known as public key cryptography. It became immediately apparent that by using asymmetric cryptography the views could be made asymmetric.

In this new attack, a public key cryptosystem such as RSA [245] is used in the payload of the virus. The virus author generates an RSA key pair specifically for the purpose of mounting the virus attack. The key pair is generated once and for all *before* the virus is deployed. The public key is placed within the virus and the corresponding private key is *not* placed in the virus. The private key is kept secret by the author. The viral payload may be triggered by a particular event or date, for instance. The payload encrypts critical host data using the public key, thereby taking the data hostage. From the definition of a public key cryptosystem, it is not possible to derive the private key from readily available information such as the public key, which may be extracted from the virus. As a result antiviral analysts will not be able to determine the private key from the virus[5] (see Figure 2.3). If there are no backups, then only the virus author will be able to restore the encrypted data because only the virus author knows the needed RSA private decryption key.

Only later did it truly sink in that it was the notion of computational intractability that made the virus so powerful. When the virus is scrutinized by an antiviral analyst the RSA public key $(e, n)$ will be found where $e$ is the public exponent and $n$ is the product of two primes $p$ and $q$. However, no matter how carefully $n$ is studied it will not reveal its prime factors $p$ and $q$, thereby breaking the symmetry.[6] For the victim to recover all of the lost data without the involvement of the virus writer and without backups, the victim would have to break RSA.

That evening the idea thoroughly congealed in my mind and I considered the best course of action. The idea had a definite academic ring to

---

[5]This means that even though the state-transition table and starting state of the virus are known, the private key will remain hidden from antiviral analysts.

[6]To be technically accurate, RSA is based on the difficulty of computing $e^{\text{th}}$ roots modulo $n$. Also, every RSA ciphertext leaks the Jacobi symbol of the plaintext. Public key cryptosystems with stronger security properties are discussed at the end of this chapter.

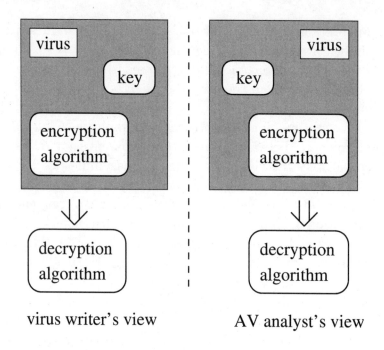

virus writer's view            AV analyst's view

**Figure 2.2** Symmetric views of the virus

it since it fell squarely into the category of denial-of-service attacks which are attacks that deny one or more users access to computer resources. The attack is a form of denial-of-service since in the absence of backups the host can no longer access the encrypted data. But, this attack had a twist to it. Since the data can be restored using the private key, the attack was suitable for extortion.

The computer science department offers an optional master thesis course that is geared towards students who want to pursue a particular research topic. It seemed to me that this discovery merited a master's thesis, but in the end the decision would ultimately fall on the shoulders of a faculty member. It had the potential of killing two birds with one stone: develop a prototype while satisfying course credits towards the degree. The challenge, then, was to solicit the involvement of an Ivy League faculty member to help investigate a computer virus with an unprecedented payload.

On the following day, a staff member of the computer science department named Alice Cueba took the time to assist me in seeking a thesis advisor for the idea. Alice knew all the visiting professors as well as all the full-time faculty members, some of whom were on sabbatical. She has

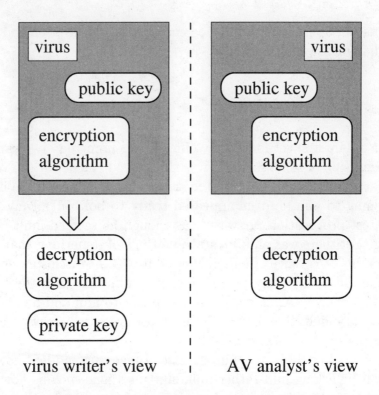

**Figure 2.3** Asymmetric views of the virus

seen more undergraduates and graduates through their educational careers than I can imagine, and I knew that if anyone could pull some strings to find someone willing to get involved in this questionable research topic it was she. Alice spoke with Professor Galil and together they suggested that I contact Professor Blaze and a guest of the department named Moti Yung. At the time Moti was a researcher at the IBM T. J. Watson Research Center. Soon after I met Moti for the first time, and I will never forget the encounter.

Fear gripped me as I approached his office. The idea had already been laid bare via e-mail and his true intentions for the meeting could not be ascertained. Academia is riddled with burnouts, student-haters, and petty thieves of ideas, so I had no idea what to expect. For the first time in my life I had opted to come clean with a hacking idea and it felt like I was confessing to something that I hadn't even done. Would he belittle the idea? Would he publish it himself? Would he interrogate me about my past history and then seek my expulsion through the Dean's office? The answer to all these questions was no. Amid walls of books and mountains of papers Moti addressed me as a would-be peer and had me utterly disarmed within an hour....

* * * * *

When Adam first set foot in my office it was immediately clear that he was on a mission of some sort. He was shifty-eyed and sat at the very edge of his seat. On occasion he would look over his shoulder to see if anyone was listening to him, and he appeared ready to bolt out of my office at the slightest provocation. It wasn't as though he seemed guilt-ridden or anything. Yet there was an unmistakable tinge of something that weighed heavily on his conscience. In all likelihood it was the disclosure of the idea that made him feel uneasy rather than my affiliation with the computer science department. After all, I was a stranger to him and he had openly admitted via e-mail that he was interested in researching ways of taking other people's data hostage, *literally*.

I did what I could to put him at ease. I made no sudden movements[7] and began by asking him rather mundane questions such as how long he had been at Columbia and who his faculty advisor was. He replied by saying that he'd been there for a year and that Steven Feiner was his advisor. We talked briefly about Feiner's work in computer graphics, and the conversation slowly moved on to the city of Manhattan, and then onto where Adam did his undergraduate studies. Overall it seemed as if Adam wasn't quite sure what he was getting himself into, but on some level it appeared as though he believed he was doing the right thing.

What Adam did not realize was that I was already interested in attacks on computer systems. It is from such threats that security requirements are identified, and they stimulate the development of new and improved models and tools for securing computer systems. I welcomed the opportunity to talk with him about computer viruses, since I had predicted long ago that they will become increasingly vicious, dynamic, and virulent. Viruses were the primary motivation for an earlier work that I did with Ostrovsky on how to withstand mobile virus attacks [215]. This threat model grew into what is now known as the proactive security model, which allows for dynamic and non-monotone corruption of machines on a network. Researchers have to be at least one step ahead of the game in order to safely handle new attacks. This belief suggests that novel threats

---

[7]Slight exaggeration.

have to be exposed, through scientific publications, conferences, and so forth, so that the necessary infrastructures are developed. Several questions had occupied my mind upon reading his e-mail and meeting him for the first time.

How do you deal with a student who has just rediscovered in a negative light the enormous power of public-key cryptography? Public-key cryptography is the power of breaking symmetries between parties such that one party can compute something whereas another party cannot. This power is what makes modern cryptography a science that constantly surprises and mystifies. It is a science in which seemingly paradoxical and unsolvable problems are solved, problems like "how to flip a coin over the telephone."

How do you deal with a student whose apparent goal is to *improve* computer virus attacks and capabilities? After all, virus study is dangerous and represents a threat in and of itself since experimentation can lead to accidental viral infections. Great care must be taken to isolate any and all machines that are used for experimentation.

How do you deal with a student who has a solid background in engineering but doesn't even know the basics of modular arithmetic? Number theory is at the very heart of modern cryptography. He was well versed in continuous mathematics as any student of electrical engineering should be, yet he had never even heard of the extended Euclidean algorithm when I first met him. This became clear after I realized that, despite having applied public key cryptography to virus attacks, he didn't even know how to compute an RSA private exponent given the public exponent and the two private primes.

These questions would all be answered in time. When Adam asked me if I would be his master's thesis advisor, I gladly accepted the position.[8] His academic interest in pioneering virus attacks seemed genuine. It nonetheless became quickly apparent that his understanding of computer viruses exceeded the norm, and this suggested that he had conducted extensive experimentation on his own. I advised him to start learning about number theory, so he went out and bought Underwood Dudley's book on the subject [96]. Every so often he'd hit a roadblock of some sort when trying to understand a cryptosystem that he'd never seen before, and I would always explain it to him.

---

[8]The cryptovirus attack first appeared in A. Young, "Cryptovirology and the Dark Side of Black-Box Cryptography," Master's Thesis, Comp. Sci. S6902, Columbia University Dept. of Comp. Sci., Summer, 1995, advisor: Moti Yung.

It was a special time for me, because I found that I was learning as much from him as he was from me. It is the type of student-teacher relationship that every faculty advisor strives for. However cliché it may be, Einstein's statement that "imagination is more important than knowledge" could not be truer with respect to scientific exploration. Adam's enthusiasm for malicious software drove him to study branches of mathematics that he probably would have never learned otherwise. As for where the research was heading, I did not know. Yet all of the ingredients for a promising student were present, so I decided to build on his natural enthusiasm for the subject, and decided that whatever he would learn and whatever direction his research would take him would be up to him.

Going forward I decided to lay down only a minimal set of principles as well as a general framework for our collaboration. It was to be a scientific endeavor rather than a rogue operation. There would be no accidental release of viruses. In fact, there would be no public disclosure of executable code at all.

We also discussed the rationale behind publishing information warfare attacks. I explained that the wisdom of the open research community as a whole, due to peer reviews, competition, and collaboration, is vast and that the scrutiny of ideas helps to make systems more secure. Closed research communities have proven to fail in the past. A classic case is the secret design behind the Clipper chip that fell from grace due to the attacks that were found against it. Only the input/output specification and the chips themselves were made available, yet attacks were nonetheless found based on the size of its parameters [28] as well as the binding of its authentication [104]. I explained to him that I agreed to investigate cryptovirology because it is interesting in its own right, and because I believed in the importance of researching defenses against cryptovirology.

From this point on working with Adam was like working with any of my previous graduate students. The motivation and insight that researchers have on cryptography varies greatly from person to person. Some people are driven by the underlying mathematics, some by system security aspects, some by theoretical considerations, and still others by practical every-day considerations. Adam approached cryptography from a completely different angle than others, and it was a new perspective for me.

During the course of our research we began referring to the virus as a *cryptovirus*. I coined the term *cryptovirus* to describe them since it accurately describes their modus operandi. *A cryptovirus is a computer virus that contains and uses a public key.* The original definition stipulates that the author knows the private key, but this aspect of the definition can be weakened. Polymorphic viruses have used symmetric encryption for a long time, and it is fitting to employ a new name for viruses that use public key cryptography. Cryptoviruses are unique due to their ability to perform one-way cryptographic computations that only the virus writer can undo.

* * * * *

And so it was that the first cryptovirus was researched under the auspices of Columbia University. In the weeks that followed we met regularly in the Mudd building alongside Amsterdam Avenue. During our collaborations we realized two shortcomings in the attack. First, in order for the virus to encrypt a significant amount of data it would be necessary to break the data into chunks that could be encrypted using RSA. Since RSA encryption is slow in comparison to symmetric ciphers, this meant that the attack would take a long time for the virus to carry out. Also, if the virus writer were to simply give the private key to the victim then the victim could publish the private key and foil any attempts to extort other victims. The virus writer could instead demand that he or she be given the ciphertext in order to perform the decryption, but this would require a huge file transfer. It is also quite possible that by exposing the host data to the virus writer, its value would significantly diminish.

We discovered that all of these shortcomings could be resolved in one fell swoop. In this more refined attack, the virus does not encrypt host data directly with the public key. Instead, it generates a symmetric key uniformly at random and then encrypts the host data using this key. The public key in the virus is then used to encrypt the symmetric key. This is known as *hybrid encryption*. If the victim wants the data back, the victim has to send the virus writer the ciphertext of the symmetric key. The virus writer then decrypts the ciphertext using his or her own private key and then sends the symmetric key to the victim. To preserve that attacker's anonymity an anonymous remailer can be used to carry out the transaction. The attack will only work if there are no backups of the host data, and if the virus was not being observed while mounting the attack. Since the symmetric key is chosen uniformly at random for each victim, publication of the symmetric key is not likely to be of any use to other victims.

With a solid and carefully planned viral payload, we set out to create the first cryptovirus. A Macintosh SE/30 computer was chosen as our test bed. The latest copy of the GNU multiprecision library was obtained, and was modified as necessary to compile on a Macintosh. Only a small fraction of the GNU multiprecision library was needed, yet it was still large enough that it comprised the majority of the cryptovirus. Part of the virus was written in ANSI C and part of it was written in Motorola assembly language. Before the first version of the virus was compiled, assembled, and linked, logic was included to prevent replication on any machine other than the SE/30. It was of the utmost importance that it not escape. It would have been incredibly embarrassing for Columbia University if it did.[9] The virus was not polymorphic and was not designed to bypass any antiviral software whatsoever. As an added precaution, a snippet of the virus was taken and used as a search string. Antiviral searches were performed regularly using this custom virus definition to keep the virus in check.

The hybrid cryptosystem for the virus consisted of RSA and TEA. To generate symmetric keys randomly, AT&T's truerand was used [166]. Truerand was critical since any weakness in it might give rise to a way for victims to derive some or all of the bits of the symmetric key used in the attack. Any weaknesses in truerand, TEA, or RSA would imply a weakness in the cryptovirus attack.

Truerand can be invoked *ad infinitum*, producing an endless stream of random numbers. As a result the cryptovirus can be viewed as a probabilistic algorithm with access to randomness that is generated by a physical device. The original cryptovirus used the raw outputs of truerand to generate the symmetric encryption key. However, an *entropy extraction* algorithm should be applied to the output of truerand to remove any potential bias.

Table 2.1 gives a synopsis of the speed of the Macintosh cryptovirus. The cryptovirus contained a 512-bit RSA public modulus. This is a bit small by modern standards. RSA key lengths of 768 or 1024 bits should be used today. The virus generated 384 random bits. This was used to derive Initialization Vector (IV) information and two 128 bit symmetric keys denoted by $k_1$ and $k_2$. The virus computed a checksum using cipher feed-back mode (CFB) on a file entitled 'payroll' that the fictitious virus

---

[9]I had grown very fond of my alma mater after meeting Moti and it seemed that Columbia was sticking its neck out to accommodate my abnormal, albeit academic research interests.

| | | |
|---|---|---|
| system boot (no attack) | < | 16.7 msec |
| infect a program | ≈ | 1 sec |
| infect file 'System' | ≈ | 4 sec |
| perform RSA encryption | = | 66.7 msec |
| generate 384 random bits | = | 6.4 sec |
| system boot (w/ attack) | = | 11.92 sec |
| TEA encr. rate (1 round) | = | 47k bytes/sec |
| TEA encr. rate (3 rounds) | = | 15.7k bytes/sec |

**Table 2.1**  Running time of the virus

| code size | bytes | source language(s) |
|---|---|---|
| attack routines 'main' | 434 | ANSI C |
| TEA encryption routine | 88 | Asm |
| truerand size | 124 | Asm |
| misc. attack code | 804 | ANSI C |
| global data | 560 | N/A |
| modified GNUmp lib | 4,372 | ANSI C |
| entire attack routine | 6,382 | ANSI C/Asm |
| main virus routine | 614 | Asm |
| total virus size | 6,996 | ANSI C/Asm |

**Table 2.2**  Size of the virus

author demanded. The block cipher that was used in CFB was TEA in encryption-decryption-encryption mode. The EDE mode first encrypts the plaintext with $k_1$ then decrypts the result with $k_2$ and then encrypts that result using $k_1$. A keyed cryptographic checksum $h$ that uses keys $k_1$, $k_2$ can be implemented using CFB as follows.

$$h(IV, k_1, k_2, m) = last(CFB(IV, k_1, k_2, m)) \tag{2.1}$$

The checksum is computed on a message $m$. The function *last* denotes the final ciphertext block in the CFB ciphertext. A nice aspect of this checksum algorithm is that it requires very little code above and beyond the code needed to perform CFB encryption.

The virus then encrypted the confidential file entitled "e-money" using
TEA in EDE mode. The original file was overwritten with the ciphertext
in the process. The checksum, initialization vector information, and the
two TEA keys were encrypted using the 512-bit RSA public key. The IV
that is used in the encryption of the file "e-money" and both keys are
needed by the victim to recover the file "e-money."

In this hypothetical cryptovirus attack, the author demands the file
"payroll" from the victim. The author does not help the victim unless
the proper file "payroll" and the RSA ciphertext are obtained. Upon
receiving the 512-bit RSA ciphertext from the victim, the virus author
decrypts it using the RSA private key, thereby recovering the checksum,
IV information, and both TEA keys. The author computes a checksum on
the provided file using the IV and both keys that were recovered from the
RSA ciphertext. The file "payroll" is accepted as being valid if and only
if the resulting checksum matches the checksum from the decrypted RSA
ciphertext. If the "payroll" file is valid then the two TEA symmetric keys
are given to the victim to allow the victim to decrypt the file "e-money."
The virus computes the checksum and asymmetrically encrypts it along
with the TEA keys to prevent the victim from sending an alternate version
of the "payroll" file.

Speed was an important factor in benchmarking the cryptovirus, since
as indicated by the table it took a noticeable amount of time to generate
the 384 random bits. Table 2.2 shows the size of the resulting cryptovirus.
The virus was written in Motorola assembly language and ANSI C.

With a prototype in hand as well as data on its performance, we wrote
a paper about it that was submitted to the IEEE Symposium on Security
& Privacy.[10] The paper was accepted and was presented on May 7, 1996
[332].[11] To notify the scientific community of this threat, a message was
posted to the sci.crypt newsgroup that explained the use of asymmetric
cryptography to mount a reversible denial of service attack [330].

Since the time of the conference, a number of reports, presentations,
books, and so on, have discussed *cryptoviral extortion*. Many of these discussions define cryptoviral extortion as a "virus that encrypts the victim's
files," without mentioning anything specific about the type of encryption

[10]See the call for papers in [285]. Certain members of the program committee were
vehemently opposed to its publication. The notion of a digital facehugger was apparently perceived as "vulgar" and non-scientific.

[11]The paper was presented in the session entitled *Biologically Inspired Topics in
Computer Security*. The program for the conference appears in [206].

algorithm that is used by the virus (e.g., symmetric, asymmetric, hybrid). In one example [86], it is stated that a "cryptovirus" has a payload that encrypts files with a secret key, making the contents inaccessible to the owner. In the cryptoviral extortion attack that we designed, the cryptovirus either (1) encrypts files with a *public key*, or (2) encrypts a session key with a *public key* and then encrypts files using the session key. Asymmetric encryption is *central* to a *secure* (from the perspective of the virus writer) cryptoviral extortion attack since the decryption key cannot be recovered from an old copy of the cryptovirus. Viruses that do not employ asymmetric cryptography do not mount the cryptoviral extortion attack as defined in [332].

Initially, the combination of software attacks and cryptographic techniques appeared to be quite powerful and this has proven to be even more so today. What we noticed over the years is that advanced and provably secure malware attacks are made possible by advances in cryptographic models and algorithmic constructions. Examples of such advances include: trapdoor functions, semantic security of encryption, cryptographically strong pseudorandomness, the random oracle model, and so forth. These are cornerstones for building secure cryptosystems and proving that they are so. Our research has shown that these tools can be used to devise attacks that are not detectable and that bestow unusual powers to the attacker. This is not unlike using missiles to take down missiles, i.e., fighting fire with fire.

Later on in this book we describe cryptotrojan attacks that leak private keys to the attacker. The approaches that are taken to prove the security of the attacks are reminiscent of approaches used in proving the security of many modern cryptosystems. We investigated cryptovirology and then moved on (without even realizing it at first) to a subject that we later called *kleptography*. From there we moved to other subjects that turned out to be closely related. Scientific exploration is hard to control and even harder to predict, and our joint research has led us to places that we did not expect to go. But it has been our experience that this is the way that things usually turn out in research.

The remainder of this book is not going to read like the text in Chapters 1 and 2. The purpose of these first two chapters was to expose some of the motivation and history behind cryptovirology. This is where the pedal hits the metal, so to speak. The remainder of the text is saturated with equations and algorithms. However, scattered throughout are ideas and attacks that are explained at a relatively high level. So, we encourage

readers to keep reading and not be discouraged by the technical details.
To us, playing the role of the *bad guy* is tremendous fun and we hope that
readers will get a kick out the book, however sinister it may seem.

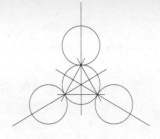

# Chapter 3

# Tools for Security and Insecurity

Cryptosystems and cryptographic protocols rely on various tools to be implemented properly. Perhaps the most basic tool is a *random bit generator*.[1] Random bit generators are used to randomly generate symmetric keys, private keys, padding, and so on in cryptography. They form the cornerstone of algorithms designed to protect computer systems and the cornerstone of algorithms that are designed to subvert computer systems. A poor random number generator could lead to a weak or otherwise guessable private key. A poor random number generator could lead to a guessable symmetric key and thereby diminish the effectiveness of a cryptovirus attack.

The survey books on cryptography that appeared in the 1990s gave the impression that crypto is a panacea for the Internet and its needs. However, experience has shown that this is far from the case [260]. For example, symmetric ciphers were analyzed in detail and proposed as solutions to common problems, yet little direction was given on how to arrive at *truly random* symmetric keys. This led to implementations containing very strong components as well as weak ones and security almost always defaults to the weakest link.

The first part of this chapter describes various physical phenomena that have been proposed in the literature as sources of randomness. It is common practice to misuse such sources by utilizing cryptographic hash

---

[1] In fact, randomized algorithms in general require access to quality random numbers to run properly. Examples include the ubiquitous Quicksort and the randomized algorithm for computing square roots modulo a prime $p$ when $p$ has no special form.

functions as entropy extractors. The nature of this questionable practice is discussed in some detail.

John von Neumann's classic algorithm for unbiasing a biased coin is one of the earliest known entropy extraction algorithms.[2] In this chapter it is shown how to apply this algorithm to an entropy source that behaves like a biased coin. A simple extension to Neumann's algorithm is then given along with references to other approaches. Common sense dictates that the more entropy sources that can be used, the better, so an approach is given to combine multiple sources of entropy securely. This approach has the property that the resulting bit stream is perfectly random provided that at least one of the entropy sources behaves like a biased coin and that is provably quasi-random otherwise.

It is often the case that sources of physical randomness provide random bits at a rate that is too slow for most applications. As a result efficient algorithms are needed that can convert a small number of truly random bits into a larger number of pseudorandom bits. Such algorithms are called *pseudorandom number generators* and the general topic is addressed in this chapter.

It is an unfortunate fact that even when random numbers are generated properly they are often misused. For example, OpenSSL suffered from a classic wrap-around bug in which the numbers from 1 to $n$ were chosen in such a way that the smallest of these numbers were more likely to be chosen than the rest [233, 329]. This occurred in the selection of witnesses for the Rabin-Miller probabilistic primality test. Uniform sampling is a general subject that is important in designing secure malware as well. For example, a worm may need to choose a server uniformly at random from a set of three servers in order to decide which server to infect. Furthermore, the worm may only have a random bit generator at its disposal to make the selection. A common programming mistake is to generate two bits to get a number $x$ between 0 and 3 inclusive, and then let the final answer be $x \bmod 3$. This is wrong since 0 will occur with a higher probability than 1. Uniform sampling techniques solve this problem and for this reason the topic of uniform sampling is covered.

Even when used correctly, random bits are often utilized in a wasteful fashion. This problem can be avoided by the judicious selection of efficient algorithms for the problem at hand. As a case in point, the problem of shuffling a deck of cards is covered. It is shown how successively choosing a card from the deck randomly uses up more random bits on average

---

[2]In fact, it might even be the first published entropy extraction algorithm.

than applying an unranking algorithm from algorithmic combinatorics. This particular example is clearly applicable to on-line casinos, but is also applicable to designing secure polymorphic viruses. A polymorphic virus often needs to randomly permute instructions and may need to select a random subset of machine registers to use in a decryption algorithm that deciphers the bulk of the virus.

The chapter concludes with a discussion of how general advances in cryptography lend strength to malicious software attacks. It is shown how semantic security against plaintext attacks and adaptive chosen-ciphertext security affect the cryptovirus extortion attack from the perspective of the attacker. Also, the subject of mix networks is addressed. Mix networks constitute a fundamental building block in secure on-line voting protocols, electronic money protocols, and so on, and they are also crucial in carrying out malicious software attacks in a way that protects the perpetrator, be it a person or finite automaton.

## 3.1  Sources of Entropy

Computer programs utilize entropy sources to generate random numbers. Often user input is used as an entropy source. For example, the RSA toolkit SecurPC, which ran on Microsoft Windows 95, derived random seeds based on keyboard and mouse timings. This data is collected during a period of several minutes in which the user "bangs on the keyboard" [248]. Aside from being a hassle from the user's perspective, the security of this approach is questionable to say the least. Reliance on user-supplied entropy should be avoided or minimized whenever possible since it is vulnerable to attacks and can provide a false sense of security. This holds true for normal security applications as well as for malicious software.

Desirable sources of entropy are those that are firmly rooted in physical phenomena that are not affected by the actions of users. The emission from radioactive material has been proposed as entropy source [124]. Although this may be a very solid source of randomness, it requires specialized hardware that does not come with typical personal computer systems.

An attractive candidate for entropy is AT&T's truerand (described in Chapter 2) since it is based on physical phenomena and is likely to work on any PC equipped with a CPU crystal and a real-time clock crystal. Truerand increments a counter in a busy-waiting fashion until a timer interrupt causes the loop to terminate. This effectively pits the real-time clock signal against the microprocessor signal and in theory captures their discrepancies in the resulting counter value.

Another attractive entropy source is the air turbulence that exists within hard drives. The seek time for a drive is the time it takes the read/write head to move over the track that it is going to read or write to. Once in position, the disk must rotate so that the desired sector falls under the read/write head. This is called the *rotational latency* or *rotational delay* [221]. Seek times and rotational delay are governed by physical phenomena and are affected by such things as chaotic air turbulence that is generated within the confines of high-speed hard disk drives [81]. A typical way to extract entropy from this source is to measure the time it takes to perform a disk read, for instance. Davis surmised that the movement of a hard disk arm perturbs the flow of air inside the drive, thus creating chaotic turbulence. To implement programs that extract this type of entropy, one has to be conscious of the fact that most operating systems cache disk accesses. It is prudent to measure hard disk entropy by making low level read/write calls.

Using hard disks as entropy sources was carefully studied at Lucent Technologies [139]. Jakobsson et al devised an approach to extracting randomness from hard disks based on multiple drive phenomena. They derived experimental results using a Sun Ultra-1 with a Cheetah disk and were able to generate between 5 and 577 random bits per minute depending on the type of phenomena that was used. They subjected the resulting bits to a battery of tests, and they passed with flying colors.

Designing software that avoids the use of specialized hardware is even more important in the case of malicious software than in normal scenarios. Consider computer viruses, for example. By their very nature they propagate from machine to machine, some of which may lack the needed specialized hardware and all of which are hostile environments to the virus. Such programs clearly cannot assume the presence of specialized hardware random number generators.

## 3.2   Entropy Extraction via Hashing

It is not an uncommon practice to collect randomness from entropy sources to produce a byte stream and then hash this byte stream to derive a "random" stream of bits. This heuristic is most likely based on the premise that since the outputs of cryptographic hash functions look random, they are random. When hash functions are used as such, they are being used as *entropy extractors*.[3]

Consider the SHA-1 cryptographic hash function, for example [211]. SHA-1 takes as input a variable length byte stream and outputs a 160-bit hash value. SHA-1 is based directly on the MD4 algorithm [242]. MD4 is a customized hash function designed with the explicit purpose of hashing with optimized performance in mind. The original MD4 design goals were to:

1. Make finding a collision difficult, taking about $2^{64}$ operations to do so (collision intractability).

2. Make finding a message yielding a pre-specified hash value difficult, taking about $2^{128}$ operations to do so (non-invertability).

Despite the fact that finding collisions was supposed to be difficult, a collision in MD4 was in fact found [94]. This demonstrates the danger of relying on primitives that cannot be proven to be correct.

Collision resistance and non-invertability were also the design criteria used in devising SHA [201]. SHA was not designed to output "random-looking hash values" and it was not designed to "extract truly random bits from inputs with a sufficient amount of entropy." The fact that it may appear to do so on the surface is immaterial from the standpoint of security. Properties (1) and (2) above were designed to provide sufficient conditions for using a hash function to heuristically protect against existential forgeries in digital signature schemes.

The use of SHA-1 to extract 160 "random" bits from the collected entropy strings is perilous since there is no evidence to suggest that the SHA-1 function does in fact do this. This use of SHA-1 assumes that it is a magic box that can magically extract entropy from the input string and output a truly random 160-bit string. The following quote is from a paper by Juels et al [148]:

---

[3]Adam encountered this practice firsthand while reviewing the RNG code for a company during a consulting engagement. The client used SHA-1 as an entropy extractor and the resulting entropy was used to generate random permutations. The client company shall remain nameless.

> *Timings of human interaction with a keyboard or mouse are*
> *currently the most common source of random seeds for cryp-*
> *tographic applications on PCs.    After a sufficient amount*
> *of such timing data is gathered, it is generally hashed*
> *down to a 128-bit or 160-bit seed.    This method relies*
> *for its security guarantees on unproven or unprovable as-*
> *sumptions about the entropy generated by human users* [97]
> <u>*and the robustness of hash functions as entropy extractors.*</u>

The danger of using a complex algorithm to produce strong random numbers in the absence of a theoretical foundation or analysis was noted in
RFC 1750 [97]:

> *Another serious strategy error is to assume that a very complex*
> *pseudo-random number generation algorithm will produce strong*
> *random numbers when there has been no theory behind or anal-*
> *ysis of the algorithm.*

There has been no theory or analysis behind SHA-1's ability to extract
entropy from its input. The complexity of the SHA-1 algorithm in no way
justifies its use as a magic box.

Consider the case in which entropy is taken from two sources. The
first source is a weak source derived from user input (e.g., message arrival,
mouse inputs, etc.) and potentially guessable inputs such as the system
time. The second source is a strong source of entropy such as a hardware
RNG. There is strong reason to suspect that the clock input is poor indeed.
The following is from RFC 1750 [97]:

> *Computer clocks, or similar operating system or hardware val-*
> *ues, provide significantly fewer real bits of unpredictability than*
> *might appear from their specifications.*

Suppose that 24 bytes are derived solely from the weak source and 24 bytes
are taken directly from the strong source. Finally, suppose that these two
sequences are concatenated and fed as input to SHA-1 to produce a 20-byte
value. The use of SHA-1 in this fashion could in fact result in a seed that
is significantly less random than 24 bytes from the strong entropy source.
It is conceivable that SHA-1 mixes this low-quality randomness with the
high-quality randomness and outputs bits having a degree of randomness

that is somewhere between the two extremes. An extreme, albeit remote, possibility is that SHA-1 will derive virtually all of the resulting entropy from the weak source. Again, since there is no proof regarding SHA-1's true behavior as an entropy extractor, anything seems possible.

## 3.3  Unbiasing a Biased Coin

The notion of a biased coin is by and large an abstraction used by theorists to articulate the behavior of a source of entropy. A real coin may certainly be biased based on how it was minted. But in the context of computer security, a biased coin is a general term for an entropy source that has a fixed bias towards outputting binary 1's or binary 0's.

As it turns out, the existence of a biased coin is enough to guarantee access to *perfectly random bits*. For many people, particularly those in the computer security field, the mere mention of perfect anything borders on taboo. Yet, in this case it is safe to say so. The math speaks for itself and the proof of this statement is given in this chapter. The subtlety lies in whether or not a given source of entropy in fact behaves like a biased coin or not.

### 3.3.1  Von Neumann's Coin Flipping Algorithm

A biased coin is a coin that has a fixed probability of heads, denoted by $p_h = 1/2 + \delta$, where $\delta$ is a Real number contained in the interval [-1/2,1/2]. The value $\delta$ is referred to as the bias of the coin. Let $p_t$ be the probability of tails. Hence, $p_t = 1 - p_h$. For example, if a coin comes up heads with probability 51% then $\delta = 1/100$. If the coin comes up heads with probability 49% then $\delta = -1/100$.

The standard approach to removing bias is to use Neumann's classic unbiasing algorithm [309]. The problem of unbiasing a biased coin is one whose fundamental nature is matched only by its elegant solution. It is instructional to consider the problem using a concrete example. Suppose that we are given a coin that comes up heads with probability 5/8. Neumann's solution is as follows. A series of experiments are performed in which the coin is tossed twice in succession. If in a given experiment the result is heads followed by tails, then the result of the toss is heads and no more experiments are performed. If in a given experiment the result is tails followed by heads, then the final outcome is tails and no more experiments are performed. If in a given experiment the tosses are the same, then another experiment is performed. This is depicted in Table 3.1.

Observe that the probability of heads is the same as the probability of tails. So, given that the two tosses are not the same the answer will be heads with probability 1/2. The answer is therefore always correct when an experiment terminates. An interesting aspect of this algorithm is that the numerical value of the bias is not needed to generate fair coin tosses. The probability that a given experiment will terminate with an answer is $15/64 + 15/64 = 30/64$. Although it is possible that this method will never terminate when executed, the chances of this is negligible for a bias of 1/8. Since the algorithm might never halt but always outputs the correct answer when it does halt, it belongs to a class of algorithms known as *Las Vegas algorithms*. The algorithm is tractable for any bias that is not overwhelmingly close to heads or tails.

The following claim regarding Neumann's algorithm can be proven.

**Claim 1** *When the input bits to Neumann's algorithm are generated by a biased coin, Neumann's algorithm outputs a heads with probability 1/2.*

To see this, consider the case that a value is output in iteration $j$. Since the two input bits for iteration $j$ are generated by a biased coin it follows that the two flips are independent events. In iteration $j$, Neumann's algorithm outputs heads with probability $(1/2 + \delta)(1/2 - \delta)$. It outputs tails with probability $(1/2 - \delta)(1/2 + \delta)$. It follows from the commutative property of multiplication that these probabilities are equal.

| Outcome | Probability | Result |
|---------|-------------|--------|
| heads-heads | 25/64 | do over |
| tails-tails | 9/64 | do over |
| heads-tails | 15/64 | heads |
| tails-heads | 15/64 | tails |

**Table 3.1** Unbiasing using Neumann's algorithm

### 3.3.2 Iterating Neumann's Algorithm

There has been a significant amount of research on improving the efficiency of Neumann's algorithm[4] [148, 222]. Rather than reiterating one of these algorithms, a simple example of how to slightly improve Neumann's method will be given. In the improvement described in Table 3.2, Neumann's algorithm is modified to accept four bits at a time instead of two. A result of heads is indicated by a binary "1" and a tails is indicated by a binary "0."

The middle column shows the output when Neumann's algorithm is applied to the input nibble.[5] For example, if the input is 0001 then the first two zeros causes a rejection, and the 01 causes a zero to be output. The rightmost column shows the output when Neumann's method is generalized to taking 4 bits as input. Observe that in each row the rightmost column has at least as many bits listed as the middle column, and sometimes more so. It follows that this approach has a higher bandwidth than Neumann's algorithm.

To see the utility of this increased bandwidth algorithm, suppose that this improved algorithm is supplied with a very long stream of input bits. We would expect it to produce more perfectly random bits than Neumann's classic algorithm would.

The correctness of the improved algorithm will now be analyzed. Recall from probability theory that if $A$ and $B$ are two events in a uniform probability space, the conditional probability of $A$ given $B$ is defined as follows.

$$Pr[A|B] = \frac{Pr[A \cap B]}{Pr[B]}$$

The following are probabilities of outputting 0 and 1 when one bit is output.

$$Pr[0 \ is \ output \mid one \ bit \ is \ output] = \frac{p_t^2 p_h^2}{2p_h^2 p_t^2} = \frac{1}{2}$$

---

[4]For example, the work of Juels et al shows how to simulate the maximum number of coin flips for a given number of die rolls.

[5]One nibble equals four bits.

| Input | Neumann | Improved Neumann |
|-------|---------|------------------|
| 0000  | -       | -                |
| 0001  | 0       | 00               |
| 0010  | 1       | 10               |
| 0011  | -       | 0                |
| 0100  | 0       | 01               |
| 0101  | 00      | 00               |
| 0110  | 01      | 01               |
| 0111  | 0       | 01               |
| 1000  | 1       | 11               |
| 1001  | 10      | 10               |
| 1010  | 11      | 11               |
| 1011  | 1       | 11               |
| 1100  | -       | 1                |
| 1101  | 0       | 00               |
| 1110  | 1       | 10               |
| 1111  | -       | -                |

**Table 3.2** Improved Neumann Algorithm with 4-bit input

$$Pr[1 \text{ is output} \mid \text{one bit is output}] = \frac{p_h^2 p_t^2}{2p_h^2 p_t^2} = \frac{1}{2}$$

It remains to consider the case that two bits are output. Below, the probability for 00 is derived.

$$Pr[00 \text{ is output} \mid \text{two bits are output}] = \frac{p_t^3 p_h + p_t^2 p_h^2 + p_h^3 p_t}{4(p_t^3 p_h + p_t^2 p_h^2 + p_h^3 p_t)} = \frac{1}{4}$$

It is straightforward to show that the conditional probability is 1/4 for 01, 10, and 11 as well.

### 3.3.3  Heuristic Bias Matching

A crucial observation in Neumann's classic algorithm is that the bias must be the same for both flips in a given execution of Neumann's algorithm for the output bit to be unbiased. This suggests that great care should be exercised when applying Neumann's algorithm to a given entropy source.

Neumann's method can be heuristically applied to remove bias in the output of truerand using the following algorithm. (Truerand is discussed in Chapter 2.) In the first step truerand is invoked to obtain the 16 least significant bits of the counter $i$. Let $s_1$ denote these 16 bits. Truerand is then invoked again to obtain another set of 16 bits $s_2$. The least significant bits from each of these two sets are used as a Neumann experiment, then the two penultimate bits are used as a second experiment, and so on. For concreteness, suppose that $s_1$ and $s_2$ are as follows:

$$s_1 = 0100111010001011$$

$$s_2 = 0101111100101010$$

Experiment 1 results in 10, experiment 2 results in 11, experiment 3 results in 00, and so on. A result of 10 is interpreted as a randomly chosen binary 1 and a result of 01 is interpreted as a randomly chosen binary 0. A result of 00 or 11 is regarded as a failed experiment. Let $p_{i,j}$ denote the probability that a binary 1 occurs in the $j^{\text{th}}$ bit of the $i^{\text{th}}$ trial, where $j = 0, 1, ..., 15$ and $i = 1, 2, 3, 4, ....$ Consider the following two assumptions:

1. $p_{i,j} = p_{i+1,j}$ for $i = 1, 3, 5, 7, ...$ and $j = 0, 1, 2, ..., 15$.

2. for all $i$ there exists a $j$ contained in $\{0, 1, 2, ..., 15\}$ such that $p_{i,j}$ is neither overwhelming nor negligible.

Assumption (1) implies that truerand behaves consistently across pairs of invocations, which is necessary for correctness. Assumption (2) implies that in each trial $i$ there is at least one probability $p_{i,j}$ capable of producing a fair toss.[6] For example, suppose that $p_{i,15} = 1$ for $i = 1, 2, 3, ....$ In this case the random number generator will never output a bit based on bit position $j = 15$. If for all $i$, $p_{i,j} = 1$ for $j = 0, 1, 2, ..., 15$ then truerand would not provide any randomness at all.

This approach demonstrates the notion of heuristic bias matching. A series of "random" positive integers are obtained from a timing-sensitive entropy source. The source should not be based on user inputs, and there should be reason to believe that the source behaved in the same basic way

---

[6]This assumption can actually be weakened a little since truerand need only provide such a probability sufficiently often.

to produce each of these numbers. The integers are such that the entropy is arguably concentrated in the least significant bits. The most significant bits may have no entropy at all. Pairs of these integers are obtained from the source. To apply Neumann's algorithm, the least significant bits are run through Neumann's algorithm, then the second least significant bits, and so on. Of course, this is only a heuristic. But, one would expect that the biases may in fact match up this way. *If they do, then perfectly random bits will result.* To guard against the possibility that the biases do not match up, multiple entropy sources should be used and a general approach such as Santha and Vazirani's algorithm (described in Section 3.4) should be employed to combine the sources.

## 3.4   Combining Weak Sources of Entropy

Consider a true RNG predicated on the "randomness" derived from keyboard latency. What if the user breaks his or her arm and has to type methodically with one hand?[7] This may eliminate some if not all the randomness for a time. What if a hardware-based RNG suffers a breakdown, thus rendering the hardware RNG unavailable? Such a solution would then have to rely entirely on other sources of randomness until the failure is rectified.

A solid approach to generating pseudorandom bits based on physical randomness is given in Figure 3.1. The two dark gray boxes are separate sources that are believed to provide a measurable amount of true entropy. Each source is treated separately and the output of each source is sent through an unbiasing algorithm as indicated by the light gray boxes. The operating system RNG could, for instance, be the Intel hardware RNG. This RNG uses two free-running oscillators, one that is fast and one that is much slower. A thermal noise source is used to modulate the frequency of the slower clock signal. The slower clock triggers measurements of the faster clock. The drift between the two is used to generate bits, which may be biased [149]. The Intel hardware RNG applies Neumann's algorithm internally to produce an unbiased stream (in theory). This is why the output of the Intel RNG does not go through a light gray box in Figure 3.1.

The three bit streams produced by the three light gray boxes are then

---

[7]Look for key, press key, look for key, press key (commonly referred to as *hunting and pecking*).

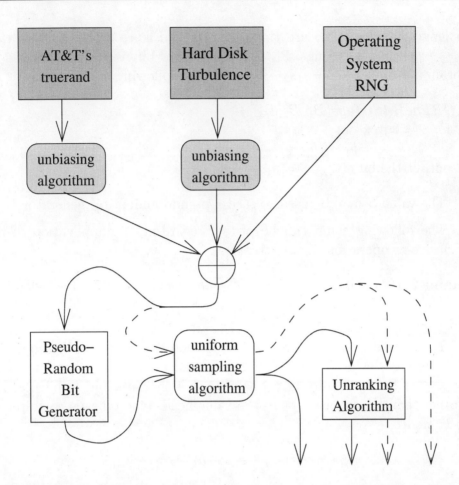

**Figure 3.1** Sound approach to generating and using randomness

bitwise exclusive-or'ed. This is indicated by the $\oplus$ symbol. Observe that if one of the physical sources of randomness behaves like a biased coin then exactly one of the streams going into $\oplus$ will be completely random. This is what makes this random number generation method robust. Suppose that all but one of the sources is compromised, either due to device failure or a malicious adversary. *As long as one of the streams is truly random, the output of the $\oplus$ operation will be truly random.* If a source were to shut down, then the stream that it would normally contribute to $\oplus$ can be set to all zeros. This will have a null effect on the bitwise XOR operation.

In fact, it is sufficient that in the bitwise XOR operation, one bit in each bit position be completely random. This will now be analyzed. Let $B_i = b_{i,1} b_{i,2} \cdots b_{i,k}$ denote the bit string that is output by Neumann's algorithm when applied to entropy source $i$. Each string $B_i$ is $k$ bits in length. Since there are three sources in Figure 3.1, it follows that $1 \leq i \leq 3$. The strings $B_1, B_2$, and $B_3$ are bitwise exclusive-or'ed to obtain a $k$-bit seed $S = s_1 s_2 \cdots s_k$ using the following algorithm.

$XORTheBitStrings(B_1, B_2, B_3)$:
1. for $j = 1$ to $k$ do:
2.                  $s_i = b_{1,j} \oplus b_{2,j} \oplus b_{3,j}$
3. output the bit string $S = s_1 s_2 \cdots s_k$

The value $S$ may be used to seed a pseudorandom bit generator.[8]

The following claim can be proven regarding the application of the exclusive-or operation to the streams.

**Claim 2** *If for all $j$ where $1 \leq j \leq k$ there exists an $i \in [1,3]$ such that $b_{i,j}$ is chosen uniformly at random, then $S$ is a truly random $k$-bit string.*

To see this, consider bit position $j$ where $1 \leq j \leq k$. Without loss of generality, let $b_{i,j}$ be a bit that is chosen uniformly at random, with $1 \leq i \leq 3$. Let $p_h$ denote the probability that the three bits in bit position $j$ other than $b_{i,j}$ exclusive-or to the value heads where heads corresponds to 1. Hence,

$$p_h = Pr[b_{1,j} \oplus b_{2,j} \oplus b_{3,j} \oplus b_{i,j}] = 1$$

The probability that $s_j = 1$ is $\frac{1}{2}p_h + \frac{1}{2}(1 - p_h) = \frac{1}{2}$. This is the probability that bit $b_{i,j} = 0$ and $p_h$ results in heads plus the probability that bit $b_{i,j} = 1$ and $p_h$ results in tails.

Observe that the perfect randomness in each bit in $S$ is closely related to the security of each plaintext bit in a Vernam ciphertext.[9] The unconditional security of the One-time pad holds regardless of the probability distribution over the message space.

In addition to being provably secure when a biased coin is available, this solution produces quasi-random bits when such a coin is not available, provided that enough sources of weak entropy are used. This follows immediately from the work of Santha and Vazirani [253], who weaken the

---

[8]Other $k$-bit strings may need to be obtained as well, for example, to compute the primes $p$ and $q$ in Blum-Blum-Shub.

[9]Gilbert Vernam published the One-time pad cryptosystem in 1926 [308] and it wasn't proven to provide perfect secrecy until some 30 years later [270].

assumption that a biased coin is available. The pseudorandomness results from the fact that several weakly random bit streams are bitwise exclusive-or'ed with each other. The basic idea may be illustrated using several examples. Consider the two entropy sources in Table 3.3.

Consider the first row in Table 3.3. A final result of heads occurs if source 1 results in heads and source 2 results in tails, or if source 1 results in tails and source 2 results in heads. This is $\frac{5}{8}\frac{2}{8} + \frac{3}{8}\frac{6}{8} = \frac{28}{64} = \frac{7}{16}$. A coin-flip that results from the XOR of the bits from the two sources is in every case the same or better than the best flip in either of the two sources.[10]

It is important not to misinterpret Figure 3.1. Relying on three sources alone may not always be a good idea. This is especially true if the sources are poor. However, when only a small amount of physical sources is available some form of unbiasing should be performed on each before exclusive-or'ing the resulting bit streams. If only one entropy source is available and the source is known to be reliable then it can be used to form multiple arrays of bytes. These byte arrays can be run through the Santha-Vazirani algorithm to extract quasi-random bits.

The Santha-Vazirani algorithm is a good way to combine weak entropy sources to guarantee that the randomness improves. However, the state of the art in entropy extraction has advanced considerably in recent years. There is a wealth of scientific literature on the subject [207, 266, 267, 296, 297, 298, 299]. Entropy extraction is an area of theoretical computer science unto itself. It has far more applicability than to cryptography alone since truly random numbers are needed to run randomized algorithms such as Quicksort properly. Entropy extraction algorithms have their own set of

---

[10]A coin flip that is heads with probability 3/8 is in some sense just as erroneous as one with probability 5/8 since the absolute values of the biases are identical.

| $p_h$ source 1 | $p_h$ source 2 | $p_h$ under XOR |
|---|---|---|
| 10/16 | 12/16 | 7/16 |
| 10/16 | 4/16 | 9/16 |
| 4/8 | 5/8 | 4/8 |
| 2/16 | 4/16 | 5/16 |
| 1 | 5/8 | 3/8 |
| 12/16 | 14/16 | 5/16 |

**Table 3.3** Entropy from the XOR of two sources

assumptions, not unlike the factoring assumption, Diffie-Hellman assumption, and so on. It is a subject that has been largely neglected in texts dealing with cryptography. Given the robust nature of modern entropy extraction algorithms, there is little reason not to employ them to arrive at provably random seeds for PRNGs.[11] Were a company to advertise both the entropy source assumptions and the intractability assumptions that their products relied upon, that company would truly raise the bar in the computer security industry.

It is unfortunate that entropy extractors are largely, if not entirely, ignored by the software industry. They are often dismissed as being too slow or otherwise not necessary. To the contrary, the Santha-Vazirani algorithm is even faster than using most hash functions such as SHA-1 to extract entropy. It simply performs the bitwise XOR operation on collected entropy streams. Also, the speed is in many cases irrelevant. *The proper way to generate random bits is to work hard to get a truly random seed and then let the faster pseudorandom number generator do the rest.* All that is needed is a truly random seed and perhaps a couple more randomly chosen parameters in order to operate a secure cryptographic pseudorandom number generator properly.

# 3.5  Pseudorandom Number Generators

Subsection 3.5.1 presents a pseudorandom number generator that has undergone standardization. It does not enjoy provably secure properties, but constitutes a sound heuristic approach to the problem. The approach is ideal for applications that demand a high volume of pseudorandom bits per second. Subsection 3.5.2 covers PRNGs that have provably secure properties under well-accepted intractability assumptions.

## 3.5.1  Heuristic Pseudorandom Number Generation

The algorithm below is a U.S. Federal Information Processing Standard (FIPS) approved method to pseudorandomly generate keys and initialization vectors for use with DES. It is from the ANSI X9.17 standard [135].

---

[11]The assumptions regarding the nature of entropy sources have been weakened considerably.

$ANSIX917PRBG(s, m, k)$:

input: a random 64-bit seed s, integer $m$, and a DES EDE key $k$

output: $m$ pseudorandom 64-bit strings $x_1, x_2, ..., x_m$

1. compute $I = E_k(D)$ where $D$ is a 64-bit representation of the
                date/time in as fine a resolution as possible.

2. for $i = 1$ to $m$ do:

3.              $x_i = E_k(I \oplus s)$

4.              $s = E_k(x_i \oplus I)$

5. output $(x_1, x_2, ..., x_m)$

This approach is a sound way to generate pseudorandom bits provided that DES is replaced by a more modern cipher such as AES. Any programmer that employs this method for pseudorandom bit generation by replacing DES with AES is employing a sound primitive.

## 3.5.2    PRNGs Based on Reduction Arguments

A definitive source for provably secure techniques regarding pseudorandom number generators and related primitives is *Pseudorandomness and Cryptographic Applications* by Michael Luby [177]. The definition of a pseudorandom bit generator (PRBG) is given below.

**Definition 1** *Let $k, \ell$ be positive integers such that $\ell \geq k + 1$ and $\ell$ is a specified polynomial function of $k$. A $(k, \ell)$-PRBG is a function from $k$-bit strings to $\ell$-bit strings that can be computed in polynomial time (in $k$). The input to the PRBG is a $k$-bit seed $s_0$ and the output is an $\ell$-bit string that is pseudorandom.*

A simple and relatively fast $(k, \ell)$-PRBG is the Blum-Blum-Shub generator [30]. It uses the parameters $p, q$, and $n$. The values $p$ and $q$ be two large distinct primes and $n = pq$. These two primes must be kept secret. The Blum-Blum-Shub generator is defined as follows. Let $s_0$ be a quadratic residue modulo $n$. The pseudorandom bit stream is found by computing $z_i$ for $i = 1, 2, 3, ..., \ell$.

$$z_i = (s_0^{2^i} \bmod n) \bmod 2$$

It was originally shown that the output of the Blum-Blum-Shub generator could be $\epsilon$-distinguished from $\ell$ truly random bits if and only if there exists an unbiased Monte Carlo algorithm that solves the quadratic residues problem (see Appendix B.3.5) having an error probability of at most $\delta$, for any $\delta$ greater than zero.[12] An even stronger result was shown by Vazirani and Vazirani [307]. They proved that this PRBG is secure under the weaker assumption that factoring is intractable.

The Blum-Blum-Shub PRBG is also regarded as being secure when the $log_2(log_2(n))$ least significant bits of $s_0^{2^i}\ mod\ n$ are used (instead of just the least significant bit). So, when $n$ is a 768-bit composite, the 9 least significant bits can be used in the pseudorandom bit stream.

Why is this a favorable approach to generating bits pseudorandomly? The answer to that question is simple. Whereas DES, AES, and so forth have only been around for a few decades or less, brilliant mathematicians have been trying to solve the factoring problem for centuries... and have yet to publish a solution.

A provably secure pseudorandom number generator (PRNG) will operate in a secure fashion if and only if the following three conditions hold:

1. The secret PRNG parameters must be kept secret. This includes the initial seed (and the primes, as in the case of the Blum-Blum-Shub PRNG, etc.).

2. The parameters for the PRNG must be correct: This means that the seed must be chosen perfectly at random (and the primes in Blum-Blum-Shub must be chosen correctly, etc.).

3. The underlying computational intractability assumption (or assumptions) must hold. In the case of the Blum-Blum-Shub PRNG, this means that factoring must in fact be hard.

If any of the above conditions do not hold then the PRNG may be compromised.

## 3.6   Uniform Sampling

Often a problem requires that a number be chosen randomly or pseudorandomly from a set that has a number of elements that is not a power of 2. When this is the case random bit generators, be they pseudo or otherwise, cannot be used directly to generate the needed number. What

---

[12]Thus, polynomial indistinguishability holds under the quadratic residuosity assumption.

is needed is an algorithm that utilizes the available random bit generator to sample from such sets uniformly at random.

For example, suppose that a computer worm propagates on a local area network by randomly selecting a machine to infect from the set of machines that are adjacent to the current host. If six such machines are connected directly to the host, then such an algorithm will be needed.[13] This problem boils down to using a coin to simulate the rolling of a fair six-sided die. The die roll can be simulated perfectly as follows. The coin is flipped three times to obtain a 3-bit number. This number is uniformly distributed between 0 and 7 inclusive. If the number is between 0 and 5 then the number is output. Otherwise, the three bits are thrown out and this procedure is repeated. Since all 6 faces of the die are equally likely, this method samples $\{0, 1, 2, 3, 4, 5\}$ uniformly at random. Uniform sampling techniques are needed when a random bit generator is available and when elements must be sampled from a set that has a cardinality that is not a power of 2.

This general uniform sampling algorithm is as follows. Let $RBG(i)$ denote a perfectly random bit generator that returns a string consisting of $i > 0$ truly random bits.

Input: Integer $N \geq 1$
Output: $R$ chosen uniformly at random from [0,N-1]
$Choose1toNRandomly(N)$:
1. Let $T$ be the smallest power of 2 such that $T \geq N$
2. compute $R = RBG(log_2(T))$
3. if $R < N$ then output $R$ and halt
4. goto step (2)

The following claim regarding uniform sampling can be proven.

**Claim 3** *Assuming that the function $RBG()$ returns random bit strings, the function Choose1toNRandomly() outputs $R$ drawn uniformly at random from [0,N-1].*

To see this, observe that the strings that are output by $RBG$ are chosen independently at random. Suppose that $Choose1toNRandomly$ halts with $R$ in iteration $j$. Let $p_{i,j}$ denote the probability that $R = i$ with $0 \leq i < N$ in iteration $j$. Clearly $p_{i,j} = 1/T$. Since step (3) is

---

[13]It is in fact possible to view the whole world in terms of computer viruses!

the only step that outputs a value, and since this value is $R$ it follows that Choose1tnNRandomly outputs $R$ drawn uniformly at random from $[0, N-1]$.

In a given iteration of $Choose1toNRandomly$, the value $R$ will be less than $N$ with probability $N/T$. So, the probability that a given iteration causes a repeat in step (4) is $1 - N/T$. Since $T$ is the smallest power of 2 such that $T \geq N$, it follows that $N/T > 1/2$. So, the probability that no answer is found after $j$ iterations is,

$$\left(1 - \tfrac{N}{T}\right)^j < \left(1 - \tfrac{1}{2}\right)^j = \tfrac{1}{2^j}$$

It follows that $Choose1toNRandomly$ is an efficient Las Vegas algorithm. Observe that $Choose1toNRandomly$ will never loop if $N$ is a power of 2. This implies that the algorithm is efficient even when random bit strings are needed. This makes the function ideal for use as a public function in an Application Programming Interface (API). Note that this function is how users obtain random numbers in Figure 3.1. This is indicated by the solid arrow emanating from "uniform sampling algorithm" that terminates at the bottom of the figure. The dotted arrow that leaves the "uniform sampling algorithm" and that terminates at the bottom of the figure indicates that applications have direct access to pseudorandom sampled values.

In OpenSSL [233], the function BN_rand_range() generates a cryptographically strong pseudorandom number $rnd$ in the range $0 \leq rnd < range$. BN_pseudo_rand_range() does the same, but is based on the function BN_pseudo_rand(). The function BN_rand_range() was added[14] in OpenSSL 0.9.6a and the function BN_pseudo_rand_range() was added in OpenSSL 0.9.6c.

int BN_rand_range(BIGNUM *$rnd$, BIGNUM *$range$);

int BN_pseudo_rand_range(BIGNUM *$rnd$, BIGNUM *$range$);

The functions return 1 on success, 0 on error. The error codes can be obtained by ERR_get_error().

---

[14]It was included in the function BN_is_prime_fasttest() to fix the bug that was pointed out [329].

## 3.7  Random Permutation Generation

Generating random permutations is a fundamental problem in computing. On-line casinos need to generate random permutations over $\{1, 2, 3, ..., 52\}$ to properly shuffle a deck of cards. Computer worms benefit from choosing random permutations over the set of machines on a network to arrive at an unpredictable hit list. This allows worms to attempt to travel from one existing machine to another, rather than simply choosing IP addresses randomly to try to propagate to. This is important since many heuristic antiviral network monitors are effective against stupid worms that ping non-existent Internet addresses. Malicious software is difficult to detect when it looks, smells, tastes, and feels like all the benign software around it.

### 3.7.1  Shuffling Cards by Repeated Sampling

The following algorithm shuffles a deck of cards in-place and is thereby very memory efficient. Initially, $deck[i] = i$ for $i = 1, 2, 3, ..., 52$.

CardShuffle():
1. for $i = 1$ to 51 do:
2.     j = number drawn uniformly at random between $i$ and 52 inclusive
3.     card = deck[j]
4.     deck[j] = deck[i]
5.     deck[i] = card

Assuming that a random (or pseudorandom) bit generator is available, step (2) above can be implemented using Neumann's method. For example, when $i = 1$ a 6-bit number $r$ is generated. If the number is between 0 and 51 inclusive, then we set $j = r + 1$. Otherwise, we generate another 6 bits and repeat. From Lemma 3 it follows that $j$ will be drawn from the correct probability distribution.

It remains to consider the running time of CardShuffle(). Suppose that a fair coin is available. How many times would one expect to have to flip it to get heads? The answer is 2. Suppose that a biased coin is available that comes up heads with probability 3/4. How many times would one expect to have to flip it to get heads? The answer is 4/3. The expected number of random bits needed to shuffle using CardShuffle() is found by summing the expected number of bits needed in each iteration.

The expected number of bits needed per iteration is given below. The number immediately before the colon is $i$.

$$
\begin{array}{llll}
1: 6 * \frac{64}{52} & 2: 6 * \frac{64}{51} & 3: 6 * \frac{64}{50} & \cdots \quad 20: 6 * \frac{64}{33} \\
21: 5 * \frac{32}{32} & 22: 5 * \frac{32}{31} & 23: 5 * \frac{32}{30} & \cdots \quad 36: 5 * \frac{32}{17} \\
37: 4 * \frac{16}{16} & 38: 4 * \frac{16}{15} & 39: 4 * \frac{16}{14} & \cdots \quad 44: 4 * \frac{16}{9} \\
\end{array}
$$

$$
\begin{array}{llll}
45: 3 * \frac{8}{8} & 46: 3 * \frac{8}{7} & 47: 3 * \frac{8}{6} & 48: 3 * \frac{8}{5} \\
& 49: 2 * \frac{4}{4} & 50: 2 * \frac{4}{3} \\
& 51: 1 * \frac{2}{2}
\end{array}
$$

For example, in the first iteration when $i = 1$, one would expect to have to use $6(64/52)$ bits to draw the first card in the shuffle. Observe that $6 * 64 = 384$ factors out of the top row, $5 * 32 = 160$ factors out of the second row, and so on. The top row is equivalent to the following,

$$
6 * 64 \left( \tfrac{1}{52} + \tfrac{1}{51} + \tfrac{1}{50} + \cdots + \tfrac{1}{33} \right)
$$

The rightmost term is the difference between two Harmonic numbers, namely $H_{52}$ and $H_{32}$. The $n^{\text{th}}$ Harmonic number $H_n$ is defined by,

$$
H_n = 1 + \frac{1}{2} + \cdots + \frac{1}{n} = \sum_{k=1}^{n} \frac{1}{k}
$$

This definition is from *Concrete Mathematics* by D. Knuth et al [122]. Clearly all Harmonic numbers are rational. The above expression is equivalent to,

$$
384(H_{52} - H_{32}) + 160(H_{32} - H_{16}) + 64(H_{16} - H_8) + 24(H_8 - H_4) + 2 + \tfrac{8}{3} + 1
$$

After simplifying, the following expression is obtained.

$$
384 H_{52} - 224 H_{32} - 96 H_{16} - 40 H_8 - 24 H_4 + 5 + \tfrac{2}{3}
$$

These five Harmonic numbers are given below [111].

$$H_4 = \frac{25}{12} \quad H_8 = \frac{761}{280} \quad H_{16} = \frac{2436559}{720720}$$

$$H_{32} = \frac{586061125622639}{144403552893600} \approx 4.0585$$

$$H_{52} = \frac{14063600165435720745359}{3099044504245996706400} \approx 4.53804$$

The expected number of random bits needed to shuffle a single deck is 355.9 using this method.

## 3.7.2   Shuffling Cards Using Trotter-Johnson

Algorithms to generate and enumerate permutations fall under the category of algorithmic combinatorics. Ranking and Unranking algorithms allow computer scientists to efficiently store, generate, and use combinatorial objects. Consider the problem of storing a particular permutation of $n$ objects in a computer. If the objects are numbers, for instance, one could simply store them in an array. However, a more efficient way is to establish a bijection between the $n!$ combinatorial objects and the natural numbers from 0 to $n! - 1$ and subsequently store the natural number that uniquely identifies the object.

When a Ranking function is supplied with a combinatorial object it returns the object's rank (a natural number that uniquely represents the object). When a rank is given to an Unranking function, it returns the corresponding combinatorial object. An example of such a bijection will go a long way to illustrate this concept. Consider the problem of establishing a bijection between $\{0, 1, 2, ..., 9\}$ and the $\binom{5}{3}$ subsets of $\{1, 2, 3, 4, 5\}$ containing three elements. Table 3.4 depicts a co-lex ordering that defines such a bijection.

The Trotter-Johnson algorithm is a minimal-change algorithm for generating the $n!$ permutations. It is a well-known algorithm developed in the early 1960s by Trotter and Johnson [142, 301]. In this algorithm, $\pi$ is a permutation over $\{1, 2, 3, ..., n\}$. The value $r$ is a rank of such a permutation, hence, $r \in \{0, 1, 2, ..., n! - 1\}$. Shimon Even and Kreher and Stinson wrote excellent introductory texts on algorithmic combinatorics [98, 163].

| T | rank(T) |
|---|---|
| [3,2,1] | 0 |
| [4,2,1] | 1 |
| [4,3,1] | 2 |
| [4,3,2] | 3 |
| [5,2,1] | 4 |
| [5,3,1] | 5 |
| [5,3,2] | 6 |
| [5,4,1] | 7 |
| [5,4,2] | 8 |
| [5,4,3] | 9 |

**Table 3.4**  Co-Lex ordering for 3-element subsets

TrotterJohnsonUnrank(r,n):
1. $r_2 = 0$
2. $\pi[1] = 1$
3. for $j = 2$ to $n$ do:
4.     $r_1 = \lfloor \frac{rj!}{n!} \rfloor$
5.     $k = r_1 - jr_2$
6.     if $r_2$ is even then
           for $i = j - 1$ down to $j - k$ do:
7.             $\pi[i + 1] = \pi[i]$
8.         $\pi[j - k] = j$
9.     else
10.            for $i = j - 1$ down to $k + 1$ do:
11.                $\pi[i + 1] = \pi[i]$
12.        $\pi[k + 1] = j$
13.        $r_2 = r_1$
14. output $\pi$ and halt

This algorithm is the natural way to select a particular ordering of the 52 cards in a deck. The actual value of 52! is needed to implement shuffling based on unranking. When expressed in decimal the value of 52! is,

80658175170943878571660636856403766975289505440883277824000000000000

Expressed in hexadecimal, the value of 52! is

2FDE529A3274C649CFEB4B180ADB5CB9602A9E0638AB2000000000000

The abundance of zeros on the right side of these numbers is due to the fact that every other number in $1 * 2 * 3 * 4 * 5 * \cdots * 52$ is evenly divisible by 2 and every other fifth number is evenly divisible by 5. The number of binary digits needed to express 52! is exactly 226.

Given the above value for 52!, Trotter-Johnson unranking can be used to shuffle as follows. A random 226-bit number $r$ is chosen. If the number is less than 52! then it is supplied to Algorithm 2.18 with $n = 52$. The algorithm will return the shuffle $\pi$. If $r \geq 52!$ then $r$ is discarded, another 226 bits are chosen randomly, and this process repeats.

Multiprecision libraries such as OpenSSL contain routines for testing if one big number is less than another. To test if $x < y$ the algorithm scans the bits of $x$ from the most significant bits to least significant bits. The algorithm does this with $y$ at the same time. The algorithm makes a determination if and when two bits differ.

Now consider the running time of this approach. Observe that,

$$52! \approx 80.658175 \times 10^{22}$$

$$2^{226} \approx 107.839787 \times 10^{22}$$

So, one would expect to have to generate a sequence of 226 bits about 1.337 times. It follows that using TrotterJohnsonUnrank, about 302.2 random bits will be needed on average to shuffle a single deck. Since $302.2 < 355.6$, it is more efficient to use TrotterJohnsonUnrank to shuffle cards. When 50,000 shuffles are performed we would expect TrotterJohnsonUnrank to use up about 1.8 megabytes of randomness.[15] The iterated approach would use up approximately 2.12 megabytes of randomness. The unranking algorithm helps to pave the way for using PRNGs based on rigorous mathematical foundations that tend to be more computationally demanding than *ad hoc* constructions.

Finally, if combinatorial objects need to be selected uniformly at random then the output of the uniform sampling algorithm can be used as input to a combinatorial unranking algorithm. This is depicted in Figure 3.1. The rounded box labeled "uniform sampling algorithm" is used to generate a rank $r$ uniformly at random that is supplied to the unranking algorithm.

---

[15]This is using the common definition of a kilobyte in which 1 kilobyte equals 1,024 bytes (not 1,000 bytes).

## 3.8 Sound Approach to Random Number Generation and Use

The algorithms that were presented for unbiasing coin flips and performing uniform sampling are Las Vegas algorithms. That is, they will always output the correct answer, but strictly speaking there is no guarantee that they will ever halt. Since well-designed functions return error codes anyway, it makes sense to make these algorithms Monte Carlo. To do so, the number of attempts to arrive at an answer can be fixed to, say, 32,000. If they don't arrive at an answer then they halt with failure. Otherwise, they halt at or before 32,000 iterations have passed with the correct answer. This way, the calling function can handle failures gracefully, and we can say something meaningful about the worst-case running time of the algorithm.[16] As of this writing the OpenSSL functions BN_rand_range() and BN_pseudo_rand_range() are still of the Las Vegas type.

Figure 3.1 depicts four output arrows. Two are from the uniform sampling algorithm and two are from the combinatorial unranking algorithm. These give direct access to random and pseudorandomly sampled values as well as random and pseudorandomly generated combinatorial objects. The truly random output of the uniform sampling algorithm gives the calling application access to truly random bits. This call can be used to test the quality of the random seeds that are used to seed the pseudorandom number generator. This may be ascertained by subjecting the bit stream to FIPS-140 statistical tests, among others.[17] The uniform sampling function allows applications to generate coin flips, die rolls, roulette wheel spins, and so on. Finally, the unranking function allows applications to generate random/pseudorandom permutations over sets, random/pseudorandom subsets, and so on. *The nice aspect of this API is that at the lowest level, only the uniform sampling algorithm is visible to application programmers. This should help ward off programming errors that result from incorrect sampling.*

Developing a design document and documenting code is clearly good software engineering practice. Yet, this seldom ever occurs in practice. Companies are often riddled with deadlines and wind up with off-the-cuff implementations all the time. However, security software should be

---

[16]This may seem like nitpicky advice. However, we would like to think that when libraries such as OpenSSL are used to control access to nuclear arsenals such measures are taken.

[17]That is, the monobit test, the poker test, the runs test, and the long runs test.

designed so that third parties can easily verify its correctness. Part of this involves articulating the design and commenting the code, and part of it involves creating a well-designed application programming interface. Adam has seen in a number of consulting engagements no design documents whatsoever, poorly documented code, and to top it all off, random number generation code that is intimately merged with other code that performs such things as socket connections. This hampers efforts to verify the implementation and can be very time-consuming to analyze. Code that performs the functionality described in Figure 3.1 should be implemented in a completely standalone fashion.

## 3.9 RNGs Are the Beating Heart of System Security

Random number generators constitute the very foundation of secure computing machines. If one were to break or otherwise be able to predict the output of an RNG that is used, it would likely yield unadulterated access to the machine or sensitive data. A random number generator is a prime target for carrying out insider attacks. A Trojan horse that lives in and attacks a random number generator could potentially give the author unfettered access to private keys, symmetric keys, and the like. This is in fact the very heart of kleptographic attacks since it employ cryptotrojans that hide in random number generators and that masquerade as producers of truly random bits.

Military and government agencies would do well to employ the algorithm of Santha and Vazirani to produce seeding material. This will hedge against the threat of insider abuse, a topic that is gaining widespread interest in DARPA and ARDA. Applications that rely on a single source of entropy are paving the way for potentially devastating insider attacks. By exclusive-or'ing the bit streams from multiple sources, this threat is minimized. A malicious software program will also benefit from taking this approach, since it will prevent the program from relying entirely on the random number generator provided by the operating system. It is conceivable that the random numbers produced by the operating system are logged or are otherwise predictable. A computer host is an environment that is hostile to malware and as such malicious software will benefit from taking some entropy directly from available peripherals.

Given that truly random seeds are critical for the operation of IN-

FOSEC devices, one has to wonder why there are no FIPS standards encompassing how they are generated. The ANSI X9.17 standard covers a heuristically sound way to generate pseudorandom bits, but this technique was proposed by the Banking Industry and does not cover how the initial seed is derived. A U.S. government standard that encompasses a sound method for extracting entropy from multiple sources would improve the security of computer software on a very large scale. Neumann's algorithm dates back to the middle of the last *century*. Formal results on weakening Neumann's assumptions can be traced back to the early 1980s, and research on the subject has continued.

## 3.10   Cryptovirology Benefits from General Advances

The original Macintosh cryptovirus was a proof-of-concept that had substantial room for improvement. For example, instead of using the outputs of truerand directly, it could have applied Neumann's algorithm or a more advanced entropy extractor to the output of truerand. Ideally, a cryptovirus would also utilize such sources as hard disk turbulence and the RNG that is provided by the underlying operating system. Although the simple extortion attack did not require a large number of random bits, it should have nonetheless applied an entropy extractor to several different sources of entropy. In this section a number of improvements and extensions to the cryptovirus attack are discussed.

### 3.10.1   Strong Crypto Yields Strong Cryptoviruses

In all likelihood the RSA cipher as originally defined is secure enough to mount the cryptovirus extortion attack. However, improved public key cryptosystems exist. A known drawback to RSA is that each RSA ciphertext $c = m^e \bmod n$ leaks the Jacobi symbol of $m$ with respect to $n$ [175]. (See Appendix B.2 for an explanation of the Jacobi symbol.) The Jacobi symbol of $m$ with respect to $n$ is either 1 or $-1$. Since $e$ is odd, it is not hard to see that,

$$J(m/n) = J(m/n)^e = J(m^e/n) = J(c/n) \qquad (3.1)$$

Since the Jacobi symbol must be one of two different values, a single bit of information about $m$ is leaked in every ciphertext. Ideally, no poly-time computable function of the plaintext should be efficiently computable given the ciphertext. In this example the computable function has a certain semantic meaning, namely the Jacobi function. But other efficiently computable functions with semantic meaning may exist. Another drawback to RSA is that it is deterministic. Every time that a particular message $m_1$ is encrypted in RSA the exact same ciphertext $c_1$ will result. This means that it is possible to guess the plaintext in a given ciphertext and then verify the guess. For example, suppose $c_1 = m_1^e \bmod n$ is known. If $m_2$ is suspected as being the plaintext it can be encrypted to obtain $c_2 = m_2^e \bmod n$. If $c_2 = c_1$ then $m_2 = m_1$. When a user encrypts short messages there is the risk that someone else can guess the plaintext and verify the guess. A heuristic way to prevent adversaries from guessing the plaintext and then verifying is to shrink the message space and include a random bit string in each encryption. This makes each plaintext message map to more than one ciphertext message. However, a provably secure approach is more desirable. In the more general case it should not be possible to select two messages and distinguish between their encryptions.

These observations lead to two notions of security: semantic security and message Indistinguishability, respectively. As it turns out, when the adversary is allowed to be any probabilistic poly-time algorithm these two definitions of security are equivalent. To avoid such vulnerabilities a semantically secure cryptosystem can be used [117]. An encryption algorithm is semantically secure against plaintext attacks if for all probability distributions over the message space, anything that a passive adversary can compute efficiently about the plaintext given the ciphertext can also be efficiently computed without the ciphertext given *any* historical information about the plaintext.

An efficient public key cryptosystem called Optimal Asymmetric Encryption Padding (OAEP) has been proposed [19] that can be implemented given any trapdoor one-way function such as RSA. Its security was proven within the random oracle model[18] [18]. When a cryptosystem is used that is semantically secure against plaintext attacks to encrypt a symmetric key, no partial information about the symmetric key is revealed in the resulting ciphertext. Such a cryptosystem therefore provides more security than using RSA as originally defined. In computer security, the standard approach is to formalize the capabilities of the adversary in a

---

[18]The security of OAEP has recently been reinvestigated in [109, 272].

*threat model*, develop an algorithm to deal with the possible presence of the adversary, and then *prove* that the algorithm is secure within that threat model. The bottom line is that a cryptosystem is only guaranteed to be secure within the threat model that it is designed to handle and may well succumb to more powerful adversaries should they exist.[19]

Semantic security against plaintext attacks guarantees that an adversary that tries to determine some additional partial information concerning a plaintext given the corresponding ciphertext along with existing partial information cannot do so. However, there exists an even more powerful type of adversary than this. For example, in the case of the cryptovirus extortion attack what has not been considered is a group of victims that is prepared to pay multiple ransoms, that use the virus writer as a decryption oracle, and that choose the public key ciphertexts based on previously decrypted ciphertexts. This amounts to what is called an *adaptive chosen-ciphertext attack*. This illustrates some of the subtleties in designing secure systems. A cryptosystem that is semantically secure against plaintext attacks is not necessarily semantically secure against adaptive chosen-ciphertext attacks. However, it turns out that OAEP is secure against adaptive chosen-ciphertext attacks.

This reasoning implies that cryptoviruses benefit directly from general advances in cryptology. Even though the original cryptovirus did not use multiple entropy sources and an entropy extractor, and even though it did not use OAEP, it is straightforward to utilize these more advanced techniques to design secure cryptoviruses.

## 3.10.2   Mix Networks and Cryptovirus Extortion

Arguably, the weakest aspect of the extortion attack from the perspective of the virus writer is obtaining the ransom without getting caught. To this end, it may be best to avoid demanding cash entirely. If the virus writer seeks information alone, then a more attractive alternative is possible. Methods exist that enable two mutually distrusting parties to communicate securely over a network in an anonymous fashion. The basic vehicle for doing so is called a *mix network* [54]. A mix network forms the basis for anonymous remailing systems and is a fundamental building block for many cryptographic protocols [55, 119, 137, 295]. In a nutshell a mix network is a service that lets users send messages anonymously to other users, and that makes the correlation of output messages with input

---

[19]Side channel analysis and kleptographic attacks must also be considered.

messages nearly impossible. Mix networks fall into two major catagories: synchronous mixes and asynchronous mixes. In practice asynchronous mixes are ideal for anonymizing e-mail traffic, whereas synchronous mixes are best for randomizing message traffic in batches. It is typically easier to produce formal proofs of security for synchronous mixes than for asynchronous mixes, and as a result synchronous mixes tend to be employed in protocols such as electronic voting. This allows ballots to be cast in a provably anonymous fashion. Asynchronous mixes are arguably easier to deploy on a large scale and rely on a number of heuristic defenses against particular attacks.

A mix network consists of a collection of $N$ mix net nodes. The basic idea behind an asynchronous mix is to take an incoming message, send it from node to node along a randomly chosen path, and then send it to its final destination. It is necessary to use encryption to prevent correlations based on content as well as to fix the length of each message so that correlations based on size are not possible. This implies that large messages need to be broken down into smaller pieces, and short messages need to be padded out to the requisite length. The fixed sized messages are encrypted using a probabilistic public key cryptosystem. Therefore, even if the same message is sent through the network on more than one occasion it will look different each time with overwhelming probability. Not only are outsiders a threat to mix networks, but insiders are a threat as well. A properly designed mix net is still secure even if a fixed fraction of the nodes are operated by malicious persons that collude in order to track messages. Assuming that a sufficient number of messages go in and out of a given node at any given time it is important that the message go through multiple honest nodes to make the probability of tracing it negligible. A mix network is depicted in Figure 3.2.

Onion routing is a common method for implementing asynchronous mix networks. In an onion routing system, each of the $N$ nodes has a key pair. A user selects a random traversal among the $N$ nodes and successively encrypts in reverse-order the message using the public keys corresponding to the nodes that the message will traverse. In choosing the traversal, the same node can be chosen multiple times and therefore loops are possible in the path that the message takes. The layers of the resulting ciphertext are peeled away by performing decryption as the message travels through the network. By padding with random bytes it is possible to accomplish this in such a way that the length of the transmitted message is always the same.

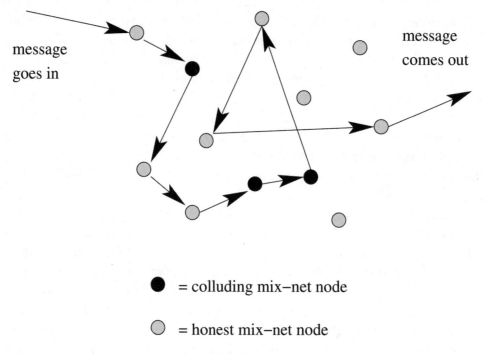

message
goes in

message
comes out

● = colluding mix–net node

◯ = honest mix–net node

**Figure 3.2**  Asynchronous mix network

Over time a given mix net node may receive 1,000 incoming messages. These are decrypted, the order of them is mixed, and the resulting messages are sent out. The original packet headers are discarded and the messages are sent in newly constructed packets. This prevents trivial matching based on packet headers. If a message is decrypted entirely then it is sent to the final recipient. This way, a given input message to the node may end up being any of 1,000 different outgoing messages (see Figure 3.3).

It is also possible for a mix node to decrypt a message, determine the next intended recipient, and then re-encrypt the message using the public key of the recipient. When this re-encryption is probabilistic, it makes it more difficult for the original sender to identify his or her own message as it moves through the mix network.

An asynchronous mix network must have a sufficiently large message volume at all times. If only a handful of messages is traveling through the network then correlation is trivial. There are numerous attacks on mix networks that have been described in the literature.[20] For example, an active

---

[20]Lance Cottrell described several attacks against asynchronous mix networks [75].

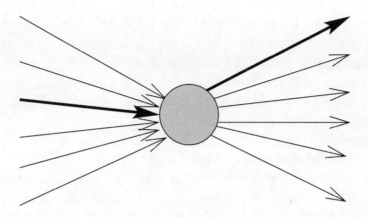

**Figure 3.3**  Mixing in a mix network node

adversary may try to determine the partial path of an unknown message by sandwiching it between messages of the adversaries' own choosing. The object is to fill the queue of messages in the mix with custom-made messages, all except for the one that needs to be traced. The adversary then watches the messages as they leave the node to determine where the sandwiched message goes. The adversary takes note of how many messages each intended recipient receives. This is enough to determine where the sandwiched message went.

A novel solution to this problem has been proposed [112]. The idea is to regard the mix net nodes as probabilistic algorithms and let them affect the paths that messages take. The way this is accomplished is by flipping coins, and with a certain probability sending a given message on a short, randomly chosen *inter-mix detour*. When a detour occurs it has the effect of adding a few new layers back onto the message in question. This mechanism has the novel property that even the sender does not know for sure what path his or her message will take within the mix network. The probability that a given message is sent on a detour must be low enough to keep the message volume from growing out of control.

Methods have been devised to not only allow anonymous messages to be sent, but also to allow anonymous replies [112]. In the cryptovirus attack, the virus can instruct the victim to place the victim's email address on a public bulletin board. To avoid embarrassment, the virus can tell the victim to first encrypt the e-mail address using the public key in the virus. The e-mail address can be chosen specifically for dealing with the virus writer and therefore not reveal the identity of the victim. The virus writer periodically scans the board for such ciphertexts, and decrypts

them when found. The virus writer then sends the demand anonymously
to the victim. Provided that the ransom is information, the victim can
include the ransom within the anonymous reply. As long as the ransom
itself does not reveal the identity of the victim, the attack preserves the
victim's anonymity. A mix network is therefore a powerful building block
for carrying out cryptovirus attacks.

To apprehend the virus writer, law enforcement bodies may seek to
subpoena the administrators of each node in the mix network. Such a
subpoena might call for the current private key and all previous private
keys of each of the administrators. If all of the needed private keys and
message traffic were obtained, this would allow law enforcement to trace
any given message. However, if each mix net node adhered to a de facto
mix net protocol standard, generated new key pairs every so often, and
deleted all previous private keys and coin tosses, then the subpoena would
likely not help law enforcement. Also, if the nodes spanned multiple countries then the tracing effort would be hampered even more due to legal
complications.

The fact that mix net nodes traditionally decrypt incoming messages
and then re-encrypt them when they are sent out, implies that the individual private keys of each mix net administrator can be used to trace
message traffic. A recent method known as *universal re-encryption* has
been proposed as a basis for a provably secure mix network [120]. By
using a cryptosystem such as ElGamal that allows re-encryption without
first decrypting, it is possible to have the mix net nodes randomize the incoming messages in an oblivious fashion. With respect to the virus attack,
this implies that there are no administrator private keys for law enforcement to subpoena. If a re-encryption mix net node does not store the
random permutation that it used in a mix operation, then the permutation is effectively lost forever.[21] This property makes re-encryption mixes
very attractive to criminals that need to communicate anonymously.

Various indirect methods exist to achieve financial gain through extortion. For example, a determined attacker may premeditate an extortion
attempt by purchasing several shares of a small public company, provided
that a substantial number of shares are up for sale. Once the attack is
carried out the victim can be forced to purchase a high volume of shares
from the small company. This has a tendency to drive the share price
up, at which point the attacker can cash out. The obvious drawback to

---

[21]Unless all of the inputs and outputs of the re-encryption mix network are obtained.

this method is that all of the outstanding shareholders may be regarded as suspects.

## 3.11   Anonymizing Program Propagation

An important issue that has been glossed over is the anonymity of the actual virus propagation. Strictly speaking, given enough snapshots of the states of machines on a network it is theoretically possible to trace the flow of a virus or worm perfectly. So, an interesting theoretical question is how to design a virus or worm that cannot be traced. Intuitively it would seem that a solution along these lines would make use of some form of mix network.

At first sight Figure 3.4 may appear to be quite silly. It looks like an artery or something out of a Dr. Seuss book, but it is quite illustrative of a new concept that will now be introduced. Consider a simple generalization of a mix network in which it is programs that are mixed instead of simply messages. Suppose further that programs can submit themselves to the mix network. In this case a program can choose a destination, jump into the mix, and then reappear at the destination much like the bug does in the figure. This in itself would not be very useful unless the program had a way of gaining control when it arrives at its destination. This could be accomplished by having the client programs for the mix network automatically run the programs that are received from the network.

This system is somewhat similar to the worm that was researched at the Palo Alto Research Center (see Appendix A.1) with one critical difference: a program's starting location cannot be ascertained at all once the program travels through the network.[22] A nice feature to have would be a program that submits itself to the mix and that can either choose the destination machine explicitly or let the mix choose the final machine based on its own random coin flips. This latter approach allows programs to literally *disappear* without a trace from one machine and show up at some random location that the program itself could not have predicted accurately. This aspect would make viruses and worms very happy.

The system can be construed as a distributed operating system in which the processes may optionally be distributed anonymously among many machines. It may at first sight appear to be suicidal for users. In many respects this is in fact the case. However, a virtual machine with

---

[22]The program could be designed to reveal this information deliberately, however.

C C MICHAEL & ELISA YOUNG

**Figure 3.4** A mix that mixes programs

a security kernel that verifies the signature on programs before running them can be used to implement execution rights and access control.

The system has some very interesting implications for digital copyright issues. Suppose that the system is based on a mix that enables anonymous messages to be sent along with anonymous replies [112]. Also, suppose that a program is written that uses private information retrieval (see Section 6.2) to search for a particular MP3 song and retrieve it. The program can contain a specific query as well as the database administrator algorithm. The program runs the database administator algorithm on the query and the database of the machine when it arrives.[23] If this program shows up on a machine through the mix, takes an MP3, and then disappears back to

---

[23]The scheme can utilize tagged private information retrieval (see Section 6.4) and use a questionable encryption scheme (Subsection 6.6.2) to "encrypt" the response to the query. A sting operation can be performed by pirates against law enforcement in which witnesses of non-encryption are revealed to refute the validity of ciphertexts that are "evidence."

where it came from, is the owner of the machine at fault in a legal sense? If the database consists of public domain songs as well as commercial songs then the owner of the machine will never have any way of knowing if a commercial song has ever been taken off the machine or not.

In this respect the system acts like a *passive file server* since programs can show up out of nowhere, take files, and jump back into the mix. The only overt action that the mix client does that makes file sharing possible is to send control to programs that arrive from the mix. This overt action can be eliminated without hindering public file sharing capabilities. The system can be *designed* to check for the requisite level of access control, but *contain* a rather convenient bug that accidentally allows world *read* permissions to commercial MP3s. Can users be liable for not finding bugs in their software and fixing them? Can companies be liable for selling or distributing buggy software? Should laws be passed to force users not to trust the world? The mix-based distributed operating system just described is hackable by design.[24] The cryptographic agent that moves through it is designed to hide what it is doing. This is an example of how cryptography can be maliciously used by software pirates to violate copyright laws.

---

[24]In terms of world read permissions.

# Chapter 4

# The Two Faces of Anonymity

The ability to communicate anonymously and do things in an anonymous fashion is a mixed blessing. Criminals that perform criminal operations in an anonymous way minimize their risk of getting caught and voters that cast ballots anonymously do so without fear of persecution. Anonymity mechanisms, however simple in design, can be regarded as technologies unto themselves. The need for communicating anonymously and performing anonymous activities has extended into the digital realm and there currently exist advanced cryptographic algorithms for anonymously sending e-mails, voting, and purchasing items over the Internet. The potential for abuse of such technologies is immense and the first part of this chapter sheds some light on many of the possibilities. The chapter concludes with a description of a cryptotrojan attack that utilizes an anonymous communication channel. By carrying out the attack, the Trojan horse author is able to steal login/password pairs from a host machine in a way that greatly diminishes the risk of getting caught.

## 4.1 Anonymity in a Digital Age

Mechanisms that provide anonymity serve the common good in a variety of ways. For example, the ability to cast ballots anonymously helps protect voters against government persecution in response to their choices in electoral candidates. Other modes of communication that involve anonymity include tip lines for law enforcement agencies, newspaper classified ads, and suggestion boxes. The way in which these anonymity mechanisms serve the common good is clear. Tip lines help prevent citizens who may know the criminal from being discovered by the criminal, and also help lesser accomplices reveal crimes without fear of prosecution. Likewise, suggestion boxes help customers and patrons speak candidly about the products and services of a company or store without running the risk of being identified and mistreated.

### 4.1.1 From Free Elections to the Unabomber

The ability to carry out actions in an anonymous fashion is not without its drawbacks. For instance, a terrorist can take credit for a bombing by sending a letter to a news agency, calling from a pay phone, and so forth. These approaches are risky for criminals since they can leave behind a trail of fingerprints, eyewitnesses, skin tissue, and so on. The mail system is subject to even worse abuses, as evidenced by the Unabomber and Anthrax attacks in the United States.

The migration of anonymity mechanisms to the digital realm is likely to have a growing impact on both the beneficial and malicious capabilities they provide. Cryptographic on-line elections have the potential to be more accurate, more secure, and timelier. This paves the way for society to resolve issues by voting on a much larger scale, thereby more accurately capturing the true consensus of the population. On the flip side of this coin, a terrorist can claim credit for a bombing by sending a message to a news agency via an anonymous remailer. This eliminates the possibility of leaving a physical trail for forensic scientists. Terrorists can also coordinate their activities using anonymous remailers and can conceivably assign tasks to individuals without ever even meeting them in person.

### 4.1.2 Electronic Money and Anonymous Payments

Cash is a payment medium that is favored by many consumers due to the anonymity that it provides. Purchasing items with cash preserves the anonymity of the buyer and seller. When a consumer purchases an item with a debit or credit card, the consumer's identity and often the item or items that are purchased are revealed and recorded. This information is often sold to marketing agencies for profit and is used to solicit more sales via targeted advertising.

The downside to cash from the consumer's perspective is that it is easy to steal. A mugger that steals a wallet containing cash will profit from the criminal act. If the wallet contains a debit card then the criminal is at a loss since the personal identification number is needed to get at the money. Consumers therefore face a tradeoff when deciding to carry either cash or debit cards. Cash guarantees anonymity but runs the risk of being stolen. Debit cards are resilient against theft but expose the consumer to aggressive advertising.

Cryptography may well hail as the savior in this dilemma. Electronic money is a technology that combines the anonymity of cash with the security and convenience offered by debit cards. The concept of e-money takes getting used to, since it implies that streams of zeros and ones can replace paper money. E-money is one of the most involved applications of public key cryptography.

One of the benefits of e-money is that it can be protected from destruction. Once downloaded to a smart card, the e-notes can be copied to a home computer. If the smart card is destroyed then a backup will reside on the computer and vice versa. This is not the case with paper money. Since e-notes can be duplicated one would think that forging them would be trivial. However, this is not the case since the underlying algorithms are designed to protect against *double-spending* [53]. Once a note is spent it renders all other identical copies null and void. When considering the evolution of currency, the migration to e-money makes sense. The problems associated with bartering perishables for non-perishables were solved using coins. The problem of lugging around hundreds of pounds of coins was minimized using paper money. Assuming that smart cards become ubiquitous, e-money may become a cheaper payment medium overall compared to paper money. Unlike printing dollar bills, e-money takes a fraction of a second and very little energy to mint.

Electronic payment systems remain a very active area of research today since there are numerous problems to deal with in order to arrive at an acceptable solution [9, 37, 53, 130, 168, 212, 214, 303, 313]. For example, divisibility is important since many items are valued at fractions of a dollar. Efficiency is an issue since too much protocol interaction may render solutions impractical to use. A fundamental security requirement is that it must not be possible to counterfeit e-notes. An important problem to consider in deploying a secure payment system is that the security of the entire system often degenerates to that of the security level of the weakest link. This is often the case in the theory of secure systems. In many situations it is important to augment a payment scheme using mix networks [138]. Perhaps the most intriguing technological advantage to e-money over paper money is that the unforgeability aspect can be proven based on well-established intractability assumptions.

The anonymity provided by cash payments is attractive to criminals as well. Criminals often prefer to conduct transactions using cash due to the difficulty of tracing it in small quantities. As a result, serial numbers and watermarks are used when needed to help track the movement of U.S. treasury notes. The countermeasure to these traceability mechanisms is money laundering. It is not uncommon for small-time crooks to buy expensive goods at a department store in one state and then return them in another state in order to move large sums of money safely.

### 4.1.3   Anonymous Assassination Lotteries

Since truly anonymous e-money is not traceable it would provide an ideal medium for money laundering. It would be possible to leave the country with millions of dollars tucked away safely within an average-sized wallet. This has the potential to fill the treasuries of crime syndicates and terrorist groups to unprecedented levels. When combined with anonymous remailers, the potential for abuse of e-money is even worse. So begins the manifesto of Jim Bell, civil libertarian [186]:

*A few months ago, I had a truly and quite literally "revolutionary" idea, and I jokingly called it "Assassination Politics": I speculated on the question of whether an organization could be set up to legally announce that it would be awarding a cash prize to somebody who correctly "predicted" the death of one of a list of violators of rights, usually either government employees, officeholders, or appointees. It could ask for anonymous contributions from the public, and individuals would be able (to) send those contributions using digital cash.*

The idea combines the notion of e-money with anonymous remailers to create a treacherous lottery. Cash would flow in through anonymous mix networks and each winner would receive his or her share of the pool in an anonymous reply. The combined technologies also make it possible for criminals to pay for each other's services by sending e-money to each other using anonymous remailers. This makes it impossible to coerce criminals in custody to divulge the identity of accomplices *since they won't know the identities of their accomplices*. Hence, the sum of both technologies is greater than the two.

### 4.1.4   Kidnapping and Perfect Crimes

To illustrate this even further, consider the problem that a kidnapper faces in collecting the ransom money. Even if the kidnapper sends the delivery person on a wild goose chase to the final drop-off point, the kidnapper may still get caught. This situation is risky from the kidnapper's perspective since it makes certain assumptions about the surveillance capabilities and overall manpower of law enforcement. But with e-money, this is not the case. The kidnapper can insist that the ransom be paid using e-money that is encrypted under the kidnapper's public key. Like in the cryptovirus attack, the kidnapper can insist that the encrypted e-money be sent using an anonymous remailer in an anonymous reply. This is known as the perfect crime [311].

Armed with this foresight, cryptographers have devised algorithms for implementing electronic money with safeguards that prevent these abuses [50, 140]. These safeguards typically involve key escrow, and therefore utilize a predetermined group of escrow authorities. When needed, the escrow authorities can collaborate and thereby trace the flow of e-money notes. They therefore have the ability to revoke the anonymity provided by the underlying system. Kidnappers that try to use e-money with revocable anonymity would face even worse traceability issues than with cash. In the case of assassination politics the identities of the lottery participants could be ascertained.

Sometimes it is amazing how science fiction novels foreshadow future technology. The text below is from the chapter entitled "The Logicality of Liking" from Book II of the 1975 novel *The Shockwave Rider* [43]. It bears a striking resemblance to mixes with revocable anonymity.[1]

> *"What sort of trick?"*
> *"Sometimes it's known as going to the Mexican Laundry."*
> *"Ah. You route a credit allotment—to avoid either tax or recriminations—into and out of a section of the net where nobody can follow it without special permission."*

Given the existence of anonymous e-cash schemes that provide for revocable anonymity, one might assume that the threat of assassination politics and perfect crimes is eliminated. However, this assumption is fundamentally flawed since it makes the implicit assumption that there is

[1]Special thanks to C. C. Michael for pointing this out.

an entity that is capable of controlling all payment mediums. This need not be the case.

Suppose that an offshore organization (for example, a small foreign country) creates a digital currency. Using encryption, signatures, and mix networks it would be possible to buy and sell products and services using the currency on the Internet in a confidential and untraceable fashion (similar to "BlackNet" [184]). This organization can design the payment system to be completely anonymous.[2]

Any country or organization that does this is likely to thrive. It would become a repository for crime syndicates worldwide and would probably amass an endowment in short order that would permit it to invest in legitimate businesses. Other countries could pass legislation that would make using the foreign e-money illegal, but cryptography would greatly inhibit law enforcement's ability to enforce such laws. Under these circumstances, the threat of anonymous assassination lotteries and perfect crimes remains alive. In Bruce Sterling's book *Islands in the Net* [292], Grenada is a pirate cove that closely resembles this sort of country.

## 4.1.5   Conducting Criminal Operations with Mixes

Mix nets and anonymous money are powerful technologies for conducting criminal activities (see Subsection 3.10.2). One can surely expect an immense amount of interest from law enforcement agencies and intelligence agencies whenever a mix network is deployed. It was only a matter of time until strong cryptography became a household technology. It is quite possible that robust mix networks will come next. Traditionally, it is open standards that gain the most widespread and rapid adoption. *An open standard for a mix network, should one be drafted and highly utilized by the general public, could prove to be the single most liberating and at the same time life-threatening Internet technology to date.* Various peoples live out their entire lives in fear of persecution. Mix networks have the potential to help make freedom of speech a reality worldwide.

In fact, something very similar to such a widespread open protocol already exists. The people at Nullsoft[3] developed the gnutella protocol in late 1999. The gnutella protocol is currently utilized by an immense number of people round-the-clock to share files on the Internet. Many of these files are copyrighted MP3 songs. Needless to say these sorts of programs

---

[2]Perhaps under suitable computational intractability assumptions.

[3]The creators of Winamp.

have been the bane of the recording industry for some time now. Unlike its predecessor, Napster, the gnutella protocol is *completely decentralized* and allows each user to be a file sharing server. This makes it exceptionally hard to apprehend those who illegally duplicate and distribute copyrighted material. It is possible to design a protocol akin to the gnutella protocol that preserves the anonymity of the recipients of copyrighted material. For example, users could connect to offshore servers using a mix network. This would allow citizens in countries with stringent copyright laws to violate copyright laws in an undetectable fashion. Furthermore, if the sharing were performed at a packet switching layer, the new protocol could serve as a general mix net packet switch *and* a medium for distributing MP3s. This would serve hardened criminals and casual copyright violators alike. Due to the immense number of packets relating to MP3 transfers, the network would always be highly utilized and a high level of anonymity would be assured for everyone. Perhaps the biggest technical challenge is handling the needed PKI for such a service.

An anonymous e-mail service based on a cryptographically secure mix net when combined with e-cash is a criminal's dream: criminals can operate in cells, coordinate criminal acts by sending each other anonymous e-mails, and pay for each other's services by sending each other e-cash via anonymous e-mail, *all without ever knowing each other's true identity.* In cryptographic terms, it is a way of *secret-splitting* criminal operations.[4] This is a policeman's worst nightmare. Even if one criminal is apprehended there would be no way to use that prisoner to track down his or her accomplices... simply because the prisoner would honestly not know who the accomplices were. Interrogators love to lie to captives to get them to divulge facts that law enforcement needs. In fact they are permitted to do so under U.S. law. They need only read the criminal his or her Miranda rights and then slap 'em around a bit to prevent the criminal from taking the fifth. However, they cannot lie about leniency in regards to sentencing. Given enough pressure many criminals break. With mix nets and anonymous cash, breaking the prisoner may be a fruitless endeavor.

Using mix nets securely is a complicated business. Imagine the following Trojan horse attack on a mix net. A malicious entity, Mitch, deploys an e-mail client with a stegotrojan in it. Two criminals, Alice and Bob, both use this infected e-mail client to send and receive e-mails. Suppose

---

[4]Certain crimes can even be split down to the level where each slice is hardly a criminal act in and of itself. The ability to amass chemicals in small quantities comes to mind.

that each copy of the client has a unique identifier $ID$. Each time a client sends out an e-mail it steganographically encodes two $ID$s in the header information. One $ID$ is that of the client that constructed the e-mail. The other $ID$ is that of the $ID$ in the most recently received e-mail packet.

In this attack it is assumed that Alice and Bob use the infected clients on a regular basis for benign communications. Also, suppose that they have never communicated by e-mail before and that on a single occasion Alice sends Bob e-mail through an e-mail anonymizer wherein the e-mail describes a premeditated criminal act. Bob's client will eventually receive the e-mail, perhaps through his digital pseudonym. Alice's $ID$ will go out in stego form in Bob's next e-mail. For instance, it may go to a user named Carol. If the header data that is going to Carol is in plaintext form then Mitch, who is passively eavesdropping on the network, will be in a position to learn that the anonymous e-mail that Bob received was in fact sent from Alice. The point of this attack is that hackers and intelligence agencies can use stegotrojans to foil the anonymity that is provided by mix nets. There are a myriad of other ways to do this. Criminals and honest users alike would do well by verifying the design used in all of their hardware and software, especially network related software. *In the absence of doing so, the safest assumption to make is that all of your communications will be traceable.* This attack does not necessarily imply that Mitch will be able to read the message that was sent from Alice to Bob through the mix net. It could be encrypted using Bob's public key. However, due to the steganographic tag in the e-mail header, the ciphertext could be traceable. This may constitute enough probable cause to arrest and interrogate Alice or Bob.

Violating the anonymity afforded by mix nets is a serious issue. It has the potential for ruining the privacy in electronic voting protocols. There exist numerous provably secure cryptographic protocols for voting in the scientific literature. Many are based on the existence of secure anonymizing capabilities. In a matter of years companies are likely to produce e-voting software and tout it as being 100 percent secure, accurate, and timely. Given the presidential election tally screw-up in Florida recently, it may end up being adopted. If such technologies become the norm, the threat of stegotrojans and government corruption could then more easily give rise to an Orwellian society.

The use of Linux or a similar free operating system may help in preventing stegotrojan attacks. Operating systems that are based on Unix exist in the public domain. Their source code can be verified. They can then be compiled and used. However, care must be taken that the underlying computer and compiler do not contain Trojans. A clever attack in this regard is presented in Section 9.3.

## 4.2   Deniable Password Snatching

Given the ideas behind assassination politics and the perfect crime it seemed only natural that other dark applications of anonymity could be found. These two threats do not involve malware *per se* and can be categorized as protocols that are conducted by malicious individuals. The cryptovirus attack merges malware with mix networks and could easily make use of e-money if such currency were known to be untraceable.

The concept of a cryptovirus is a simple one. Place a public key in a virus and let it perform one-way operations on the host system that only the author can undo. It is really the payload of a cryptovirus that gives it an edge, since the public key in no way assists in viral replication. The discovery of the cryptovirus attack led us to ask ourselves the following question:

*In what other novel ways can malicious software, when gifted with the public key of the author, mount attacks on its host with improved efficacy?*

The question itself suggests that all existing cryptographic tools need to be analyzed from the perspective of degrading system security rather than improving it. The notion of anonymity had already proven fruitful in the perfect crime, assassination politics, and the cryptovirus attack. It was only natural to question whether or not its uses had been exhausted. This led to our work on deniable password snatching [334].

### 4.2.1   Password Snatching and Security by Obscurity

Consider a typical Trojan horse program that steals the login/password pairs of users. The Trojan horse program hooks into the system's authentication mechanism and captures such pairs as they are entered by the users. The login/password pairs are often stored in a file with an obscure name in a remote location on the file system. In some operating systems it is even possible to designate the file as being invisible, which makes it harder to detect. The attacker then accesses the machine at a later time and downloads the pilfered login/password pairs. From the attacker's perspective this attack is risky for two reasons:

1. Someone else may find the hidden file and infiltrate the accounts, thereby endangering the author of the Trojan horse. The assumption that others will not read data in the file by virtue of the fact that the file is hidden is dangerous. It is an instance of *security by obscurity*, a discouraged cryptographic practice.

2. The Trojan horse may be discovered by system administrators and alarms may be put in place that sound whenever the hidden file is read. So, the Trojan author is sticking his or her neck out by issuing commands to download the hidden file.

Security by obscurity is discouraged among cryptographers but it is a principle that applies to computer security in general. Security should not depend on the secrecy of the design nor the ignorance of the attacker [13].

## 4.2.2   Solving the Problem Using Cryptovirology

The virus writer can readily overcome both of these problems. To carry out the attack, a cryptotrojan that contains the public key of the virus writer can be used. To solve the first issue, the Trojan horse encrypts each login/password pair using the public key contained within the virus. The data can be encrypted using the RSA-based OAEP cryptosystem, for instance. The resulting ciphertext is stored in a hidden file as before. The hidden file can be designed to contain $M$ ciphertext values at all times and hence remain fixed in size. To implement this, an index $i$ is stored at the beginning of the file (see Figure 4.1). The value $i$ stores the index of the next ciphertext to be overwritten. It will range from 0 to $M - 1$ inclusive and when $M - 1$ is reached the value for $i$ will then wrap back around to zero. This way, the Trojan will overwrite the oldest entries in the file when it is full. By doing so the entries will always be kept up-to-date. If the Trojan is in place for months on end and users change their passwords, the Trojan will overwrite the old passwords in favor of the new ones. It is important to keep the file from constantly increasing in size to keep it from drawing unwanted attention.

In the deniable password-snatching attack the file is initially filled with $M$ ciphertexts corresponding to the encryptions of $M$ randomly chosen messages. The starting value for $i$ is a number chosen uniformly at random between 0 and $M - 1$ inclusive. These starting conditions help obfuscate the activity of the Trojan immediately upon deployment.

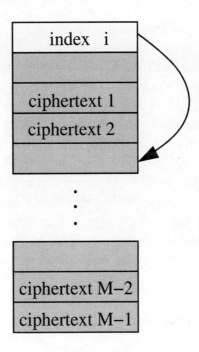

**Figure 4.1**  Hidden login/password file

The notion of anonymity leads to the solution of issue (2). The fact that the login/password pairs are securely encrypted paves the way for using an anonymous distribution channel. The idea is to covertly give the hidden file to the general public. This can be done without compromising the stolen passwords since only the Trojan horse author can decrypt the file.

For concreteness, consider a scenario in which the Trojan author plans on returning to the machine to download the hidden file to a floppy disk. In this attack the Trojan horse is designed to unconditionally copy the hidden file to every writable floppy disk that is inserted into the machine that has a sufficient amount of free space. To make the password data as unnoticeable as possible, it is written to the last few unused sectors of the floppy disk. These sectors must remain unused in the eyes of the file system. If the sectors were marked as allocated then users might discover the file due to loss of disk space. The Trojan horse author must be sure not to write to the floppy disk until the hidden file is safely recovered from the floppy using a low-level disk editor. As a result of this approach, lots of users may inadvertently receive a copy of the hidden password file. Since it is public key encrypted they will not be able to decipher it.

This attack illustrates that malware often needs to collect and store data that is obtained from the host environment. To make malware difficult to detect it should be fixed in size and this suggests that *circularly linked lists are ideal data structures for storing data that needs to be kept up-to-date in malware.*

The biggest problem that remains in this attack from the perspective of the Trojan horse author is installing the Trojan horse program in the first place. One way to do this is to write a virus that installs the Trojan horse program. For example, the author can store the infected program on a floppy. To install the Trojan horse, the floppy is inserted into the host machine and the infected program is run. The virus will migrate from the executable on the floppy to the host machine on its own. If the author is caught at this time then he or she can claim to be an innocent victim of the virus.[5]

## 4.2.3  Zero-Knowledge Proofs to the Rescue

There are a couple of effective defenses against this deniable password-snatching attack. If a Public Key Infrastructure is available and users are outfitted with smart cards, then they can conduct zero-knowledge interactive proofs to authenticate without using login/password pairs. It can be shown via a simulation argument that an eavesdropper that observes ZKIP authentication sessions learns absolutely nothing that will allow the eavesdropper to impersonate other users. Another solution is to use timed cryptographic tokens such as RSA's SecurID product. This battery-powered token computes hash values and displays them on the token in regular intervals. Each user must also choose a personal identification number (PIN) to use along with the token. To authenticate to a host system a user transmits both the PIN and the current hash value. Like ZKIPs, the solution is secure against eavesdroppers that learn the PIN and hash values, provided that the SecurID token remains in the custody of the user. The SecurID token is a tamper-resistant device that stores secret information that is used to compute the hash values. The existence of these robust authentication technologies implies that the utility of the deniable password-snatching attack is likely to wane as time goes on.

However, the attack is general in nature and can be used for stealing

---

[5]Such an argument is not likely to work when you are a known cryptovirologist, however.

data other than login/password pairs. The method works equally well for stealing any kind of information on host machines. Assuming that a benign communication channel exists, a Trojan on a compromised machine can broadcast public key encrypted data over the channel. Benign channels include steganographic channels, subliminal channels, dummy fields in packet headers, and so on. In this case only the Trojan author will be able to decipher the broadcast.

### 4.2.4   Improving the Attack Using ElGamal

By using a specific type of public key cryptosystem the attack can be improved slightly. Ideally, the Trojan horse author would like the administrator of the host machine to be as oblivious to the activities of the Trojan horse as possible. This includes not letting the administrator know how many passwords, if any, were stolen before the discovery of the Trojan horse.

This can be accomplished by using the ElGamal cryptosystem [110] modified appropriately [304] to be semantically secure under plaintext attacks[6] (see Appendix C.2.2). Recall that $x$ is the private key and $(y, g, p)$ is the corresponding public key in ElGamal. The ciphertext of $m$ is the pair $(a, b)$. One of the most useful properties of ElGamal is that its ciphertexts are malleable under multiplication. By multiplying $b$ by some other plaintext $m_1$ the encrypted plaintext becomes $mm_1 \bmod p$. Also, it is possible to rerandomize ElGamal ciphertexts as follows. Choose a value $k_1 < q$ randomly and compute $(a', b') = (ag^{k'} \bmod p, by^{k'} \bmod p)$. This changes the appearance of $(a, b)$ completely and $(a', b')$ decrypts to the same value as $(a, b)$.

In regular intervals the Trojan horse can be designed to perform this rerandomization to all $M$ ciphertexts regardless of whether or not any new passwords are stolen. Also, the decision to steal each login/password pair can be probabilistic. As a result, with some very small probability the Trojan will never encrypt any login/password pairs. This approach will hamper the sysadmin's attempt to determine if any passwords have been stolen before the discovery of the Trojan horse. If disk backups are continually taken then system administrators will have a chance of catching a glimpse of the previous activities of the Trojan horse. For example, a dump of virtual memory could expose the virus while it was encrypting a given user's password. However, if all of the backups miss

---

[6]In this attack the malware designer cannot be used as a decryption oracle.

these small windows of opportunity, then it could not be proven that any passwords had been stolen prior to the discovery of the Trojan. All $M$ entries will change regardless of whether or not the Trojan snatches a single password.

As in turns out the deniable password-snatching attack can be improved even more. By observing the password-snatching Trojan in action it is possible to witness it encrypt passwords and transmit them. It is possible to redesign the Trojan so that even when the Trojan is monitored at runtime it is not possible to tell if it is actually encrypting anything. The improved attack utilizes a new notion that we call *questionable encryptions*. See Section 6.6 for details.

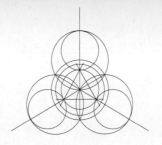

# Chapter 5

# Cryptocounters

A common trigger used in viruses to decide when to attack is a counter value. Such viruses typically do not trigger until it has propagated itself a certain minimum number of times. The Den Zuk virus contains such a trigger [289]. When counters are used only to measure the number of viruses in the wild, a good approach is to utilize two different generation counters. One counter would store the generation number of the virus that is incremented by one in each child a given virus has. This would provide the height $h$ of the family tree. The other counter would be used to measure the average number of children that each virus has (see Chapter 1). This mechanism could be used as a tool for measuring replication performance of viruses in real-world infections.

However, antiviral analysts would likely benefit more than virus writers from the incorporation of counters in virus code since they would receive better population samplings. To solve this malware problem, a method is needed to implement such counters in a way that the viruses can increment the counters but that only the virus writer can read the actual counter values. A *cryptocounter* is a cryptographic primitive that solves this problem.

In this chapter a simple cryptocounter scheme is presented based on the ElGamal public key cryptosystem. Drawbacks to this approach are then given, followed by an improved approach based on the Paillier public key cryptosystem. The chapter concludes with discussion of even more ways to implement a cryptocounter.

## 5.1   Overview of Cryptocounters

Informally, a *cryptocounter* is a probabilistic public key encryption that encrypts a counter value that anyone can increment or decrement but that can only be decrypted using the appropriate private key. Put another way, it is a malleable ciphertext that allows the plaintext to have 1 added to it or 1 subtracted from it. The increment and decrement operations can be performed by anyone without even knowing the plaintext value and without first decrypting the encryption of the counter value.

The typical threat model for the operation of a cryptocounter is the *honest-but-curious* model. In this model, it is assumed that the machine that increments the cryptocounter does so properly, and does not change the counter in unexpected ways. For instance, if the algorithm normally increments the cryptocounter once every hour, the machine does not maliciously increment it twice every hour, and so on. It is assumed that the machine that operates on the cryptocounter ciphertext is passive and merely observes any and all computations regarding the counter. The machine may do its best to try to learn the counter value based on these observations, hence the term *curious*. In this sense the machine is a form of passive adversary. But, the machine does not interfere with the normal operation of the counter, which is a capability that active adversaries have.

By placing a cryptocounter within the virus, there is an added level of protection over the use of a plaintext counter. The counter value that the cryptocounter encrypts will never be revealed. This holds even if snapshots of the cryptocounter are taken on a regular basis. Such snapshots can occur as the result of coredumps and so forth. It is necessary to monitor the operations on the cryptocounter each step of the way in order to keep track of the current counter value.

Consider a virus that stores two cryptocounters to help keep track of the number of viruses in the wild. It is relatively safe to assume that before the virus is discovered, the host machine will not corrupt the counter value and will not interfere with the virus when it increments the counter. Also, it is prudent to assume that once the virus is found several system administrators may examine their logs to try to determine the counter values. Assuming that the snapshots are spaced out reasonably far enough, the snapshots are not likely to reveal the counter values that the viruses contain.

## 5.2 Implementing Cryptocounters

In this section two methods for implementing cryptocounters are given. This first is based on the ElGamal public key encryption algorithm. Although conceptually very simple, this approach has a significant drawback when counter values are large. The second approach is almost as simple as the first. It is a counter based on the Paillier public key cryptosystem. The Paillier cryptosystem is described and it is shown how to use Paillier to implement a simple cryptographic counter.

### 5.2.1 A Simple Counter Based on ElGamal

It is straightforward to utilize the ElGamal public key cryptosystem to implement a rudimentary cryptocounter. In the semantically secure version of ElGamal (see Appendix C.2.2) the message space consists of all messages $m$ such that $m^q = 1 \ mod \ p$. Here $q$ is a large prime that divides $p - 1$ evenly. Since the cryptosystem is malleable under multiplication modulo $p$, the plaintext can be multiplied by values modulo $p$ without ruining the decipherability of the ciphertext. So, a simple counter can be implemented using the public key $(y, g, p)$ as follows.

The plaintext is initially set to $g^1 = g$. By choosing $k_1$ randomly, the first counter value is computed to be the pair $(a_1, b_1)$ that is equal to $(g^{k_1} \ mod \ p, y^{k_1}g \ mod \ p)$. To increment the counter by 1, the ciphertext $(a_2, b_2)$ can be computed by setting $(a_2, b_2) = (a_1, b_1g \ mod \ p)$. Similarly, $(a_3, b_3) = (a_2, b_2g \ mod \ p)$. When this ciphertext is decrypted, the plaintext is found to be $g^3 \ mod \ p$. This is illustrated in Table 5.1.

However, there is a problem with this approach since it paves the way for correlation attacks against the virus. For example, consider a generation counter that is incremented by one in each child. Suppose that a virus on machine A has a child on machine B and that this virus has a child on machine C. The ciphertexts on $A, B, C$ would be $(a_1, b_1), (a_2, b_2), (a_3, b_3)$, respectively. Observe that the equalities $a_1 = a_2 = a_3$ hold. The problem is that $b_3/g = b_2 \ mod \ p$ and $b_2/g = b_1 \ mod \ p$. So, the path of the virus can be ascertained based on the relationships between $b_1$, $b_2$, and $b_3$.

This problem can be solved by rerandomizing the ciphertexts each time the counter is incremented. This makes correlation impossible due to the semantic security of the underlying cryptosystem. This approach will now be described. The plaintext is initially set to $g^1 = g$. By choosing $k_1$ randomly, the first counter value is computed to be $(a_1, b_1) =$

| ciphertext value | $i = 1$ | $i = 2$ | $i = 3$ |
|:---:|:---:|:---:|:---:|
| $a_i =$ | $g^{k_1} \bmod p$ | $a_1$ | $a_2$ |
| $b_i =$ | $y^{k_1} g \bmod p$ | $b_1 g \bmod p$ | $b_2 g \bmod p$ |

**Table 5.1**  Flawed ElGamal Cryptocounter

$(g^{k_1} \bmod p, y^{k_1} g \bmod p)$. To increment the counter by 1, the ciphertext $(a_2, b_2)$ is computed by choosing $k_2 < q$ randomly and setting $(a_2, b_2) = (a_1 g^{k_2} \bmod p, b_1 y^{k_2} g \bmod p)$. When this ciphertext is decrypted, the plaintext is found to be $g^2 \bmod p$. To see that this works, note that $\frac{b_2}{a_2^x} = \frac{y^{k_1} g y^{k_2} g}{g^{k_1 x} g^{k_2 x}} = \frac{g^{x k_1} g g^{x k_2} g}{g^{k_1 x} g^{k_2 x}} = g^2 \bmod p$. To increment the counter again, the ciphertext $(a_3, b_3) = (a_2 g^{k_3} \bmod p, b_2 y^{k_3} g \bmod p)$ is computed using a randomly chosen value $k_3 < q$, and so on. This is illustrated in Table 5.2. This method stores the actual counter value in the exponent of $g$. The counter value $i$ therefore corresponds to the ElGamal plaintext $g^i \bmod p$.

Suppose that the cryptocounter ciphertext $(a_i, b_i)$ is obtained from a virus. By performing ElGamal decryption the plaintext $m = b_i / a_i^x \bmod p$ is found. Since $m = g^i \bmod p$, computing $i$ is equivalent to computing the base $g$ discrete logarithm of $m$. Provided that $i$ is not exponentially large, this can be done by testing whether or not $g^i = m \bmod p$ for $i = 1, 2, 3, \ldots$ until the equality holds.

## 5.2.2  Drawback to the ElGamal Solution

The drawback to this counter is that there is no trapdoor for the counter value. The value for $i$ must be found by brute-force after $g^i \bmod p$ is computed via decryption. Consider an application in which the counter value is not always incremented by one. If at some point the counter is incremented by an exponentially large value, it will take exponential time to determine the exact counter value during decryption. When used for implementing virus generation counters this drawback may not be very sig-

| ciphertext value | $i = 1$ | $i = 2$ | $i = 3$ |
|:---:|:---:|:---:|:---:|
| $a_i =$ | $g^{k_1} \bmod p$ | $a_1 g^{k_2} \bmod p$ | $a_2 g^{k_3} \bmod p$ |
| $b_i =$ | $y^{k_1} g \bmod p$ | $b_1 y^{k_2} g \bmod p$ | $b_2 y^{k_3} g \bmod p$ |

**Table 5.2**  ElGamal Cryptocounter

nificant, but in other applications it may well be. Cryptographic counters like this one can be used in a variety of ways. They are ideal mechanisms for securely gathering statistics on untrustworthy host machines and are general tools for securing mobile agents.

### 5.2.3 Cryptocounter Based on Squaring

The ElGamal cryptocounter is trivial to decrement by anyone. To decrement $(a_i, b_i)$ one need only compute $(a_i, b_i g^{-1} \bmod p)$ and then rerandomize the new pair. This drawback can be heuristically avoided using the following variation of the counter. It is very similar to the ElGamal cryptocounter in terms of choosing exponents randomly, rerandomizing, decrypting the counter, etc. However, instead of using the prime $p$, the modulus $n$ is used where $n$ is the product of two secret primes. The value $g \in \mathbb{Z}_n^*$ is chosen such that it has order $\lambda(n)/2$. Hence, $g$ is a quadratic residue modulo $n$.

The counter value 0 is represented by a randomly chosen quadratic residue $a$ modulo $n$ that is kept secret. To increment the counter by 1, both $a_i$ and $b_i$ are squared modulo $n$. Thus $a^2$ corresponds to a counter value of 1, $a^4 \bmod n$ corresponds to a counter value of 2, and so on (see Table 5.3).

Just as in the ElGamal cryptocounter there is no trapdoor here. To determine the counter value the pair $(a_i, b_i)$ is decrypted using $x$ and the resulting plaintext is $a^{2^i} \bmod n$. The counter value is $i$ and this can be found by brute force. A brute force approach is to start with $a$, square it repeatedly and stop when a value is found that matches the plaintext of $(a_i, b_i)$.

Consider the problem of decrementing the counter without $a$ and without knowing the factorization of $n$. This can be trivially accomplished by reverting to a previously stored cryptocounter pair if one is available. If no previous snapshots of the cryptocounter are available, then the counter value can be modified by setting $b_i = b_i w \bmod n$ where $w$ is a quadratic

| ciphertext value | $i = 0$ | $i = 1$ | $i = 2$ |
|---|---|---|---|
| $a_i =$ | $g^{k_0} \bmod n$ | $a_0^2 g^{k_1} \bmod n$ | $a_1^2 g^{k_2} \bmod n$ |
| $b_i =$ | $y^{k_0} a \bmod n$ | $b_0^2 y^{k_1} \bmod n$ | $b_1^2 y^{k_2} \bmod n$ |

**Table 5.3** Squaring Cryptocounter

residue modulo $n$. However, this modification is not likely to be meaningful since $a$ is kept secret.[1] Decrementing a cryptocounter pair directly without any previous copies amounts to computing a square root of $a_i$ and a square root of $b_i$ modulo $n$, which is intractable.

## 5.2.4    The Paillier Encryption Algorithm

Perhaps one of the simplest and most elegant solutions to the problem of implementing a cryptocounter is to use Paillier's public key cryptosystem [216]. The Paillier cryptosystem constitutes a one-way trapdoor under the computational composite residuosity assumption (see Appendix B.3.3). The Paillier cryptosystem is semantically secure against plaintext attacks under the decision composite residuosity (DCR) problem (see Appendix B.3.4).

The value $n$ in Paillier is the product of two large primes $p$ and $q$, the same as in RSA. The Paillier cryptosystem is based on the following two properties of Carmichael's $\lambda$ function.

1. For any $w$ contained in $\mathbf{Z}_{n^2}^*$, the congruence $w^{\lambda(n)} \equiv 1 \ mod \ n$ holds.

2. For any $w$ contained in $\mathbf{Z}_{n^2}^*$, the congruence $w^{n\lambda(n)} \equiv 1 \ mod \ n^2$ holds.

In RSA the public exponent $e$ in the public key $(e, n)$ is relatively prime to $(p-1)(q-1)$. Typically, the value $e$ is shared by all the users. Paillier's cryptosystem is quite a bit different since it does not employ $e$. Instead, the cryptosystem utilizes an integer $g$ that has order $v$ modulo $n^2$ with $v$ satisfying the following congruence.[2]

$$v \equiv 0 \ mod \ n \tag{5.1}$$

The value $g$ is shared by all the users. The public key is $(n, g)$ and the private key is $\lambda(n)$.

---

[1] In fact, by using two different counter constructs such as this one and the ElGamal one at the same time, by making the counter values equivalent, and by incrementing them in lock-step, a redundancy check is implemented. The check is verified by decrypting the cryptocounters and making sure they both store the same count. This makes it harder for an active adversary to falsify a previous counter value.

[2] The value $g$ is said to have *order* $v$ modulo $n^2$ if and only if $v$ is the smallest positive integer satisfying $g^v \equiv 1 \ mod \ n^2$.

The following is how to encrypt a message $m$, which is an integer satisfying $m < n$. A value $u$ is chosen uniformly at random from $\mathbb{Z}_n^*$ and the ciphertext $c$ is computed as follows,

$$c = g^m u^n \bmod n^2 \qquad (5.2)$$

The function $L(x) = \frac{x-1 \bmod n^2}{n}$ is used for decryption. The following equation shows how to decrypt $c$ to recover $m$.

$$m = L(c^{\lambda(n)} \bmod n^2)L(g^{\lambda(n)} \bmod n^2)^{-1} \bmod n \qquad (5.3)$$

It remains to show that decryption succeeds for all messages $m$. By Euclid's division rule, given positive integers $g^{\lambda(n)}$ and $n^2$ with $n^2 \neq 0$, there exist unique integers $q$ and $r$, with $0 \leq r < n^2$ such that $g^{\lambda(n)} = qn^2 + r$. In this equation $q$ is the quotient and $r$ is the remainder upon dividing $g^{\lambda(n)}$ by $n^2$. The value $r$ equals $g^{\lambda(n)} \bmod n^2$. By reducing both sides modulo $n$ this implies that,

$$g^{\lambda(n)} \equiv r \bmod n \qquad (5.4)$$

By property (1),

$$g^{\lambda(n)} \equiv 1 \bmod n \qquad (5.5)$$

By transitivity, equations 5.4 and 5.5 imply that $r \equiv 1 \bmod n$. Hence, $g^{\lambda(n)} \bmod n^2$ is congruent to 1 modulo $n$. So, there exists an integer $\beta < n$ such that $g^{\lambda(n)} \bmod n^2 = 1 + \beta n$. Hence,

$$g^{\lambda(n)} \equiv 1 + \beta n \bmod n^2 \qquad (5.6)$$

By subtracting 1 from both sides it follows that $g^{\lambda(n)} - 1 \equiv \beta n \bmod n^2$. This implies that $g^{\lambda(n)} - 1 \bmod n^2 = \beta n \bmod n^2$. Define $t_1$ to be $g^{\lambda(n)} - 1 \bmod n^2$. So, $t_1 = \beta n \bmod n^2$. By applying the division rule again, it follows that there exists a $k_1$ such that $\beta n = k_1 n^2 + t_1$. So, $t_1/n = \beta - k_1 n$. By reducing both sides modulo $n$, it follows that $t_1/n \equiv \beta \bmod n$. Since $t_1/n = L(g^{\lambda(n)} \bmod n^2)$ this implies that

$$\beta \equiv L(g^{\lambda(n)} \bmod n^2) \bmod n \qquad (5.7)$$

By raising both sides of equation 5.2 by $\lambda(n)$ and reducing modulo $n^2$ it follows that $c^{\lambda(n)} \equiv (g^m u^n)^{\lambda(n)} \bmod n^2$. From property (2), the value $u^{n\lambda(n)} \equiv 1 \bmod n^2$. Hence,

$$c^{\lambda(n)} \equiv (g^{\lambda(n)})^m \bmod n^2 \qquad (5.8)$$

Now, by substituting equation 5.6 for $g^{\lambda(n)}$ in equation 5.8 it follows that $c^{\lambda(n)} \equiv (1 + \beta n)^m \bmod n^2$. The Binomial Theorem describes the expansion of the binomial $(1 + \beta n)$ on the right side of this equation. But, since this equation is reduced modulo $n^2$, every term will be zero except for the first two terms of the expansion. As a result, $c^{\lambda(n)} \equiv 1 + m\beta n \bmod n^2$. So,

$$c^{\lambda(n)} - 1 \equiv m\beta n \bmod n^2 \qquad (5.9)$$

But this implies that $c^{\lambda(n)} - 1 \bmod n^2 = m\beta n \bmod n^2$. Define $t_2$ to be $c^{\lambda(n)} - 1 \bmod n^2$. By the division rule, there exists a $k_2$ such that $m\beta n = k_2 n^2 + t_2$. Hence, $t_2/n = m\beta - k_2 n$. By reducing both sides modulo $n$ it follows that $t_2/n \equiv m\beta \bmod n$. Since $t_2/n = L(c^{\lambda(n)} \bmod n^2)$ this implies that,

$$L(c^{\lambda(n)} \bmod n^2) \equiv m\beta \bmod n \qquad (5.10)$$

By substituting equation 5.7 for $\beta$ in equation 5.10 it follows that,

$$L(c^{\lambda(n)} \bmod n^2) \equiv mL(g^{\lambda(n)} \bmod n^2) \bmod n \qquad (5.11)$$

Multiplying both sides by $L(g^{\lambda(n)} \ mod \ n^2)^{-1} \ mod \ n$ results in the plaintext $m$.

Since the quantity $L(g^{\lambda(n)} \ mod \ n^2)^{-1} \ mod \ n$ is always the same each time that a ciphertext $c$ is decrypted, this value can be computed once and for all. So, let $\psi = L(g^{\lambda(n)} \ mod \ n^2)^{-1} \ mod \ n$. The user can then store $(\lambda(n), \psi)$ as his or her private key. Equation 5.12 shows how to decrypt $c$ using $\psi$.

$$m = \psi L(c^{\lambda(n)} \ mod \ n^2) \ mod \ n \qquad (5.12)$$

As in RSA, the Chinese Remainder Theorem can be used to speed up decryption. A variant of Paillier's scheme has been proposed that makes some efficiency improvements regarding the size of Paillier ciphertexts [79].

### 5.2.5   A Simple Counter Based on Paillier

The way to utilize this cryptosystem as a cryptocounter is straightforward. The counter is initially set to $m = 1$. To encrypt this counter value, $u_1$ is chosen randomly and the ciphertext is computed to be $c_1 = g^1 u_1^n \ mod \ n^2$. To increment the counter by one, $u_2$ is chosen randomly and the value $c_2 = c_1 g u_2^n \ mod \ n^2$ is computed. In general, $c_i = c_{i-1} g u_i^n \ mod \ n^2$. This rerandomization guarantees that each counter value is encrypted in a semantically secure fashion.

The benefit of this approach as opposed to the ElGamal solution is that no comparisons are necessary when $c_i$ is decrypted. The value $i$ is found immediately. A depiction of what a cryptocounter looks like when viewed on an untrusted machine is given on the right side of Figure 5.1.

## 5.3   Other Approaches to Cryptocounters

The Paillier cryptocounter is efficient in the sense that the counter value can be computed in poly-time even if the counter value is exponentially large. The Paillier cryptosystem constitutes an additive homomorphism under multiplication modulo $n^2$ since the product of two ciphertexts yields a ciphertext containing a plaintext that is the sum of the two original plaintexts. A cryptocounter was proposed by Katz et al that does not rely on this property [152]. Their construction shows how to implement a cryptocounter given any encryption scheme that is homomorphic over the

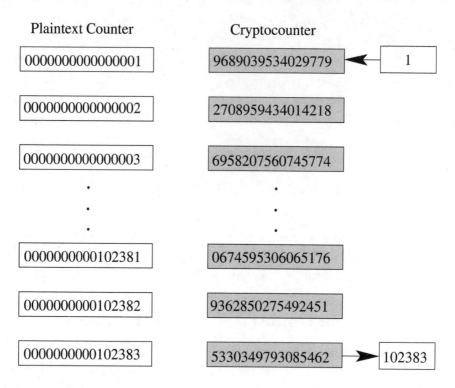

Plaintext Counter            Cryptocounter

**Figure 5.1**  Plaintext counter vs. cryptocounter

additive group $\mathbb{Z}_2$. As a result, cryptocounters can be constructed based on the *quadratic residuosity assumption*.

In summary, cryptocounters can be implemented based on the Decision Diffie-Hellman problem, the problem of distinguishing $n^{th}$ residues modulo $n^2$, and the composite quadratic residuosity problem. So, if the Decision Diffie-Hellman problem is found to be tractable, for example, then one of the other settings might still provide a secure foundation for this primitive. It is also quite possible that cryptocounters can be synthesized based on other intractability assumptions as well.

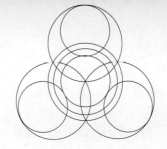

# Chapter 6

# Computationally Secure Information Stealing

Perhaps the two biggest fears that the victim of a computer virus has is that information has been covertly stolen or that data files have been deleted or altered by the virus. This chapter focuses exclusively on the former fear. Such viruses are among the most insidious since they can steal information for an indefinite period of time before ever being noticed.

More specifically, the problem of designing malware to *securely* and *privately* steal information is considered. The chapter begins with a straightforward cryptovirological approach that utilizes the public key of the malware author. However, this approach has a significant drawback since the virus code reveals the data that it is trying to steal. This drawback forms the motivation for a stronger model to privately obtain information. This strong model is known as the private information retrieval (PIR) problem. The notion of a PIR scheme is given and various approaches to solving this problem are mentioned.

A computationally secure PIR scheme is then described that has some very desirable properties from an operational standpoint. A few variants of this scheme are presented, thereby developing a heuristic solution that is amenable for use in real-world malware. Such malware is capable of privately stealing information without revealing anything about the information that is sought and without revealing anything about what is taken.

The notion of private information retrieval is closely related to a new notion that will be introduced in this chapter called *questionable encryptions*. An algorithm that produces questionable encryptions of data may, depending on its inputs, produce valid encryptions or fake encryptions that are actually just random numbers. It is related to private information retrieval since it is intractable to distinguish between the two cases and since a virus that sends questionable encryptions to the author may not be sending encryptions at all.[1]

Several constructions for a questionable encryption scheme are described as well as an instantiation based on the Phi-Hiding technique. It is shown how to use questionable encryptions to improve the deniable password-snatching attack described in Section 4.2. A further improvement of the deniable password-snatching attack is given based on the notion of *malware loaders*. Malware loaders are programs that contain enough functionality to load secure malware modules obtained from the network. By themselves they reveal very little regarding the ensuing attack since the modules that are loaded contain the code that is specific to the attacks that are conducted. They form a way of compartmentalizing malware functionality to allow attacks to deploy the truly malicious code from the safety of anonymizing networks.

The chapter concludes with a brief discussion of the *cryptocomputing* problem. A cryptocomputer is a primitive that has the potential to greatly improve antipiracy technologies as well as malware technologies in the same fell swoop. It is an ambitious new direction for cryptography, since a cryptocomputer is a virtual machine that can perform general computational operations on plaintext data that is hidden within ciphertext without ever exposing the plaintext in the process.

# 6.1   Using Viruses to Steal Information

Consider the problem of designing a virus to steal information from a host system. A typical scenario involves a *tag string* that can be used to identify the associated information that is desired by the virus author. For example, if the host contains a salary database indexed by the employee name, the virus can be designed to steal the salary information of a given employee. In the case that the virus writer wants to get the skinny on an employee named Billy Bob, someone that the virus writer feels is overly compensated, the virus writer could design the virus to search for the string "Billy Bob" and steal the associated salary information. The database would contain the entry "Billy Bob, $130,000." Upon matching the string "Billy Bob" contained in the virus with the entry "Billy Bob"

---

[1]Hence, there is a form of cryptographic obliviousness at work.

in the database, the virus knows it found the correct database entry. The virus then copies the value 130,000 into an internal viral storage area. Once found, the virus could delete the tag "Billy Bob" within itself in an attempt to hide that which was sought.

The virus certainly accomplishes its stated goal, yet it nonetheless suffers from some obvious drawbacks:

1. Stolen Data Revealed: The data is stored within the virus in the clear. This implies that its value will be available to anyone who obtains the virus down the road. In this example the string "130,000" is stored in plaintext form in the virus.

2. Tag Information Revealed: Even if the tag is deleted once the data is pilfered, previous snapshots of the virus will reveal the tag that the virus used. Hence, people may still be able to figure out it is Billy Bob's salary that was obtained.

Drawback (1) may be trivially resolved [332]. To fix this problem a randomly generated public key is placed within the virus, thus forming a cryptovirus. When the salary is found, it is asymmetrically encrypted and the resulting ciphertext is stored within the virus. This ciphertext is toted around until the author obtains the virus, extracts the ciphertext, and decrypts it using his or her private key.

As it turns out, drawback (2) can be resolved as well. The solution is non-trivial and forms the bulk of this chapter. What is needed is a private information retrieval algorithm that can privately retrieve Billy Bob's salary without revealing the tag string "Billy Bob." This information-stealing method is applicable to malware in general, not just viruses. It is equally useful in designing password-snatching Trojans and other Trojans that steal data.

## 6.2   Private Information Retrieval

In its most basic form, the private information retrieval (PIR) problem is for one party to retrieve the entry in a database that is maintained by one or more other parties without revealing which entry is sought. The formal problem is as follows. A database consists of $n$ entries, each of which stores a single binary digit. The database can be represented by a bit string $B = b_1 b_2 \cdots b_n$. The problem is to submit a query $i$ to the database administrator,[2] where $1 \leq i \leq n$ in such a way that the $i$ is not revealed to the database administrator, yet $b_i$ is returned in response to the query. Hence, bit $b_i$ is privately retrieved from the database.

This technology has obvious applicability in practice. For example, consider a high-tech company that wants to obtain a patent but does not want to reveal to the database administrators the exact technology that the company is interested in. If the company could privately retrieve the patent, then this problem would be solved.

The obvious solution to this problem is to simply return the contents of the database in response to the query. However, for large databases this solution is obviously inefficient. The notion of private information retrieval (PIR) was proposed by Chor et al and independently by Cooper et al [61, 71]. The proposed solutions can be broken down into two basic security categories: those that are *information theoretically secure*,[3] and those that are *computationally secure.*

To date the information theoretically secure solutions involved two or more database administrators that possess copies of the same database and that collectively process the queries of a user. A solution that is information theoretically secure cannot be broken under any circumstances, provided that the entity that supplies the query does not collude with database administrators and provided that the database administrators do not communicate with each other. It is analogous to multiprover proof systems [20].

A solution that is computationally secure is secure only under certain computational intractability assumptions. Schemes that fall under this latter category tend to be more efficient in terms of data storage overhead, since to date the information theoretic solutions assume that the database is replicated two or more times.

Chor and Gilboa demonstrated that it is possible to arrive at a subpolynomial communication complexity with minimal database replication when it is assumed that user inputs are private under a computational intractability assumption [60]. Kushilevitz and Ostrovsky showed that database replication can be avoided entirely [165]. They designed a single-database computational PIR that has subpolynomial communication complexity. It is based on the quadratic residuosity assumption (see Appendix B.3.5). Chachin, Micali, and Stadler presented a two-round computation-

---

[2]Or administrators, in the case that multiple instances of the database are maintained.

[3]This is also often referred to as being unconditionally secure.

ally secure PIR that assumes the existence of a single database [48]. Their solution is polylogarithmic in $n$, the size of the database. It is based on two new complexity assumptions (see Appendix B.3.6 and B.3.7). The scheme is remarkably efficient *and elegant*, partly due to the fact that it is only computationally secure, when compared to other PIR schemes. For this reason it will be described in this chapter.

## 6.2.1 PIR Based on the Phi-Hiding Problem

The Phi-Hiding PIR scheme consists of three algorithms. These are a query generator, a database algorithm, and a response retriever. The query generator encrypts the query $i$ in such a way that bit $b_i$ can be privately retrieved from $B$. Of course, $i$ is not encrypted in the usual sense, but it is nonetheless concealed from the database administrator. The outputs of this algorithm are a query $q$ that hides $i$ as well as a secret $s$ that can be used to recover bit $b_i$. The database algorithm takes the database $B$ as input as well as $q$ and applies the query to each entry in the database. The end result of this computation is a response $r$. The value $r$ is returned in response to the query. Finally, the values $r$ and the secret $s$ are supplied to a response-retrieving algorithm. This algorithm outputs bit $b_i$. This PIR is a two-round scheme since $q$ is given to the database administrator in round one and $r$ is returned in round two.

The intuition behind the scheme is as follows. A schema is given that allows a sufficiently large prime number $p_j$ to be constructed deterministically for each database entry $j$. Hence, the database entries $1, 2, ..., n$ will correspond to primes $p_1, p_2, ..., p_n$. With overwhelming probability these primes will be distinct. The user wants to obtain the bit in entry $i$ of the database without revealing $i$. The prime that is used to obtain this bit is $p_i$. A composite $m$ is then constructed that is tailored after this prime. It is crafted in such a way that $p_i$ divides $\phi(m)$ evenly, yet $m$ is difficult to factor even when $p_i$ is known. A value $x$ is then chosen uniformly at random from $\mathbb{Z}_m^*$. With overwhelming probability $x$ will not have $p_i^{\mathrm{th}}$ roots modulo $m$. A value in $\mathbb{Z}_m^*$ that does not have $p_i^{\mathrm{th}}$ roots modulo $m$ is construed as a binary zero. Hence, with overwhelming probability $x$ will be a binary zero. The database administrator is given the schema to compute the primes as well as $x$. The administrator uses the schema to compute $p_1, p_2, ..., p_n$ and sets $x_0 = x$. To retrieve the entry, the administrator computes $x_j = x_{j-1}^{p_j^{b_j}} \bmod m$ and returns $x_n$ to the user. With overwhelming probability, $x_n$ will not have $p_i^{\mathrm{th}}$ roots modulo $m$ unless $b_i = 1$. Hence, with overwhelming probability the transformations on $x$ will leave $x_n$ as a binary zero unless $b_i = 1$ in which case $x_n$ with have a $p_i^{\text{th}}$ root, thereby making $x_n$ a binary one. So, there is a forced correlation between bit $b_i$ and whether or not $x_n$ has $p_i^{\text{th}}$ roots or not.

The scheme utilizes a security parameter $k$. This value must be chosen such that $k > (log\ n)^2$. It is not uncommon in a formal cryptographic algorithm to provide $1^k$ as input. Recall that this is the binary string that consists of $k$ binary 1's. The reason for this is to provide a suitable setting for measuring the running time of the algorithm. When $1^k$ is provided as input, it becomes meaningful to say that the algorithm runs in time that is polynomial in the length of its input, no matter how tiny the usual inputs to the algorithm are. So, this custom is utilized in the descriptions of these algorithms.

The algorithm for the query generator is given below. It utilizes the subroutines $PrimeGenerator$ and $PhiHide$ that are subsequently described. Also, the parameter $f$ is covered in Appendix B.3.6.

$QueryGenerator(n, i, 1^k)$:
input: integer $n$ (number of bits in the database $B$)
        integer $i$ satisfying $1 \le i \le n$
output: a query $q = (m, x, Y)$ where:
             $m$ is a composite that is $k^f$ bits in length
             $x$ contained in $\mathbb{Z}_m^*$
             $Y$ which consists of $k^3$ $k$-bit strings
      secret $s$ which is the factorization of $m$
1. generate random $k$-bit strings $y_0, y_1, ..., y_{k^3-1}$
2. set $Y = (y_0, y_1, ..., y_{k^3-1})$
3. compute $p_i = PrimeGenerator(n, i, Y, 1^k)$
4. compute $(Q_1, Q_2) = PhiHide(f, p_i, 1^k)$
5. compute $m = Q_1 Q_2$
6. choose $x$ randomly from $\mathbb{Z}_m^*$
7. output $q = (m, x, Y)$ and $s$ and halt

Algorithm $PrimeGenerator$ generates a prime in a deterministic fashion based on the values $a$ and $Y$. It utilizes a deterministic primality testing algorithm [5].

$PrimeGenerator(n, a, Y, 1^k)$:
input: integer $n$ (number of bits in the database $B$)
        integer $a$ satisfying $1 \le a \le n$

$Y$ which consists of $k^3$ $k$-bit strings

output: a $k$-bit prime $p_a$

1. for $j = 0$ to $2^{k-\log n}$ do:
2.     set $A$ to be the $(\log n)$-bit representation of $a$
3.     set $J$ to be the $(k - \log n)$-bit representation of $j$
4.     set $\sigma_{aj} = A||J$
5.     compute $z_j = \sum_{\ell=0}^{k^3-1} y_\ell \sigma_{aj}^\ell \mod 2^k$
6.     if $z_j$ is prime then output $p_a = z_j$ and halt
7. output $p_a = z_j$ and halt


A composite integer $m$ is said to $\phi$-hide a prime $p_a$ if $p_a$ divides $\phi(m)$ evenly. It is implicitly assumed that $m$ is difficult to factor completely. Algorithm $PhiHide$ is used to $\phi$-hide $p_a$ within the composite $m$.

$PhiHide(f, p_a, 1^k)$:

input: integer $f$
       $k$-bit prime $p_a$

output: the factorization $s = (Q_1, Q_2)$ of a composite $m = Q_1 Q_2$ where
        $m$ is $k^f$ bits in length

1. repeatedly choose a random $(k^f - k)$-bit integer $q_1$ until
       $Q_1 = p_a q_1 + 1$ is prime
2. choose a random $k^f$-bit prime $Q_2$
3. output $s = (Q_1, Q_2)$ and halt


The tractability of $PhiHide$ holds under the Phi-Sampling assumption (see Appendix B.3.7). Under the Extended Riemann Hypothesis, algorithm $PhiHide$ runs in expected polynomial time in $k^f$. The database administrator runs $DatabaseAlgorithm$ that takes the database $B$ and query $q$ as input.

$DatabaseAlgorithm(B, q, 1^k)$:

input: database $B = b_1 b_2 \cdots b_n$ consisting of $n$ bits
       query $q = (m, x, Y)$

output: a response $r$ contained in $\mathbb{Z}_m^*$

1. set $n = |B|$
2. set $x_0 = x$
3. for $j = 1$ to $n$ do:
4.     compute $p_j = PrimeGenerator(n, j, Y, 1^k)$
5.     compute $e_j = p_j^{b_j}$

6.     compute $x_j = x_{j-1}^{e_j} \; mod \; m$

7. output $r = x_n$ and halt

The value $r$ is then sent back to the entity that submitted the query $r$. Once obtained, the entity runs algorithm *ResponseRetriever* on $r$ and the secret $s$.

*ResponseRetriever*$(n, i, (q, s), r, 1^k)$:

input: integer $n$ (number of bits in the database $B$)

        integer $i$ satisfying $1 \leq i \leq n$

        query $q = (m, x, Y)$

        secret factorization $s = (Q_1, Q_2)$

        response $r \in \mathbb{Z}_m^*$ obtained from database administrator

output: a bit $b$ such that $b = b_i$ with overwhelming probability

1. compute $p_i = PrimeGenerator(n, i, Y, 1^k)$

2. compute $t = \frac{(Q_1 - 1)(Q_2 - 1)}{p_i}$

3. compute $w = r^t \; mod \; m$

4. set $b = 0$

5. if $w = 1$ then set $b = 1$

6. output $b$ and halt

The probability that a random element in $\mathbb{Z}_m^*$ has a $p_i^{\text{th}}$ root modulo $m$ is exponentially small in $k$. Observe that *ResponseRetriever* returns $b = 1$ if and only if $r$ has $p_i^{\text{th}}$ roots modulo $m$.

## 6.2.2   Security of the Phi-Hiding PIR

For a retrieval scheme to truly constitute a computationally secure PIR it must satisfy two properties. It must satisfy the *correctness* property as well as the *privacy* property. Informally, the correctness property states that with overwhelming probability it should be possible to efficiently construct a query, run the query on the database, and decrypt the query efficiently such that the proper bit is obtained. The privacy property states that there does not exist a circuit that can take the query as input and discern $i$ from it. The formal definition of a computationally secure PIR will now be given.

**Definition:** Let the three private information retrieval algorithms denoted by *QueryGenerator*, *DatabaseAlgorithm*, and *ResponseRetriever* be efficient algorithms. These algorithms constitute a polylogarithmic computationally secure PIR scheme if there exist constants $a, b, c, d > 0$ such that,

1. Correctness: for all $n$, for all $n$-bit strings $B$, for all $i \in \{1, 2, 3, ..., n\}$, and for all $k$, after the ordered execution of the following steps:

    (a) $(q, s) = QueryGenerator(n, i, 1^k)$

    (b) $r = DatabaseAlgorithm(B, q, 1^k)$

    $Pr[ResponseRetriever(n, i, (q, s), r, 1^k) = b_i] > 1 - \frac{1}{2^{ak}}$.

2. Privacy: for all $n$, for all $i, j \in \{1, 2, 3, ..., n\}$, for all $k$ such that $2^k > n^b$, and for all $2^{ck}$-gate circuits $A$, after the ordered execution of the following steps:

    (a) $(q_1, s_1) = QueryGenerator(n, i, 1^k)$

    (b) $(q_2, s_2) = QueryGenerator(n, j, 1^k)$

    $Pr[A(n, q_1, 1^k) = 1] - Pr[A(n, q_2, 1^k) = 1] < \frac{1}{2^{dk}}$.

   The correctness assumption says that a computationally secure PIR need only work correctly nearly all of the time, not absolutely all of the time. In short it says that the failure probability must be negligible in $k$. The privacy property says that there should not exist an adversary circuit $A$ that can distinguish a query containing $i$ from a query containing $j$ with non-negligible probability. It also shows that $Q$ is efficient under the Phi-Sampling assumption (see Appendix B.3.7).

   The proof that the aforementioned scheme constitutes a polylogarithmic PIR will not be given here. We refer the reader to the original paper on the scheme [48]. The non-trivial aspect of the proof is in showing that privacy holds. The proof that privacy holds is by contradiction. For the sake of contradiction it is assumed that the privacy condition does not hold for $(D, Q, R)$. From this assumption it follows that an adversary circuit $A_1$ exists that violates the privacy property. It is then shown how to use $A_1$ as an oracle in a guessing circuit $C_1$ that violates the Phi-Hiding assumption (see Appendix B.3.6). This leads to a contradiction since the underlying premise is that the Phi-Hiding assumption holds. Hence, the assumption that the privacy condition does not hold is in error. The guessing circuit $C_1$ performs Lagrange interpolation to find $y_0, y_1, ..., y_{k^3-1}$ based on the input prime $p$, $i$, and randomly chosen $k$-bit numbers $a_1, a_2, ..., a_{k^3}$.

### 6.2.3 Application of the Phi-Hiding Technique

It is instructive to analyze the performance of the Phi-Hiding scheme in a practical scenario. Consider a database that consists of $2^{36}$ bits and hence $n = 2^{36}$ entries.

$$2^{36} \; bits = 2^{33} \; bytes = 2^{23} \; kbytes = 2^{13} \; MB = 2^3 \; GB$$

This may therefore be thought of as the problem of privately obtaining a single bit from an eight gigabyte hard drive.

Since $k$ must be greater than $(log\ n)^2$ it follows that $k$ must be chosen such that $k > 36^2 = 1296$. For simplicity suppose that $k = 1296$. The query contains $Y$ which consists of $k^3$ strings, each of which is $k$-bits in length. Since $2^{33}$ bits equals 1 gigabyte this corresponds to,

$$\frac{(36^2)^4}{2^{33}} = \frac{4^8 9^8}{2^{33}} = \frac{2^{16} 9^8}{2^{33}} = \frac{9^8}{2^{17}} \; GB$$

It follows that $Y$ is about 328 gigabytes long. A query that is 328 gigabytes would present significant problems in many practical settings.

The Phi-Hiding PIR has a communication complexity that is polylogarithmic in $n$ times a polynomial in the security parameter $k$. It is this polynomial dependence that may lead to such a large query. Choosing $k$ as such is overkill and this is duly noted in the original paper.

Relaxing the restriction that $k$ be greater than $(log\ n)^2$ is one way to make this PIR more viable in practice. However, other relaxations may also be considered. Minimizing the size of the query is critical in mobile agent applications, and in viruses in particular since the size of a virus has everything to do with how hard the virus is to find. This provides the motivation for the closely related PIR scheme that is presented in the next section.

## 6.3 A Variant of the Phi-Hiding Scheme

This variation of the Phi-Hiding PIR utilizes a security parameter $k$ that may be chosen independently of $n$. In general it is prudent to choose $k \geq 160$. The approach is essentially the same, except that a random oracle assumption is used. The random oracle assumption allows the query $q$ to be shrunk considerably. As always care must be taken when instantiating a random oracle. A simple hash function such as SHA-1 will rarely suffice.

It should provide an enormous number of output bits (not just 160 as in SHA-1) and correlations should not be possible.

Let $RandPrime_k$ be a random function with domain $\{0,1\}^*$. This function is implemented using a random oracle $H$ as follows. When $RandPrime_k(s)$ is invoked on an input bit string $s$, $RandPrime_k$ in turn invokes $H(s)$. The output of $H$ is a bit string that is countably infinite in length. At the time the oracle was created, each bit in $H(s)$ was chosen with probability $1/2$. The random function $RandPrime_k$ samples $H(s)$ $k$-bits at a time and tests for primality using a deterministic primality test [5]. It samples at most $k^3$ strings from $H(s)$ each of which is $k$-bits in length. The first $k$-bit sequence that is prime forms the output of $R$. If no prime is found, then the last $k$-bit string is output. This is analogous to the original Phi-Hiding scheme that essentially makes $k^3$ attempts at finding a random $k$-bit prime.

The expected running time of $RandPrime_k$ can be ascertained based on the Prime Number Theorem (see Appendix B.2). For a given input string $s$ the probability that no prime is found is at most about $(1 - \frac{1}{k})^{k^3}$. It follows that $RandPrime_k$ has an efficient expected running time.

$QueryGenerator2(n, i, 1^k)$:

input: integer $n$ (number of bits in the database $B$)

　　　integer $i$ satisfying $1 \leq i \leq n$

output: a query $q = (m, x, Y)$ where:

　　　　　$m$ is a composite that is $k^f$ bits in length

　　　　　$x$ contained in $\mathbb{Z}_m^*$

　　　　　$y$ which is a $k$-bit string

　　　secret $s$ which is the factorization of $m$

1. generate a random $k$-bit string $y$
2. set $I$ to be the $(log\ n)$-bit representation of $i$
3. compute $p_i = RandPrime_k(y||I)$
4. compute $(Q_1, Q_2) = PhiHide(f, p_i, 1^k)$
5. compute $m = Q_1 Q_2$
6. choose $x$ randomly from $\mathbb{Z}_m^*$
7. output $q = (m, x, y)$ and $s$ and halt

$DatabaseAlgorithm2(B, q, 1^k)$:

input: database $B = b_1 b_2 \cdots b_n$ consisting of $n$ bits

　　　query $q = (m, x, y)$

output: a response $r$ contained in $\mathbb{Z}_m^*$
1. set $n = |B|$
2. set $x_0 = x$
3. for $j = 1$ to $n$ do:
4.      set $J$ to be the $(\log n)$-bit representation of $j$
5.      compute $p_j = RandPrime_k(y||J)$
6.      compute $e_j = p_j^{b_j}$
7.      compute $x_j = x_{j-1}^{e_j} \bmod m$
8. output $r = x_n$ and halt


$ResponseRetriever2(n, i, (q, s), r, 1^k)$:
input: integer $n$ (number of bits in the database $B$)
       integer $i$ satisfying $1 \le i \le n$
       query $q = (m, x, y)$
       secret factorization $s = (Q_1, Q_2)$
       response $r \in \mathbb{Z}_m^*$ obtained from database administrator
output: a bit $b$ such that $b = b_i$ with overwhelming probability
1. set $I$ to be the $(\log n)$-bit representation of $i$
2. compute $p_i = RandPrime_k(y||I)$
3. compute $t = \frac{(Q_1-1)(Q_2-1)}{p_i}$
4. compute $w = r^t \bmod m$
5. set $b = 0$
6. if $w = 1$ then set $b = 1$
7. output $b$ and halt

This scheme is nearly identical to the original Phi-Hiding PIR scheme. The only significant difference is how the primes $p_1, p_2, ..., p_n$ are chosen. They are still chosen deterministically, yet they are chosen by applying a random oracle to a randomly chosen seed $y$. The efficiency of this approach is readily apparent since the query is the same as before except that it contains $y$ instead of $Y$. The value $y$ is $k$-bits in length whereas $Y$ is $k^4$ bits in length.

The privacy aspect differs in certain respects from the privacy proof of the original Phi-Hiding scheme. Let $A_1$ be the adversary circuit that violates the privacy condition. A guessing circuit $C_1$ may be constructed that (i) uses $A_1$ as an oracle, and that (ii) solves the Phi-Hiding problem. The inputs to $A_1$ must not look suspicious, otherwise $A_1$ can balk and not complete the needed operation. So, whatever inputs $C_1$ concocts, they must conform to the inputs that $A_1$ expects. Hence, $C_1$ must be able to *simulate* these inputs in such a way that they conform to what $A_1$ expects. Given that this scheme is in the random oracle model, it makes sense to consider simulators for other random oracle cryptosystems.

Bellare and Rogaway gave an elegant formalization of a common cryptographic technique known as the Fiat-Shamir heuristic [18]. They showed how to convert any atomic proof system[4] with knowledge error $1/2$ in the random oracle devoid model into non-interactive zero knowledge proof system with knowledge error $1/2^{k(n)}$ where $k(n)$ is a given security parameter. The construction is attractive since it permits the adversary to make $2^{k(n)}$ oracle queries in an attempt to break the non-interactive zero-knowledge proof system. The salient aspect of this construction that is relevant to this PIR is what is known as the *random oracle completion operation*. Bellare and Rogaway allow the simulator to prescribe a small (polynomial sized) piece of the oracle, and have the rest *magically* filled out at random.

The random oracle completion operation, or ROC for short, takes as input $(u,v)$ and returns an oracle $R$ that is random subject to the constraint that $R(u)$ is prefixed by $v$. The random string completion operation, or RSC for short, is an operation that takes a string $v \in \{0,1\}^*$ as input and appends to it a countably infinite sequence of random bits. So, conceptually, the output of $R$ on input $u$ is $v$ followed by $RSC(v)$.

The operations ROC and RSC can be utilized in the guessing circuit $C_1(m,p)$ that takes the composite $m$ and the $k$-bit prime $p$ as input. The approach is as follows. The value $y$ is chosen to be a random $k$-bit string and $u = y||I$ is computed. Here $I$ is the (*log n*)-bit representation of $i$. A series of $k$-bit strings are generated randomly until one is found that is prime. This prime is then replaced by $p$. This sequence of $k$-bit values forms the bit string $v$. The ROC operation is performed to compute $R = ROC(u,v)$. The RSC operation then defines the bits that follow $v$ in the output of $R$. The oracle $R$ is then used as the oracle in the random function *RandPrime*.

Assuming that the problem instance $(m,p)$ is chosen randomly, this approach produces primes $p_1, p_2, ..., p_n$ that are drawn from the probability distribution that the adversary circuit $A_1$ expects. Of course, one of these primes is in fact $p$ from the problem instance $(m,p)$. In this fashion, $A_1$ is duped by $C_1$ into solving the Phi-Hiding problem.

This computational PIR solves the space problems associated with the PIR query $q$. However, it does not minimize the running time of the database algorithm. This may prove to be too burdensome in some

---

[4]For any language $L$ contained in NP.

settings, yet perhaps not in others. It is an interesting research problem to develop a more computationally efficient private information retrieval scheme.

## 6.4   Tagged Private Information Retrieval

The random oracle based PIR presented in Section 6.3 is a space efficient way to privately obtain a single bit from a database of bits. It is of course possible to define $w$ databases $B_1, B_2, ..., B_w$ and perform the PIR scheme $w$ times, once for each database. This allows the user to obtain all $w$ bits corresponding to entry $i$ in each database. This effectively forms a single database containing $n$ entries, each of which contains a $w$-bit string.

However, this scheme is still somewhat abstract and leaves much to be desired in terms of applying it in many practical situations. There may be some situations in which the needed entry may be referenced by an index $i$, but a more likely scenario is one in which the needed entry is associated with a particular tag string rather than an index $i$ that is contiguous with the other entries. For instance, consider a hacker that wishes to obtain the password of BobbyB142 and no one else. The database consists of the user names as tags and the passwords as database entries. The hacker would like to construct a Trojan horse that privately retrieves the password of BobbyB142 without revealing that his password is sought. The Trojan could be resident and apply the database administrator algorithm to each password that is entered. The Trojan will steal Bobby's password each time he enters it.

The PIR in Section 6.3 can be retrofitted to solve this problem. It can be employed by viewing the database as multiple 1-bit databases. The index sequence $i$ can consist of the binary representations of all current user names. There will of course be huge gaps in this index sequence. It is clearly more desirable to come up with a custom tagged PIR for this problem. This PIR will now be described. The tagged database $B$ is defined as follows,

$$B = ((t_1, \bar{b}_1), (t_2, \bar{b}_2), ..., (t_n, \bar{b}_n))  \qquad (6.1)$$

Here the $t_i$'s are each $W_1$ bits in length and the $\bar{b}_i$'s are each $W_2$ bits in length. The value $\bar{b}_j = (b_{j,1}, b_{j,2}, ..., b_{j,W_2})$ for $1 \le j \le n$. The problem is to obtain string $\bar{b}_i$ privately from the database administrator.

*QueryGenerator*3$(n, t_i, 1^k)$:

input: integer $n$ (number of bits in the database $B$)
  integer $t_i$ where $|t_i| = W_1$

output: a query $q = (m, x, Y)$ where:
  $m$ is a composite that is $k^f$ bits in length
  $X$ consisting of $W_2$ values from $\mathbb{Z}_m^*$
  $y$ which is a $k$-bit string
  secret $s$ which is the factorization of $m$

1. generate random $k$-bit string $y$
2. compute $p_i = RandPrime_k(y||t_i)$
3. compute $(Q_1, Q_2) = PhiHide(f, p_i, 1^k)$
4. compute $m = Q_1 Q_2$
5. for $j = 1$ to $W_2$ do:
6.     choose $x_j$ randomly from $\mathbb{Z}_m^*$
7. set $X = (x_1, x_2, ..., x_{W_2})$
8. output $q = (m, X, y)$ and $s$ and halt


*DatabaseAlgorithm*3$(B, q, 1^k)$:

input: database $B$
  query $q = (m, X, y)$

output: a response $R$ consisting of $W_2$ values from $\mathbb{Z}_m^*$
1. set $n$ equal to the number of entries in $B$
2. for $j = 1$ to $W_2$ do:
3.     set $x_{0,j} = x_j$
4. for $j = 1$ to $n$ do:
5.     compute $p_j = RandPrime_k(y||t_j)$
6.     for $\ell = 1$ to $W_2$ do:
7.         compute $e_{j,\ell} = p_j^{b_{j,\ell}}$
8.         compute $x_{j,\ell} = x_{j-1,\ell}^{e_{j,\ell}} \bmod m$
9. output $R = (x_{n,1}, x_{n,2}, ..., x_{n,W_2})$ and halt


*ResponseRetriever*3$(n, t_i, (q, s), R, 1^k)$:

input: integer $n$ (number of entries in the database $B$)
  integer $t_i$ where $|t_i| = W_1$
  query $q = (m, X, y)$
  secret factorization $s = (Q_1, Q_2)$
  response $R = (x_{n,1}, x_{n,2}, ..., x_{n,W_2})$
output: a bit string $\bar{b}$ such that $\bar{b} = b_i$ with overwhelming probability

1. compute $p_i = RandPrime_k(y\|t_i)$
2. compute $t = \frac{(Q_1-1)(Q_2-1)}{p_i}$
3. for $j = 1$ to $W_2$ do:
4.       compute $w = x_{n,j}^t \bmod m$
5.       set $b_{i,j} = 0$
6.       if $w = 1$ then set $b_{i,j} = 1$
7. output $\bar{b}$ and halt

The scheme generalizes the random oracle PIR in the obvious way. It uses a series of elements from $\mathbb{Z}_m^*$ to record the desired database entry. Each bit in the retrieved string corresponds to a $p_i^{\text{th}}$ root or non-root. No security argument will be given for this particular scheme. However, it is clear that it is based on the Phi-Hiding problem and gets its security from the intractability of distinguishing higher order residues from non-residues.

The tagged information retrieval algorithm can also be conceptually viewed as a logic circuit. This perspective will be given here; however, it is emphasized that this is for illustrative purposes only and in no way captures the essence of the Phi-Hiding scheme from a cryptographic standpoint. The object is to design a cryptographic pattern matching and storage circuit. If we disregard the cryptographic aspect of this problem, the corresponding circuit can be realized in a straightforward fashion using *logic synthesis*.[5]

Suppose that the tag $t_i$ is 4-bits long and the associated data $b_i$ is also 4 bits long. The circuit contains $t_i$ in hardwired form. This is depicted in Figure 6.1. For concreteness suppose that $t_i = 1110$, as in the figure. These bits are encrypted in the tagged information retrieval scheme. Also, the circuit initially contains a 4-bit register $x$. Each value is initially zero as depicted in the figure. The value $x$ corresponds to $X$ in the tagged information retrieval query.

To operate correctly the circuit must match the input tag with the hardwired tag $t_i$. If they match the corresponding data, $b_i$ should be copied into the 4-bit register $x$. If they don't match, then the register values should remain unchanged. The problem can be broken down into two parts: a pattern-matching circuit and a bit-writing circuit. Consider the pattern-matching circuit. The goal is to produce a binary 0 if the input tag matches the hardwired tag $t_i$ and zero otherwise. This can be implemented by first bitwise XORing the tag bits. If they all match then

---

[5]Logic synthesis is typically covered in an introductory undergraduate course in electrical engineering.

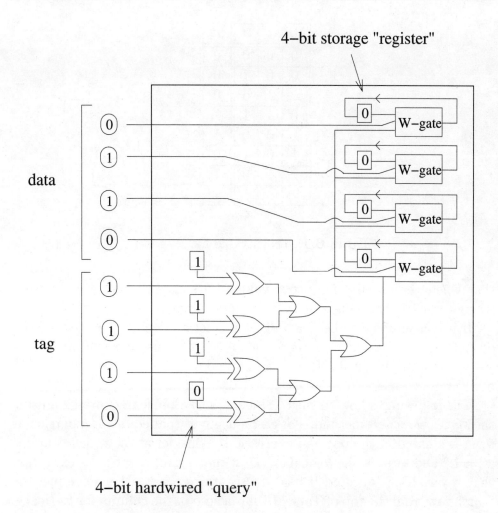

**Figure 6.1** Informaton retrieval circuit

all the resulting bits will be zero. If the bits in a single bit position differ then at least one of the resulting bits will be one. So, by ORing all the resulting bits, the result of the OR will be zero if and only if all bits match. Let the resulting signal bit be denoted by $s$.

The signal $s$ can be used to decide whether or not to copy the associated data bits into the 4-bit register $x$. This is the job of the W-gates, which stands for *writing gates*. When $s = 0$ the W-gates should cause $x$ to assume the value of $b_i$. When $s = 1$ the W-gates should leave $x$ unchanged. This design gives rise to the truth table given in Table 6.1.

In Table 6.1, $b$ denotes one of the bits in $b_i$, $x_i$ denotes the corresponding bit in $x$, and $x'$ denotes the value that $x_i$ will be changed to. Note

| b | x | s | $x'$ |
|---|---|---|---|
| 0 | 0 | 0 | 0 |
| 0 | 0 | 1 | 0 |
| 0 | 1 | 0 | 0 |
| 0 | 1 | 1 | 1 |
| 1 | 0 | 0 | 1 |
| 1 | 0 | 1 | 0 |
| 1 | 1 | 0 | 1 |
| 1 | 1 | 1 | 1 |

**Table 6.1**  Truth table for W-gate

that whenever $s = 0$, the output value $x'$ assumes the value of $b$. Also, whenever $s = 1$ the value $x'$ assumes the value of $x$.

It is conventional in boolean algebra to let $xs$ denote the logical AND of $x$ and $s$ where $x$ and $s$ are boolean values. It is also conventional to let $x + s$ denote the logical OR of $x$ and $s$ and $\bar{s}$ to denote the logical NOT of $s$.

The following is how to turn Table 6.1 into a boolean expression using the *sum-of-products* method. For each output $x'$ that equals 1, a particular term is created in the boolean expression. Consider a row which contains $x' = 1$. The term is the logical AND of the variables with the exception that a variable is negated if its entry contains a zero. For example, the fourth row from the top of Table 6.1 has a zero in the column for $b$. Hence, the term for this row is $\bar{b}xs$. All of the resulting terms are then ORed together. The truth table therefore gives rise to the following boolean equation.

$$x' = \bar{b}xs + b\bar{x}\bar{s} + bx\bar{s} + bxs \tag{6.2}$$

This boolean expression is implemented in a circuit called W-gate that is given in Figure 6.2.

It is instructive to consider the operation of the circuit in Figure 6.1. Suppose that the circuit is initially given $(t_1, b_1)$ where $t_1$ is the 4-bit tag and $b_1$ is the 4-bit data value. After this input is processed the circuit is given the input pair $(t_2, b_2)$ and then $(t_3, b_3)$. Let $(t_1, b_1) = (1010, 1100)$, $(t_2, b_2) = (1110, 0110)$, and $(t_3, b_3) = (0101, 1110)$. Since $1010 \oplus 1110 =$

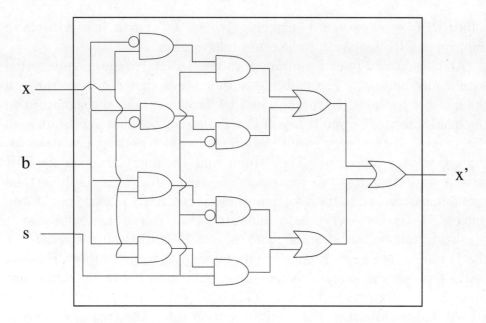

**Figure 6.2** W-gate for information-stealing circuit

0100 it follows that $s$ will be 1 for $(t_1, b_1)$. From the truth table it is evident that the value $x$ does not change whenever $s = 1$. So by the time $(t_2, b_2)$ is fed as input to the circuit, $x$ is still 0000. Now consider the input $(t_2, b_2)$. Since $1110 \oplus 1110 = 0000$ it follows that $s$ will be zero for $(t_2, b_2)$. From the truth table it is clear that the value $x$ is set to be $b$ whenever $s = 0$. So, by the time $(t_3, b_3)$ is fed as input to the circuit, $x$ will be 0110. Finally, consider the input $(t_3, b_3)$. Since $0101 \oplus 1110 = 1011$ it follows that $s$ will be 1 for $(t_3, b_3)$. From the truth table it is evident that the value $x$ does not change from 0110.

The amazing thing about the Phi-Hiding scheme is that it effectively implements this circuit without ever revealing the bits that are compared and stored. The tag $t_i$ and $x$ are encrypted from the start. Yet, the cryptocircuit nonetheless can both compare bit strings and then store data whenever a match occurs.

## 6.5   Secure Information Stealing Malware

The computational PIR in Section 6.4 is usable for both honest and malicious purposes. As previously described it can be used to implement a robust PIR based password-snatching Trojan. Of course, it is possible to implement PIR Trojans to take other information as well.

An elegant end-to-end solution is to use a PIR Trojan in conjunction with a mix network. The malware author sends signed queries through the mix net to the PIR Trojan. The PIR Trojan verifies the signature on the queries using the public key of the Trojan author that is contained in the Trojan. If the query is authentic and recent (checking time-stamps, etc.), then it is processed. The Trojan runs the query through the PIR scheme and computes the corresponding result $R$. This result is then communicated back to the Trojan author. It is already in encrypted form, but can be further encrypted to hide its form. To see this, note that it consists of values drawn from $\mathbb{Z}_m^*$ and this can be statistically detected. So, the Trojan asymmetrically encrypts it and sends it to the author. This can be done via return anonymous remailing, publishing it to a bulletin board through the mix net, and so on. This is an extremely powerful *infowar* attack since in all aspects of the information theft, the true intentions of the attacker are cryptographically concealed.

There is no reason why some or all of the tag string $t_i$ cannot be dynamic data as well. For example, the last few bits of the tag can be the current date and time. This allows the PIR to privately obtain timely information rather than just static information.

This PIR scheme is very useful in mobile agents to privately retrieve data in untrusted hosts' systems. It can be used by viruses to steal data without revealing that which is sought, provided that the database is defined to contain a large number of entries (some or all of an entire hard drive, for instance).

## 6.6  Deniable Password Snatching Based on Phi-Hiding

The Phi-Hiding scheme can be used to improve the deniable password-snatching attack (see Section 4.2). A drawback to the deniable password-snatching attack is that it is possible to observe the Trojan properly encrypt login/password pairs at run-time. A transcript of this activity itself forms strong evidence that can be used in a court of law. This possibility can be reduced significantly.

## 6.6.1  Improved Password-Snatching Algorithm

The improved deniable password-snatching attack is as follows. It is based on the tagged information retrieval scheme that is described in Section 6.4. The Trojan horse contains $n$ prime numbers $p_1, p_2, p_3, ..., p_n$ and $n$ composites $m_1, m_2, m_3, ..., m_n$ with the property that $m_i$ Phi-Hides $p_i$ for $1 \leq i \leq n$. These parameters are chosen according to the Phi-Hiding PIR scheme. Let $H(\cdot)$ be a random function that maps $\{0,1\}^*$ onto the set $\{p_1, p_2, ..., p_n\}$. Hence, a given input string $s \in \{0,1\}^*$ will satisfy $H(s) = p_i$ where $1 \leq i \leq n$ with probability $1/n$. The random function $H$ is included in the Trojan. Only the Trojan horse author knows the factorization of the $n$ composites. The Trojan horse also contains $n$ circularly linked lists $L_1, L_2, ..., L_n$ as well as $n$ indexes $I_1, I_2, ..., I_n$ that serve as pointers into these lists. Each element of a list is used as a storage location for the ciphertext of a single login/password pair. It is assumed that each login/password pair can be represented using $W_2$ bits. The linked lists are employed in a *least recently used* fashion. Hence, older ciphertexts are replaced by newer ones.

Let $s$ denote the login for a login/password pair that is obtained by the Trojan. Upon obtaining the login/password pair, the Trojan computes $p_i = H(s)$. The Trojan concatenates the login with the password and then pads the resulting string with leading zeros to derive a $W_2$-bit string $\bar{b}$. This string is effectively the desired database entry in the tagged information retrieval scheme. The Trojan then generates a tuple $X = (x_1, x_2, ..., x_{W_2})$ randomly, where each element of this tuple is contained in $\mathbb{Z}_{m_i}^*$. The Trojan then applies the tagged information retrieval scheme to this tuple as if it were part of a query for a database entry $\bar{b}$. In other words, for each bit in $\bar{b}$ that is a binary "1," the corresponding element in the tuple is exponentiated to $p_i$ modulo $m_i$. The tuple that results from this process is an encryption of the login/password pair. The Trojan stores this encryption as follows. The Trojan overwrites the entry in $L_i$ that is pointed to by $I_i$ with the newly formed encryption. The Trojan advances index $I_i$ and then awaits a new login/password pair. Note that when the index reaches the end of the list, advancing it amounts to setting it back to zero. Also, the Trojan unconditionally copies all $n$ linked lists to the last few unused sectors of every writable floppy that is inserted into the machine.[6]

---

[6] Or distributes the lists using some other channel (e.g., steganographic channel, subliminal channel, transmission over a mix network, broadcast channel, etc.).

It would be possible to carry out this attack by using only one big circularly linked list, one Phi-Hidden prime, and one composite that hides the prime. To see why this is a bad idea, consider the case in which a given user logs into the machine quite often. When this happens the single list would be saturated with this user's login/password pair. When multiple lists are used only one of the lists would be saturated. The use of hashing with multiple circularly linked lists ensures a good spread of snatched passwords, and the least recently used nature guarantees that the passwords are up-to-date.

## 6.6.2   Questionable Encryptions

At first sight it may appear that the attack that uses multiple linked lists is needlessly complicated. Also, it might not be clear why this snatching attack is better than the original deniable password-snatching attack that copies asymmetrically encrypted login/password pairs to the disk. The reason that this attack is an improvement is due to the subtle nature of what constitutes *theft*. For a law enforcement officer to frisk a citizen, there must be probable cause. For the judicial system to convict a citizen, there must be proof that a crime has been committed. The Phi-Hiding password-snatching attack helps cast doubt as to whether or not thievery has occurred.

Consider the ElGamal based deniable password-snatching attack. The Trojan contains the ElGamal public key $(y, g, p)$. For concreteness, let this be the version of ElGamal that is semantically secure against plaintext attacks. Hence, suppose that $g$ has order $q$ where $q$ is prime and $p = 2q+1$. Let $G$ be the prime order subgroup of $\mathbb{Z}_p^*$ that is generated by $g$.

Observe that it is possible to sample values $y \in G$ without knowing the private key $x$ such that $y = g^x \bmod p$. This implies that the Trojan author could conceivably gift the Trojan with a public key without even knowing the corresponding private key. A defendant that claims that he or she does not know the private key could in fact be telling the truth. It is quite possible that no one knows the private key in this case. However, it is straightforward to verify that the order of $y$ modulo $p$ is $q$. Hence, it is possible to verify that $y$ is a public key, whether someone knows the private key $x$ for $y$ or not.

What this means is that by observation, it is possible to witness the Trojan leak asymmetric ciphertexts in the deniable password-snatching attack, whether they can be decrypted or not. So, it is possible to prove in some sense that sensitive data has been transmitted outside of the machine. *This is not the case in the Phi-Hiding password-snatching attack.*

In the Phi-Hiding password-snatching attack, either $p_i$ divides $\phi(m_i)$ or not. This is not subject to debate. It is either true or it isn't. Hence, if for all $i$ it is the case that $p_i$ does not divide $\phi(m_i)$ then the Trojan is not asymmetrically encrypting anything at all. When this is the case, sensitive information is *not* being transmitted outside of the host machine. Proving that the Trojan snatches passwords amounts to proving that one of the primes $p_i$ divides $\phi(m_i)$. The presumed intractability of this is closely related to the Phi-Hiding assumption. Under this scheme, it is possible for the Trojan author to deploy a Trojan in which none of the primes are Phi-Hidden. If prosecuted, the Trojan author can *prove* that none of the primes are Phi-Hidden by revealing the prime power decomposition of the $n$ composites in the Trojan. We argue that the Phi-Hiding password-snatching attack is one of the best ways to snatch passwords from a fielded machine since it places the burden of proof on the prosecution in a very strong way. It is fitting to say that this Trojan satisfies the *questionable encryption* property, for lack of a better term. The reason that this term seems appropriate is that it is questionable as to whether the Trojan is encrypting anything at all.

A natural question to ask is whether or not the deniable password-snatching Trojan satisfies the questionable encryption property when RSA is used. Consider the case that the login/password pairs are encrypted using RSA with a deterministic padding scheme or are encrypted using OAEP. Also, suppose that $e$ is the typical value of $2^{16} + 1$ which is prime. The Trojan author can deliberately choose $p$ and $q$ such that $gcd(e^2, \phi(pq)) = e$. Without loss of generality, let $0 = p - 1 \bmod e$ and $0 \neq q - 1 \bmod e$. Adleman, Manders, and Miller presented a generalization of Tonelli's algorithm to compute $r^{\text{th}}$ roots modulo a prime where $r$ is a small prime [4] (see also [174]). Recall that there are $r$ roots in the complete solution set in this case.[7] This algorithm is efficient when $e$ is small and can be used to compute $e^{\text{th}}$ roots modulo $p$. When the factorization of $n = pq$ is known it follows that there exists an efficient algorithm to compute $e^{\text{th}}$ roots modulo $n$ in this case. In OAEP the correct root will be immediately apparent by verifying the OAEP checksum field that results from hashing. In RSA, the correct root will also likely be apparent by looking for padding bits, an ASCII value that appears to

---

[7]See page 161 of [12].

be a login/password pair, and so on. With such a small value for $e$ this approach does not exhibit the questionable encryption property.

By setting $e$ to be significantly larger than $2^{16} + 1$, for example, by making it a 160-bit prime, the RSA cryptosystem exhibits the questionable encryption property. The reason for this is twofold. First, observe that deciding whether or not $e$ divides $\phi(n)$ evenly is a decision problem that is intimately related to the Phi-Hiding problem. Second, when $e$ does in fact divide $\phi(n)$ evenly, it is intractable for the malware author to perform decryption correctly. This follows from the fact that to date, there is no known algorithm for efficiently computing $e^{\text{th}}$ roots mod $p$ with such a large prime $e$. For details the reader is referred to a section in Bach and Shallit entitled, "Computing d-th Roots" [12]. However, the questionable encryption properly need not rely on the inability of the private key holder to compute $e^{\text{th}}$ roots. To see this, consider the following alternative. The value $e$ can be set to be the product of numerous small, distinct, and odd primes. As before the value $e$ should be at least 160 bits. In this case it is possible to efficiently compute $e^{\text{th}}$ roots modulo $p$. However, the questionable encryption property still holds due to the fact that there are far too many roots for the private key holder to check. An asymmetric encryption function that exhibits the questionable encryption property is a specialized instance of *cryptocomputing* since it is possible to observe the function compute a value, but there is no way to tell if the resulting value is an asymmetric ciphertext or not.

The following are two additional ways to implement questionable encryptions. The first is based on the Goldwasser-Micali cryptosystem (see Appendix C.1.9). Recall that the GM cryptosystem uses a pseudosquare $y$ modulo $n$ where $n$ is the public modulus. The malware designer can choose $y$ to be a quadratic residue modulo $n$ instead of a pseudosquare. It is not hard to see that all of the values in a GM ciphertext will then be randomly chosen quadratic residues. Hence, the malware author will not be able to decipher anything. The author can later prove this by revealing a square root of $y$ and also the factorization of $n$ if the author so desires. This root serves as a witness that there is no trapdoor value for GM that reveals the plaintext. It follows that questionable encryptions can be implemented under the quadratic residuosity assumption. This approach is related to the computationally secure PIR of Kushilevitz and Ostrovsky [165].

The second approach is heuristic in nature. Let $(y, g, p)$ be an ElGamal public key, let $g$ and $p$ be fixed system parameters, and let $G$ be the group generated by $G$. The value $y$ can be chosen by computing $y = H(s)$. Here $s$ is a large randomly chosen seed and $H$ is a random function with domain $\{0,1\}^*$ (instantiated using a hash function). The range of $H$ is equal to $G$. The questionable encryption property holds under the presumed intractability of computing a triple $(x, y, s)$ satisfying,

$$g^x \bmod p = y = H(s) \ \ and \ \ y \in G \tag{6.3}$$

The pair $(y, s)$ serves as a witness that no one knows the trapdoor value associated with $y$. This follows from the fact that if $x$ is also known to the malware author then a valid triple must have been found.

A questionable encryption scheme is a form of oblivious transfer and can be regarded as a variant of *all-or-nothing disclosure* [38, 39]. However, these two notions differ in a couple of ways. A questionable encryption scheme can operate as an asymmetric cipher that is applied repeatedly and independently to many pieces of data, not data defined within the scope of a single protocol as is the case of all-or-nothing disclosure.

Court systems often rely on precedent in dealing with a case. The following is a way to establish a public precedent in regards to questionable encryptions. A virus writer can deploy a virus that computes questionable encryptions of sensitive data and that publishes these encryptions on the Internet. The virus can be designed so that it does not in fact encrypt anything. Once there has been a suitable amount of press coverage, the virus writer can anonymously reveal the factorization of $n$. This may put many people at ease. There would likely be even more press coverage that mentions that quite surprisingly the virus does not encrypt anything at all. With any luck this occurrence will cast a substantial amount of doubt in subsequent court cases involving questionable encryptions.

A public key cryptosystem that exhibits the questionable encryption property is a general tool for malware. It makes it such that encryptions are *questionable* in the sense that there is no way of knowing whether or not asymmetric encryptions are really being computed. For example, the SETUP attack on RSA key generation can utilize RSA with a 160-bit prime $e$. If it is the case that $gcd(e, \phi(n)) = e$, then the malware author can later reveal the factorization of $n$ and show that there never was a SETUP attack being performed despite the fact that the basic functionality needed to mount a SETUP attack is present.

The notion of questionable encryptions has potentially serious implications for copyright law. Consider a provider that illegally transmits copyrighted material to a recipient. For example, a recipient gives the provider a public key and the provider sends the recipient copyrighted material (e.g., MP3 music files) encrypted under the recipient's public key.

Now consider how a questionable encryption scheme can minimize the legal risk for the recipient. Suppose that a questionable encryption scheme is used as the delivery mechanism. If the recipient gives the provider a fake public key that produces a nonce under the asymmetric encryption algorithm, then the recipient receives random numbers instead of copyrighted material and hence the provider and recipient have not violated any copyright laws. In this case the provider is providing a random number generation service. If the public key is real, then the recipient has knowingly elicited copyrighted material that the provider had no right to give.

In this copyright violation scheme, only the recipient can initiate a copyright violation, and only the recipient knows if a violation is even occurring. Strictly speaking, the provider is not knowingly or willingly violating any copyright laws. The use of questionable encryptions for copyright violations therefore adds an extra hurdle to the successful prosecution of rogue *recipients* of copyrighted material.

It is natural to investigate how law enforcement bodies could try to catch copyright violators. Suppose that an undercover officer registers a real public key with the provider. If the officer later obtains copyrighted material from the provider, then strictly speaking it was the officer that enacted the copyright violation, not the provider. It seems that the officer would have to monitor another user: (1) generate a real public key, (2) register the public key with the provider, and then (3) obtain and decrypt the received ciphertext. This approach would clearly show that the recipient is in violation of the law. However, it is more difficult to show that the provider knowingly duplicated and transferred copyrighted material. In this regard, the notion of questionable encryptions adversely affects the enforceability of copyright laws. Recording industry groups would have a much harder time prosecuting people that use protocols like Gnutella if the underlying data delivery system were designed to use a questionable encryption algorithm.

An issue that was glossed over is the case that the copyrighted material is bulky. For example, a copyrighted file may be 2 to 3 megabytes in size. To deal with bulk data encryptions, a secure number-theoretic pseudorandom number generator can be used. The seed is encrypted with the questionable encryption scheme and the pseudorandom sequence that results from the seed is bitwise XORed with the plaintext. Observe that the seed is lost when the fake public key is used in the questionable encryption. Hence, the resulting ciphertext stream is polynomially indistinguishable from a random bit string with respect to the key holder and everyone else.

### 6.6.3  Deniable Encryptions

The notion of a *deniable encryption* was put forth by Canetti, Dwork, Naor, and Ostrovsky [52] and it is related to the notion of questionable encryptions. The utility of computing deniable encryptions is motivated by the following possibility. Consider a situation in which the transmission of encrypted messages is intercepted by an adversary who can later ask the sender to reveal the random choices[8] used in generating the ciphertext, thereby exposing the plaintext. An encryption scheme produces *deniable encryptions* if the sender can produce fake random choices that will make the ciphertext appear to be an encryption of a different plaintext, thereby keeping the true plaintext secret. Similar requirements can be formulated with respect to attacking the receiver and with respect to attacking both parties. A construction was given based on the existence of a trapdoor permutation.

Deniable encryption has several applications. For example, it can be incorporated in current protocols for incoercible and receipt-free voting in a manner that eliminates the need for a physically secure communication channel. It also underlies recent protocols for generalized incoercible multiparty computation that have no physical security assumptions. Also, deniable encryption provides an elegant and simplified construction of a multiparty protocol that is adaptively secure.

One of the differences between deniable encryptions and questionable encryptions is as follows. In a questionable encryption the receiver has a witness that the value is an encryption or a witness that the value is not a witness under a particular PKCS. In a deniable encryption the receiver can effectively present a witness for each possible interpretation of the plaintext. Another difference lies in the setting. A questionable encryption scheme must be such that it produces questionable encryptions while the encryption algorithm is under surveillance. In the deniable encryption setting this is not the case since the sender and receiver share secret information and only the transmitted messages, not the actual computations,

---

[8]As well as the secret key if it exists.

are assumed to be observable. In other words, the sender is allowed to compute privately without an adversarial onlooker. These two notions are different and solve different problems yet they are related in the following way: they both permit the recipient to refute the contents of the ciphertext. In questionable encryptions the recipient can claim that nothing is encrypted at all and in the deniable encryption case the recipient can claim that almost any string is encrypted.

## 6.7   Malware Loaders

The notions of deniable password snatching (that is, subtly broadcasting asymmetric ciphertexts wherein only the attacker can decrypt them), questionable encryptions, and private information retrieval clearly assists an attacker to receive information in such a way that (1) everyone receives the information but only the attacker can decrypt it, and (2) for all anyone knows, the ciphertexts are not ciphertexts but actually nonces, thus implying that information leakage may not have occurred.

Recall that in the original deniable password-snatching attack, the attacker uses a virus to install the cryptotrojan on the host machine. The attacker's only recourse if apprehended in this phase is to claim to be an innocent victim of the virus. This does not bode well for the attacker, since the virus will contain a Trojan that contains functionality for leaking information (although deciding if it really does is still intractable). Any prosecutor would likely try to make the case that the questionable encryptions were in fact encryptions. Since the information retrieval phase can be cryptographically improved, it is natural to ask if the malware deployment phase can be improved as well. In this section this question is answered in the affirmative. The idea utilizes the notions of an operating system, code signing, and signal monitoring. For concreteness it will be described within the context of snatching passwords, although other forms of information stealing are possible.

The attacker randomly generates a symmetric key and a key pair for a digital signature scheme. The symmetric key and digital signature verification public key are placed within a cryptotrojan. The cryptotrojan is designed to operate as follows. When running it constantly listens in on a public broadcast channel. This channel can be a public channel on the Internet, for example. The channel can even be a steganographic channel in graphics files within yet another more visible channel such as Usenet. When it receives a message it decrypts it using the symmetric key. The cryptotrojan then checks the structure of the plaintext data that results. If it is not in the form of a message, followed by a signature on the message, then it is rejected. If it is, then the signature on the message is verified using the public key.[9] If the signature is valid then the message is regarded by the cryptotrojan as an authentic message from the attacker.

The Trojan then executes the message as a child process. In UNIX this can be done using *fork* and *exec*, for example. The Trojan is thus acting like an operating system that uses code signing to check for authentic code. Since the Trojan loads and runs the process it seems natural to refer to it as a *malware loader*. The attacker constructs a *module* that the attacker wants the host system to run. This module is really just a self-contained program. The attacker digitally signs the module using the private signing key, encrypts the module and signature on it with the symmetric key, and then broadcasts the resulting binary string over a subtle public broadcast channel. The Trojan receives the signed and encrypted module from the broadcast channel and runs it only if it is authentic.

One module that the attacker can send is the questionable encryption password snatcher. This module questionably encrypts login/password pairs and broadcasts them on a subtle outgoing public channel. Another module can be a private information retrieval module that accepts queries and then scans information connected to peripherals to construct the response. The response is then broadcast on the subtle outgoing public channel. Like in the original deniable password-snatching attack, the cryptotrojan can be deployed via self-replicating malware.

The attack is a major improvement for the following reason. If the attacker is caught red-handed distributing the self-replicating malware that contains the cryptotrojan then half of the attack code will not be found on the attacker's person. This hampers things greatly from a legal perspective, since the attacker can claim that while yes, self-replicating code was being installed, its payload was only an operating system, which in itself can be quite harmless.

## 6.8 Cryptographic Computing

In some sense PIR schemes can be considered to be a specialized problem in cryptographic computing. It is the problem of performing secret string matching and string variable assignment while under the scrutiny

---

[9]Timestamps can also be used to guard against replay attacks.

of untrusted observers. This section covers the more general concept of cryptographic computing.

Cryptographic computing is an area of cryptography that is in its infancy. It is a new, ambitious direction for the field. Originally cryptography sought to provide confidentiality for inert data. Cryptocomputing is concerned with performing useful computations on encrypted data without having to decrypt it, not just the secure transport and storage of encrypted data. This functionality is applicable to software piracy protections schemes as well as secure mobile agents, viruses, worms, and so on.

In fact there is a very close relationship between piracy protection and secure mobile agent theory. They both adhere to the same premise that the underlying machine that is running the software is untrustworthy in some way. The most basic problem is observability: the underlying code can be scrutinized using debugging tools and hence the underlying algorithm can be learned and replicated elsewhere. This presents problems when a company wishes to deploy an unpatented algorithm that they wish to keep as a trade secret. It also poses a problem when a mobile agent is sent off to do work on a public network since the agent and the data it gathers is subject to the scrutiny of untrusted observers. The field of secure mobile agents is gaining in popularity, as evidenced by young workshops such as the IEEE International Conference on Mobile Agents (that had its sixth meeting last year). There has even been enough work in the area of cryptographic mobile agents to warrant general surveys on the subject [231].

However, the notion of performing useful computations in untrusted environments is at least as old as public key cryptography itself. In as early as 1978, around the time that the RSA algorithm was discovered, a sufficient mathematical framework for performing secure computations on an untrusted machine was proposed [100, 244]. Specifically, it was noted that the existence of an additive homomorphism over the ciphertexts of a public key encryption function $E$ defined over an appropriate domain as well as the existence of a multiplicative homomorphism over the ciphertexts would be sufficient to enable general computations over encrypted data akin to that which can be performed by Turing machines. In other words, the primitive would consist of operations $(E, \oplus, \otimes)$ such that for all plaintexts $m_1$ and $m_2$,

$$E(m_1) \oplus E(m_2) = E(m_1 + m_2) \qquad (6.4)$$

$$E(m_1) \otimes E(m_2) = E(m_1 * m_2) \qquad (6.5)$$

The additive homomorphism is denoted by $\oplus$, and the multiplicative homomorphism is denoted by $\otimes$. Interestingly, it is a trivial exercise to identify a multiplicative homomorphism for the RSA function, but the existence of an additive homomorphism for RSA is unknown.

If these primitives were to exist then they could be used to implement a universal logic gate such as a NAND or NOR gate. The gate would not operate on plaintext bits, but instead it would operate on ciphertext bits. For instance, the NAND gate would take as input two ciphertexts that each encrypt a single bit and it would return a ciphertext corresponding to the logical NAND of the two input plaintext bits. This would occur without ever decrypting the input ciphertexts. It is well known that any combinatorial circuit can be synthesized based on a universal gate. It is also well known that any Turing machine can be efficiently simulated by a Boolean circuit [315].

The practical utility of such a primitive may be brought into question, since an encrypted bit would likely occupy 768 or more ciphertext bits in the machine, and each operation is likely to involve multiple modular exponentiations, for instance. However, it would certainly be possible to implement small circuits to perform simple yet useful computations on untrusted hosts.

It is safe to say that researchers have been investigating the existence of these primitives for more than 20 years. However, it is important to bear in mind that this is a quest for a general-purpose cryptographic computing machine, not a machine that needs to solve a particular problem. In the mid-1980s the open research community began investigating dedicated cryptographic computing algorithms.

One such cryptocomputing algorithm appeared in 1986 [2, 99]. The idea was to disguise an instance of a hard problem, such as the discrete-logarithm problem, and have an untrusted machine solve it. The approach allows Alice to hide information from Bob while getting Bob to do some useful work. Alice has $y$ and wants to know the value $x$ such that $y = g^x \bmod p$. Bob has a magic computer and has a good chance of being able to solve the problem by brute force. Alice would like Bob to solve the problem for her, but does not want Bob to learn $x$.

Here is how the two of them can accomplish this. Alice chooses $r < q$ randomly and computes $y_r = yg^r \bmod p$. She sends $y_r$ to Bob and Bob computes the discrete logarithm of this value using the base $g$ and the modulus $p$. So, Bob computes $v = x + r \mod q$ and sends this value to Alice. Alice recovers $x$ by computing $x \equiv v - r \equiv x + r - r \mod q$. Bob has no way of knowing what the value of $x$ is. Similar results have been shown for the quadratic residuosity problem and the primitive root problem [1, 2].

A problem that is closely related to computing with encrypted data is the problem of performing secure multiparty computation. The first example of this is the famous Millionaire problem: Alice and Bob each have an integer number and they want to know who holds the greater number without having to disclose the numbers to one another. This was first addressed by Andrew Yao [325] in 1982. The more general context is the following. Two or more parties want to determine some property about the pieces of information they hold while keeping them private. The main results in the domain were achieved by Andrew Yao [326] in 1986 for the two-party case.

In 1987 Goldreich et al showed how to securely implement any desired multiparty functionality [116]. The security is guaranteed, provided either a majority of the players are honest or all parties are *semi-honest*. In other words, all parties send messages according to the protocol, but keep track of and share all intermediate results. Much attention has been paid to the important issue of minimizing the number of rounds of computation in this model. There is a wealth of literature regarding secure multiparty computations [14, 15, 16, 56, 57, 58, 105, 106, 107].

A working group, organized by DARPA, met in October 1996 to discuss security issues regarding the execution of code on machines that are operated by untrusted parties. In 1997 a workshop was held on the subject [80]. It was geared towards developing the semantics, structures, and security assumptions that form the basis for single-party secure computation. It was concluded that numerous approaches lacked formal grounds for security, and that they typically relied on ad hoc or otherwise hidden security assumptions.

In 1997 Sander and Tschudin proposed a method to compute with encrypted functions to overcome the problem of protecting mobile code from its host [250, 251]. Techniques were presented to achieve non-interactive computing with encrypted programs in certain cases and give a complete solution for this problem in certain instances. In particular they gave a protocol that allows non-interactive evaluation of encrypted polynomials over the ring of integers modulo $N$ where $N$ is a smooth (that is, $N$ has no large prime factors). The results are based on the use of homomorphic encryption schemes and function composition techniques. In particular they utilize an additive scheme of Lipton and Sander [176] that is polynomial time indistinguishable under the assumption of the hardness of the Power Residue Hypothesis, which is a generalization of the Quadratic Residue Hypothesis to residues of higher degree.

It is argued that this primitive may be usable in mobile agents that need to remotely sign their output. The agents would thereby be able to create *undetachable digital signatures*. However, they remark that there are still outstanding technical obstacles that need to be overcome in order to achieve this goal. Research that is related to this was presented in Financial Crypto '02 by Stern et al who gave a method for computing with encrypted rational numbers [103].

The first formal result regarding generalized cryptographic computing was presented in 1999 by Sander et al [252]. It was shown how in one round a protocol for secure evaluation of circuits can be performed in polynomial-time for $NC^1$ circuits (Nick's Class). The protocol involves an input party sending encrypted input to a second party (a cryptocomputer). The second party evaluates the circuit (or a known circuit over its additional private input) non-interactively, securely, and obliviously, and provides the output to the input party without learning it. This directly applies to protection against reverse engineering since under well-established intractability assumptions the reverse engineer provably learns nothing about the program that is being executed. An implementation is presented that is based on the quadratic residuosity problem. This improved on previous results that are specialized to the case of $NC^1$ circuits and that require a constant number of communication rounds. The scenario also coincides with computing with encrypted data when the input is transformed into an output while remaining encrypted throughout the computation. The algorithm utilizes a probabilistic encryption method that is random self-reducible. The paper also gives a new provably secure public key scheme that allows the computation of the logical AND operation using encrypted data. This scheme is homomorphic over a semigroup (instead of a group) and thus also expands the range of algebraic structures that can be encrypted homomorphically.

The work on one-round secure computation has been ongoing [47]. Cachin et al investigate one-round secure computation between two distrusting parties as well: Alice and Bob each have private inputs to a common function, but only Alice, acting as the receiver, is able to learn the output. The protocol is limited to one message from Alice to Bob followed by one message from Bob to Alice. The solution has an advantage over the Sander et al cryptocomputer since it works for polynomial-depth circuits. However, for the purposes of generalized mobile agent computing the solution has a drawback that it cannot iteratively receive inputs and compute values based on previously stored results. All of the inputs must be present at the time the computation commences. The authors propose a remedy to this based on symmetric cryptography but it has various inherent limitations. The solution nonetheless provides stronger evidence regarding the feasibility of executing mobile code in untrusted environments.

# Chapter 7

# Non-Zero Sum Games and Survivable Malware

Today, computer viruses, Trojans, and worms are summarily removed from computers when found. Even in the case of the One-half virus that is designed to make safe removal difficult, disinfection is still possible without damaging the host system. Antiviral programs seldom attempt to remove a virus unless they believe there are no harmful consequences for doing so. But what if the consequence extends beyond the infected computer in question? Put another way, what if the removal of a virus on one machine will cause damage on another remotely located machine? If harmful consequences result from removing malware then the payoff for removal becomes a negative quantity in game theoretic terms. Of course, leaving the malware on the system may have a payoff that is even more negative. This begs the question as to whether or not there exist malware enforceable games between the host and the malware that have a higher payoff for the host when the malware is allowed to remain after discovery.

> *The unspoken dream of every virus writer is to design a virus that cannot be safely removed even after discovery.*[1]

It is this that would constitute a true digital disease. This chapter investigates how various technologies can achieve this end when appropriately combined.

A dedicated attacker may have a rather serious goal in mind. For example, the attacker may want to factor someone's RSA key, or compute a discrete logarithm. Attacks along these lines are presented in this chapter.

---

[1]Of course, this could be our own demented dream. Who really knows?

An attacker that is simply carrying out a prank may simply want to give people a hard time. Under these circumstances survivability among malware helps to ensure that the attack lasts even after the virus is discovered and antivirus software is deployed. Such attacks hinge on the fact that not everyone is going to apply antiviral solutions on time, and some might not get around to it at all.[2] By distributing the *bargaining chips* that the virus has among several machines (for example, sensitive information that is damaging if disclosed), the virus can be made to be more survivable. In this situation, when Alice deletes the virus from her machine, the viruses that still reside on Bob and Carol's machines may exact revenge by anonymously posting stolen data from Alice's machine. The notion of distributing data among viruses and having them coordinate their attack efforts with each other is well known [332].

## 7.1   Survivable Malware

The ultimate goal of designing a survivable virus has been noted in the literature [332]. This notion was inspired by a creature called the *facehugger* that appeared in the science fiction movie *Alien* [265]. The facehugger is a parasitic alien that attacks humanoids for the purposes of perpetuating the alien species. It has the appearance of a small octopus with a long, powerful tail. It wraps its fingerlike legs around the host's head and its long tail around the host's neck, threatening the flow of air to the lungs. Once attached to the face of the victim, it slides a tube through the victim's mouth. The victim falls unconscious and remains in hibernation while retaining the ability to breathe normally.

The lifecycle for the alien species is as follows. The facehugger implants an embryo into the living host that gestates in the victim's abdomen. Eventually the host dies since the embryo grows into a baby drone that breaches the lining of the stomach. When the monstrous drones grow up, they herd together more humanoids for the facehuggers. Once in a blue moon a facehugger implants the embryo of a new queen. The queen in turn lays eggs that hatch into facehuggers.[3]

The facehugger is a fascinating alien creature. Any attempt to remove

---

[2]Some may even leave deliberately neglected and hence hackable machines on the net to assist other hackers.

[3]Interestingly enough, a cyborg robot in the movie *Alien* regarded the alien species as nothing short of perfection. This view is maintained even as the entire spaceship crew is slowly killed off.

it causes it to tighten its tail and suffocate the host. Any attempt to lacerate it will cause it to bleed its acidic blood that will eat through any and all flesh. It even eats through metal. The facehugger maliciously forces a symbiotic relationship with its host.

In fact, there exists an even earlier fictional precedent for a facehugger-like entity.[4] What's more, it takes the form of rogue *software* that travels through the network. The following is from the chapter entitled "Collapse of the Stout Party" in Book II of the 1975 novel *The Shockwave Rider* [43]:

> *"Remember what you said about a tapeworm?"*
>
> *"Oh my God. That was a joke. You mean they spat in our eye again?"*
>
> *"See for yourself, It's kind of—uh—fierce, isn't it?"*
>
> *"Fierce is only half of it. Well, I guess it better claim its first victim. You found it. You go tell Mr. Hartz to abandon the attack on Hearing Aid."*
>
> *"What?"*
>
> *"You heard me. Carry the good news from Y to X! Tamper with this thing, and—and my God! The data-net would be in chaos in one minute flat or maybe sooner! Hurry!"*

Could a digital analog to the facehugger ever be devised? This, of course, is not known, yet various technologies when combined appropriately do suggest that something similar might be possible. A protocol is given in Section 7.3 that is a step in this direction. It was presented at West Point and was published in the proceedings of IEEE Information Assurance '03 [331]. The protocol constitutes a distributed cryptovirus attack in which the virus initiates a two-player game between copies of itself and the victimized machine. Game theory is used to analyze the consequences for ignoring or meeting the demands of the distributed virus.

Game theory grew out of work at RAND Corporation, Stanford University, and the work of John von Neumann. It is a mathematical study of rational decision making, and involves the payoffs received in simplified multiplayer games. Of particular interest in this chapter is a class of games called *two-player non-zero sum* games. The most celebrated such game is the famous *Prisoner's Dilemma* in which two players find themselves in a situation in which there is no guaranteed way to win: true

---

[4]Special thanks to C. C. Michael for pointing this out.

collaboration is the only way to guarantee minimal losses by both. However, in a commercial society such collaboration does not exist between competing companies. This suggests that companies are optimal targets for game-theoretic virus and worm payloads.

## 7.2   Elements of Game Theory

In order to analyze the effectiveness of the attack that is presented, some basic notions in game theory [178] are needed. Table 7.1 is standard notation for a two-player non-zero sum game. In the game there are two players, the column player and the row player. The column player selects either column 1 or column 2 and the row player selects either row 1 or row 2. The selections occur simultaneously and the payoff for each is listed in the entry that results from the two selections. The row player receives the payoff on the left and the column player receives the payoff on the right. For instance, if the column player selects column 2 and the row player selects row 1 then the row player is paid $b_1$ and the column player is paid $b_2$. Payoffs can be positive, zero, or even negative, indicating indebtedness on behalf of the player.

A game is a *constant sum game* if $a_1 + a_2 = b_1 + b_2 = c_1 + c_2 = d_1 + d_2$. A game is a zero-sum game if it is a constant sum game and $a_1 + a_2 = 0$. When a game is not a zero-sum game it is a non-zero sum game. There are several famous non-zero sum games including Prisoner's Dilemma [305], Chicken, Battle of the Sexes, and so on. This attack involves a particular type of non-zero sum game that has a trivial solution.

The Prisoner's Dilemma is a well-known non-zero sum game that exemplifies a dichotomy between cooperation and rational decision making that can occur. This classic game theory problem is as follows.

|        | Column 1   | Column 2   |
|--------|------------|------------|
| Row 1  | $a_1, a_2$ | $b_1, b_2$ |
| Row 2  | $c_1, c_2$ | $d_1, d_2$ |

**Table 7.1**  Payoff matrix for a two-player non-zero sum game

*Two suspects A and B are in prison. The police have insufficient ev-
idence for getting a conviction. The two suspects are separated and each
one is offered the same deal: confess, and provided the other prisoner remains silent, there is no penalty. In this case the other prisoner will get
10 years to life. If both prisoners remain silent then each gets a 6-month
prison term. If both prisoners confess, then each gets 5 years to life.*

The payoff matrix for this game is given in Table 7.2. A rational
approach to this problem from A's perspective is as follows. Clearly either
B confessed or B did not confess. If B confessed and A does not, then
A gets 10 years. But, if A confesses, then A only gets 5 years. If B did
not confess, then by confessing A goes free. If A does not confess, then in
this case A gets 6 months. To avoid heavy losses it is best for A to rat on
B and confess. Assuming that they both behave rationally they will each
confess and serve 5-year sentences. But, if they cooperate, they each do 6
months.

Merrill Flood and Melvin Dresher of RAND first discovered this para-
dox in 1950. Albert W. Tucker wrote about it in a Stanford University
memo in 1950 that didn't appear until later [305].

## 7.3   Attacking a Brokerage Firm

The applications of utility theory and probabilistic decision making have
been growing recently in secure systems research. For example, in Financial Crypto '03 the utility of a thief who seeks to exploit a single
vulnerability to attack multiple installations was investigated [255]. The
issue that is addressed here takes utility theory in a slightly different direction. Game theory is used as an integral part of the attack itself that
is mounted on the host. The attack in this section builds on the notion of
a cryptovirus by adding a novel property: it is possible that the payload
of the virus will survive even after the virus is discovered. The payload

|                    | Prisoner A confess | Prisoner A deny |
|--------------------|--------------------|-----------------|
| Prisoner B confess | $-5, -5$           | $0, -10$        |
| Prisoner B deny    | $-10, 0$           | $-.5, -.5$      |

**Table 7.2** Payoff matrix in the Prisoner's Dilemma

has a chance to survive since it initiates a two player non-zero sum game between the host system and *remote* copies of the virus. The host system, which in this case is a brokerage firm, is forced to play the game under the threat that sensitive information on the host system will be disclosed by the malware.

The attack differs from the extortion attack in the following way. In the extortion attack, the victim is denied access to its own valuable information and has to pay to get it back, whereas in the attack that is presented here the victim retains access to the information but its disclosure is at the discretion of the computer virus. The attack therefore assumes that the critical host data satisfies a different property altogether.

It has been argued that whereas PKI adoption will do much to establish trust between individual people in public networks, it will also do much to establish trust for malware in public networks [331]. PKI paves the way for malware to be able to verify the compliance of remote victims by having the virus verify digital signatures, and public key cryptography allows viruses to send secure messages to other viruses.

## 7.3.1   Assumptions for the Attack

The victim of this particular attack is a stock market brokerage firm that conducts on-line trading. It is assumed that this firm has its own public key infrastructure and it is also assumed that the Securities and Exchange Commission (SEC) has its own PKI. Also, the clients of the brokerage firm belong to their own PKIs as well. It is necessary that all of these PKIs trust one another (that is, that they be cross-certified).

In this hypothetical scenario, trades occur in a very straightforward fashion. A client sends a signed message to the brokerage firm to request a trade in his or her account. Provided the signature is valid and the funds/shares are available the firm agrees to perform the transaction. At this point the firm signs the buy/sell request and sends the signed request to the trading floor. The SEC, acting as an overseer of all public trades, sends the outcome of the trade to the firm via a signed message. If a buyer/seller was found and the trade was carried out, then the SEC confirms its legitimacy. The brokerage firm forwards this signed response to the client at which point the client verifies it. This way, clients who may not be legally permitted to buy and sell stocks directly can do it securely through the brokerage firm for a small fee.

Another infrastructure that is assumed for this attack is an anonymous mix network (see Subsection 3.10.2). Since the attack amounts to an illegal act it is assumed that the mix network is vast. This may occur through the development and widespread adoption of a de facto mix network industry standard, for instance. To avoid the threat of a subpoena being issued that allows law enforcement to demand the private keys of the mixes, a re-encryption mix net can be used [120]. With such a service, seizing the machines of the mix net administrators would not help in apprehending abusers. The mix network in this attack is used in conjunction with a readable and writable public bulletin board. An example of such a public bulletin board is a Usenet newsgroup. It is assumed that the virus can both read from and write to the bulletin board anonymously. Servers currently exist that take e-mail messages and post them to the Usenet newsgroups and many users employ these servers to post anonymously. The assumptions are as follows:

1. A PKI encompasses the SEC, the brokerage firm, and the clients of the firm (for example, three cross-certified PKIs).

2. Clients send digitally signed buy/sell stock requests through the firm, and the SEC returns to clients, through the firm, signed responses to trade requests.

3. There exists a large anonymous mix network that is not controlled by law enforcement bodies.

4. There exists a public readable/writable bulletin board that accepts posts from the mix network and that is operated in such a way that it cannot be inhibited by law enforcement.

5. There exists a viral *grace period* in which the distributed viruses can freely post to the board in an inconspicuous and uninterrupted fashion.

6. The infection tree of the virus is difficult to reconstruct. This is necessary to conceal the location of the viral instances. In general a virus does not need to store any information relating to its previous host.

## 7.3.2 The Distributed Cryptoviral Attack

The attack is carried out by a distributed cryptovirus that tries to find three suitable host machines. The viral attack may be broken down into three phases: replication that leads to the infection of three suitable host machines, preparation for the attack, and then playing the two-player game.

All reading and writing to the bulletin board by the viruses is done through the mix network. For simplicity it is assumed that the messaging system is both timely and reliable. The following are the steps in the cryptovirus attack protocol:

1. Phase I: The cryptovirus is released into the wild. It is designed to do nothing but replicate for a specified period of time. For example, it will do nothing but replicate until a particular date. This allows the virus to secure entry into a large number of potential host systems.

2. When the virus activates on the particular date it analyzes its host to ascertain how well it will support the two-player game. For the machine to be an acceptable host it must fall into one of two categories: it must either be a brokerage machine or a reclusive machine. A brokerage machine is a machine in a brokerage firm that has sensitive information D available to the virus. Information D must have the property that it would be severely damaging to the firm if it were disclosed to the public. A reclusive machine is a machine in a remote area that preferably undergoes little if any scrutiny.

3. Phase II: If the host is a brokerage or reclusive machine then the virus posts a message to the bulletin board. The message indicates whether the host is a brokerage or reclusive machine and contains a randomly chosen identifier for the virus. The identifier can be a randomly chosen 512-bit number, for instance. These identifiers will be unique with overwhelming probability.

4. Each virus on a brokerage machine then goes about selecting two viruses on distinct reclusive machines to carry out the attack. Let $V_b$ denote a virus on a particular brokerage machine. For $j$ ranging from 1 to 2, $V_b$ selects (e.g., at random) a posting of a reclusive virus, takes note of its identifier, and posts a message inviting the reclusive virus to engage in the attack with $V_b$. The reclusive virus reads the post of $V_b$ and responds with one of two different posts: it accepts the invitation of $V_b$ to act as virus $V_{r,j}$, or rejects. It rejects if and only if it accepted a previous invitation. This step amounts to a handshaking protocol in which $V_b$ establishes the IDs for $V_{r,1}$ and $V_{r,2}$ and vice versa.

5. $V_{r,1}$ reads the bulletin board and finds the message in which $V_{r,2}$ accepts the invitation of $V_b$. $V_{r,2}$ reads the bulletin board and finds the message in which $V_{r,1}$ accepts the invitation of $V_b$. This way each virus $V_b$, $V_{r,1}$, and $V_{r,2}$ knows the IDs of the other two viruses. When $V_b$ posts a message to $V_{r,1}$ it includes a from field that includes the ID of $V_b$ and includes a to field containing the ID of $V_{r,1}$. This allows the viruses to communicate with each other unambiguously.

6. Each of the three viruses ($V_b$, $V_{r,1}$, and $V_{r,2}$) generates a key pair and gives the public key to the other viruses by posting it to the bulletin board. To prevent man-in-the-middle (MITM) attacks it is necessary that all viral activity goes unnoticed before the attack. From then on every viral posting is first signed and then encrypted for the intended recipient, and the signatures on all messages are verified before being accepted as valid. Note that the ciphertext postings need not have identifiers visible on the outside. The viruses can attempt to decrypt any and all ciphertexts to distinguish valid postings from random data.

7. Once all three public keys have been posted, $V_b$ chooses a pad R randomly and then encrypts D using the Vernam cipher, thereby obtaining the ciphertext C. $V_b$ then transmits R securely to $V_{r,1}$ and C securely to $V_{r,2}$ over the bulletin board.

8. $V_b$ instructs the brokerage firm to establish a new account for the virus (if necessary). Either by making the attack known to the firm, or in secret, the virus allocates an account for itself containing say, $10,000.

9. Phase III: By communicating in a signed and encrypted fashion over the bulletin board, $V_{r,1}$ and $V_{r,2}$ collectively select a publicly tradable stock to purchase and request that a single share be purchased. This share can be selected uniformly at random from all tradable shares or can be chosen according to a specified algorithm. The collaborative decision-making process can be accomplished by having $V_{r,1}$ and $V_{r,2}$ conduct fair coin tosses [31, 33] over the bulletin board. This guarantees fair coin tosses even if the coin flips of one of the viruses are compromised. The virus insists that the resulting share be held under the *street name* of the firm.

10. The desired transaction is conveyed to $V_b$ by $V_{r,1}$ and $V_{r,2}$ using

the bulletin board. $V_b$ either performs the transaction in secret (if it has control over the trading system), or failing that, it informs the brokerage firm of the desired stock transaction by displaying a message to the broker, for example.

11. The brokerage firm's trading system either carries out the purchase or does not. If it does, then either $V_b$, or the firm acting as $V_b$, encrypts the signed SEC response under the public keys of $V_{r,1}$ and $V_{r,2}$ respectively and publishes the two resulting ciphertexts in two different postings.

12. $V_{r,1}$ expects to find a posting on the bulletin board from $V_b$ consisting of a signed SEC response. If a valid signed response is not received within time $T$ (e.g., two days) by $V_{r,1}$, then $V_{r,1}$ posts R in plaintext form to the bulletin board. Similarly, $V_{r,2}$ expects to find a posting on the bulletin board from $V_b$ consisting of a signed SEC response within time $T$. $V_{r,2}$ posts C in plaintext form to the bulletin board if the SEC signed response is not received on time. So, if the two encrypted SEC messages are not posted then anyone with access to the bulletin board will be able to bitwise exclusive-or C with R and recover the sensitive data D, thus ending the two-player game in Phase III.

13. If the initial trade request is processed, then eventually another request is made by $V_{r,1}$ and $V_{r,2}$. By keeping track of the account internally, the virus can issue sale transactions in addition to buy transactions.

The attack is depicted in Figure 7.1. The purpose of using street names is to keep the transactions fluid, as in typical firm/client relationships.[5] Over time such a virus may make many transaction requests, which may be to either buy or sell shares.

Note that when the virus asks the firm to purchase one share of XYZ, the firm can always obtain a fresh signature as follows. The firm can sell one share of XYZ if it already has one to spare, or failing that, it can sell short on one share. The firm can then buy the share of XYZ back

---

[5]The issue of who to make the blackmailed stock out to was pointed out by Michael L. Gershman when this attack was presented at an NYU course entitled *Cryptographic Protocols* in the summer of 2003. The course was taught by Dr. Markus Jakobsson from RSA Labs.

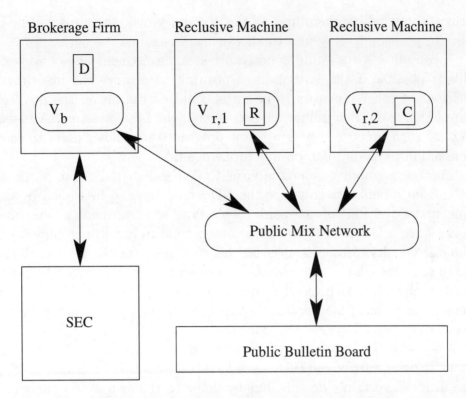

**Figure 7.1** Distributed cryptoviral attack

from the open market and obtain the fresh SEC signature that the virus expects. So what can really be gained in this attack? If nothing else, the virus has secured the opportunity to prove its worth as an intelligent investment advisor. The goal in this particular attack is not to give the virus writer direct monetary gain,[6] but to give the distributed malware *purchasing power*. The virus will develop a portfolio history based on its transaction requests. The firm must comply with the requests under threat of sensitive information disclosure, and hence the firm must observe the series of requested transactions. Over time the virus may prove its worth as a portfolio manager. In the event that the virus develops a solid track record the firm may actually start purchasing shares at the request of the

---

[6]The virus could be programmed to demand that the firm buy tens of thousands of shares of a particular company to raise the stock value of each share. This would benefit a virus writer if the virus writer already held lots of shares.

virus without selling them first. If the account grows, the virus will be in a better position to levy unorthodox demands against its victim.[7]

A computer virus could conceivably steal investment advice as well. This is possible if the virus is in a position to observe the investment decisions of other investors. The virus could eavesdrop on the buy/sell transactions and then mimic the decisions of the best investors. An ideal host for such functionality is a client program that allows users to send transaction requests to an on-line brokerage firm.

Another possibility is for the virus to demand that the firm purchase a CD from a bank. In this case the CD would have to be signed by the bank under the PKI of the bank. This type of investment differs from stocks since a CD cannot be cashed out prematurely without suffering a financial penalty. However, even in this case the firm can try to sell the CD to someone who actually wants it in order to obtain the cash that was spent on the CD.[8] An interesting question is whether or not there exists a financial investment mechanism that truly locks the buyer in and prevents the transference of the asset in question.

Also, what is to prevent the firm from notifying the SEC that the attack is being carried out? This would certainly foil the malware attack. The firm can certainly do this, but by doing so the firm would likely run the risk of the attack being made public. Hacker attacks can be very embarrassing to large companies and it is not uncommon for companies to cover them up and even suffer losses to do so.

### 7.3.3  Security of the Attack

On an algorithmic level it is possible to select various primitives for use in this attack that are provably secure by themselves. For example, the Optimal Asymmetric Encryption Padding (OAEP) algorithm used in PKCS #1 can be used to perform encryption, and PKCS #1 can be used for signing the messages that the viruses send each other [249]. Also, a provably secure mix network can be selected. However, it is difficult to analyze the exact security of this hybrid cryptographic protocol, except against specific attacks. This results from the complexity of combining all of the underlying primitives.

To allow confidential and authenticated communications between $V_{r,1}$,

---

[7]The virus will have thus crossed the line from malware to beneficial software, and making it unhappy implies the loss of valued investment advice.

[8]This was pointed out by C. C. Michael at Cigital.

$V_{r,2}$, and $V_b$ it might be tempting at first to include three separate key pairs in the initial virus. However, this is not a secure approach since the key pairs will exist in all future offspring of the virus and will therefore provide no privacy in Phase III of the attack. However, by having the viruses generate key pairs in Phase II the key exchange is subject to a man-in-the-middle attack. For this reason it seems necessary that the viruses operate in secret from when the virus is released up until the beginning of Phase III.

The reason that $V_b$ utilizes the Vernam cipher is to try to protect the privacy of the brokerage firm. Since the One-time pad is information theoretically secure, an administrator that finds $R$ will not learn anything about the plaintext $D$ without the ciphertext $C$. The same applies for $C$. This mechanism, combined with the use of mix networks, gives the brokerage firm the assurance that $D$ is stored in a secret-splitting fashion. Other approaches can be used to accomplish this as well. For example, an $m$-out-of-$n$ secret sharing scheme [21, 22, 40, 42, 59, 101] can be used in which any $m$ out of $n$ viruses can collaborate and reconstruct $D$.

A corollary of this attack is that $V_b$ can be removed without affecting the overall game that is initiated. Virus $V_{r,1}$ and virus $V_{r,2}$ expect SEC signed messages in response to their trade initiations. The viruses do not care who actually obtains and sends these signatures. A broker can carry out all of the tasks that $V_b$ performs in Phase III manually. It is a matter of semantics to say that the malware is removed by removing $V_b$. This will not change the fact that the information needed to reconstruct $D$ will be exposed to the general public if the SEC responses are not received.

### 7.3.4  Utility of the Attack

Many stock portfolios specialize in particular markets such as pharmaceuticals, computer technology, energy, and so on. For this reason the demand to purchase a tradable stock chosen randomly from all tradable stocks is likely to be perceived negatively. As a result the perceived payoff for making the purchase that the virus selects will likely be negative irrespective of any potential return on investment. If it were known a priori that this two-player game were only going to be played once, a suitable characterization for the game might be the one given in Table 7.3.

The column player is the victimized brokerage firm and the row player is the distributed cryptovirus. Column 1 is the choice to buy the stock that the virus requests. Column 2 is the choice to refuse the transaction.

|         | Column 1 | Column 2 |
| ------- | -------- | -------- |
| Row 1   | 1,−1     | 0,−10    |
| Row 2   | 0,−10    | 0,−10    |

**Table 7.3** Payoff matrix for virus and firm

Row 1 is the choice to issue a buy request. Row 2 is the choice to publish sensitive data D.

The game differs from a traditional two-player game since the choice that the virus makes is in fact contingent upon the choice that the firm makes. The payoffs may be reasoned as follows. The firm suffers a −10 penalty if D ends up being published. This happens if the firm denies the buy request or if the virus simply decides to publish D. The virus may as well select row 2 and publish D if the column player chooses column 2. Strictly speaking, due to this conditional move, this matrix is more of a payoff matrix than a two-player game. Also, the salient feature of the payoff matrix is the partial ordering of the payoffs as opposed to the specific values given in Table 7.3.

This "game" is nonetheless not a zero-sum game since $0 + (−10) = −10$. It is not a constant sum game since $1 + (−1) = 0$ does not equal $0 + (−10) = −10$. The game is therefore a non-zero sum game. But it is arguably one of the less interesting non-zero sum games since there is no conflict of interest. When played once the optimal strategy for each player is clear. The solution to the game is row 1, column 1. However, for the firm, winning amounts to cutting the firm's losses whereas for the cryptovirus winning amounts to successfully coaxing the firm to purchase a stock.

It is difficult to speculate on the game when it is repeated multiple times. There are numerous factors to take into account including how often the virus makes requests, how many shares are in each request, and so on. If the firm denies every request and eliminates the virus, then the firm can guarantee a loss of no worse than −10. But, if the firm processes the requests and the virus ultimately publishes D anyway, then the losses could be even more. If the damage that would result from the publication of D far outweighs the purchase of a few stocks, then it may be best to cater to the virus, at least for a time. On the other hand, one should not immediately discount the possibility that the virus will make sound investment decisions. It is not unthinkable that some day a real-time trading engine could be created that would cause the firm to eagerly wait for the valued investment advice of the cryptovirus. Once such a stance is established, the virus could make uncanny demands such as who to hire and fire in the firm.

The utility of this attack from the malware author's perspective is clear. It amounts to an on-line agent that is capable of automatically making and executing the author's investment decisions. The author can communicate with the agent over the same bulletin board using public key cryptography and make manual decisions on behalf of the agent. This allows the author to exercise control over the victim with very minimal real-time interaction, thereby minimizing the author's chances of being apprehended. If the investments are lucrative, the attack amounts to a free lunch for both the firm and the author. If they are not lucrative, then the firm loses money and the author loses nothing.

There are several issues that are left open. For example, are there well-defined and well-studied games in game theory that directly apply to this particular malware attack? Are there ways to improve the attack[9] so that the victimized firm is certain that D will not be published if the transaction is honored?

## 7.4  Other Two-Player Game Attacks

There are other two-player games that can be initiated by malware as well. Two such attacks are described in this section. They both utilize the notion of a distributed virus that carries out its payload by having its individual instances communicate with each other securely.

### 7.4.1  Key Search via Facehuggers

The notion of using viruses to solve computationally difficult problems is well known. For instance, a virus can by brute force try to determine the DES key that was used to produce a particular symmetric encryption [320]. Also, viruses can be used to steal CPU time to try to factor composites, compute discrete logarithms, and so on.

In this subsection a particular cryptovirus attack is detailed that is geared towards solving the discrete logarithm problem in a prime order subgroup. The prime order subgroup discrete-log problem is believed to

---

[9]Questions such as this were raised by Shabsi Walfish during the NYU lecture.

be intractable and is the basis for many cryptographic algorithms such as DSA. Recall that the DSA private key is $x$ and the DSA public key is $(y, g, p)$ (see Subsection C.2.7). DSA utilizes a public prime $q$ that is 160 bits in length. The order of $g$ modulo $p$ is $q$ and hence $q$ divides $p - 1$ evenly.

The attack utilizes the approach of Feigenbaum et al to hide information from an oracle [1, 2, 99] (see Section 6.8). The virus writer chooses $r < q$ randomly and computes $y_r = yg^r \bmod p$ thus randomizing $y$. It is simple enough to place $y_r = yg^r \bmod p$ in a virus and let the offspring try to compute the base $g$ discrete log of $y_r$. If it is found, then it can be posted to a bulletin board so that the virus writer can obtain it. Since the virus writer knows $r$, the virus writer can recover $x$ from the posting. This allows the virus writer to try to determine someone's DSA private key $x$ in $y = g^x \bmod p$ by brute force in such a way that the owner of the public key has no way of knowing that the private key has been compromised.

Consider the case that one of these viruses is found. The virus would likely be chewing up a fair amount of CPU time, and would be a nuisance in general, and would simply be removed. So in this straightforward attack a machine is lost whenever the virus on that machine is found, that is, there is one less machine to perform the distributed brute-force computation.

However, if the virus were more like a facehugger then there would be consequences for removing it. The goal then is to devise a mechanism that optimizes the number of machines that are actively trying to solve the discrete logarithm problem instance. The following is a virus attack that seeks to achieve this goal. We call the virus a *facehugger* and give a very high level description of it.[10]

To mount the attack the virus writer chooses $r < q$ randomly and computes $y_r = yg^r \bmod p$. The value $(y_r, p, g, q)$ is placed within the virus. It is assumed that the virus is given a grace period in which it can infect many machines and remotely store sensitive data without hindrance, and so on. The virus operates much like the virus in the attack on the brokerage firm. Each virus generates a large random identifier $ID$, each virus generates a key pair, and they communicate securely[11] with each other over a mix network and bulletin board, and so on. The identifiers serve as digital pseudonyms. Each virus searches its host for sensitive host data $D$ that would be damaging if published. This data is encrypted using

---

[10]We thank C. C. Michael for helpful discussions regarding this distributed cryptoviral attack.

[11]That is, they timestamp, sign, and encrypt their messages.

the Vernam cipher. The resulting ciphertext $C$ and One-time pad $R$ are securely sent to the two other viruses involved in the attack on the host.

So far the attack is almost exactly the same as the attack on the brokerage firm. However, the attack would be on a much larger scale since any host machine that contains sensitive data $D$ is a viable host for the attack. Brokerage firms are not sought after explicitly. Let the total number of viruses be denoted by $N$ and for simplicity assume that all $N$ machines contain sensitive data. The viruses partition the key space into $N$ roughly equal partitions each of which is a contiguous set of numbers. The viruses are each responsible for making their respective hosts search a given partition. Let $s_1$ denote the starting value for the partition of a given virus $V_1$.

It is important not to overload a virus in terms of the Vernam ciphertexts and One-time pads that it stores from other virus attacks. To avoid this the viruses carefully arrange the way they store the sensitive data. The arrangement of viruses can be expressed as a bipartite graph (see Figure 7.2). Each virus is represented by two vertices of the same color. The figure shows the case of $N = 5, 4, 3$ from left to right.

Although it is not shown in the figure, the vertices are labeled using the identifiers of the viruses. The vertex at the top has the highest value for $ID$, the one below that has the second highest value for $ID$, and so on. When a virus computes a One-time pad and Vernam ciphertext it sends them to the two viruses indicated by the directed edges.

The bipartite graphs in the figures are all quite similar since each vertex connects to the two vertices directly below it and to the right, except for the bottom two vertices. The bottom vertex always connects to the top two vertices on the right. The vertex second from the bottom always connects to the top and bottom vertices on the right. Also, the

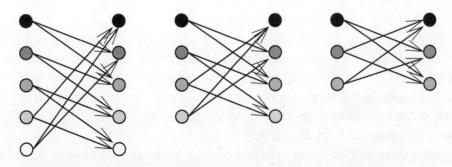

**Figure 7.2** Bipartite arrangement of the facehugger

arrangement is constructed such that each virus is responsible for storing a Vernam ciphertext from one machine and a One-time pad from another.

When the grace period ends each virus immediately begins searching the keyspace. For example, $V_1$ immediately starts searching the partition that begins with $s_1$. Virus $V_1$ checks to see if $y_r = g^{s_1}$, $g^{s_1}g$, $g^{s_1+1}g$, and so on. The partition is exponentially large so the virus, which is polynomially bounded, will not finish the search. If the logarithm of $y_r$ is found, then it is posted to the bulletin board.

Each virus also demands that two other hosts conduct searches. Consider the case that $V_1$ stores the Vernam ciphertext $C_2$ and One-time pad $R_3$ corresponding to the senstive data on two other infected machines $M_2$ and $M_3$, respectively. Also, let the viruses on these machines be denoted by $V_2$ and $V_3$, respectively. $V_1$ demands that $V_2$ and $V_3$ search the key space as well. This is accomplished by having $V_1$ send each of these two machines challenge sequences. The following is how the challenge sequences for $V_2$ are constructed. It is the same for $V_3$.

At regular intervals (e.g., once every couple of hours or so) $V_1$ chooses $r_1, r_2 < q$ randomly, chooses $j$ randomly from $\{0, 1, 2, ..., 2^{20} - 1\}$, and then flips a coin. If the result is heads then $V_1$ sets $w = r_2$ and $t = y_r g^{r_1} \bmod p$. If the result is tails then $V_1$ sets $w = r_1 - j \bmod q$ and $t = g^{r_1} \bmod p$. $V_1$ sends the pair $(t, w)$ to $V_2$ securely.

If there exists an $i$ contained in $\{0, 1, 2, ..., 2^{20} - 1\}$ such that $t = g^{w+i} \bmod p$ then $V_1$ expects $V_2$ to respond with $i$. If no such $i$ exists then $V_1$ expects $V_2$ to respond with "no exponent found." Failure to produce a valid answer, that is, $i$ such that $0 \le i < 2^{20}$ or "no exponent found" after time $T$ elapses always results in the publication of $C_2$ in retaliation. For concreteness let $T = 2$ hours. This interval must be chosen to give plenty of elbow room for $V_2$ to solve two challenge sequences at once.

If the result is heads and $V_2$ responds with $i$ then $V_1$ checks to see if $g^{w+i} \stackrel{?}{=} t = y_r g^{r_1} \bmod p$. If this equality does not hold then $V_1$ publishes $C_2$ to the bulletin board. If the equality does hold then $V_1$ publishes $w + i - r_1 \equiv x + r \bmod q$ to the bulletin board. This allows the virus writer to recover $x$ since the virus writer knows $r$. If the result is heads and $V_2$ responds with "no exponent found" then $V_1$ assumes on faith that there is no $i$ contained in $\{0, 1, 2, ..., 2^{20} - 1\}$ such that $g^{w+i} = t \bmod p$ and so $V_2$ passes the challenge sequence.

Now consider the case that the result is tails. If $V_2$ responds with "no exponent found" or a value for $i$ such that $j \ne i$ then $V_1$ publishes $C_2$

to the bulletin board in retaliation. If $i = j$ then $V_2$ passes the challenge sequence.

So what is really going on here? $V_1$ is conducting a sting operation of sorts against the host of $V_2$. With 50 percent probability a sequence is sent to $M_2$ for which, if $V_2$ is still running properly on $M_2$, $V_2$ will find the discrete logarithm and give it to $V_1$. With 50 percent probability $M_2$ is given a portion of the keyspace to search. $M_2$ has no way of knowing which is the case. So, it can do no better than guess. To be uncooperative the operator of $M_2$ can refuse to send a discrete logarithm when one is found. However, the operator will be caught with probability $1/2$. This interactive protocol is intimately related to the notion of a *proof of work*. Informally speaking, a proof of work allows a prover to demonstrate to a verifier that the prover has performed a certain amount of computational work in a specified interval of time [136].

The operator of $M_2$ can decide to ignore $V_1$'s challenge sequences entirely under the assumption that only $C_2$ will be published and not the One-time pad $R_2$. However, this increases the chances that both $C_2$ and $R_2$ will become available, thus compromising $C_2 \oplus R_2$. $M_2$ will still receive challenge sequences from the other virus, unless it has been tampered with.

The attack is intriguing since it creates a form of deadlock when the victims do not trust each other. For instance, if the operator of the machine that hosts $V_1$ decides to be a good samaritan and delete the Vernam ciphertext and One-time pad that $V_1$ is storing, there is no reason to believe that the operators of the machines that store the ciphertext and One-time pad that $V_1$ sent out will reciprocate. They might in fact publish them. This can cause the good samaritan to loose the game.

The payload of the facehugger forces victims to perform intensive computations under the threat of sensitive information disclosure. This would clearly be a hassle and a nuisance for the victim. It is related to the use of puzzles to defend against connection depletion attacks [146]. However, it uses puzzles as a malicious payload rather than a defense. Also, the payload is not simply destructive since these intensive computations are geared towards breaking a public key.

There are also other issues to consider. For example, when the viruses are never found this scheme creates needless extra work for the virus. This results from the phoney challenge sequences that must be searched. However, when the viruses are brought to near extinction the virus has a chance to continue the search on machines in which the virus has been discovered. Open issues include ways of improving the attacks as well as identifying new attacks along these lines.

A similar sort of attack can be carried out against composite public keys. Let $n = pq$ be the product of two large primes $p$ and $q$. This could be a Rabin public key, an RSA public key, and so on. The virus contains $n$ and attempts to discover the factorization of $n$. Already a complication exists since if the owner of the public key $n$ learns that a virus is trying to break it, the owner will immediately revoke the public key $n$. However, if the virus writer has a ciphertext $c$ that was computed using $n$, then breaking $n$ is still useful in trying to decrypt $c$. The attack will not be described in detail, but the general idea will be sketched out.

In the attack the virus writer tries to obtain two *ambivalent roots* of a quadratic residue modulo $n$. The values $x$ and $y$ are ambivalent roots of $x^2 \bmod n$ if $x^2 \equiv y^2 \bmod n$ and $x \neq \pm y \bmod n$. These two values allow $n$ to be factored since $gcd(x + y, n)$ or $gcd(x - y, n)$ is a non-trivial divisor of $n$.

The virus writer places $a = x^2 \bmod n$ in the virus and hopes that the viruses will find a $y$ that is ambivalent with respect to $x$. Also, the virus contains a random function $H$ that maps $\{0, 1\}^*$ onto the set $\mathbb{Z}_n^*$. Let $H_j(s) = H(J||s)$ where $J$ is the 20-bit binary representation of $j$ and $s$ is any input string. It may be assumed that $H_j(\cdot)$ is publicly known.

The victim's machine is challenged by the virus as follows. The virus chooses $r_1$ randomly from $\mathbb{Z}_n^*$, $w$ randomly from $\mathbb{Z}_{n^2}^*$, $j$ randomly from $\{0, 1, 2, ..., 2^{20} - 1\}$, and flips a coin. If the result is heads then the virus computes $t = ar_1^2 \bmod n$. If the result is tails then the virus computes $t = H_j(w)^2 \bmod n$. The virus sends the challenge $(t, w)$ to the victim.

If the victim does not respond with $i \in \{0, 1, 2, ..., 2^{20} - 1\}$ or "no root found" on time then the sensitive data is published in retaliation. If the victim responds with $i \in \{0, 1, 2, ..., 2^{20} - 1\}$ then the virus checks to see if $H_i(w)^2 \bmod n \stackrel{?}{=} t$. If this does not hold then the sensitive data (either the Vernam ciphertext or the One-time pad) is published. If this does hold and the coin toss resulted in heads then $H_i(w)/r_1 \bmod n = \sqrt{a}$ is asymmetrically encrypted under the public key of the virus writer that is contained in the virus. This ciphertext is published to a bulletin board so that the virus writer can obtain it. If $H_i(w)/r_1$ is ambivalent with respect to $x$ then the virus writer can factor $n$ using $H_i(w)/r_1$ and $x$.

## 7.4.2   Catalyzing Conflict Among Hosts

An ancient strategy when three warring factions are mutually at odds is to get the two opposing factions to obliterate each other and then take out the one that is left standing, if any. A surviving faction will likely have suffered severe losses in the initial battle. This strategy can be extrapolated to cryptovirus attacks as well. The basic idea is to infect two remote systems that are operated by owners that oppose each other. The viruses securely transfer sensitive host data to each other to initiate a two-player game and then announce that this has been done. The two owners must then complete the two-player game that the virus initiated.

Consider such an attack against two companies. The cryptovirus asymmetrically encrypts sensitive information from company A and transmits it to another copy of the virus located at company B. The virus at B decrypts the ciphertext with its private key. Similarly, the virus at B steals sensitive information from B, asymmetrically encrypts it, and then transmits the ciphertext to the virus at A. The virus at A decrypts it with its private key. When all of the information has been transferred, the distributed cryptoviruses alert their respective victims of the presence of the newfound information on their system.

If the information that was transferred is damaging when disclosed and if A and B are in direct competition, then A and B have entered into an exacerbated state of conflict. A and B are then left to arrive at a solution. In this situation the virus can be removed but its payload may only be considered removed if and when A and B complete the two-person game that the distributed cryptovirus started. Viruses that force their victims to play games with each other are unique since they exploit naturally occurring distrust among victims.

# 7.5   Future Possibilities

These attacks constitute plausibility results regarding survivable malware. The following are basic ideas that form the basis for such attacks:

1. *Implementing the virus as a distributed algorithm.* The virus resides on multiple machines that are networked. This gives robustness against the possibility that the virus attack will be terminated since deleting or compromising one or two viruses may not halt the attack (fault-tolerant viruses).

2. *Having the viruses utilize a bulletin board.* This allows the viruses to communicate to each other by reading and writing to a single location that they are all aware of.

3. *Having the viruses utilize a mix net.* This allows the viruses to conceal their locations from everyone including each other and therefore helps to keep them from being discovered.

4. *Having the virus employ split (or threshold) encryption.* This protects the privacy of the victim(s). Without some measure of privacy certain victims may not hesitate to pull the plug on the virus altogether and ignore the viral demands.

5. *Having the virus employ asymmetric cryptography.* This allows the viruses to exchange public keys, digitally sign data, and encrypt data using a public key. Hence, the viruses can establish authenticated and confidential channels with each other through the mix net and over the bulletin board.

6. *Having the viruses generate shared randomness.* Cryptographic coin flipping protocols allow the viruses to generate randomness in a way that is robust against a small number of viruses being compromised. In some sense it allows the distributed viruses to perform distributed decision making with the benefit of having an honest random (Turing machine) tape.

7. *Having the victims victimize each other.* This defers blame and some degree of culpability away from the virus. It provides victims with an alternate means of dealing with the payload; namely, by having the victims reconcile their differences out-of-band. Such conflicts can be instigated by certain non-zero sum games.

Another extension that can be made to this type of distributed malware is *secure multiparty computations.* These are cryptographic protocols that allow a number of parties to securely evaluate a circuit and they have some very robust security properties with respect to privacy, faults, and so on. By having a distributed virus employ such protocols, they would be able to perform secure distributed computations even when some of the viruses are compromised.

Looking even further ahead, consider the following possibility. Intelligent agents are slowly becoming integrated with our everyday lives.

When we call a company that provides some form of service (for example, a bank) we often get connected to electronic helpers. These agents use voice recognition to answer our questions, perform transactions, and even offer advice on achieving problem resolution. A chilling thought is the possibility that the back-end software of such an agent is a victim of an ongoing distributed cryptovirological attack. The virus could directly influence the actions of such an agent. The thing about distributed cryptoviruses that use mix nets is that *there is essentially no way to find out where they are on the net*. One could argue that the first step in achieving power is the accumulation of wealth. The overall threat is a foreseeable possibility since we are increasingly allowing machines to make decisions for us.

Fears that machines might evolve and subsequently replace people appeared in S. Butler's novel *Erewhon*. It was published in 1872 [46] and challenged the moral hypocrisy of Victorian England and its ecclesiastical institutions. In *Automata*, S. F. Wright describes machines that take over all human activities and eventually eliminates the entire species [322]. Also, the Colossus computer from the 1966 novel *Colossus* [143, 254] and the Skynet computer in the movie *The Terminator* [51] threaten the extinction of all mankind.

The distributed cryptovirus attacks may appear to be sensational, and for our time they most certainly are. However, they are perhaps no less sensational than how a pair of cell phones would have appeared to the inventor of the telegraph. In today's computing environments these attacks are perhaps most relevant as thought-provoking possibilities rather than realizable threats.

# Chapter 8

# Coping with Malicious Software

This chapter is likely to seem quite out of place in this book. Nevertheless, after dedicating so many chapters of this book towards malicious software attacks we felt obliged to present some results on how to defend against these attacks. This chapter is not a how-to manual to recover from a viral infection. Rather, a number of proactive and reactive security measures are given to combat the spread of self-replicating malware. Antiviral heuristics are presented along with their counter-heuristics, their counter-counter-heuristics, and so forth, to illuminate the challenges facing viral containment. The chapter also includes heuristics for identifying cryptoviruses and cryptotrojans wherever they may reside. These heuristics are based on the fact that cryptoviruses and cryptotrojans must contain a public key which has certain mathematical properties.

## 8.1 Undecidability of Virus Detection

A number of real-world problems that would be nice to be able to solve are in fact not solvable. For instance, it would be useful to be able to determine algorithmically if on input[1] $M$ and $w$, where $M$ is an arbitrary given Turing machine and $w$ is an arbitrary given input string, whether or not $M$ accepts[2] $w$. This is known as the *halting problem*. It is a *decision problem* since the answer comes in the form of yes or no. To solve this problem it would be necessary for the Turing machine to answer

---

[1] To be precise, the input is a Gödelization of $M$ and of $w$.

[2] Turing machine $M$ accepts $w$ if $M(w)$ terminates in a final state.

correctly for all possible input machines and all possible inputs to those machines. Such a program would be an invaluable tool for assessing the correctness of programs, since a program is correct if and only if it always outputs the correct answer and halts on all inputs. However, using a Cantor diagonalization argument Alan Turing proved that no such Turing machine exists [306]. This is not a complexity issue; it is a computability issue since the problem as stated is not solvable at all.

It is an unfortunate consequence in the theory of secure computing that the same applies to testing whether or not an arbitrary program is infected with an arbitrary virus. Adleman proved that if an algorithm exists that can detect the presence of viruses in the general case, then an algorithm exists that solves the halting problem. Since the halting problem is Turing undecidable, this proves that the problem of detecting viruses is Turing undecidable [3].

Regardless of this fundamental limitation to virus detection, methods are needed to identify viruses since hackers continue to write and release computer viruses. As a result heuristics have been developed and deployed to identify both known viruses and viruses that are yet to be written. By virtue of being heuristic in nature they each fail in specific cases, but they nonetheless raise the bar in terms of what is necessary to spread viruses successfully.

To deal with these heuristics, virus writers have reacted by developing their own suite of heuristics to bypass antiviral heuristics. These heuristics constitute counter-heuristics and some of them are surprisingly general in nature. However, these in turn have led to the development of counter-counter-heuristics in antiviral software, and so on. The end result has been an ongoing tug-of-war between detection and evasion methods.

## 8.2   Virus Identification and Obfuscation

There are several challenges surrounding the design of robust computer viruses and worms and designing algorithms to detect viruses and worms wherever present. The first part of this section covers the issue of string matching. String matching is often used by antivirus programs to positively identify viral strains. But, it is also a method that is used by viruses to identify themselves. Viral self-identification is necessary to prevent overpopulation and to prevent a host from being infected multiple times. The development of string matching antiviral programs lead to the development of polymorphic viruses, which are viruses that are specifically designed to foil string matching antiviral programs. The notion of a polymorphic virus is covered at the end of this section.

### 8.2.1   Virus String Matching

By definition, a virus spreads by copying a possibly altered version of itself to other programs, which in turn continue the viral replication. An unavoidable problem in designing such viruses is the possibility of multiple infection. How does a virus know if it already infected a given program? If the virus has no way of knowing this, then it may end up infecting the same program so many times that the user notices a suspicious loss in disk space.

Some viruses were programmed not to care about multiple infections. For example, the Israeli virus will infect a host multiple times [289]. This implies that viruses need an algorithm for identifying whether or not a given executable is already infected. This decision problem is exactly the same decision problem that antiviral software faces when analyzing the same executable. The virus writer can include within the virus an efficient algorithm for solving the decision problem and use it to prevent multiple infections. But the drawback to this is that if the virus is ever discovered it solves the problem of identifying the virus in the wild for the antiviral analyst. A viral detection algorithm is therefore a mixed blessing for both parties:

1. virus writer: prevents the virus from infecting programs multiple times and thereby minimizes the chances that the virus will be discovered due to loss of disk space. But, at the same time it gives a detection algorithm to antiviral analysts when the virus is found.

2. antiviral analyst: lowers the chance that a user will find the virus due to unexplained loss of disk space. But once found it has the benefit of solving the problem of identifying the virus in the wild (assuming it is well written).

Viruses that are indiscriminate about the executables they infect are very dangerous since they have the potential to bring down host systems by their replication alone. The fallout due to the famous Internet Worm is a case in point [287, 288].

It is possible to slow the rate of infection to prevent a virus from being discovered right away, without including a self-detection mechanism.

This can be accomplished by limiting the timeframe in which the virus replicates on a given machine [302]. To limit the timeframe the virus stores a circularly linked list internally to keep track of the most recently infected machines. Each list element contains a timestamp and a machine name.[3] The virus is designed to replicate for a specified time interval $\mathcal{I}$ on any given machine (e.g., $\mathcal{I} = 2$ days). When it is executed it obtains the name of the machine that it is currently on. If the name is not contained in the linked list then it overwrites the oldest element in the list with the current machine name and the current time, and then infects another program on the machine. If the name is contained in the linked list then the timestamp $\mathcal{T}$ for that element is retrieved. If the current time exceeds $\mathcal{T}$ plus $\mathcal{I}$ then the virus does not infect anything and sends control to the host. Otherwise, the virus infects another program. This method minimizes the excess infections that occur due to backtracking, but does prevent a given program from being infected more than once.

Designing a self-detection algorithm involves some subtle issues. For example, it is tempting to include an ID string in a virus at a known offset from the end of the virus. When the virus appends itself to the end of a host, the ID string is at a known offset from the end of the program. However, it is naive to assume that a program is infected if and only if the ID appears at the given offset since the program could have become infected *by another virus*.

The simplest viruses copy themselves to host applications without significantly altering themselves. When this occurs there is an easy way for viruses and antiviral programs to determine if a given executable is infected. The basic method for doing so is called *pattern matching* [69]. The idea is to take a string of bytes from the virus that does not change from generation to generation and use it to find other instances of the virus. By checking an executable for the presence of this substring it can be determined whether or not the executable is infected. Antiviral programs called *scanners* perform this scanning process. If the string is sufficiently long and the pattern it contains is unique this method will detect the presence of the virus in infected programs.

The approach is not flawless since the string may appear naturally in certain programs. For instance, this can occur in programs that perform complicated copy-protection operations that contain a large amount of binary data, and so on. As a result this method sometimes produces false positives. However, this method can never produce a false negative when

---

[3]A machine name can be a hard drive label, IP address, and so on.

used to identify known viruses.[4] String matching is performed correctly every time and the string will never be missed.[5] As a result a string matcher that claims to detect all known viruses will never indicate that a program is free of infection when in fact the program is infected.

A countermeasure to scanners is to design the virus so that it does not contain any of the strings contained in the database. This is incredibly easy for a virus writer to do: the virus writer infects a program with the virus and then subjects the program to all available antivirus tools to see if the virus is found. A scanner is capable of detecting a deployed virus only after the needed search string is included in the list of search strings. It is often the case that a new virus is detected only after it mounts a successful attack on a host. Consequently, scanners are not very proactive in identifying viruses. The measure is occasionally proactive since a new virus sometimes reuses the code of other viruses or contains trivial modifications and as a result succumbs to an existing search string.

To perform comprehensive viral scanning it is necessary to perform the lowest level read operations that are possible, since a surprising number of hiding places exist for viral code. For example, most file systems break a disk down into clusters that are fixed in size (e.g., 1024 bytes). An executable seldom occupies an integral number of clusters exactly and as a result there are often unused bytes at the end of executables. The number of unused bytes is dictated by the difference between the physical end-of-file marker and the logical end-of-file marker. The 1963 virus, among others, takes the liberty of storing data in this area [283].

Also, hard disks are typically designed to support multiple operating systems by allowing the disk to be divided into multiple partitions. Computers are often sold with only one preinstalled operating system and one low-level partition for the operating system. In some cases there is still space left over for another tiny partition. Assuming a virus is not too large it could turn this free space into a partition for itself without encroaching on the resident operating system at all. In the case of a multipartite virus this implies that the boot sector phase of the virus would appear to occupy no space at all from the perspective of the operating system. Such viruses gain control from the ROM code of the computer before the boot sector of the operating system is even executed.

---

[4]Stealth viruses (explained later) are an exception to this rule since they have the potential to alter the scanner's perception of the true binary data in the program.

[5]Polymorphic viruses are a different case. The question here is whether or not a program contains a particular substring.

On MS-DOS systems this physical boot sector is called the master boot record (MBR) and is exploited by the Monkey virus [283]. In general, boot sector viruses are very dangerous since they gain control of the computer before anything else [289]. This illustrates that malware can sometimes be overlooked by scanners that obtain their data through operating system read calls.

Antivirus scanners have proven to be an effective reactive security measure against viruses and are widely used to check executables, boot sectors, RAM, and so on. Many are even sophisticated enough to first decompress and then scan files compressed using popular compression programs. Antiviral products that scan for viruses often include software that is capable of disinfecting programs. Since the viruses they search for have already been carefully analyzed, in many cases it is possible to algorithmically remove them from the host program. However, whenever possible, infected programs should be deleted and backups should be reinstalled.

### 8.2.2   Polymorphic Viruses

A straightforward countermeasure to viral scanning is designing a virus to modify its own coding sequence. In laboratory experiments, Fred Cohen produced viruses that had no common sequences of over three bytes between each subsequent generation by using encryption [67, 69]. Such viruses are called *polymorphic viruses*, otherwise known as *evolutionary viruses*.

Numerous polymorphic viruses have appeared in the wild. For example, the Tremor virus is a polymorphic virus that has almost 6,000,000,000 forms [283]. A polymorphic virus typically consists of two parts: a header and a body. When dormant, the body remains in encrypted form. When activated, the header is the first section of code to receive control from the operating system. The header decrypts the body in memory. Once the body is decrypted the header transfers control to the body. The body then performs the normal viral operations. When the body is finished it sends control to the host program (see Figure 8.1).

The header stores the symmetric key needed to decrypt the body. This key can be chosen uniformly at random in each generation of the virus and the plaintext of the body can be encrypted using the new key. The new key is stored in the decryption header to ensure that decryption will proceed correctly. By making certain assumptions about the randomness of the resulting ciphertexts, it may be argued that detecting the virus using search strings requires that the search string be taken from the header.

Virus writers have a variety of methods for making the decryption header change as well. Some approaches for this are more effective than others. One obvious method is to employ several different ciphers and randomly select among them. This is a good approach but may in some cases lead to unacceptably large viruses.

Another common approach is to weave dummy instructions between the instructions that constitute the decryption algorithm. Most processors support a NOP instruction that literally does nothing. It is shorthand for no-operation and has many uses. On RISC machines these instructions cause the program to wait until all pending bus activity is completed. This allows synchronization of the pipeline and prevents instruction overlap. It is not uncommon on CISC machines to see NOP instructions woven within the sections of a switch statement to improve the performance of the instruction cache by aligning each section on a new cache line.

There are also a number of arithmetic dummy instructions. For instance, the additive identity element 0 can be used in an ADD instruction. The assembly language instruction ADD $a\ell, 0$ adds the value 0 to the machine register $a\ell$ and clearly does not change $a\ell$. The instruction MUL $a\ell, 1$ multiplies the value in $a\ell$ by 1 and also preserves the value in $a\ell$. There are dummy instructions for logical operations as well. For example, OR $a\ell, 0$ performs a bitwise logical OR operation and does not change the value in $a\ell$.

Another type of dummy instruction is any instruction that operates on registers that are not used in the underlying algorithm. For example, many algorithms do not require the use of all of the data registers at once on the target microprocessor. In this case the addition, multiplication, and so on, of any number in that register has a null effect. All of these dummy instructions have the potential to foil string-matching scanners.

There exist a number of tools that antiviral analysts use that specifically search for such dummy instructions. These tools typically have false positive rates that are very high and as a result make them unsuitable for use by the average user. They nonetheless greatly minimize the time needed for *skilled analysts* to find polymorphic code.

A better way to obfuscate the decryption header is to replace instructions with other instructions that perform the same operation and to exploit the fact that many instructions can be reordered without affecting

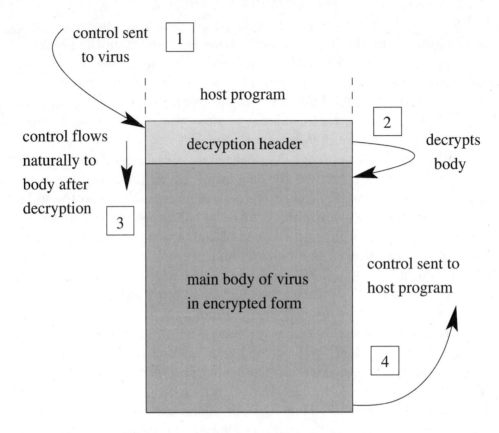

**Figure 8.1**  Typical polymorphic virus

the overall correctness of the algorithm [282]. For example, on Intel processors there are many ways to set register $a\ell$ to zero, including:

1. MOV $a\ell$,0

2. SUB $a\ell$,$a\ell$

3. XOR $a\ell$,$a\ell$

4. AND $a\ell$,0

In the case that code can be reordered, the virus can choose an ordering randomly when creating a modified decryption header. For example, the value $x + y + z$ can be derived by computing $t_1 = x + y$ and then by computing $t_2 = t_1 + z$. Alternatively, it can be derived by computing $t_1 = y + z$ and then $t_2 = t_1 + x$. This works since integers are commutative under addition.

When four instructions are completely interchangeable there are 4! ways to order them. Implementing this correctly is subtler than it seems since to be truly correct, one of the 4! permutations must be chosen uniformly at random. A typical random number generator will output a random byte or byte sequence. Such a generator can therefore be used to implement a random bit generator. To choose one of the $4! = 4*3*2*1 = 24$ permutations uniformly at random the following Las Vegas algorithm can be performed. Five random bits are taken from the random bit generator. These 5 bits constitute a number chosen uniformly at random between 0 and 31 inclusive. If the number is less than 24 then it is used to select the permutation. Otherwise another 5 bits are generated and the process is repeated.

Once this number is found it is necessary to translate it into the appropriate permutation over the four instructions, for example, $(0, 2, 1, 3)$. There are well-known methods in algorithmic combinatorics to efficiently translate such numbers into the combinatorial objects they represent. These are referred to as *unranking* algorithms. When working with permutations the Trotter-Johnson algorithm is an efficient way to perform ranking and unranking [142, 163, 301].

Register usage is another aspect that is easily randomized. On the Motorola 68000 Microprocessor there are eight general-purpose data registers. A given decryption algorithm may only require the use of four data registers. There are $\binom{8}{4}$ ways of selecting four distinct registers from the set of eight registers. Kreher and Stinson give a comprehensive overview of ranking and unranking algorithms for $k$-element subsets (that is, binomial coefficients) [163].

Choosing the set of registers to use uniformly at random may seem like a good heuristic, but with a bit more effort a better approach may be as follows. To make the code less conspicuous, the set of registers should be chosen according to the way the host uses them. This may be accomplished by analyzing the host, calculating the probability distribution over the registers, and then selecting the set of registers to use based on that probability distribution. If for whatever reason a given compiler never uses a particular register, then the decryption header will never employ that register either, thereby making heuristic detection via inhomogeneous code less likely.

Another approach to heuristically obfuscating a decryption header is to interleave another algorithm within the header. For example, by weaving within the header an arbitrary algorithm such as Mergesort and having it

sort legitimate data, it may be considerably more difficult to determine
that the header performs decryption. In the end all of these heuristics
succumb to reverse engineering by an analyst or a carefully crafted program that specifically looks for this type of obfuscation.[6] However, a virus
writer's goal is often to simply bypass all *existing* antiviral programs and
not worry about what will be developed further down the road.

It has been observed that since many viruses execute before the host, it
is often possible to positively identify polymorphic viruses by letting them
decrypt themselves [197]. The general idea is to emulate the operation of
the host program for the first few thousand or so instructions and then scan
the resulting executable for the presence of known polymorphic viruses.
The method is called *generic decryption* and involves three components:
a CPU emulator, an emulation control module, and a scanner. The CPU
emulator is designed to emulate a particular CPU such as a Pentium IV
processor. The emulation control module determines such things as how
many instructions will be emulated[7] and is also responsible for making
sure that no damage is done to the underlying machine as a result of the
presence of malware. For example, writes to the disk may be prevented
or otherwise contained. The scanner is applied to the code at regular
intervals during the emulation to attempt to detect malicious software.
Generic decryption can be performed on the fly along with traditional
scanning methods to help identify polymorphic viruses wherever present.

A countermeasure to generic decryption is to make the virus decrypt
its body with some fixed probability. The virus could generate a random
number and with some probability not decrypt its main body at all. For
example, when the virus gains control in a given invocation of the host
program, it could roll a six-sided die. If the result is "1" then the virus
could decrypt itself and then try to replicate. If the result is not "1" then
it could simply send control back to the host.

Another countermeasure to generic decryption is to make the virus
gain control at a randomly determined offset within the host program. Implementing this countermeasure is more complicated than it seems since
simply overwriting portions of the host will likely lead to crashes. As
usual, the bulk of the virus could be stored at the end of the executable.
The problem then remains to modify the host to send control to the virus.
One approach to accomplishing this is to choose an offset within the host

---

[6]This further motivates the study of the cryptocomputing problem.
[7]Due to the halting problem there is no general way to determine if a program will
halt or not.

randomly and overwrite the code at that location with a jump instruction. The original code would need to be stored within the virus, and the overlaid jump instruction would send control to the virus unconditionally. When the virus finishes executing it repairs the host by overwriting the jump instruction with the original host code and then sends control back to where it normally would have been. This has been demonstrated experimentally (see Appendix A.4).

This approach is not without its risks, however. The jump instruction and the viral code that follows it should preserve the state of the program. Register values should be pushed onto the stack, and so on, and popped when the virus completes. Also, if the jump instruction is too long it might overwrite code that forms an entry point for another jump instruction within the host. This could cause the host program to crash as a result of the inserted jump instruction. The virus would have to heuristically analyze the host to make certain that this cannot occur. If the host were naturally polymorphic, this analysis would be just as hard as the problem faced by antiviral programs. Finally, race conditions could cause faulty behavior within the host. If the jump instruction were written over an atomic action that operates on a semaphore and if the viral operation exacerbates the race-condition, then the infected host could crash or produce erroneous results.[8]

Another general heuristic for detecting polymorphic viruses is to look for changes in memory where the code for the currently running executable resides [218]. Symantec developed a tool that interprets the program one instruction at a time and that takes note of every byte in the program's code space that changes. This method is a solid countermeasure, but has certain weaknesses. For example, it is possible to make the virus create multiple encryption layers with decryption headers in the host. These small headers can decipher the rest of the binary executable and therefore almost every byte of the program in memory can be changed. Another issue to deal with is programs that spawn child programs.[9]

An unavoidable aspect of making a virus difficult to detect is that by doing so it becomes harder for the virus to detect itself. This makes it difficult for the virus writer to prevent multiple infections. The more a

---

[8]There are a myriad of other problems that could arise as well. For example, the inserted jump could alter a checksum, cause a digital signature verification to fail, and so on.

[9]For example, processes often *fork* and *exec* in UNIX thereby creating more heap zones that need to be analyzed.

virus writer strives to make the virus undetectable, the more difficult it becomes for the virus to detect itself. This leads to the aforementioned trade-off wherein the virus writer has to decide whether or not to include a virus detection algorithm within the virus. Assuming that multiple infections are not tolerable, the true threat model that a virus writer faces is that of preventing the virus from being discovered in the first place.

## 8.3 Heuristic Virus Detection

Viruses perform actions that are not typical of normal programs. As a result there are several heuristics that can be used to detect them whenever they are present. For example, a virus replicates by definition. Word processors, web browers, and e-mail programs do not replicate. So, any program that contains code that adds code to another program could in fact be infected with a virus. However, there are certain obvious exceptions to this rule. For example, software companies often release fixes to their software in the form of patches. These patches are programs that add or overwrite code to a program on the machine. Software patches allow portions of large programs to be repaired without reinstalling the entire program.

In this section several virus detection heuristics are described. These include the detection of code abnormalities such as unusual program entry points and unusual program behavior such as self-replicating code. The section concludes with ways of detecting cryptographic functions in binary progams. These latter heuristics are designed to help detect cryptoviruses and cryptotrojans.

### 8.3.1 Detecting Code Abnormalities

Scanners are excellent protection mechanisms for viruses that have already been discovered. However, virus writers often subject viruses to antiviral scanners before releasing them, thus guaranteeing that they do not contain any of the known search strings. More often than not such viruses are only discovered as a result of the activation of their payloads. It is therefore desirable to be able to detect new viruses before they have a chance to sabotage computer systems. This motivates the need for proactive antiviral mechanisms that heuristically detect computer viruses.

One approach to proactively detecting viruses relies on the fact that many viruses append themselves to the end of executables and change the entry point to point to themselves. In bulky programs this initial jump may be abnormally large and thereby indicate the presence of a virus. Some viruses change the entry points to very unusual locations and this forms another heuristic for viral detection.

Weber, Schmid, Geyer, and Shatz at Cigital Labs devised a handful of clever methods for detecting malware [314]. Their methods were implemented in a toolkit called the Portable Executable Analysis Toolkit, or PEAT for short. PEAT is designed to detect malware that has been added to programs after they have been compiled, and is based on the premise that hand-crafted malware introduces statistical discrepancies when it appears within an otherwise homogenous binary executable.

When a compiler creates a program it often creates jump tables for functions and has internal jumps and subroutine calls throughout. However, when malware is appended there will typically be only one jump into the added malware and one jump out to send control back to the host. In this case there may be a noticeable lack of flow control instructions between the malware and its host. PEAT looks for flow control anomalies such as this to help identify malware. Also, most programs are written in high-level languages, whereas malware is typically written in assembly language and as a result tends to be more compact and efficient. When malware is attached to a homogenous executable there is often a statistical difference in the instruction frequencies between the two regions. PEAT searches for these variations and reports them to the user. The PEAT toolkit has a false positive rate that is too high for most end-users but is ideal for reducing the time needed for skilled analysts to identify malicious code.[10]

## 8.3.2 Detecting Abnormal Program Behavior

By definition viruses copy possibly altered versions of themselves into host programs. Many antiviral programs exploit this intrinsic property of computer viruses to identify new strains. By looking specifically for executable code that modifies other executable code there is a chance that new strains will be identified before they have a chance to execute their payloads. At

---

[10]A number of other companies provide antiviral software that perform viral scanning, heuristic detection, and disinfection. Such products include Symantec Antivirus and McAfee VirusScan. These products typically have lower false positive rates than PEAT against known viruses but higher false negative rates against new viruses.

the heart of every operating system is an operating system services layer that provides exactly this functionality.

Modern operating systems provide a set of service routines to applications that enable the applications to make full use of the computer and its peripherals. For example, there are well-defined operating system routines to read keystrokes from the keyboard, read and write data to disk drives, and so forth. By providing developers with a standard interface to common peripherals, the specifics of particular peripheral devices may be ignored without hindering their usability. This standard interface therefore provides a level of abstraction for software developers and eases the overall software development process. Device drivers help bridge the gap between operating system calls and the underlying peripheral machinery. The operating system expects to be supplied with a device driver whenever a new device is attached to the system. This provides operating system developers with their own level of abstraction. The amount of code needed to interface directly with device drivers is often substantial and so the operating system service routines help to minimize the amount of code used in individual applications.

Application programs typically access operating system routines using software interrupts. To invoke an operating system routine such as reading in a keystroke from the keyboard, the program typically places various parameters in CPU registers and then executes a software interrupt instruction (e.g., INT 21h). The CPU then temporarily suspends the operation of the program and looks up the address of the operating system routine for that interrupt in the interrupt vector table (see Figure 8.2). Control is then sent to the address and the operation is carried out. When the operating system routine is finished it returns control back to the calling program by executing an interrupt return instruction (e.g., IRET). The values that are returned are typically left for the calling program in CPU registers. For instance, the values may indicate whether or not a key was pressed and which key was pressed, if any.

Many viruses propagate by first opening the target executable file with write permissions followed by a call to write to the file. It would therefore make sense to scan executables for a software interrupt that opens executables for writing followed by a software interrupt that attempts to write to the file. However, in the case of polymorphic viruses this will not always work since the interrupt instructions could be encrypted.

A heuristic solution to this problem is to monitor at run-time all attempts to open files with write permissions and all attempts to write data

Interrupt Table

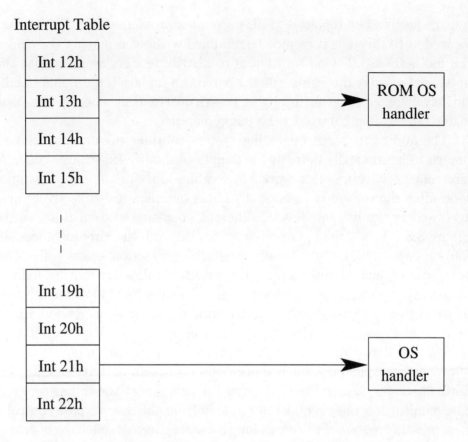

**Figure 8.2**  Operating system software interrupt handling

to the disk.  An effective way to carry out this form of monitoring is to modify the operating system service routines to be more suspicious of the applications that call them.  *Interrupt patching* is a standard systems programming technique that can be utilized to add such functionality to otherwise trusting operating system service routines.

To patch an interrupt, an interrupt handler is loaded into memory in a persistent and non-relocatable block.  The entry in the interrupt table corresponding to the operating system routine being patched is overwritten with the starting address of the new interrupt handler.  When the handler finishes executing it sends control to the address that was originally contained in the interrupt table.  Many operating systems have service routines for manipulating the interrupt vector table.  Common functions include returning the interrupt handler address for a particular interrupt and setting the interrupt handler address for a particular interrupt.

On occasion a bug is found in a native operating system routine and the routine needs to be replaced. This presents a problem when the routine is located in ROM since it cannot be modified without replacing the chip on the motherboard.[11] One solution is to distribute a software update that patches the buggy interrupt. Such a patch can replace the original handler entirely by executing an interrupt return instruction when it completes instead of sending control to the buggy handler.

The ability to patch operating system routines provides a good approach to heuristically detecting attempts to modify executable code. An interrupt activity monitor works by loading antiviral interrupt handlers soon after the computer is booted. These handlers are collectively managed and typically span several different operating system routines (see Figure 8.3). When they gain control they analyze the circumstances surrounding the call and often maintain state information across calls. They take note of such things as opening executable files for writing followed by attempts to write to the file. In general, monitors look for attempts to write to any sector containing executable code such as device drivers, boot sectors, and so on [185, 289]. They also typically look for attempts to reformat floppy disks and other potentially malicious acts.

When a suspicious sequence of events occurs an activity monitor will normally display a message to the user that implicates the calling program. The monitor may also request permission from the user to pass control to the operating system service routine. If the user agrees to let the operation continue, control is then sent to the original address that was listed in the interrupt table (see Figure 8.4). This way, users have a chance to stop a virus before it writes itself to another program.

One of the dangers in using activity monitors is that if the alerts occur too frequently, the user may then become desensitized to them. Alerts may arise when a software patch is applied, when a new program is compiled, when a program utilizes a copy protection scheme that causes the program to write to itself (e.g., WordPerfect [185]), and so on. This form of "cry wolf" makes it more likely that users will allow a virus to spread in spite of warnings from an activity monitor. Unlike scanners, activity monitors are designed to identify both existing and future viruses, and as a result activity monitors are prone to yield false negative results. False negatives are guaranteed due to the undecidability of viral detection.

How do viruses deal with this heuristic countermeasure? There are

---

[11]The contents of EEPROM chips can actually be changed by users, but this often requires explicit user intervention. It is a very security-intensive operation since malware can be burned into the chip.

Interrupt Table

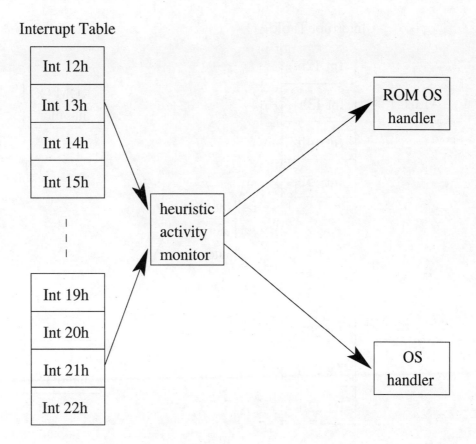

**Figure 8.3** Heuristic interrupt monitor

a variety of ways that viruses bypass activity monitors. A boot sector virus can gain access to the interrupt table before activity monitors and as a result learn the starting addresses of the operating system routines that it needs to call. Once learned, the virus can call them directly when needed or temporarily modify the interrupt table to contain the original addresses. However, it is not uncommon for activity monitors to patch operating system routines that manipulate the interrupt table. In this case the boot sector virus could manipulate the interrupt table directly.

Another viral defense against activity monitors that boot sector viruses can take is to create a viral patch that encompasses all of the interrupts that the virus will need to invoke (see Figure 8.5). In this situation the virus does not need to utilize the interrupt table at all. It therefore makes all the difference in the world which program gains access to the interrupt table first: the virus or the activity monitor. As a result the interrupt table has traditionally formed a battleground in older PC operating systems.

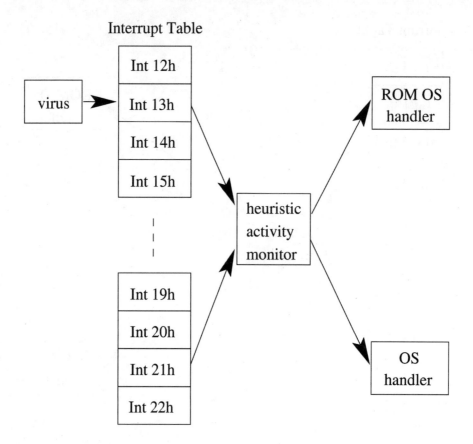

**Figure 8.4** Virus detected by activity monitor

A challenge for viruses is to be able to call operating system routines on a machine that is already running an activity monitor. Such a situation arises when an infected program is run for the first time on a machine that is judiciously guarded by an activity monitor. The reason that this is a non-trivial undertaking is that when the operating system routine is patched with an activity monitor, the starting address of the operating system routine is overwritten in the interrupt table with the starting address of the activity monitor. The starting address for the operating system routine is typically stored somewhere within the activity monitor to allow control to be transferred to the operating system routine. *Tunneling* is a method in which a virus tries to recover the starting address of the original operating system routine by heuristically analyzing the activity monitor code [239, 283]. If all of the needed addresses are successfully recovered, the virus can call the original operating system routines directly and circumvent the activity monitor completely.

Interrupt Table

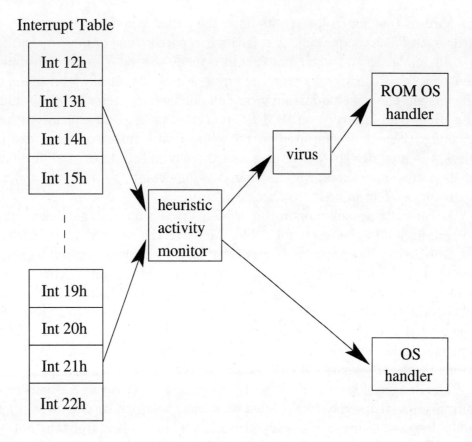

**Figure 8.5** Virus bypassing an activity monitor

A cumbersome and oftentimes risky way to avoid this type of activity monitor is to implement all of the needed operating system functionality directly within the virus [185]. This way there is no need to utilize the operating system services. However, this is very difficult to do while keeping the size of the virus at a minimum.

Viruses that patch operating system interrupts are invoked frequently since they gain control whenever an application makes a service request. The fact that they gain control frequently makes it easy for them to infect programs since they can infect the currently running program as opposed to performing a directory search. Many of the early viruses replicate by infecting interrupt handlers [289]. Some cleverly written memory-resident viruses only write themselves to other executables during normal write operations. On disk drives that have lights, this implies that the light goes on only when the light would normally go on and as a result makes such viruses difficult to detect.

Viruses that patch interrupts have the added benefit of being able to utilize *stealth* methods [283]. A stealth virus patches one or more operating system read calls and when an attempt is made to read a sector containing the virus (e.g., the boot sector), the virus returns the uninfected version of the image. The Pakistani Brain virus camouflaged its presence by patching the BIOS read interrupt on IBM PC machines [289]. Consequently, when an integrity check is computed on a machine that is infected with a stealth virus, the integrity check will pass and thereby fail to detect the presence of the virus. This threat implies that it is important to boot from a clean operating system in order to check for viruses.

In carefully designed operating systems it is quite difficult for viruses to gain access to the interrupt table. Many of the early viruses had free reign over the interrupt table since the early personal computers were not designed with the threat of computer viruses in mind. One of the primary reasons why these early viruses were so successful is that older PC operating systems were based on a very weak trust model. This model assumed that each machine was used by a single trustworthy user [289]. The model did not take into account large exchanges of software and as a result these early viruses flourished.

The danger of viral replication is minimized in operating systems that run in protected kernel mode, such as UNIX. Security kernels were originally designed to provide provable security. They evolved from the notion of a reference monitor[12] that was described in the Anderson Report [6]. A reference monitor is an abstraction of the access checking function of object monitors [121]. The main idea behind a security kernel is to have a small nucleus of operating system software that is tasked with administering the security policy of the entire system. Provided that the kernel is small, the verification effort is much less than what would be required to verify a complete operating system [85].

A security kernel operates in a separate address space that is not accessible to user programs. Privileged operations such as starting I/O and halting the CPU are available exclusively to the kernel. User programs request services from the kernel via *system calls*. System calls are used to cause the kernel to read from the keyboard, read/write to disk drives, and so on. System calls are usually implemented as hardware traps that change execution mode of the CPU and the current address space mapping. The kernel validates the parameters supplied by user programs before they are used in order to guarantee the correctness of the system. All parame-

---

[12]The notion of a reference monitor was suggested by Roger Schell.

ters that are passed are copied into the kernel address space [169]. Open research on security kernels began in the early 1970s and a number of prototypes were implemented soon thereafter [256, 290, 312].

In the UNIX operating system, programs inherit the access privileges of the user that is currently logged in. As long as the user avoids logging in as root whenever possible, it is very difficult for a virus to gain total control of the machine. Usually when a virus succeeds at becoming root it succeeds due to the exploitation of a bug that exists in the underlying operating system.

### 8.3.3  Detecting Cryptographic Code

Cryptographic malware is a subset of all malicious software. Examples of malicious software that do not employ cryptography include the *cookie-monster* virus. Its name derives from the cookie monster on the television show *Sesame Street*. It would flash up the message "I want a cookie" on the monitor. The word "cookie" had to be fed to the virus to keep it quiet [185]. A cookie monster Trojan that ran on PDP machines was also reported [129]. The relationship between cryptography and malware may be depicted by way of a Venn diagram (see Figure 8.6). Polymorphic viruses that employ trivially breakable symmetric encryption still fall within the intersection, yet due to their simplistic nature they should probably be plotted more towards the malware set as opposed to the cryptographic code set.

It follows that one way to heuristically detect cryptoviruses is to heuristically detect the presence of cryptographic code. The absence of cryptographic code implies that absence of cryptoviruses, cryptotrojans, and so on. In considering this problem, a number of heuristics immediately come to mind. For example, many cryptographic libraries test primality by first performing trial division using small primes. It is not uncommon for a primality-testing program to store an array constant consisting of all prime numbers that fit within 16 bits. These are ordered from smallest to largest (e.g., $2, 3, 5, 7, 11, 13, 17, ...$). It is possible to detect such implementations using a form of string matching. Basically, this sequence of primes is searched for taking into account little endian and big-endian machine architectures. However, the majority of cryptovirus attacks that have been presented do not involve primality testing (the exception is the RSA SETUP attack). So this cryptographic code detection heuristic is likely to be of little use in those cases.

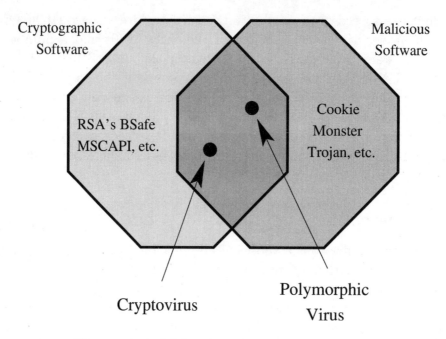

**Figure 8.6**  Malware and cryptographic code

In a similar vein it is straightforward to detect many symmetric ciphers as well. These algorithms have fixed constants in the form of substitution boxes and permutation boxes. When in plaintext form, they are relatively easy to detect using string-matching techniques. The ability to detect decryption algorithms is crucial in detecting advanced polymorphs. The heuristic detection of Feistel transformations can also indicate the presence of cryptographic hash functions. This helps to infer semantics about the program in question since it reveals some of the underlying cryptographic functions that are used.

A general heuristic[13] to detect public key cryptography implementations is to look for the presence of the Karatsuba multiplication algorithm [150]. The Karatsuba algorithm is an efficient algorithm for multiplying two large numbers together. It follows the divide-and-conquer paradigm and has a complexity of $O(n^{log_2 3})$ where $n$ is the size in bits of the numbers being multiplied.[14] The classic multiplication algorithm that is taught in grade school has a running time of $O(n^2)$.

Karatsuba is used in many cryptographic libraries since it speeds up

---

[13]This heuristic was developed by Adam at Cigital Labs.

[14]This may be proven by setting up the recurrence relation and solving it.

RSA, ElGamal, DSA, and a wealth of other algorithms. The algorithm is given below. For simplicity it is assumed that $|x| = |y| = 2^\alpha$ for some integer $\alpha > 0$. The notation $|x|$ denotes the bit length of $x$.

Karatsuba(x,y):
1. if $|x| \leq 16$ then return $(x * y)$
2. $m = |x|/2$
3. compute $a$ and $b$ such that $x = a2^m + b$
4. compute $c$ and $d$ such that $y = c2^m + d$
5. $t = \text{Karatsuba}(a, c)$
6. $u = \text{Karatsuba}(a + b, c + d)$
7. $v = \text{Karatsuba}(b, d)$
8. output $(tv2^{2m} + (u - t - v)2^m + v)$ and halt

The reason that Karatsuba is faster than the classical approach is that it divides a problem into three problems of half the size.

The recursive structure of Karatsuba lends itself to a simple detection heuristic. The heuristic requires that the *call graph* of the program in question be constructed from the binary code. There is ongoing research in the area of reconstructing call graphs from binary programs [62, 63, 64, 65]. A call graph is a directed graph where each vertex is a function and each directed edge is a pointer to a function that the vertex calls. There are a number of algorithms and packages available that can be used to construct the call graph for a given program. If such a graph contains a cycle, then it contains a recursive function call. In a straightforward implementation, Karatsuba will have the calling structure depicted in Figure 8.7.

Since Karatsuba calls itself exactly three times, one would expect it to contain a single function that sends control to the Karatsuba entry point exactly three times. An algorithm like Mergesort that divides a problem into two problems of half the size would contain a function that called Mergesort exactly twice, and so on. This implies that Karatsuba can be singled out to a degree. Detecting whether or not a directed graph contains a cycle is an elementary problem. It can be accomplished by performing a breadth-first search of the graph, while maintaining a list of vertices that have been visited. When a back-edge is found that leads to a vertex that has already been visited, a cycle has been found. By storing the parent of each vertex in a parent array, the cycle can be traversed backwards and written down.

It is worth noting that a generalization of Karatsuba exists. Also, large integer multiplication can be performed using Strassen multiplica-

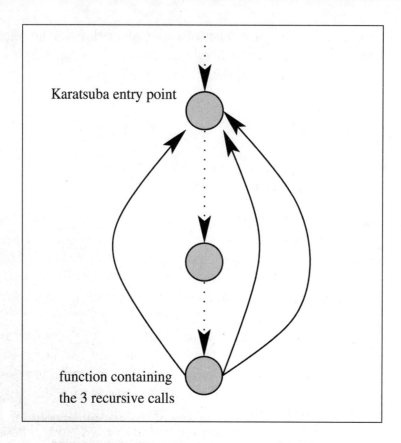

Karatsuba entry point

function containing
the 3 recursive calls

**Figure 8.7** Recursive structure of karatsuba

tion. This method is based on the Fast Fourier Transform and is a good candidate for parallel implementation. Thus, other recursive structures can be heuristically searched for as well.

Another potential approach to detecting cryptoviruses and cryptotrojans is to search for the public keys they contain. Shamir and Someren investigated approaches for algorithmically searching for RSA public and private keys in bulk data [268]. This was within the context of *lunch time* attacks where an attacker gets brief access to a machine and wants to search for cryptographic keys quickly. This notion is useful for detecting malware that uses such keys as well. In this section heuristics are given for detecting various types of public keys. Consider discrete log trapdoor. A discrete logarithm based key pair typically comes in 3 forms:

1. $((y, g, p), x)$ where $y = g^x \bmod p$, $ord_p(g) = p - 1$, $p - 1$ has large prime divisor

2. $((y, g, p), x)$ where $y = g^x \mod p$, $ord_p(g) = (p-1)/2 = q$ where $q$ is prime

3. $((y, g, p, q), x)$ where $y = g^x \mod p$, $ord_p(g) = q$, where $q$ is prime

In all three pairs, the first tuple is the public key and $x$ is the private key. In form (2) $p$ is a safe prime. Here $ord_p(g)$ denotes the order of $g$ modulo $p$. In form (1), $g$ generates $\mathbb{Z}_p^*$. In forms (2) and (3), $g$ has order $q$ and generates a prime order subgroup of $\mathbb{Z}_p^*$.

Multiprecision integers are typically stored in one's complement format in cryptographic libraries. Typically, $p$ is 768 or 1024 bits in length. The value $y$ is almost always the same length as $p$. The value $g$ is sometimes chosen randomly, but a common heuristic in choosing a generator $g$ is to try $g = 2, 3, 4, 5, 6, ...$ until one is found. It is believed that the factorization of $p - 1$ must be known to test if a value is a generator. This heuristic is likely to work when $g$ is chosen uniformly at random. The idea is to heuristically identify these parameters in embedded code based on the fact that they are typically high-entropy strings of specific lengths. Certain assertions exist based on the mathematical relations. These assertions are listed below for each form:

1. The value $p$ is prime: This is a somewhat weak assertion, but it is worth noting that this form is old-fashioned. ElGamal encryptions that use such keys are not semantically secure against plaintext attacks.

2. The value $p$ is prime, $(p-1)/2$ is prime, $g^{(p-1)/2} = 1 \mod p$.

3. The value $p$ is prime, $q$ is prime, $q$ divides $p-1$ evenly, $g^q = 1 \mod p$, $q$ is typically 160 bits in this setting (e.g., DSA).

Checking for such assertions has the potential of minimizing false positives. For example, if form (3) is satisfied, there is a good chance that a public key has been found.

It is worth articulating the failure probability for form (3) above, since this is the one with the lowest false positive rate. A random value in $\mathbb{Z}_p^*$ will have order $q$ with probability about $q/p$. This is found by dividing the number of elements in $G$ by the number of elements in $\mathbb{Z}_p^*$. Here $G$ is the prime order subgroup of $\mathbb{Z}_p^*$ generated by $g$. Typically, $q$ is 160 bits and $p$ is say, 768 bits. So, this probability is about $2^{160}/2^{768} = 2^{-608}$. Note that the public key $y$ will also have order $q$ modulo $p$. Hence, the heuristic need only find $y$ or $g$. This probability is so astronomically small that if this assertion holds, a public key will most certainly have been found in the software.

In DSA, the prime $p$ varies from 512 to 1024 bits in multiples of 64 bits. One would expect 768 or 1024 to be used the most. The following heuristic can be used to search for DSA public keys of the form $(y, g, q, p)$ in binaries. It runs in time polynomial in the length of the binary code that is analyzed. However, it is somewhat computationally intensive and so is most practically applied when a binary has been found that is believed to contain a Trojan, virus, worm, and so on, and the malware is not identified by other means, for example, commercial antiviral software.

This heuristic searches for $(y, q, p)$ from $(y, g, p, q)$ where $y^q = 1 \bmod p$. The reason that we do not search for $g$ is that $g$ can be very small (10 bits or less, and so on). But, for a randomly chosen private key $x$, $y$ will almost certainly be as long as $p$ in bits.

The heuristic assumes that big numbers are stored on byte boundaries. It can be coded to handle big endian and little endian architectures. For simplicity assume that the bytes are ordered from most significant to least significant. The heuristic can handle one's complement and two's complement big integers, since the numbers are the same when they are positive. All public key parameters are positive.

In this example we will assume that $p$ is 1024 bits and $q$ is 160 bits. Hence, $p$ is 128 bytes and $q$ is 20 bytes. The following is the heuristic to find prime order subgroup trapdoors in binaries:

1. Scan the binary for 1024-bit primes $p$. This is done by checking the first 128 bytes, then shifting one byte, testing primality, shifting one byte, testing primality, and so on. The end result is a list $L_p$ of 1024 bit primes. For a random byte stream, the Prime Number Theorem implies that 1 in 1024 values will be prime naturally. Remove all values from $L_p$ that have low entropy.

2. Scan the binary for 160-bit primes $q$. This is the same as in step 1, except that it is for a different size prime. Let the resulting list be $L_q$. Remove all values from $L_q$ that have low entropy.

3. Scan the binary for 1024 bit values $y$ that have high entropy. Let the resulting list be $L_y$. This list may be quite large.

4. For each possible 3-tuple $(y, q, p)$ where $y \in L_y$, $q \in L_q$, and $p \in L_p$,

compute $y^q \bmod p$. If this quantity equals 1 then output $(y, q, p)$ for this tuple. Note that multiple 3-tuples might be output in this step.

In general, if a single 3-tuple is output, a prime order subgroup public key has been found in the binary.

## 8.4   Change Detection

Computer viruses must invariably change their hosts in some way in order to infect them. As a result one way to detect infections is to look for changes in executables. It may be tempting to simply consider the size in bytes of executables in order to detect changes since by adding code to a program one would think that the resulting program would be larger than the original. But this is not necessarily the case. If the binary code in the host executable is redundant then it can be compressed to make the added viral code less noticeable.

For example, a virus could be written that performs Huffman compression and decompression [134] and that has space reserved internally for a Huffman tree. When an executable is considered for infection, the Huffman tree for the executable is computed and the compression ratio is calculated. If the size of the compressed executable plus the size of the virus is less than or equal to the size of the original executable, then the virus decides to infect the executable. The virus then compresses the executable and pads it as necessary so that the resulting data when combined with the virus is the same length in bytes as the original executable. It is necessary that such a virus gain control before the host program to prevent the infected executable from crashing. When the virus gains control it performs its normal viral operations, decompresses the host, and then sends control to the host.

### 8.4.1   Integrity Self-Checks

File sizes alone are therefore not sufficient for identifying changes to executables. A better approach is to utilize cryptographic integrity checks [68, 70]. A program can perform cryptographic integrity checks at runtime to help ascertain whether or not the program has been changed in any way. A simple approach is to compute a cryptographic hash of the executable after the program is compiled and include the hash value inside a routine that is appended to the program, much like a Trojan horse program. This program will recompute the hash on the body of the executable at run-time and compare the result with the internally stored value. The routine sends control to the body of the executable if and only if the hash values are equal. The design of self-checking software is a well-studied area [70, 327].

A drawback to cryptographic integrity checks is that they notify the user of changes only after they occur. This line of defense therefore falls into the category of being reactive in nature. Also, it is critical that the initial cryptographic hash values are computed on executables that are known to be virus-free. To prevent false alarms it is necessary to update the hash values whenever software updates are applied. In environments in which programs are frequently added and updated this solution may prove cumbersome.

There exists a subtler problem with integrity self-checks. Consider a virus that replicates as follows. Once control is sent to the host the virus immediately gains control and searches the file system for two programs to infect. Once found, the virus infects both of them and then disinfects itself from its host in memory.[15] The virus then sends control to its host. If the host performs an integrity check on itself in memory then it will pass since it is in the same pristine form that it would be if it were never infected. *It passes since the host is no longer infected.* Like other viruses, this virus will also benefit from an exponential infection rate since it performs two infections each time it disinfects itself. The virus therefore demonstrates a fundamental weakness in viral self-checking. The self-disinfection defense constitutes a mixed blessing, both from the perspective of the virus writer and from the perspective of antiviral analysts:

1. *virus writer:* Has the benefit of preventing the virus from being discovered by hosts that perform integrity self-checks. However, it assists antiviral analysts in devising a cure for the virus.

2. *antiviral analyst:* Has the drawback of preventing executables that perform integrity self-checks from finding the virus. But once found, it reveals the steps necessary to safely remove the virus.

## 8.4.2   Program Inoculation

Activity monitors form a solid proactive measure to prevent viruses from spreading in the first place. However, the numbing alerts that they present

---

[15]And from the disk image, if possible.

to the user can negatively impact the success of the measure. Another proactive measure is to *inoculate* programs against specific viruses [289]. Inoculation is a procedure that protects a given program from being infected in the first place. It only works against viruses that actively prevent multiple infections in a given host. In this procedure an executable is modified in such a way that it appears to the virus as if it is already infected. More often than not this involves appending data to the end of the application that contains data at a particular offset that leads the virus to believe that a copy is already in the host. The appended data is benign and serves only to fool the virus into thinking that the application is already infected.

The main problem with this solution is that there may be far too many viruses to protect against. Also, if this method is applied to an executable that checks its own integrity then it may fail to run in response to the modification. The addition of the benign data to the code will with overwhelming probability cause cryptographic integrity checks to fail.

### 8.4.3 Kernel Based Signature Verification

To be most effective the integrity checking should be conducted externally on the program rather than internally. External integrity checking programs exist that take snapshots of vulnerable programs and sectors when they are first installed. Some time later these programs take new snapshots and compare them with the old ones. If a new snapshot does not match the corresponding old snapshot then the user is notified. Such snapshots duplicate the executable code exactly and therefore identify changes perfectly. This form of external checking is most effective when it is applied from within a secure kernel. For reasons of efficiency a cryptographic hash can be used in lieu of raw images. Before running an application, the kernel computes the cryptographic hash of the file and compares the result with the internally stored value in the kernel space. The program is executed if and only if they match.

Although this method is a clear improvement, it does not prevent programs from being altered after leaving the manufacturer and before installation on the user's machine. A powerful end-to-end solution to this problem combines the notion of a secure kernel with digital signatures [85, 87]. In this method the kernel stores the root and CA digital certificates of the PKI used to certify the application that is to be run. The manufacturer digitally signs the application and releases it along with the digital signature and certificate that are needed to verify the signature. When the user runs the application, the certificate and signature are given to the kernel. The kernel verifies the authenticity of the certificate using the internally stored CA certificate and also checks a Certificate Revocation List if necessary. Once the certificate is deemed valid it is used to verify the signature on the application. The application is run if and only if the certificate and signature are valid. When a signature is valid the user can be overwhelmingly certain that the program has not been tampered with.

This form of integrity checking will never produce false positive results. If the digital signature is invalid, then the application has been changed without a doubt. However, there is a negligible chance that a false negative will result. A malicious user or program can change an application and still have the signature verify correctly with an exponentially small probability.

In retrospect it is safe to say that the early viruses spread rampantly only because of the initial short-sightedness of PC manufacturers. With the Internet revolution and the proliferation of secure kernels in desktop PCs, virus writers today face hurdles that they really should have been facing two decades ago. It is a classic case of existing yet neglected technology. Public key cryptography promises to close this gap even further and provide more secure and more reliable computing environments in the years to come.

# Chapter 9

# The Nature of Trojan Horses

Up until this point the book has focused largely on self-replicating programs. The exception to this is the deniable password-snatching attack described in Section 4.2 that is carried out by a Trojan horse program. The remainder of the book focuses exclusively on Trojan horse programs.

The term *Trojan horse* is a fitting one for describing malicious software and is based on a Greek myth. According to legend, the Greeks were unable to penetrate the city of Troy using siege machines and other weapons of war. So, they devised a plan. They built a huge wooden horse with a hollow belly and filled it with Greek warriors that were poised for attack. The Greeks pushed the horse to the outskirts of Troy and then sailed away. The Trojans assumed that it was a peace offering and brought the horse inside the city to celebrate the presumed departure of the Achaeans. The citizens rejoiced and drank heavily throughout the evening and much of the night. The Greek warriors took the city by surprise under cover of dark.

Computer Trojan horses are much the same. They are invisible to the naked eye. They appear within otherwise attractive or harmless programs. They require some form of user or operating system intervention to activate, and they do something that the user does not expect. The purpose of this chapter is to convey a basic principle that underlies the design of Trojan horse programs, the principle being that Trojans are designed to exploit resources and access permissions that are inherent in their hosts. By virtue of being one with the host program the Trojan inherits these resources and access permissions and exploits this to achieve its goal. In the case of password snatchers the goal is to securely and subliminally leak login/password pairs to the Trojan author. In the case of kleptographic attacks the goal is to securely and subliminally leak private keys to the attacker, and so on.

To further illustrate this principle, key questions that attackers ask themselves are addressed. Such questions are along the lines of, "If I could place a Trojan in program X, how could I program it to exploit the system?" It was this sort of thinking that led to the kleptographic attacks in the chapters that follow.

## 9.1   Text Editor Trojan Horse

Consider a multiuser operating system that has an installed text editor that is free for use. Users can run the text editor, create and modify text, and save their files to disk. However, suppose further that this program can be executed but not modified or deleted by the users, as in typical multiuser operating systems such as UNIX.

This program has certain unique privileges. It has read access to every text file that users create or open for editing. As such it is an ideal target for a Trojan horse program that is geared towards stealing the private data of others. When a Trojan is installed in this program it can store data from one user and make the data available to the Trojan horse author. It could have devastating effects if, for example, top secret data were leaked to someone that had only secret clearance or lower. This type of attack was described in the visionary Anderson report of 1972 [6].

## 9.2   Salami Slicing Attacks

In November of 1987 an article was published in the *Globe and Mail* that described a talk given by Sergeant Ted Green, an officer of the Ontario Provincial Police.[1] The talk described several *logic bomb* attacks and other attacks against systems. One of them was a Trojan horse attack that was clearly intended to achieve financial gain. The attack was carried out by an employee of a bank who managed to accumulate $70,000 by funneling a few cents out of every account into his own [179, 205]. This type of attack is called a *salami slicing* attack [219] since small portions of money are purloined from numerous accounts. This is necessary to prevent employees from noticing that their paychecks are a bit less than they should be. Many

---

[1]We make no guarantees about the accuracy of this article.

assets or resources can be salami sliced. For instance, CPU use can also be salami sliced. This allows malware to steal CPU time in small increments to solve computational problems in an inconspicuous fashion.

The resource that the bank Trojan has access to is money and the Trojan steals the money. The resource that the text editor has access to is the documents of many users and the Trojan steals the documents. The cryptotrojans described in Chapters 11 and 12 are inserted into cryptosystems that have access to private keys which are also stolen. All of these Trojans exploit the access privileges of their hosts and steal the assets that they have access to. So, the methodology for designing a Trojan is simple: decide what sort of asset is desired, determine which programs have access to it, and then carefully design a Trojan to secure the asset. However, actually getting the Trojan into position is a different story. This can easily be done by an insider, whereas outsiders often have to exploit bugs in the system to gain entry.

## 9.3  Thompson's Password Snatcher

Stealing login/password pairs is the bread and butter of every hacker's existence. Once a system is infiltrated, password-snatching programs are often surreptitiously installed. Such programs are often referred to as *rootkits* [132]. They are installed to ensure that access to the machine continues to be possible, even if a few accounts are terminated due to suspicious activity. Such programs have been written as DOS terminate and stay resident (TSR) programs that record all keystrokes entered via the keyboard. These programs typically patch the operating system hardware interrupt for key presses and log the key presses to a hidden file. Technically speaking, such a stand-alone program is not a Trojan horse per se since it is not directly attached to a host.

The addition of a stand-alone TSR program to a file system may be a noticeable act of espionage. For example, if the TSR program is stored in a directory of programs that are always run at boot time then its presence may be revealed. A more desirable approach from the attacker's perspective is to integrate the password-snatching code into an existing operating system program in an unnoticeable fashion.

A suitable host for a password-snatching Trojan is any program that has access to the passwords of users. A perfect example of this is the UNIX *passwd* program. The passwd program is the UNIX program that is responsible for verifying the identity of UNIX users by obtaining and verifying login/password pairs. There are two obvious approaches to mounting a Trojan horse attack against such a program. The first is to manually attach one by copying the Trojan to the end of the passwd program and altering the entry point and exit points appropriately. Another option, assuming that root access is possible, is to modify the source code for the password program, recompile it, and install the compromised version. It may be argued that this form of attack is the epitome of a Trojan horse attack.

Even this approach suffers from an obvious drawback. What if the source code for the passwd program is updated and the system administrator compiles a new version of it? If the system administrator installed the new version, the old one would be deleted and the attack would be foiled due to the system update. The use of a UNIX compiler therefore threatens the perpetuation of the Trojan horse attack. It would make sense, then, to install a Trojan horse program into the *compiler* so that whenever it is given the source to the passwd program it secretly inserts the password-snatching code. This will clearly increase the survivability of the attack.

But what if the compiler is recompiled? It is common practice to both add functionality and fix non-fatal flaws in a compiler by having it compile the revised version of itself. If such a compromised compiler is recompiled the code that secretly inserts the Trojan into the passwd program would be lost.

Ken Thompson described a somewhat involved Trojan horse attack that solves this program elegantly [300]. The idea is as follows. A normal compiler parses a source file, checks its syntax, and produces object code. This standard compiler behavior is indicated by the ellipsis in Figure 9.1.

The parameter $s$ is a pointer to a string that contains the source code. The idea is to insert a source level Trojan horse into the source code of the compiler that checks for two patterns in the string $s$. The first pattern

```
compile(char *s)
{
    ...
}
```

**Figure 9.1**  Normal compiler (ANSI C notation)

is source code corresponding to the password verification program (e.g., passwd). When this pattern is found the password-snatching source code is secretly added to the program just before it is compiled. The Trojan is, of course, not saved to the source file of the password program. The second pattern is source code corresponding to the compiler. When this pattern is found the entire compiler Trojan is secretly included in the compiler source code just before it is compiled. This code, of course, contains all of the source code for the password-snatching Trojan. This is indicated by the two "if" statements in Figure 9.2.

This Trojan is somewhat virus-like since it copies itself in its entirety into the source file for the compiler whenever the compiler is compiled. It could be added to the source for the compiler, the compiler could be recompiled, and the old compiler could be replaced with the new. This would remove all traces of the source code for the Trojan horse attack. The Trojan would remain in binary form, seamlessly integrated with the rest of the compiled instructions.

The moral of the story is that one cannot ascertain the honesty of the code that is being created even if the source code is analyzed before compilation. To be certain that no slight of hand is being performed it is necessary to analyze the binary code of the compiler. Even this is not enough, for the microprocessor itself can execute a covert series of instructions at any time, based on a previously executed sequence of opcodes or otherwise. Thompson's Trojan horse attack exploits the unique capabilities of its host:

1. It exploits the fact that compilers are used to make programs, including the passwd program and the compiler itself.

2. It exploits the fact that the passwd program has unadulterated access to login/password pairs. By transitivity the compiler has access to login/password pairs as well (in some sense).

It is only natural to ask what other Trojan horses can be concocted based on host programs with unique capabilities and responsibilities. It was this very question that drove the research behind kleptography: A key generation program has access to private keys, a public key decryption program has access to private decryption keys, a digital signature program has access to private signing keys. What types of Trojan horses can be attached to these programs that exploit the fact that they have access to private keys? This very question is addressed in the chapters that follow.

```
compile(char *s)
{
if (match(s,pattern1) == true)
  {
  compile(trojan1);
  return;
  }
if (match(s,pattern2) == true)
  {
  compile(trojan2);
  return;
  }
...
}
```

**Figure 9.2**  Compiler with Trojan (ANSI C notation)

## 9.4   The Subtle Nature of Trojan Horses

It is difficult at best to come up with a formal definition of a Trojan
horse program. Whether or not a given program is a Trojan horse can
depend completely on the perspective of the user that encounters it. Take
the reboot monitoring Trojan described in Chapter 1, for instance. This
Trojan could not be simpler in design. It is installed in a highly concealed
manner. The host of the Trojan is a program that is found on virtually
everyone's machine[2] and that gains control when the system boots. It
increments a counter by 1 each time the machine is rebooted and stores
the counter in variable in RAM and on the disk.

The Trojan is a very simple form of spyware that solves a problem
facing any hacker. For example, suppose that a hacker has a gigabyte of
data that can be used as evidence against the hacker. The data should
obviously remain encrypted almost all the time. When the hacker leaves
his or her machine for a period of time, the hacker wants to make sure that

---

[2]Such as an operating system process.

a law enforcement agent does not install a monitor on the machine.[3] Such a monitor could be used to log all of the hacker's personal passwords, and so on. So, the Trojan is used by the hacker to booby trap the machine. The hacker simply notes the counter value, turns off the machine, and then leaves. Upon returning, the hacker turns on the machine (it had better still be off!) and takes note of the counter value. If the machine had been turned on in the interim, the hacker would likely know. The hacker's program needs to be hidden since if the law enforcement agent finds it, the counter value could be adjusted to make it look as if the machine hadn't been used by anyone.

Is this rogue program a Trojan? Certainly not from the perspective of the hacker since the hacker knows what it is about. It is clearly a Trojan from the perspective of the law enforcement agent since the agent doesn't know that it is there. Given the fact that the program is designed to be hard to find and does something that *someone* doesn't expect, it seems natural that it should be classified as a Trojan. This makes it rather interesting, since it is a purely beneficial Trojan from the perspective of the hacker.

Also, there is a fine line between what constitutes a Trojan horse attack and what constitutes an honest programming mistake. In the subsections below two examples of Trojans are given that illustrate this fine line. They have the property that even when they are analyzed by skilled programmers it may not be clear whether or not they are Trojans at all. The first such example is a Trojan that is nothing more than a bug. However, this bug is bad enough that when planted properly it allows that Trojan author to break into the computer system. The second Trojan horse is a purely mathematic one. The Trojan affects the statistical distribution of the output of a random number generator in a way that makes the generator extremely sensitive to the input entropy. So, when the Trojan is given *correct* inputs it does nothing to harm the output of the random number generator. However, when the Trojan is given *poor* inputs, the Trojan adversely affects the outputs of the random number generator.

---

[3]The passwords that the hacker types in can probably be obtained via a hidden camera, but there may be crucial encrypted evidence that is never typed in or displayed on the screen.

## 9.4.1   Bugs May In Fact Be Trojans

As early as 1978 Farber and Popek described an address wraparound vulnerability in the PDP-10 TENEX system [230]. Under the right conditions, a user could force the program counter to overflow while executing a supervisor call. This resulted in a privileged-mode bit in the word corresponding to the state of the process to be activated, thereby causing control to return to the user's program in supervisor mode.

If a user forced this condition by accident, then it would constitute a bug. However, if the user forced this condition on purpose so that it could later be exploited, then it would constitute a Trojan horse. This illustrates the fine line between bugs and Trojan horse programs.

## 9.4.2   RNG Biasing Trojan Horse

The following is a Trojan horse that attacks random number generators. The Trojan horse is effectively a digital filter that accepts as input "random" bits and outputs "random" bits. Such filters are often used to remove any existing biases in the distribution over the input bits, as in the case of John von Neumann's method for unbiasing a biased coin. However, this filter is somewhat the opposite in purpose. Rather than eliminating any existing bias, this filter exacerbates any existing bias. However, if there is no bias to begin with then there will not be any bias in the output values.

The algorithm is given below. It takes as input three bits $b_1, b_2, b_3$. It outputs a single bit $B$. By supplying it with an endless stream of input bits it will produce an endless stream of output bits. It is assumed that each bit $b_i$ is produced with a fixed bias for all $i$.

$BiasExacerbator(b_1, b_2, b_3)$:
1. $B = 0$
2. if $b_1 b_2 b_3 = 111$ or $110$ or $101$ or $011$ then $B = 1$
3. output $B$ and halt

For example, the stream of bits $b_i$ may be produced by a loaded coin that produces heads with probability 51 percent. Let the probability of heads be denoted by $p_h = 1/2 + \delta$. If $\delta = 0$ then the coin is fair. If $\delta > 0$ then heads is more likely than tails. If $\delta < 0$ then tails is more likely than heads.

Let the probability of tails be denoted by $p_t$. Hence, $p_t = 1 - p_h$. The probability that *BiasExacerbator* outputs $B = 1$, denoted by $p_H$ is given below.

$$p_H = p_h^3 + p_h^2 p_t + p_h p_t p_h + p_t p_h^2 = p_h^3 + 3p_h^2 p_t \tag{9.1}$$

$$p_H = (1/2 + \delta)^3 + 3(1/2 + \delta)^2(1/2 - \delta) \tag{9.2}$$

$$p_H = \frac{1}{2} + \frac{3}{2}\delta - 2\delta^3 \tag{9.3}$$

From equation 9.3 it is clear that when $\delta = 0$ the value $p_H = 1/2$. Hence, if the input bits are not biased then the output bits will not be biased. As a sanity check note that if $\delta = 1/2$ then the value $p_H = 1$. This is what one would expect when this function is given $b_i = 1$ for all $i$.

The interesting issue is to determine under what circumstances this digital filter messes with the input distribution. Suppose that $\delta > 0$. It will amplify the input bias towards heads whenever the following inequality holds.

$$\frac{1}{2} + \frac{3}{2}\delta - 2\delta^3 > \frac{1}{2} + \delta \tag{9.4}$$

This simplifies to the following inequality,

$$\delta^2 < \frac{1}{4} \tag{9.5}$$

To solve the above inequality for $\delta$ we may take the square root of both sides. The value $\delta^2$ has two square roots, namely $\delta$ and $-\delta$ and $1/4$ has the two square roots $1/2$ and $-1/2$. Since it was assumed that $\delta > 0$ it follows that amplification towards heads will occur whenever $0 < \delta < 1/2$. No amplification occurs when $\delta = 0, 1/2$. If $\delta < 0$ it can be shown that the bias will increase towards tails whenever $-1/2 < \delta < 0$.

The interesting aspect of this filter is that it amplifies the bias in the direction that the bias is already in. For example, if the initial bias is towards heads, then the output bias is even more towards heads. If the input bias is towards tails, then the output bias will be even more towards tails.

This filter may be aptly dubbed a Trojan horse if it is appended to a random number generator. Mathematically speaking, it is totally benign when the input bits are unbiased. But, when the input bits are biased this Trojan makes the bias *even worse*. A natural question to ask is how to design finite automata to detect such a Trojan and label it as malicious. Such a program would have to somehow "understand" that the mathematics behind the algorithm makes the underlying software "less stable."

To summarize, the fact that an address wraparound vulnerability can constitute a Trojan horse is really a matter of semantics. As illustrated by the RNG biasing Trojan, whether or not a program constitutes a Trojan can also be a matter of pure mathematics.

# Chapter 10

# Subliminal Channels

Subliminal channels form the cornerstone of modern kleptography. They can be utilized in the payloads of cryptoviruses and cryptotrojans to implement robust backdoors in cryptographic algorithms. Subliminal channels were originally investigated to demonstrate a weakness in a nuclear arms control verification protocol. In this regard subliminal channels demonstrated a plausibility result: given a carefully selected cryptosystem, a sneaky Trojan horse program could be developed for that cryptosystem that leaks which missile silos contain nuclear missiles. The applications of subliminal channels grew to encompass devastating smart-card insider threats. The classic abuse of subliminal channels is in the Prisoner's Problem that was formulated by Gus Simmons. This problem is described in this chapter along with numerous known subliminal channels.

On the surface it would seem that whenever a subliminal channel exists in a cryptosystem, this is a *bad thing*. However, ironically enough, this is not the case. It has been shown that this communication channel can sometimes be used in a non-subversive and publicly advertisable way. The chapter concludes with a description of how a subliminal channel can be used to help solve the key escrow problem. In a nutshell it is often possible to utilize a subliminal channel to securely transmit a private key to the key escrow authorities in a key escrow system. In this regard, subliminal channels are entirely beneficial. This was an intriguing development since it took a subversive technology and turned it into a very useful technology.

# 10.1   Brief History of Subliminal Channels

Gus Simmons is the father of subliminal channels. His investigations into the subject began in the 1970s and it is instructional to explain[1] the origin of this fantastic cryptographic phenomenon [280]. In 1978 the Carter administration was seriously considering the adoption of a national security protocol that was designed to allow Russia to verify how many minuteman missiles the United States had fielded in the 1,000 U.S. silos without exposing which silos were actually armed. To constitute an acceptable solution to Russia, the compliance messages would have to be digitally signed in a way that would not be possible for the United States to forge. At any given time the United States was permitted to have 100 minuteman missiles residing in randomly chosen silos. Any more than this would be a violation of the SALT II treaty, a treaty devised to control the arms race [281].

The scheme that the Carter administration was endorsing was often referred to in the press as the missile shell game. This is because the 100 missiles would be shuttled randomly using trucks among the 1,000 silos on a continual basis. It was envisioned that these trucks would even haul fake payloads, such as water, to conceal whether or not a given payload actually contained a live missile. This was necessary since the trucks could be observed via spy satellites. However, simply hauling fake loads would, of course, not be enough. The trucks would all have to exhibit the same acceleration, lest they be distinguished using elementary kinematics.[2]

The proposed solution, one that would allow Russia to verify the number of minuteman missiles the United States had placed afield, utilized both sensors and cryptographic devices. The sensors were to be placed in the silos. The data acquired by the sensors would indicate the presence or absence of a missile in a given silo, thus constituting a single bit of information. This bit had to be protected so that it could not be forged or falsely attributed. Both countries agreed that the sensor technology was acceptable. Gravimetric sensors could be used to detect underground features versus voids, tilt sensors could also be used, and so on. In the proposed solution each country would provide its own cryptographic algorithm.

---

[1]Many interesting details have been omitted from the explanation in this section. Interested readers are urged to read about it from the source [280].

[2]Incidentally, this entire concept is remarkably similar to the operation of a digital mix network.

This problem was being solved at about the same time that the Diffie-Hellman key exchange was devised. Symmetric ciphers were the norm at that time. The basic idea was to have the cipher use a secret key to encrypt a message. Both the ciphertext and plaintext would be output by the device. Signature verification amounted to decrypting the ciphertext and comparing the result to the plaintext. Implicit in this approach was that it should not be possible to leak information in each ciphertext. The ability to do so could potentially compromise the identity of the silo and give the enemy the opportunity to launch a devastating first strike.

As the story goes, the NSA viewed the SALT II treaty as an opportunity to learn more about the state of cryptography in Russia. It was suggested that the Russians come up with their own cipher to place in the device. Gus Simmons saw the peril in this rationale. He called a meeting with the NSA, armed with the fact that the recently discovered Rabin cipher could be used to leak a single bit out of the device to the Russians. To sign a message in Rabin, the message is transformed into a square modulo the public key. A square root of the message is then computed using the two prime factors of the public key (see Appendix C.1.6). Four square roots exist, and so any of the four square roots can be used as the signature on the message. This was an incredibly important discovery. The device had the elbow room to leak information out from under the noses of the United States.[3] Exactly two of these roots can safely be used to leak a single bit. It is these two roots that have a Jacobi symbol of 1.

This was conveyed to the NSA and the response was largely that of disinterest. They indicated that they would never approve of such a cipher and said that a one-bit channel is insignificant. Ten bits would allow the unambiguous identification of a given silo since $2^{10} = 1024 > 1000$. Ultimately, it was the projected cost of the solution, not this channel, that caused it to be abandoned.

Gus Simmons was nonetheless determined to demonstrate the importance of his finding. He had found a major hole in the protocol used to verify the compliance of the SALT II treaty, a protocol developed by TRW and approved by the NSA. Yet, as will be shown in this chapter, this was merely the tip of the iceberg of Simmons' contributions to the subject.

---

[3]Had this channel actually been exploited, the code to do so could aptly be dubbed a Trojan horse program.

## 10.2   The Difference Between a Subliminal and a Covert Channel

The difference between a covert channel and a subliminal channel is subtle at best. Typically, the term *subliminal channel* is used to refer to an information transmission channel that can be used to send information out of (or potentially into) a cryptosystem. A covert channel, on the other hand, is a somewhat older notion that is broader in scope.

A concrete example will go a long way to explain what a covert channel is. Suppose that Alice and Bob are connected to a computer that is running a multiuser operating system. In a secure operating system that can be used for sensitive (e.g., military) applications it should not be possible for a process that Alice is running to transmit information covertly to a process that Bob is running. But, suppose that a printer is connected to this machine. Each process can make an operating system call to print data. This call will return a result code indicating success or failure. The result code will also indicate if the printer is busy printing out a document. Alice's process can utilize a special communication protocol to speak with a process that Bob is running. For example, printing out two short documents with a brief pause in between could correspond to a binary "1" and printing out one document could be a binary "0." Bob's process calls the operating system routine in a busy waiting fashion to receive bits from Alice's process.

The problem of confining a program during its execution so that it cannot transmit information to any program other than its caller is known as the *Confinement Problem*. This problem was introduced by Butler Lampson [167]. A simple example of this problem is a text editor that secretly saves some data from one user's text file and exposes the stolen data to another user. A program that cannot do this is said to be *confined*. If a process can covertly establish such a channel with a process other than its caller, then this channel constitutes a *covert channel*. Covert channels exist in all forms of software and hardware systems, and there have been efforts to develop multilevel security systems that avoid this problem.

To summarize, a subliminal channel can be categorized as a covert channel, but the converse is not always the case. Subliminal channels are particular to cryptosystems.

# 10.3  The Prisoner's Problem of Gustavus Simmons

The work in analyzing the SALT II treaty compliance led to subsequent investigations on the negative impact of subliminal channels in digital signature algorithms. The *Prisoner's Problem*[4] clearly accentuates the hazards of digital signature algorithms [274]. In the Prisoner's Problem, Alice and Bob are two inmates who wish to coordinate a jailbreak. All of their communications must pass through a warden named Willy. If Willy sees any information that appears to be ciphertext and is not a valid digital signature, he does not forward it to the receiver. The problem that the prisoner faces is to devise a way to communicate with the other prisoner via digital signatures despite the fact that Willy will read everything and verify every digital signature. It is assumed that Willy is actively looking for misbehavior by the inmates and that he will refuse to forward invalid digital signatures. This prevents the prisoners from abusing their privileges by sending ciphertexts to each other. The problem is only regarded as being satisfactorily solved provided that the following two properties hold:

1. The subliminal channel algorithm can be made *public* without compromising Alice and Bob's ability to coordinate a jail break.

2. Willy can neither read information from the subliminal channel nor even detect that it is being used.

Property (1) eliminates simplistic solutions that are not secure. For example, suppose that before going to prison Alice and Bob agreed to use the following scheme to communicate. To send a subliminal message, the sender concocts an ASCII message such that the least significant bit in each sentence matches a bit in the subliminal message. This solution hides information from Willy by virtue of the fact Willy is not privy to it.[5] Using this solution is perilous since Willy may record every transmission and later discover the steganographic channel. The attack is actually a very simple form of *steganography*. A comprehensive treatise on steganographic methods was given by Johnson, Duric, and Jajodia [141].

---

[4]Note that this is distinct from the Prisoner's Dilemma in game theory that is described in Chapter 7.

[5]This is commonly referred to as *security by obscurity*.

Simmons presented the first acceptable solution to this problem. The solution assumes that Alice and Bob both know Alice's signing private key $x$ before they are sentenced. This solution is as follows.

1. The sender Alice generates an innocuous message to be signed.

2. Alice signs the innocuous message using $x$ with the modified signing algorithm in such a way that the subliminal message is encoded within the signature that is output.

3. The signature and innocuous message are given to the warden Willy.

4. Willy verifies the signature, and after finding nothing amiss, forwards the information along to Bob.

5. Bob verifies the signature and if it is valid, Bob assumes that the signature is authentic.

6. Bob then extracts the subliminal message from the signature using $x$.

The primary difference between this solution and the aforementioned steganographic solution is that even if Willy knows the particulars of the subliminal channel, he still cannot detect the use of the channel nor read from it since he does not know $x$.

**Definition 2** *A subliminal channel is a channel that exists within a cryptographic protocol, authentication system, digital signature algorithm, and so on, that transmits additional messages to a (special) receiver that is hidden, such that the messages cannot be read by other receivers (or a warden).*

## 10.4   Subliminal Channels New and Old

Simmons demonstrated subliminal channels in the ElGamal and Schnorr digital signature algorithms [275]. The following is the subliminal channel he found in ElGamal. Let $m'$ *mod* $p-1$ be the subliminal message that Alice wants to send to Bob. It is required that $m'$ and $p-1$ be relatively prime. To sign the innocuous message $m$, Alice calculates the signature value $r = g^{m'} \bmod p$. The signature on $m$ is the pair of values $(r, s)$ where $s$ is computed as in equation 10.1.

$$s = m'^{-1}(H(m) - xr) \bmod p - 1 \qquad (10.1)$$

Bob recovers $m'$ by computing $m' = s^{-1}(H(m) - xr) \bmod p - 1$. Note that $x$ is required to recover $m'$. Clearly a sufficient portion of $m'$ must be randomly chosen, otherwise the warden could guess $m'$ and compute $x$. This would not only expose the use of the subliminal channel, but also its contents and Alice's private signing key.

## 10.4.1   The Legendre Channel of Gus Simmons

Simmons proposed a couple of narrowband channels. In this subsection a narrowband channel of Simmons will be described that is based on quadratic residuosity. It solves the Prisoner's Problem and does not require Alice to divulge her private signing key to Bob. This channel is suitable for numerous discrete-log based signature algorithms and it was described by attacking DSA in particular [277, 278].

In this attack, Alice and Bob both agree on 14 distinct large prime numbers $p_1, p_2, ..., p_{14}$ prior to being arrested. Each of these primes is greater than $q$. This channel has a bandwidth of 14 bits[6] per DSA signature. Let $m = m_1 m_2 \cdots m_{14}$ be the 14 bits that Alice wants to send to Bob subliminally. To send the message $m$, Alice repeatedly chooses $k$ in the Digital Signature Algorithm (see Appendix C.2.7) and then calculates the signature value $r$ until the following is satisfied:

$$L(r/p_i) = 1 \Leftrightarrow m_i = 1 \ \text{ for } \ i = 1, 2, 3, ..., 14 \qquad (10.2)$$

Bob can recover $m$ in a straightforward fashion. Bob applies Euler's criterion to $r \bmod p_i$ and knows that $m_i = 1$ if and only if $L(r/p_i) = 1$.

The 14 primes should each be greater than $q$ for the following reason. For simplicity consider the one bit channel that uses $p_1$ to leak one subliminal bit. If $p_1$ is large (e.g., 128 bits in length) but is still less than

---

[6]The bandwidth can be set to be a bit larger or smaller. In general the bandwidth is $O(log(log \ p))$ bits per signature.

$q$, then the following situation can occur. It is possible that $k$ will be chosen such that $r = (g^k \bmod p) \bmod q$ is evenly divisible by $p_1$. In this case, $r \bmod p_1 = 0$. It follows that $r$ is neither a quadratic residue nor a quadratic non-residue modulo $p_1$. Hence, certain values for $r$ would never be output by a digital signature device that utilizes this channel. By making $p_1 > q$ this situation cannot occur.

It is important to consider the expected running time of the Legendre channel. Since finding a suitable $k$ for a particular subliminal message is a randomized process, the running time can be estimated by considering the probability of finding a suitable $k$ for a given 14-bit message. This is a tricky point to analyze formally. One would expect that a randomly chosen $k$ in DSA will lead to an $r = (g^k \bmod p) \bmod q$ that is a quadratic residue modulo $p_i$ with probability $1/2$. This results from the fact that half of the elements in $p_i$ are quadratic residues. Under this assumption, a value $k$ will be able to leak a particular message with probability about $2^{-14}$. Another potential issue is the probability distribution over $r$ that is induced by the probability distribution over the message space. For communications to be subliminal, the attacked values for $r$ must be indistinguishable from the values for $r$ that result when $k$ is chosen uniformly at random. For the one bit version of this channel that uses only $p_1$, the values for $r$ will be indistinguishable from the ones that result from choosing $k$ uniformly at random. This follows from a theorem due to Seysen if the $r$'s are not squares over the Reals [133].

It has been assumed that DSA was designed to be a signature algorithm that is hard to abuse in the sense that it could not be used directly as a public-key system, a key exchange system, or as any system providing for confidential information exchange (see [284]). Therefore, it was surprising that Simmons found a channel in it with a bandwidth of 14 bits. If this subliminal channel were employed in a device used to verify the SALT II treaty, it would be capable of leaking the exact identity of each silo. This observation, therefore, destroys the logic behind letting the Russians choose their own cryptographic algorithm for the device for the purpose of learning more about Russian cryptography.

Simmons showed that if Alice's relationship with her accomplice has not gone south then she can use this channel to give her private key to Bob. After doing so she can utilize a channel much like the one described in Section 10.4 to establish a higher bandwidth channel with Bob. In this method the 160-bit DSA private key $x$ is divided into 16 blocks with each block consisting of 10 bits. Four bits are used to identify each of the 16 different blocks and 10 bits are used to display the contents of a given block. Since the aforementioned channel has a bandwidth of 14 bits, it can be used to leak a block and the index for the block. This can be accomplished by letting $m_1, m_2, ..., m_{10}$ be the contents of the block and letting $m_{11}, m_{12}, m_{13}, m_{14}$ be the index. So, at a bare minimum, 16 digital signatures are needed to leak an entire DSA private key.

Some algorithm is needed to choose which block to leak in a given DSA signature. An obvious approach is to choose a block uniformly at random. This approach is ideal when the DSA signing algorithm is implemented in a smart card device that has limited or otherwise restricted non-volatile memory. (This would prevent the device from cycling through the 16 blocks in order.) Given this randomized block selection approach, a natural question to ask is how many signatures on average will be required to convey Alice's private key in its entirety. As it turns out, the number of such signatures is dictated by the first moment of the *Coupon Collector's Problem* [102].

The Coupon Collector's Problem is as follows. Each time a customer buys groceries, the customer is given a coupon that is selected uniformly at random from all $N$ possible types of coupons. If a customer wants to obtain at least one of each possible type of coupon, how many times must the customer go grocery shopping on average? It turns out that the expected number of times is $N \log N$. So, in the case of leaking the DSA private key $x$, Alice could expect to have to give Bob $16 \log 16 = 64$ digital signatures. The applicability of the Coupon Collector's Problem to subliminal channels was noted in a kleptographic attack on black-box symmetric ciphers [340].

The ability to leak private keys as such has extremely important implications for smart card security. *It brings into question the wisdom behind implementing cryptography in hardware.* If DSA were implemented in a tamper-resistant device and this attack were carried out, then the manufacturer of the device could obtain the DSA private keys of anyone who uses the device. The attack is not robust against reverse engineering, since knowledge of the 14 primes implies knowledge of the private keys. But the attack nonetheless demonstrates the feasibility of creating effective subliminal channels out of thin air.

An approach to foiling this is to prevent Alice from having the luxury of choosing $k$ explicitly. By adding a trusted entity to the signature process, a protocol can be devised that prevents Alice from choosing $k$ explicitly. In the scenario of the Prisoner's Problem, the signer and the warden jointly generate the signature by having each person contribute to the randomness in the signature [276, 279]. A complication in this approach is due to the fact that the prisoner who constructs the signature can simply halt, thereby not computing a signature and converying a single bit [90].

## 10.4.2    The Oracle Channel

In Subsection 10.4.1, the probability that a random $k$ allows the 14-bit subliminal message to be leaked was argued to be $2^{-14}$. This assumption is clearly number theoretic in nature. One of the reasons that this analysis is complicated is as follows. Consider the 1-bit channel that uses $p_1$. For it to be the case that with probability $1/2$ a randomly chosen $k$ leads to an $r$ that is a quadratic residue modulo $p_1$, it is required that half of the values in $\mathbb{Z}_q$ be quadratic residues modulo $p_1$. Now consider the case in which the channel is extended to 14 primes. In this case, the event that $r$ is a quadratic residue modulo $p_1$ and the event that the same $r$ is a quadratic residue modulo $p_2$ are not independent.

A further issue to consider is that of computational efficiency. The Legendre symbol of $r$ must be computed modulo each $p_i$ to determine if $r$ leaks the desired subliminal message. Using Euler's Criterion, numerous modular exponentiations must be computed for each signature $(r, s)$ that contains a subliminal message.

Aside from these very minor technicalities, it is natural to ask why the Legendre channel works. This question is perhaps best answered by analyzing it a bit more closely. Let *LegendreChannel* denote the function that is used to decide if $r$ subliminally leaks $m_1, m_2, ..., m_{14}$ using the secret primes $p_1, p_2, ..., p_{14} > q$. Hence, this function is a boolean predicate that may be computed by running Euler's Criterion 14 times and checking the results.

$$LegendreChannel(r, (m_1, m_2, ..., m_{14}), (p_1, p_2, ..., p_{14})) = 0 \ or \ 1 \quad (10.3)$$

When *LegendreChannel* outputs 1 then $r$ leaks the 14-bit subliminal message. The inputs are a publicly displayed value $r$, a subliminal message, and a secret key in the form of 14 distinct primes. Clearly the space for $r$ and the key space should be large to make the channel secure. This brute-force channel works well for short messages due to the elbowroom in choosing $r$.

Horster, Michels, and Petersen proposed a narrowband channel that uses a One-time pad [133]. The 14-bit version of this channel will now be described. In this channel, Alice and Bob share a randomly chosen 14-bit string $b_1, b_2, ..., b_{14}$. The 14-bit subliminal message is XORed with this bit string and the resulting 14-bit Vernam ciphertext is displayed in the 14 least significant bits of $r$. Hence, $k$ is repeatedly chosen until the 14 least significant bits of $r$ happen to match this Vernam ciphertext. The predicate for this channel, which is named after Horst et al, is given below.

$$HMP(r, (m_1, m_2, ..., m_{14}), (b_1, b_2, ..., b_{14})) = 0 \ or \ 1 \qquad (10.4)$$

When $HMP$ returns 1, the 14 least significant bits of $r$ is the Vernam ciphertext of the 14-bit subliminal message. The subliminal message is recovered by decrypting the Vernam ciphertext using the One-time pad $b_1, b_2, ..., b_{14}$. Strictly speaking, this channel is not secure if it is used more than once.

A new channel will now be presented that extends the Simmons and Horster et al narrowband channels. It is based on the observation that a large space for $r$ is required as well as a large key space. The channel is as follows. A random oracle $R$ is chosen randomly and is used in the attack. As in Simmons' original attack, the parameter $k$ is repeatedly chosen until an $r$ is found that leaks the subliminal message. Let $S$ be a randomly chosen secret seed. For concreteness let $S$ be a 160-bit quantity. The value $S$ is analogous to the 14 primes in the Simmons attack. The predicate for the Oracle Channel is as follows.

$$OracleChannel(r, (m_1, m_2, ..., m_{14}), S) = 0 \ or \ 1 \qquad (10.5)$$

In the attack, the device repeatedly chooses $k$, computes $r$, and then computes the above predicate. The attack ceases when the predicate returns 1. The final values for $k$ and $r$ are the ones used in computing the digital signature that is output. The predicate is instantiated by computing $R(S||r)$ and taking the first 14 output bits of the oracle. If these 14 bits match $m_1, m_2, ..., m_{14}$ exactly, then the predicate returns 1. Upon obtaining $r$, the attacker need only take the first 14 output bits of $R(S||r)$ to recover $m_1, m_2, ..., m_{14}$.

It is instructive to consider the security of this channel. Suppose that the channel is being used in a black-box environment and that the user suspects that the device is using this channel to leak secrets. From the perspective of the device designer, the user is a distinguishing adversary that wants to be able to distinguish honest devices from those that use the subliminal channel. A worst-case scenario is one in which the device always leaks the same 14-bit message, and one in which the adversary supplies the key pair to the device and analyzes the resulting DSA signatures $(r, s)$. Note that given $x$ and $(y, g, p)$ it is straightforward to recover $k$ from $(r, s)$. So, the distinguishing adversary has access to every value for $k$ that the device uses in the signatures that it outputs.

The security parameter in DSA is 160, the number of bits in $q$. To try to distinguish, the poly-time adversary can obtain a set of signatures that has a cardinality that is polynomial in $k$. Given the limited number of outputs that are created, the likelihood that the device will generate a given value for $k$ more than once is very small. Hence, the oracle inputs will likely be distinct. This means that the oracle outputs will likely be chosen in an independent fashion. Since there are an exponential in 160 number of values for $k$ that can be used to leak a given 14-bit message, it is not hard to see that the distinguishing adversary cannot distinguish. This approach is applicable to the ElGamal Legendre channel as well as the DSA Legendre channel.

### 10.4.3  Subliminal Card Marking

Another early result on subliminal leakage of information was a subliminal attack on a cryptographic poker game protocol. Rivest, Shamir, and Adleman suggested the scheme. It utilizes a box-locking primitive based on the RSA algorithm. In the scheme Alice and Bob know the factorization of a large number $N$. Alice chooses an exponent $K$ randomly mod $\phi(N)$ such that $K$ is relatively prime to $\phi(N)$. She uses $K$ as the RSA exponent to lock cards from a virtual deck of cards in a box (by exponentiation mod $N$ with the exponent $K$). Let $E_K(M)$ denote the box-locking primitive applied to card $M$. She can unlock a box using the inverse of $K$ mod $\phi(N)$. As long as she does not give $K$ to Bob, the contents of the box is secured. Note that this primitive constitutes a commutative symmetric cipher. Bob can lock the box received from Alice, and give the result to Alice, which Alice can unlock. However, in this case Alice cannot read the contents of the box without Bob performing the unlocking procedure to reverse his locking computation. This commutative property is necessary to play this version of mental poker (for example, over the phone).

However, in 1980 Richard Lipton observed that if $M$ is a perfect square modulo $N$, then so is $E_K(M)$. The encryption primitive therefore preserves quadratic residues. In a paper by DeMillo and Merrit it was shown how this primitive can be used to mark cards $M$ [83]. For example, a player who initially encrypts $M$ has an advantage in identifying/ruling out encrypted cards by determining quadratic residuosity modulo $N$ of locked cards in which the player does not know the contents. Though this attack doesn't uniquely identify marked cards, it does give an unfair advantage to those who employ it, and may help a player cheat and win in the long run. It is clear that this attack, in some sense, constitutes a subliminal channel with a bandwidth between 0 bits and 1 bit (knowledge of the factors of $N$ is needed to use this channel).

### 10.4.4   The Newton Channel

Work on finding new subliminal channels has continued as demonstrated by the discovery of the Newton channel [7]. The following is a description of this channel. Let $p = qm+1$ be prime, and let $q$ be prime. Furthermore, assume that $m$ is a smooth integer and that $g$ generates $\mathbb{Z}_p^*$. For security it is assumed that computing discrete logs in the group generated by $g^m$ is hard. Let $c$ be the message that is to be subliminally leaked. To display $c$ in an exponentiation mod $p$ using base $g$, a value $k' \bmod (p-1)/m$ is chosen randomly, and then $k$ is solved for in $k = c+k'm \bmod p-1$. Hence,

$$k \equiv c \bmod m \qquad (10.6)$$

The user then publishes $r = g^k \bmod p$ in the usual way. For example, this could be the value $r$ in an ElGamal digital signature. The value $c$ can be computed by anyone by solving for $z$ in the following equation.

$$(g^q)^z \equiv r^q \bmod p \qquad (10.7)$$

The value $z$ can be found since the order of the subgroup of $\mathbb{Z}_p^*$ generated by $g^q$ is a smooth integer. Let $B$ be the largest prime in $m$ (i.e., its smoothness). Using the Pohlig-Hellman algorithm [224] and Pollard's Rho algorithm [227] this requires time $O(B^{1/2})$. It then follows that,

$$c \equiv z \ mod \ m \qquad (10.8)$$

Observe that this is in fact a broadcast channel since everyone is capable of computing $c$. The Newton channel can be modified to address this issue. This is done by replacing $q$ with two different primes $q_1$ and $q_2$, having the sender and receiver a priori secretly share the signing private key mod $q_2$, and having the sender keep the signing key mod $q_1$ private [7]. This, however, requires a more specialized form for the factorization of $p-1$ and may result in reducing the security of the underlying system.

So what can be done to minimize the threat of malware that exploits the Newton channel? Fortunately, the elimination of this particular channel is not difficult. By basing cryptosystems on a prime order subgroup of $\mathbb{Z}_p^*$, this particular channel can be eliminated. DSA is a perfect example of a cryptosystem that is immune to this threat.

## 10.4.5   Subliminal Channel in Composites

Yvo Desmedt noted that it is possible to choose half of the bits of the product of two primes explicitly when one is free to choose any two large prime numbers [89]. In Crypto '96 it was shown that this channel can be used by malicious software to compromise RSA key geneartion [333]. Also, a number of recent papers address the generation of RSA moduli with a predetermined portion [145, 172].

One approach to displaying data in the bit representation of the modulus $n$ is as follows. Suppose that $n$ is required to be a $W$-bit composite that is the product of two $W/2$-bit primes $p$ and $q$. Let $M$ be a $W/2$ bit integer. Hence, $M$ is $W/2$ bits long and the most significant bit is 1. The goal is to display $M$ in the bit representation of $n$ that is being randomly generated.

$DisplayM(M)$:
input: a $W/2$-bit subliminal message $M$
output: two $W/2$-bit primes $p$ and $q$
1. set $W = 2|M|$
2. generate a random $W/2$-bit string $RND$

3. set $n_1 = M\|RND$
4. generate a random $W/2$-bit prime $p$
5. solve for quotient $q$ and remainder $r$ in $n_1 = pq + r$
6. if $q$ is not a $W/2$-bit integer or if $q < 2^{W/2-1} + 1$ then goto step 2
7. if $q$ is composite then goto step 2
8. output $(p, q)$ and halt

The quotient $q$ and remainder $r$ are computed by performing division. In many cases $M$ will appear in unaltered form in the $W/2$ upper order bits of $n = pq = n_1 - r$. However, sometimes the subtraction of $r$ will cause a borrow bit to be taken from $M$ in the upper order bits. In this case $M - 1$ is displayed in the upper order bits. The subliminal message $M$ can easily be recovered in either case. Ideally $M$ should be chosen in a pseudorandom fashion, since fixing it may give rise to a weak composite that might be easily factorable. There are variations on this approach to displaying subliminal information in composites $n = pq$.

Kilian and Leighton showed how to exploit this channel to subvert a factoring based key escrow system [155]. This applies, for instance, to a PKI that is based on RSA. In such a key escrow system the users are forced to escrow their RSA private keys in order to be registered into the PKI. However, the subliminal channel in composites allows rogue users to subliminally display composites $n'$ that have unescrowed private keys within composites that have escrowed private keys. More specifically, the public modulus $n'$ of a rogue user can be displayed within the upper half of the bits in the bit representation of his or her own legitimate public modulus $n$ (see Figure 10.1). The security parameter of $n'$ is half of the value of the security parameter of $n$. When such rogue users collude, they can establish an unescrowed PKI that benefits from the certification performed in the legitimate infrastructure, since CA signatures on the legitimate composites are also signatures on the rogue composites.

This form of abuse has been dubbed *shadow public key* abuse. A shadow public key is a public key that is displayed within the bits of a legitimate public key. Note, however, that if an RSA shadow public key

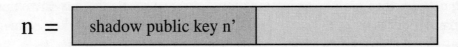

**Figure 10.1** Shadow public key attack on composites

is displayed within a legitimate composite then its security parameter will be half that of the security parameter of the legitimate composite.

A coalition of rogue users can always go outside of the system to defeat a key escrow infrastructure. However, one can envision a scenario in which a totalitarian government persecutes all persons that establish rogue certification authorities that certify unescrowed keys. In such a situation the shadow public key attack subverts the totalitarian PKI and uses it to securely distribute shadow public keys.

## 10.5   The Impact of Subliminal Channels on Key Escrow

The applications of subliminal channels have expanded significantly over the years. Using subliminal channels it was shown how to implement an RSA based key escrow system using smart card devices in a way that is transparent[7] to the end user [333]. The information needed by the key recovery agent to recover the private key of a user is encoded within the upper order bits of the public key itself and cannot be obfuscated by the user without ruining the public key. In other words, the user cannot publish the public key without publishing the means for the key recovery agent to recover the user's RSA private key. By way of a subliminal channel, the two pieces of information are inseparable. The public key is digitally signed by a device-specific signing private key contained within the device. So, the device outputs three values to the user: a public key, the corresponding private key, and a signature on the public key. The user is registered into the PKI if and only if a public key is given to the CA along with a valid signature on the public key. The signature on the public key proves that the public key was generated by the hardware device. The upper order bits of the public key is an asymmetric ciphertext that when decrypted by the key escrow authorities reveals a prime divisor of the RSA public modulus of the user.

This hardware based key escrow solution seemed so close to being the solution to software key escrow, yet no cigar. The problem is that it requires hardware. The private signing key in the device has to remain private otherwise users can forge unescrowed key pairs. The key element that was missing was a *proof* that the private key is escrowed.

---

[7]That is, it is as protocol-efficient as an unescrowed PKI.

The software key escrow problem had received a lot of attention [155, 192, 193, 246] and was the subject of a fair amount of controversy. The *fair cryptosystem* approach of Micali could be implemented completely in software, but requires that each user secretly shares his or her private key in a publicly verifiable fashion among a set of key escrow authorities. So, it is required that the user perform more protocol interaction than in the case of an unescrowed public key infrastructure. It seemed that if the hardware based key escrow system from Crypto '96 could be modified so that the device creates a single non-interactive zero-knowledge proof[8] that the private key is properly escrowed, then a more efficient protocol for software key escrow could be made.

This, in fact, turned out to be the case. It was shown that by having the user construct such a proof, the problem of software key escrow is solved [328, 337]. The key escrow solution utilizes a technique that is often referred to as *verifiable encryption* [108, 291]. The public keys of the key recovery authorities are used in constructing the non-interactive proof that in itself constitutes a ciphertext that encrypts the private key of the user. The non-interactive proof shows in zero-knowledge that the plaintext is in fact the private key of the user, and is hence recoverable by the key escrow authorities. This proof has been referred to as a *certificate of recoverability*.

The basic idea is to make entry into the public key infrastructure contingent upon providing a public key and corresponding proof of escrow to the certification authority (CA). In other words, each user is forced to escrow his or her own private key, otherwise the user will not be issued a digital certificate from the CA. The CA signs the public key if and only if the public key and proof are valid. The key escrow authorities can recover the user's private key from the public key and proof alone. In this respect, the key escrow solution does not require tamper-resistance and maintains transparency with respect to the end user. It is transparent since the certificate of recoverabilty can be sent to the CA along with the public key. The user can obtain the public key of the escrow authorities from the CA, for instance. As a result, the user never has to interact directly with the key escrow authorities.

This approach differs from the fair cryptosystem approach in a critical way: in fair cryptosystems, the user splits his or her private key into shares and gives them to the escrow authorities in a verifiable fashion, whereas in a solution based on certificates of recoverability the escrow

---

[8]In the form of a small data file (that is, a non-interactive zero-knowledge proof).

authorities generate shares of a private key, compute the corresponding public key, and have the users use the public key to construct certificates of recoverability.[9]

Numerous other verifiable encryption algorithms have been shown that mention certificates of recoverability as a particular application [11, 49, 217, 232, 264, 273]. To date, the notion of certificates of recoverability have caught on in the scientific community but has yet to make its way into the industry. In retrospect, subliminal channels were an essential step in the discovery of a protocol-efficient solution to the software key escrow problem.

Another approach to efficient key escrow has recently been proposed by Franklin and Boneh [36]. The solution is based on the notion of an identity-based cryptosystem [269]. In the Franklin-Boneh system, the public key of a user can be computed by anyone given publicly available information about the user such as name, social security number, date of birth, and so on. A set of trusted authorities computes the private key of the user and sends the private key to the user. The private key is escrowed until these authorities decide to take it out of escrow.

This system is remarkable since it is essentially certificate-free. However, some form of key revocation mechanism is needed if the private key is ever compromised. The solution differs from systems that utilize certificates of recovery since the recovery authorities must actively compute and transmit the private key for each new user. In a scheme based on certificates of recoverability, the key recovery authorities remain off-line until an actual recovery is needed. The Franklin-Boneh scheme is secure against chosen ciphertext attacks in the random oracle model assuming an elliptic curve variant of the computational Diffie-Hellman problem. The system is based on the Weil pairing [144].

---

[9]The exact algorithm varies depending on whether it is an ElGamal-based or RSA-based solution.

# Chapter 11

# SETUP Attack on Factoring Based Key Generation

The notion of black-box hardware and software and the hazards associated with them are familiar to everyone. For example, when a user installs a new commercial program there is no easy way to find out if the program is sending personal information across the Internet back to the manufacturer. Such information could include personal e-mail addresses, the name of the user's Internet service provider, what type of machine the user is using, and so on. The fear is that there might be an invasion of privacy that could among other things lead to aggressive marketing. Hardware implementations of algorithms are even more black-box in nature since the silicon housing hides the underlying circuitry.

When cryptosystems are implemented in a black-box fashion this fear is magnified tenfold. In a worst-case scenario the cryptosystem could be sending the user's secret keys back to the manufacturer. This could allow the manufacturer to do such things as decrypt the user's communications, sign documents on behalf of the user, or even gain unlawful access to the user's machine. This chapter addresses this threat by exploring ways of designing cryptotrojans that to do exactly this, in spades.

In the pages that follow, a set of attacks are presented that are specifically designed to attack black-box key generation algorithms that generate factoring based keys. Such key generation algorithms are used to generate private keys for RSA, Rabin, Goldwasser-Micali, and other public key cryptosystems [117, 237, 245]. The first set of attacks are simplistic in nature and have varying degrees of security. Drawbacks to these solutions are presented that relate to the threat of reverse engineering and that affect the security of the attacks. The chapter concludes with an improved cryptotrojan attack that does not suffer from these drawbacks. It is a kleptographic attack that applies cryptography within the cryptographic key generation algorithm to securely undermine the integrity of the device. The cryptotrojan leaks private keys to the attacker securely and subliminally through the seemingly honest output of the black-box device. The attack is secure from the attacker's perspective based on the assumed intractability of factoring. The proof of security is in the random oracle model (see Appendix B.4).

The threat of advanced kleptographic attacks is an extremely important consideration when insider attacks are possible. A cryptotrojan can be inserted into a fraction of all the black-box devices that are produced. This implies that spot reverse engineering checks, that is, choosing devices randomly and checking for the presence of cryptotrojans, will not always work since some of the devices are honest. This issue is even worse when the devices are tamper-resistant. Such chips are the epitome of black-boxes since they are designed to hide the internals from well-funded and dedicated adversaries.

Designing cryptographic devices to be tamper-resistant is an involved science and the security afforded by such devices is an active area of research [8, 10]. Tamper-resistant cryptographic microchips have been endorsed by the U.S. government, namely, in the Clipper chip and Capstone technology. The Clipper and Capstone technologies have been offered as next generation hardware-protected key escrow devices. Even software implementations can be perceived as black-boxes when users refuse to analyze the code at the assembly language level. Simply verifying a digital signature on code in no way proves that the code is free of backdoors.

This chapter is likely to be of interest to companies that manufacture smart cards and organizations that rely on smart cards for sensitive applications. It demonstrates clearly how an insider who has control of cryptographic designs or implementations can benefit from carrying out insider attacks with minimal loss of overall security. Also, this chapter is important to users who wish to use mix networks securely. When a cryptotrojan is used to generate the keys for a mix network, the author of the Trojan is often in a position to trace the flow of messages throughout the network.

Since black-box cryptosystems are central to the security of the attacks in this chapter, the definition of a black-box cryptosystem needs to be spelled out. The definition of a black-box cryptosystem incorporates the notion of efficiently computable functions and thus addresses the issue of computational complexity. Also, it captures ideas from electrical engineering since it makes the worst-case assumption that the black-box has non-volatile memory.

**Definition 3** *A* **black-box cryptosystem** *is an efficient probabilistic algorithm[1] that has readable and writable non-volatile memory. In other words, it has access to a fair coin and can store variables across multiple invocations. Furthermore, the algorithm and memory are not externally accessible. Only the input and output of the cryptosystem is accessible.*

Note that whereas a manufacturer may claim that a given microchip does not contain non-volatile memory cells, it may nevertheless contain non-volatile memory. Manufacturers could easily *lie* in this regard. The availability of non-volatile memory has a significant impact on the types of cryptotrojan attacks that can be carried out within the device, since it allows a Trojan to store values across multiple invocations of the device.

## 11.1   Honest Composite Key Generation

The key generation algorithm *GenPrivatePrimes*1 described below may be used to generate the primes $p$ and $q$ for RSA private keys, Rabin private keys, Goldwasser-Micali private keys, and so on. However, it does not check that $gcd(e, (p-1)(q-1)) = 1$ as in the case of RSA key generation. This check can be easily added. Most composite key generation algorithms output composite integers of even bit length. Typical lengths are 768, 1024, and 2048 bits. For simplicity *GenPrivatePrimes*1 will only generate $W/2$-bit primes such that $W$ is evenly divisible by 2. $W$ should be 768 or greater to provide a suitable setting for the factoring problem. It is a simple matter to multiply these two primes to derive the public key $n = pq$. The Appendices cover the notation and underlying algorithms that are used.

*RandomBitString*1():
input: none
output: random $W/2$-bit string
1. generate a random $W/2$-bit string *str*
2. output *str* and halt

---

[1]That is, a probabilistic poly-time Turing machine that may or may not utilize the random tape.

*GenPrivatePrimes1()*:

input: none

output: $W/2$-bit primes $p$ and $q$ such that $p \neq q$ and $|pq| = W$

1. for $j = 0$ to $\infty$ do:
2.     $p = RandomBitString1()$ /* at this point p is a random string */
3.     if $p \geq 2^{W/2-1} + 1$ and $p$ is prime then break
4. for $j = 0$ to $\infty$ do:
5.     $q = RandomBitString1()$
6.     if $q \geq 2^{W/2-1} + 1$ and $q$ is prime then break
7. if $|pq| < W$ or $p = q$ then goto step 1
8. if $p > q$ then interchange the values $p$ and $q$
9. set $S = (p, q)$
10. output $S$, zeroize all values in memory, and halt

Also, note that there are some elements of the ANSI C programming language in this program [154]. Text that appears between /* and */ are programmer's comments and *break* causes control to exit the innermost loop. The keyword *continue* sends control to the beginning of the next iteration of the innermost loop. Testing for primality can be performed in deterministic polynomial-time [5]. A feel for how long this algorithm will take to run can be determined using Chernoff bounds and the Prime Number Theorem (see Appendix B.2).

Observe that a $K$-bit string can have leading zeros. A $K$-bit positive integer must have a most significant bit equal to 1. The product of two $K$-bit positive binary integers with $K > 1$ is either a $2K$ bit integer or a $2K - 1$ bit integer. To see this, note that $2^{K-1}$ is the smallest $K$-bit integer. $2^{K-1}$ squared is $2^{2K-2}$, which is $2K - 1$ bits long. Also, note that $2^K - 1$ is the largest $K$-bit positive integer. $2^K - 1$ squared is $2^{2K} - 2^{K+1} + 1$, which is a $2K$ bit integer. So, in this algorithm it is entirely possible that $W/2$ bit primes $p$ and $q$ will be chosen such that $|pq| < W$ bits.

## 11.2  Weak Backdoor Attacks on Composite Key Generation

There exist several Trojan horse attacks on composite key generation. Those presented in this section are all rather simplistic in nature and have varying degrees of security. They are classic attacks in some sense since they are intuitively obvious to any cryptographer. However, none of them is as secure from the attacker's perspective as a secretly embedded trapdoor attack. They are useful to study since they exemplify important properties that a secure cryptotrojan attack against a cryptosystem should exhibit.

## 11.2.1  Using a Fixed Prime

An attacker can change the design so that the prime $p$ is fixed and known to the attacker, or an attacker can append a Trojan horse to the program that deletes $p$ after $GenPrivatePrimes1$ is called and that substitutes the fixed prime $p$. In this case the function $GenPrivatePrimes1$ may have to be invoked anew if $|pq| < W$, and so on. Either way, since $p$ is known to the attacker, the attacker can factor every public key that is generated. The modified algorithm is given below.

$GenPrivatePrimes2()$:
input: none
output: $W/2$-bit primes $p$ and $q$ such that $p \neq q$ and $|pq| = W$
1. for $j = 0$ to $\infty$ do:
2.      $q = RandomBitString1()$
3.      if $q \geq 2^{W/2-1} + 1$ and $q$ is prime then break
4. if $|pq| < W$ or $p = q$ then goto step 1
5. if $p > q$ then interchange the values $p$ and $q$
6. set $S = (p, q)$
7. output $S$, zeroize all values in memory, and halt

The rationale behind this attack is that since $q$ is chosen randomly, the modulus will look random to the casual observer. This is important since the modulus $n = pq$ will be made public, for example, by being placed in a digital certificate. An important consideration is that a user is often in a position to learn each of the primes $p$ and $q$ corresponding to his or her own public key. This holds true in the case of software key pairs that are stored in personal information exchange[2] files, for instance. However, this is not always the case for private keys that are generated and used in smart cards. If the user has access to $(n, e, d)$ where $ed = 1 \; mod \; (p-1)(q-1)$ then a well-known[3] probabilistic algorithm can be used to efficiently factor $n$. From the attacker's perspective it is always safest to assume the worst,

---

[2]For example, stored according to RSA's PKCS #12 format.
[3]Figure 4.10 in Stinson details the factoring algorithm that works given the decryption exponent [293].

and that is that $p$ and $q$ will be known to the key owner. This has the following properties:

1. *The attack is detectable*: One need only hypothesize that the attack is being carried out, obtain two moduli $n$ that are output by the device, and compute their greatest common divisor. This value will be $p$ and it will divide both moduli evenly. Note that this detection method will work even if the key owner does not have access to his or her own private key.

2. *The attack is breakable without reverse engineering*: The Euclidean algorithm can be run on two different moduli $n$ and as a result the prime $p$ can be found. So, the device need not even be reverse engineered to break the attack.

3. *The attack doesn't exhibit forward secrecy vs. reverse engineers*: In an ideal situation, the reverse engineer who recovers the algorithm and its current state should not be able to determine the previous prime numbers that the device computed. Since $p$ is revealed to the reverse engineer, this is not the case.

There are numerous variations on this attack. For example, the public modulus $n$ can be generated so that it can be factored more easily than normal. For example, $n$ could be the product of a 512-bit prime and two 256-bit primes. Again, this gives the attacker no significant advantage over other users since anyone can factor such moduli.

## 11.2.2    Using a Pseudorandom Function

The problem of detectability in the attack described in Subsection 11.2.1 can be avoided by using pseudorandom values instead of random values and having the initial seed known only to the device and the attacker. In the jargon of Turing machines, this means that the algorithm will take its randomness from a pseudorandom Turing machine tape rather than from a truly random tape. Since the pseudorandom tape is polynomially indistinguishable from a truly random tape, the sampled primes will be indistinguishable as well. It makes sense for the attacker to use a pseudorandomness primitive that is predicated on the difficulty of factoring. This way, both of the composites that are generated and the rogue pseudorandom primitive used to compute the primes will rely on the same intractability assumption. Basing the primitive on the discrete logarithm problem would make the attack rely on two potentially different intractability assumptions.

One of the goals of using pseudorandom values is to prevent the backdoor from being exploited by anyone other than the attacker. To those familiar with cryptographic primitives, it may be tempting to utilize a pseudorandom function to accomplish this goal. For example, consider the following approach. The pseudorandom function $F$ is used in the device along with a secret string $ID$ [113, 114]. The string $ID$ should be sufficiently long. For simplicity assume that $|ID| = 160$. The $ID$s for the devices should be chosen randomly, subject to the constraint that they all be unique. The function $F$ is publicly known. Recall that $F(ID, x)$ is indistinguishable from a random value, where $ID$ is secret and $x$ is a public index. The pseudorandom bit stream is formed by invoking $F$ with $x = 1, 2, 3, ....$ The index $x$ is stored in non-volatile memory within the device. Hence, the pseudorandom bit stream is $F(ID, 1)||F(ID, 2)||F(ID, 3)|| \cdots$.

So, why does the attacker have an advantage? Well, observe that at most a polynomial[4] number of devices can be manufactured. So, there are a polynomial number of distinct values chosen from all possible 160-bit strings from the database of IDs that only the attacker knows. Without knowing this database, the complexity of guessing an ID correctly is exponential.

Though conceptually simple, this approach does not provide computational forward secrecy. For example, suppose that a reverse engineer opens the device and obtains $F$, $ID$, and $i = 117$. The reverse engineer can recover the previous pseudorandom bits by computing,

$$F(ID, 1)||F(ID, 2)|| \cdots ||F(ID, 117)$$

It is therefore imperative that the device forgets its past, which is not the case in this approach. So, this particular attack has the following properties.

1. *The attack is not detectable*: Even if a user hypothesizes that this exact attack is being carried out, its presence cannot be detected without knowing $ID$.

2. *The attack is not breakable without reverse engineering*: The pseudorandom bits that are used by the key generation algorithm are

---

[4]In some reasonable parameter.

indistinguishable from random ones without knowledge of $ID$. It follows that provided that the device is not successfully reverse engineered the attack is secure.

3. *The attack doesn't exhibit forward secrecy vs. reverse engineers*: In an ideal situation, the reverse engineer who recovers the algorithm and its current state should not be able to determine the previous prime numbers that the device computed. However, since $ID$ is revealed to the reverse engineer and since $x = 1, 2, 3, ...$, this is not the case.

The third drawback above is addressed in Subsection 11.2.3. The point of this subsection is not to argue that pseudorandom functions cannot be used to attack key generation in a desirable way. The point that is being made is that a *straightforward* use of them is not very desirable. What is needed is a mode of operation that is effectively memoryless. A memoryless mode of operation is one that prevents the reverse engineer from being able to determine previous inputs to the function.

## 11.2.3    Using a Pseudorandom Generator

A solid approach to attacking the composite private key generation algorithm is to use a pseudorandom number generator $G$ (see Subsection 3.5.2) and an initial seed. The attack will be illustrated using the Blum-Blum-Shub. Define $G$ to be a $(k, 2k)$-PRBG (see Subsection 3.5.2). Define $G_H(s)$ to be the $k$ most significant bits of $G(s)$ and define $G_L(s)$ to be the $k$ least significant bits of $G(s)$. Let $s_0$ be the randomly chosen $2k$-bit initial seed that is stored within the device and that is known to the attacker.

In this attack, the input values $s_i$ for $G$ are defined by $s_{i+1} = G_L(s_i)$ where $i = 0, 1, 2, ....$ The pseudorandom bit stream that the device uses to compute private keys is defined by $G_H(s_0)||G_H(s_1)||G_H(s_2)|| \cdots$. When the algorithm outputs $(p, q)$ on a given invocation, only one seed $s_i$ is stored in non-volatile memory. Previous seeds are erased and lost. It can be shown that the attack has the following properties.

1. *The attack is not detectable*: Even if a user hypothesizes that this exact attack is being carried out, its presence cannot be detected without knowing one of the seeds.

2. *The attack is not breakable without reverse engineering*: The pseudorandom bits that are used by the key generation algorithm are indistinguishable from random ones without knowing one of the seeds. It follows that provided that the device is not successfully reverse engineered, the attack is secure.

3. *The attack exhibits forward secrecy vs. reverse engineers*: Consider the case that a reverse engineer is able to recover the algorithm and its current state. The reverse engineer will not be able to determine the previous prime numbers that the device computed. Doing so implies the ability to invert the pseudorandom generator $G$.

In practice it would not be wise to provide multiple devices with the same initial seed $s_0$. This would quite literally cause users to generate the same "random" private keys, and would not go unnoticed.

Another threat to the integrity of this attack exists that has not been addressed. Consider the possibility that a powerful engineer can effectively peer into the device, read its contents, and then repair it, replace it, or somehow guarantee that the device will appear to have been left untouched. FIPS-140 level 4 complaint smart cards are supposed to destroy the data they contain if the casing is breached. In theory, then, some form of non-intrusive reading method would be required for such smart cards. One cannot help but wonder if such a non-intrusive reading capability exists in the form of a sensitive instrument that measures a particular property of the physical device at runtime. If this were possible, then even this pseudorandom generator attack would not be secure. The powerful engineer would be able to learn the current seed and hence all future randomness that the device will employ. One can envision a covert operation in which the smart card belonging to an enemy is obtained, read, and then carried back to its place of origin. In this case all future randomness that the device will use would be known to the powerful engineer. This threat model begs the question as to whether a design exists that is secure against this threat. Such an attack is one that can be scrutinized by a reverse engineer and then be redeployed in a way that will remain secure against the reverse engineer.

Another weakness of the PRNG attack revolves around software implementations. Suppose that there exists an on-line server that generates key pairs and issues them to users. The code for the server may be digitally signed and the signature may be verified periodically. This implies that the reverse engineer cannot modify the code after successful reverse engineering without the modification being detected. In the case of the pseudorandom number generator attack, an archived core-dump would reveal an intermediate seed and hence compromise all subsequent private keys that are generated.

The remainder of this chapter describes a kleptographic attack that is robust against the exposure of intermediate seeding material. It is based on a result published in Crypto '96 [333]. The original approach focused on attacking software key generation implementations. The scheme was entitled PAP, meaning pretty-awful-privacy. This was a play on PGP, the well known pretty-good-privacy program that originally utilized RSA [343]. The goal in designing PAP was to come up with a cryptotrojan that could be deployed in a program like PGP that gave the Trojan horse writer an exclusive advantage: the ability to derive the private keys of all users. One of the tricky aspects of this approach is that the Trojan, which is in software, will be duplicated as is along with PGP. This prevents each instance of the Trojan from having unique identifiers. However, it seems that given this restriction it is difficult to arrive at cryptotrojan attacks with provably secure properties.

It has since become clear that the best way to approach the problem is to gear the attack towards hardware implementations such as smart cards. In this situation, secret seeding material can be used in the black-box environment to provide strong security guarantees. It is when the black-box is opened that the fail-safe aspects of the key generation attack take effect. It makes sense to study the problem this way, since it is then straightforward to weaken the black-box assumption to obtain a gray-box assumption. For lack of a better term, a gray-box may be regarded as a box that is difficult to look into but not impossible. A compiled program may be considered to be a gray box with respect to the average user. In so doing, the security against the successful reverse engineer in the black-box setting may be regarded as the security that is provided in the gray-box scenario. In software cryptotrojan attacks, the Trojan can search for a unique identifier in its host at run-time. For example, a fixed IP address or a guessable CPU ID can be used as an identifier. By doing this, a security analysis is formulated that accounts for both hardware and software security settings.

## 11.3    Probabilistic Bias Removal Method

One of the tools that will be needed for the kleptographic attack on composite key generation is what we call, for lack of a better term, the probabilistic bias removal method (PBRM). The method is reminiscent of the technique used to sample a set uniformly at random given a fair coin. The problem is as follows. Suppose that we have a value $x$ that is drawn uniformly at random from $\{0, 1, 2, ..., R-1\}$. Being kleptographers, we cannot display $x$ as such within the output of a cryptosystem since it is drawn from the wrong set. Suppose that the correct set to draw from uniformly at random is $\{0, 1, 2, ..., S-1\}$, where $S > R > \frac{S}{2}$. Since the correct set is a superset of the wrong set the value $x$ has in effect been drawn from the correct set, but using the wrong probability distribution. That is, $x$ will be one of $R, R+1, ..., S-1$ with probability zero. This bias towards the lower elements must be removed.

If we could somehow display $x$ in the form of a value $x'$ that is uniformly distributed in $\{0, 1, 2, ..., S-1\}$, then the modified version of $x$ will no longer look suspicious. It is required that the value $x$ be easily derivable from $x'$.

$PBRM(R, S, x)$:
input: $R$ and $S$ with $S > R > \frac{S}{2}$ and $x$ contained in $\{0, 1, 2, ..., R-1\}$
output: $e$ contained in $\{-1, 1\}$ and $x'$ contained in $\{0, 1, 2, ..., S-1\}$
1. set $e = 1$ and set $x' = 0$
2. choose a bit $b$ randomly
3. if $x < S - R$ and $b = 1$ then set $x' = x$
4. if $x < S - R$ and $b = 0$ then set $x' = S - 1 - x$
5. if $x \geq S - R$ and $b = 1$ then set $x' = x$
6. if $x \geq S - R$ and $b = 0$ then set $e = -1$
7. output $e$ and $x'$ and halt

The value $-1$ indicates *failure*. It is clear that $x$ is readily obtainable from $x'$. To see this note that $x = x'$ unless $x' \geq R$, in which case $x = S - 1 - x'$. Note that this is a Monte Carlo algorithm. If it fails, a new value for $x$ will have to be chosen.

**Lemma 1** *Let $S > R > \frac{S}{2}$, let $x$ be a value chosen uniformly at random from $\{0, 1, 2, ..., R-1\}$, and let $(e, x') = PBRM(R, S, x)$. If $e = 1$ then $x'$ is uniformly distributed in $\{0, 1, 2, ..., S-1\}$.*

**Proof** Define $E_1$ to be the event that $x < S - R$ and $b = 1$. Define $E_2$ to be the event that $x < S - R$ and $b = 0$. Define $E_3$ to be the event that $x \geq S - R$ and $b = 1$. Observe that the probability that a particular $x \in \{0, 1, 2, ..., R - 1\}$ is chosen is $\frac{1}{R}$.

$$Pr[E_1 \cup E_2 \cup E_3] = \frac{S - R}{2R} + \frac{S - R}{2R} + \frac{R - (S - R)}{2R} = \frac{S}{2R} \quad (11.1)$$

$$Pr[E_1 \cap (E_1 \cup E_2 \cup E_3)] = \frac{S - R}{2R} \quad (11.2)$$

$$Pr[E_2 \cap (E_1 \cup E_2 \cup E_3)] = \frac{S - R}{2R} \quad (11.3)$$

$$Pr[E_3 \cap (E_1 \cup E_2 \cup E_3)] = \frac{R - (S - R)}{2R} = \frac{2R - S}{2R} \quad (11.4)$$

Equations 11.1 through 11.4 give rise to the following three conditional probabilities.

$$Pr[E_1 \mid E_1 \cup E_2 \cup E_3] = \frac{\frac{S-R}{2R}}{\frac{S}{2R}} = \frac{S - R}{S} \quad (11.5)$$

$$Pr[E_3 \mid E_1 \cup E_2 \cup E_3] = \frac{\frac{2R-S}{2R}}{\frac{S}{2R}} = \frac{2R - S}{S} \quad (11.6)$$

$$Pr[E_2 \mid E_1 \cup E_2 \cup E_3] = \frac{\frac{S-R}{2R}}{\frac{S}{2R}} = \frac{S - R}{S} \quad (11.7)$$

Clearly all values for $x'$ in the interval $[0, S - R)$ are equally likely. Since there are $S - R$ possible values for $x'$ in this interval, it follows from equation 11.5 that when event $E_1$ occurs, each value $x'$ in this interval is chosen with probability $\frac{S-R}{S} \frac{1}{S-R} = \frac{1}{S}$. A similar argument holds for the intervals $[S - R, R)$ and $[R, S)$. It follows that if $e = 1$ then $x'$ is uniformly distributed in $\{0, 1, 2, ..., S - 1\}$. $\diamond$

This bias removal method is a useful tool to leak secrets out of a cryptosystem in an inconspicuous fashion.

# 11.4    Secretly Embedded Trapdoors

Recall that the fundamental weakness in the pseudorandom number generator backdoor attack is that once an intermediate seed is exposed, the future operation of the device is compromised (see Subsection 11.2.3). This weakness alone may be enough to prevent smart card companies and designers from ever mounting such an attack. Inserting a deliberate backdoor is a criminal offense that warrants jail time. However, inserting a deliberate backdoor that is exploitable by people other than the malicious designer could lead to serious breaches in national security. The study of robust backdoors is thus of great importance to intelligence agencies and hackers alike.

This problem can be solved *by thinking kleptographically*. The idea is to use cryptography to construct carefully designed cryptotrojans. These cryptotrojans may be designed into the cryptosystem by a malicious manufacturer, or they may be added to the code by hackers after deployment. Consider the key generation process. A key generation algorithm outputs a private key and a public key to the user. Only the public key gets sent across public networks. So, it is safe to assume that the Trojan horse designer will be able to obtain the public keys that the Trojan generates. This is a communications channel between the device and the attacker. Gus Simmons demonstrated the subversive power of such channels by formally investigating the notion of subliminal channels. If a prime that divides $n$ can be displayed in the binary representation of $n$ then the attacker could factor $n$. This is the heart of the attack on composite key generation and it is based on the subliminal channel that exists in composite key generation (see Subsection 10.4.5). However, simply placing the prime $p$ in the upper order bits of $n$ would allow anyone to factor $n$. This implies that $p$ should be asymmetrically encrypted using the public key of the attacker. Hence, cryptography should be employed within cryptography to gain exclusive access to everyone's private keys. This attack was first published in Crypto '96 [333]. It was later refined in Eurocrypt '97 [335]. This attack may be regarded as a cryptotrojan attack since it exploits the fact that key generation algorithms have access to private keys, and since the Trojan uses the public key of the attacker.

It is critical that cryptotrojans not interfere with the normal operation of a device. By definition a subliminal channel has a fixed bandwidth that can be utilized without hindering the device's normal operation. Cryptotrojans that exploit subliminal channels to leak ciphertexts will therefore not hinder the expected behavior of the device.  Care must of course be taken to ensure that the subliminal channel is utilized in a covert fashion. The infected black-box cryptosystem must appear normal in every way.

To discover attacks on other cryptosystems one should ask the following questions:

1. What are the outputs of the device?

2. Does the device exhibit a subliminal channel?

3. If so, what is the bandwidth of the channel?

4. What can we hide or encode within the outputs of the device without hindering its normal operation and without giving the attack away?

The key generator outputs public keys *and so it is in public keys that private keys must be displayed.*  As a result of the attack, a database of public keys is in fact a database of public keys and ciphertexts that encrypt the corresponding private keys.  Only the attacker is able to decrypt these ciphertexts.  A cardinal lesson in kleptography is that subliminal channels, wherever present, can be used by cryptotrojans to leak public key encryptions that are computed using the public key of the attacker.

The two basic threats from the attacker's point of view give rise to the following two types of adversaries.

1. Distinguishing Adversary: The goal of the distinguishing adversary is to *distinguish* an honest implementation from a dishonest implementation, assuming that neither of these particular devices has ever been reverse engineered.  It is assumed that the distinguishing adversary has successfully reverse engineered one or more devices and obtained their code and obtained the contents of their non-volatile memory.  It is assumed that the adversary has access to all public information including public algorithms, public keys, ciphertexts, signatures, and so on.

2. Cryptanalyzing Adversary: The goal of the cryptanalyzing adversary is to *break* the security of a given device that has never been reverse engineered.  This may involve factoring a public key, decrypting a public key encryption, forging a signature, and so on.  It is assumed that the cryptanalyzing adversary has successfully reverse engineered one or more devices (other than the one in question) and

obtained their code and obtained the contents of their non-volatile memory. It is assumed that the adversary has access to all public information including public algorithms, public keys, ciphertexts, signatures, and so on.

For example, a reverse engineer may have reverse engineered one chip and will try to use that information to factor the composite that is output by another chip. When the composites are generated using a kleptographic attack, the reverse engineer should not be able to factor such a composite. This should hold even if the reverse engineer can specify the inputs to the device, for example, the size of the keys that are generated. Even with the ability to adaptively select the inputs and receive the outputs, the reverse engineer should not be able to factor other peoples' composites.

Informally, a SETUP (secretly embedded trapdoor with universal protection) attack is an algorithm that can be embedded within a cryptosystem to leak encrypted secrets within the output of the cryptosystem, often through a subliminal channel that exists in that cryptosystem. This encryption is typically performed using the public key of the attacker that is contained within the cryptosystem. Since the public key is used in a trapdoor one-way function, and since it is secretly embedded within the cryptosystem, the resulting code is referred to as having a secretly embedded trapdoor. The information that is leaked through the cryptosystem is universally protected because even if the cryptanalyzing adversary is given access to the leaked ciphertext, the reverse engineered device (that is, the code for the attack and the attacker's public key), and the contents of the device's non-volatile memory, the ciphertext can only be decrypted by the attacker. This enables the attacker to maintain his or her relative advantage over other users and even successful reverse engineers. SETUP attacks are designed to gracefully handle the possibility of reverse engineering and are designed to be robust against users who try to distinguish honest devices from dishonest ones.

The following is an informal definition of a SETUP.

**Definition 4** *Let C be an honest* **black-box cryptosystem** *that conforms to a public specification. Let C′ be a dishonest version of C that contains a publicly known cryptotrojan algorithm,[5] that was implemented by an attacker A, and that may contain secret seeding information that is*

---

[5]For example, that may be obtained by successful reverse engineering, or using the algorithm from this chapter.

*not publicly known. Cryptosystem C' constitutes a SETUP version of C if the following properties hold:*

1. *Halting Correctness: C and C' are efficient algorithms. That is, they must halt in time polynomial in the length of their inputs, and*

2. *Output Indistinguishability: The outputs of C and C' are indistinguishable to all efficient probabilistic algorithms except for the attacker A who can always distinguish, and*

3. *Confidentiality of outputs of C: The outputs of C are confidential to all efficient probabilistic algorithms and do not compromise the cryptosystem that C implements, and*

4. *Confidentiality of outputs of C': The outputs of C' are confidential to all efficient probabilistic algorithms except for the attacker A, and do not compromise the cryptosystem that C' implements, and*

5. *Ability to compromise C': With overwhelming probability the attacker A can decrypt, forge, or otherwise cryptanalyze at least one private output of C' given a sufficient number of public outputs of C'.*

Property 2 utilizes the notion of polynomial indistinguishability of probability distributions, a concept that is central to proving the security of various cryptosystems. Properties 2, 3, and 4 can be made more comprehensive by requiring that they hold in an adaptive scenario in which the adversary adaptively chooses the inputs for the device and receives the public outputs. This is analogous to providing security against adaptive chosen ciphertext attacks. It follows that the above definition of a secure backdoor draws from well-studied concepts in modern cryptography.

## 11.5   Key Generation SETUP Attack

The notion of a SETUP attack was presented at Crypto '96 [333] and was later improved slightly [335]. To illustrate the notion of a SETUP attack, a particular attack on RSA key generation was presented. The SETUP attack on RSA keys from Crypto '96 generates the primes $p$ and $q$ from a skewed distribution. This skewed distribution was later corrected while allowing $e$ to remain fixed[6] [341]. A backdoor attack on RSA was also presented by Crépeau and Slakmon [77]. They showed that if the device is free to choose the RSA exponent $e$ (which is often not the case in practice), the primes $p$ and $q$ of a given size can be generated uniformly at random in the attack. Crépeau and Slakmon also give an attack similar to PAP in which $e$ is fixed. Crépeau and Slakmon [77] noted the skewed distribution in the original SETUP attack as well. The specific attack that is given in this section is based on the first author's doctoral dissertation.

When the honest algorithm $GenPrivatePrimes1$ is implemented in the device, the device may be regarded as an honest cryptosystem $C$. The advanced attack on composite key generation is specified by the algorithm $GenPrivatePrimes3$ below. This algorithm is the infected version of $GenPrivatePrimes1$ and when implemented in a device it effectively serves as the device $C'$ in a SETUP attack.

Recall that a random oracle $R(\cdot)$ takes as input a bit string that is finite in length and returns an infinitely long bit string. Let $H(s, i, v)$ denote a function that invokes the oracle and returns the $v$ bits of $R(s)$ that start at the $i^{\text{th}}$ bit position, where $i \geq 0$. For example, if $R(110101) = 01001011110101...$ then,

$$H(110101, 0, 3) = 010$$

and

$$H(110101, 1, 4) = 1001$$

and so on.

The algorithm $GenPrivatePrimes3$ contains the attacker's public key $N$ where $|N| = W/2$ bits, and $N = PQ$ with $P$ and $Q$ being distinct primes. The primes $P$ and $Q$ are kept private by the attacker. The attacker's public key is half the size of $p$ times $q$, where $p$ and $q$ are the primes that are computed by the algorithm. Each device contains a unique $W/2$-bit identifier $ID$. The $ID$s for the devices are chosen randomly, subject to the constraint that they all be unique. The variable $i$ is stored in non-volatile memory and is a counter for the number of compromised keys that the device created. It starts at $i = 0$. The variable $j$ is not stored in non-volatile memory. The attack makes use of the four constants $(e_0, e_1, e_2, e_3)$ that must be computed by the attacker and placed within

---

[6]For example, with $e = 2^{16} + 1$ as in many fielded cryptosystems.

the device. These quantities can be chosen randomly, for instance. They must adhere to the requirements listed in Table 11.1.

It may appear at first glance that the backdoor attack below is needlessly complicated. However, the reason for the added complexity becomes clear when the indistinguishability and confidentiality properties are proven. This algorithm effectively leaks a Rabin ciphertext in the upper order bits of $pq$ and uses the Rabin plaintext to derive the prime $p$ using a random oracle.

Note that due to the use of the probabilistic bias removal method, this algorithm is not going to have the same expected running time as the honest algorithm $GenPrivatePrimes1()$. A standard approach to designing randomized algorithms is to design them to be Monte Carlo as opposed to Las Vegas. That is, the running time is bounded by a fixed polynomial and the failure probability is bounded from above. This guarantees a poly-time algorithm. However, in the case of composite key generation, such an algorithm either outputs $(p, q)$ or $failure$. If the failure probability is not carefully designed in the attack, it might be possible to distinguish the honest key generator from the dishonest one based on the frequency of the $failure$ output. The ultimate goal in the attack is to make it produce outputs that are indistinguishable from the outputs of an honest implementation. It is easiest to utilize the Las Vegas key generation algorithm in which the only possible type of output is $(p, q)$.

The value $\Theta$ is a constant that is used in the attack to place a limit on the number of keys that are attacked. It is a restriction that simplifies the algorithm that the attacker uses to recover the private keys of other users.

| Constant | Properties |
|:---:|:---:|
| $e_0$ | $e_0 \in \mathbb{Z}_N^*$ and $L(e_0/P) = +1$ and $L(e_0/Q) = +1$ |
| $e_1$ | $e_2 \in \mathbb{Z}_N^*$ and $L(e_2/P) = -1$ and $L(e_2/Q) = +1$ |
| $e_2$ | $e_1 \in \mathbb{Z}_N^*$ and $L(e_1/P) = -1$ and $L(e_1/Q) = -1$ |
| $e_3$ | $e_3 \in \mathbb{Z}_N^*$ and $L(e_3/P) = +1$ and $L(e_3/Q) = -1$ |

**Table 11.1**  Constants used in key generation attack

*GenPrivatePrimes*3():

input: none

output: $W/2$-bit primes $p$ and $q$ such that $p \neq q$ and $|pq| = W$

1. if $i > \Theta$ then output *GenPrivatePrimes*1() and halt
2. update $i$ in non-volatile memory to be $i = i + 1$
3. let $I$ be the $|\Theta|$-bit representation of $i$
4. for $j = 0$ to $\infty$ do:
5.        choose $x$ randomly from $\{0, 1, 2, ..., N - 1\}$
6.        set $c_0 = x$
7.        if $gcd(x, N) = 1$ then
8.            choose bit $b$ randomly and choose $u$ randomly from $\mathbb{Z}_N^*$
9.            if $J(x/N) = +1$ then set $c_0 = e_0^b e_2^{1-b} u^2 \ mod \ N$
10.           if $J(x/N) = -1$ then set $c_0 = e_1^b e_3^{1-b} u^2 \ mod \ N$
11.        compute $(e, c_1) = PBRM(N, 2^{W/2}, c_0)$
12.        if $e = -1$ then continue
13.        if $u > -u \ mod \ N$ then set $u = -u \ mod \ N$ /* for faster decr. */
14.        let $T_0$ be the $W/2$-bit representation of $u$
15.        for $k = 0$ to $\infty$ do:
16.            compute $p = H(T_0||ID||I||j, \frac{kW}{2}, \frac{W}{2})$
17.            if $p \geq 2^{W/2-1} + 1$ and $p$ is prime then break
18.        if $p < 2^{W/2-1} + 1$ or if $p$ is not prime then continue
19.        $c_2 = RandomBitString$1()
20.        compute $n' = (c_1 \ || \ c_2)$
21.        solve for the quotient $q$ and the remainder $r$ in $n' = pq + r$
22.        if $q$ is not a $W/2$-bit integer or if $q < 2^{W/2-1} + 1$ then continue
23.        if $q$ is not prime then continue
24.        if $|pq| < W$ or if $p = q$ then continue
25.        if $p > q$ then interchange the values $p$ and $q$
26.        set $S = (p, q)$ and break
27. output $S$, zeroize everything in memory except $i$, and halt

It is assumed that the user, or the device that contains this algorithm, will multiply $p$ by $q$ to obtain the public key $n = pq$. Making $n$ publicly available is perilous since with overwhelming probability $p$ can easily be recovered by the attacker. Note that $c_1$ will be displayed verbatim in the upper order bits of $n = n' - r = pq$ unless the subtraction of $r$ from $n'$ causes a borrow bit to be taken from the $W/2$ most significant bits of $n'$. The attacker can always add this bit back in to recover $c_1$.

Suppose that the attacker, who is either the malicious manufacturer or the hacker that installed the Trojan horse, obtains the public key $n = pq$.

The attacker is in a position to recover $p$ using the factors $(P, Q)$ of the Rabin public key $N$. Rabin decryption is described in Appendix C.1.5. The factoring algorithm attempts to compute the two smallest ambivalent roots of a perfect square modulo $N$. Let $t$ be a quadratic residue modulo $N$. Recall that $a_0$ and $a_1$ are ambivalent square roots of $t$ modulo $N$ if $a_0^2 \equiv a_1^2 \equiv t \bmod N$, $a_0 \neq a_1$, and $a_0 \neq -a_1 \bmod N$. The values $a_0$ and $a_1$ are the two smallest ambivalent roots if they are ambivalent, $a_0 < -a_0 \bmod N$, and $a_1 < -a_1 \bmod N$. The Rabin decryption algorithm can be used to compute the two smallest ambivalent roots of a perfect square $t$, that is, the two smallest ambivalent roots of a Rabin ciphertext.

For each possible combination of $ID$, $i$, $j$, and $k$ the attacker computes the algorithm $FactorTheComposite$ given below. Since the key generation device can only be invoked a reasonable number of times, and since there is a reasonable number of compromised devices in existence, this recovery process is tractable.

$FactorTheComposite(n, P, Q, ID, i, j, k)$:
input: positive integers $i, j, k$ with $1 \leq i \leq \Theta$
        distinct primes $P$ and $Q$
        $n$ which is the product of distinct primes $p$ and $q$
        Also, $|n|$ must be even and $|p| = |q| = |PQ| = |ID| = |n|/2$
output: $failure$ or a non-trivial factor of $n$
1. compute $N = PQ$
2. let $I$ be the $\Theta$-bit representation of $i$
3. $W = |n|$
4. set $U_0$ equal to the $W/2$ most significant bits of $n$
5. compute $U_1 = U_0 + 1$
6. if $U_0 \geq N$ then set $U_0 = 2^{W/2} - 1 - U_0$   /* undo the PBRM */
7. if $U_1 \geq N$ then set $U_1 = 2^{W/2} - 1 - U_1$   /* undo the PBRM */
8. for $z = 0$ to 1 do:
9.     if $U_z$ is contained in $\mathbb{Z}_N^*$ then
10.        for $\ell = 0$ to 3 do:    /* try to find a square root */
11.           compute $W_\ell = U_z e_\ell^{-1} \bmod N$
12.         if $L(W_\ell/P) = +1$ and $L(W_\ell/Q) = +1$ then
13.           let $a_0, a_1$ be the two smallest ambivalent roots of $W_\ell$
14.           let $A_0$ be the $W/2$-bit representation of $a_0$
15.           let $A_1$ be the $W/2$-bit representation of $a_1$
16.           for $b = 0$ to 1 do:
17.              compute $p_b = H(A_b||ID||I||j, \frac{kW}{2}, \frac{W}{2})$
18.              if $p_0$ is a non-trivial divisor of $n$ then

19.                    output $p_0$ and halt
20.                 if $p_1$ is a non-trivial divisor of $n$ then
21.                    output $p_1$ and halt
22. output *failure* and halt

The quantity $U_0 + 1$ is computed since a borrow bit may have been taken from the lowest order bit of $c_1$ when the public key $n = n' - r$ is computed.

## 11.6   Security of the SETUP Attack

The entire proof that this attack constitutes a secretly embedded trapdoor with universal protection will not be given. However, the two non-trivial aspects of this proof will be sketched out. It is stressed that this is a proof in the random oracle model and that when the attack is implemented, it is subject to the weaknesses of the primitive used to instantiate the oracle. The proof that the attack satisfies Property 2 of a SETUP attack will be outlined. It is shown that the primes that are output by the cryptotrojan are computationally indistinguishable from the primes that are output by the honest key generation algorithm. The proof that the outputs are confidential, even against a successful reverse engineer, is then outlined. This is Property 4 of a SETUP attack and it holds using a reduction argument.

### 11.6.1   Indistinguishability of Outputs

It is assumed that the distinguishing adversary knows the cryptotrojan algorithm. This could be from prior reverse engineering endeavors. Hence, the attacker's Rabin public key $N$ is known to the adversary. Since the adversary has not reverse engineered the particular device in question the adversary does not know the value $ID$ right off the bat.

There is nothing to distinguish when $i > \Theta$, so we will consider the case that $i \leq \Theta$. The first observation is that indistinguishability does not hold against an adversary that has unbounded computational resources. Such an adversary can factor $N$ and hence knows $P$ and $Q$. This means that the adversary is capable of decrypting Rabin ciphertexts when they are embedded in the upper order bits of $pq$. The attacker can guess a value for $ID$ and then invoke the key generation device, say four times. The adversary collects the four pairs of primes that the device outputs. This data set is used to help test if the guess for $ID$ was correct or not. The adversary knows that $j$ will be zero at the beginning of each invocation. The adversary also knows that the values for $i$ will be $i$, $i+1$, $i+2$, and $i+3$. Since $i \leq \Theta$ can be guessed, the adversary will be able to verify correctly with overwhelming probability whether or not the guess for $ID$ was correct. The adversary can probe the integrity of the device's output values by performing the same computations that the device would do if it were dishonest and comparing the results with the data set. If the values do not match the data set, $ID$ may be guessed again. In time, the computationally unbounded adversary will be able to try all $ID$s and hence distinguish an honest device from a dishonest one.

The attack is, however, indistinguishable to all adversaries that are polynomially bounded in computational power.[7] Let $C$ denote an honest device that uses $GenPrivatePrimes1()$ and let $C'$ denote a dishonest device that uses $GenPrivatePrimes3()$. A key observation is that the primes $p$ and $q$ that are output by the dishonest device are chosen from the same set and same probability distribution as the primes $p$ and $q$ that are output by the honest device. So, it will be shown that $p$ and $q$ in the dishonest device $C'$ are chosen from the same set and from the same probability distribution as $p$ and $q$ in the honest device $C$.[8]

First consider the value $p$. In $C$, clearly $p$ is chosen randomly from the set of $W/2$-bit prime numbers due to the first loop. Now consider the device $C'$. Note that the substring $(ID||I||j)$ is completely unique to the $j$th iteration in the inner loop of the $i$th invocation in the unique device that contains $ID$. Since $(T_0||ID||I||j)$ is the argument to the random oracle, this means that this oracle input is different from every other oracle input, even when considering all outermost iterations and all devices. Since the output of $R(T_0||ID||I||j)$ is sampled $W/2$ bits at a time, it follows that $p$ is chosen uniformly at random from all $W/2$-bit prime numbers in $C'$. Therefore, $C'$ generates $p$ from the same set and probability distribution as $p$ in $C$.

It remains to consider the set and distribution that is used to choose $q$. In $C$, clearly $q$ is chosen randomly from the set of $W/2$-bit prime numbers. Now consider the device $C'$. If $x$ is not relatively prime to $N$ then $c_0$ is assigned the value $x$. If $x$ is relatively prime to $N$, then $c_0$ is set to be a

---

[7]Polynomial in $W/2$, the security parameter of the attacker's Rabin modulus $N$.

[8]The key to this being true is that $n'$ is a random $W$-bit string and so it can have a leading zero. So, $|pq|$ can be less than $W$ bits, the same as in the operation in the honest device before $p$ and $q$ are output.

randomly chosen element from $\mathbb{Z}_N^*$ using the four constants $e_0, e_1, e_2,$ and $e_3$. It follows that $c_0$ is a random element of $\{0, 1, 2, ..., N-1\}$. It follows from Lemma 1 that $c_1$ is a random element of $\{0, 1, 2, 3, ..., 2^{W/2} - 1\}$. Hence, $c_1$ is a randomly chosen $W/2$-bit string. Clearly $c_2$ is a randomly chosen $W/2$-bit string as well. Due to the concatenation of $c_1$ and $c_2$ it follows that $n'$ is a random $W$-bit string.

Using Euclid's division equation with quotient $q$ and $r$ as the remainder, $n' = pq + r = (2^{W/2-1} + 1)^2 + 0$ is the smallest possible value for $n'$ such that $p, q \geq 2^{W/2-1} + 1$. But this equals $2^{W-2} + 2^{W/2} + 1$ and is thus a $(W-1)$-bit quantity. The greatest possible $W/2$-bit integer is $p = q = 2^{W/2} - 1$. So, $n' = pq + r = pq + (p-1) = (2^{W/2}-1)^2 + (2^{W/2}-1) - 1$ is the greatest possible value for $n'$ such that $p$ and $q$ are $W/2$-bit integers. But this equals $2^W - 2^{W/2} - 1$ and is hence a $W$-bit quantity. This shows that the smallest and largest possible values for $n' = pq + r$ where $|p| = |q| = W/2$ and $p, q \geq 2^{W/2-1} + 1$ are contained in $\{0, 1\}^W$. Hence, all values for $n' = pq + r$ where $|p| = |q| = W/2$ and $p, q \geq 2^{W/2-1} + 1$ are contained in $\{0, 1\}^W$. It follows that for every pair $(p, q)$ such that $|p| = |q| = W/2$ and $p, q \geq 2^{W/2-1} + 1$, there are $p$ values in $\{0, 1\}^W$ that when divided by $p$ yield $q$ as the quotient. Since all $n' \in \{0, 1\}^W$ are equally likely, $q$ is chosen uniformly at random from the $W/2$ bit integers greater than or equal to $2^{W/2-1} + 1$ in $C'$. Those values for $q$ that are composite will be rejected. Hence, $q$ is chosen uniformly at random from all $W/2$-bit primes.

This can be conceptualized as follows. The $W/2$-bit prime $p$ can be fixed and the space $\{0, 1\}^W$ can be "divided" into regions containing $p$ numbers. A region consists of $qp + 0, qp + 1, qp + 2, ..., qp + p - 1$. Observe that when each of these values is divided by $p$ the quotient is $q$. Note also that there are $p$ such values. The regions are the rows below.

$$\cdots$$

| | | | | |
|---|---|---|---|---|
| $(q-1)*p+0$ | $(q-1)*p+1$ | $(q-1)*p+2$ | $\cdots$ | $(q-1)*p+p-1$ |
| $(q+0)*p+0$ | $(q+0)*p+1$ | $(q+0)*p+2$ | $\cdots$ | $(q+0)*p+p-1$ |
| $(q+1)*p+0$ | $(q+1)*p+1$ | $(q+1)*p+2$ | $\cdots$ | $(q+1)*p+p-1$ |

$$\cdots$$

A *dart* can then be thrown at $\{0, 1\}^W$. Which region if any the dart lands in determines the value of $q$. Due to acceptance/rejection no region is preferred and exactly one valid region must be selected.

The remaining tests (that make sure that $p \neq q$, etc.) are identical in $C$ and $C'$. Hence, the outputs of $C$ and $C'$ are drawn from the same set and probability distribution. This implies that the only way to distinguish is to guess the oracle input $ID$ correctly. Since $ID$ is not guessable and since it is kept secret from all adversaries in the black-box cryptosystem $C'$, it follows that the outputs of $C$ and $C'$ are indistinguishable to all computationally bounded adversaries.

## 11.6.2   Confidentiality of Outputs

An important observation is that the security parameter of the attacker's public key is half the value of the security parameter of the public key that is being generated. For instance, if the key being generated is a 1024-bit composite then the attacker's composite is 512 bits in length. This is clearly a risky scenario since if the device is reverse engineered, then the effective security parameter is 512. However, if the key that is generated is 2048 bits, then the attacker's key is 1024 bits. It is possible to modify this attack so that the attacker's public key has a higher security parameter in the SETUP attack. However, such variants will not be discussed here.[9]

Recall that Property 4 of a SETUP attack (see Section 11.4) is confidentiality against a reverse engineering adversary. In this section a reduction argument is given to prove that Property 4 holds. The claim is that there exists an algorithm that can break the confidentiality of the cryptotrojan attack if and only if there exists an algorithm that can factor efficiently. Clearly if factoring can be broken then there exists an efficient algorithm to break the confidentiality of the cryptotrojan. It remains to show the converse, namely, that if there exists an efficient algorithm that can break the cryptotrojan then factoring is easy.

In a nutshell this is proven by showing that if an efficient algorithm exists that violates the confidentiality property then either $W/2$-bit composites $PQ$ can be factored or $W$-bit composites $pq$ can be factored. This reduction is not a randomized reduction, yet it goes a long way to show the security of the cryptotrojan attack.

With regard to confidentiality it is assumed that the computationally bounded adversary has reverse engineered the device in question and hence knows the value for $ID$ that it contains. It is assumed that the device has been reconstituted and redeployed. It is also assumed that the adversary knows the current value for $i$ that exists in the non-volatile memory store of

---

[9]For example, elliptic curve cryptosystems can be used [157, 158, 162, 187, 188, 189].

the device. These are *very* generous assumptions about what the adversary knows.

To prove confidentiality of the dishonest device it is necessary to show that the adversary cannot compute $p$ in $n = pq$ when the adversary has the following view,

$$view_{C'} = (n, ID, i, N, e_0, e_1, e_2, e_3) \qquad (11.8)$$

The adversary also knows the cryptotrojan algorithm. What the adversary does not have access to is the coin flips that the cryptotrojan will generate once it has been redeployed.

The proof of confidentiality is by contradiction. Suppose for the sake of contradiction that a computationally bounded algorithm $A$ exists that violates the confidentiality property. For a randomly chosen input, algorithm $A$ will return a non-trivial factor of $n$ with non-negligible probability. The adversary could thus use algorithm $A$ to break the confidentiality of the system. Algorithm $A$ factors $n$ when it *feels* so inclined, but must do so a non-negligible portion of the time.

It is important to first set the stage for the proof. The adversary that we are dealing with is trying to break a public key $pq$ where $p$ and $q$ were computed by the cryptotrojan. Hence, $pq$ was created using a call to the random oracle $R$. It is conceivable that an algorithm $A$ that breaks the confidentiality will make oracle calls as well to break $pq$. Perhaps $A$ will even make some of the *same* oracle calls as the cryptotrojan. However, in the proof we cannot assume this. All we can assume is that $A$ makes at most a polynomial[10] number of calls to the oracle and we are free to "trap" each one of these calls and take the arguments.

Consider the following algorithm $SolveFactoring(N, n)$ that uses $A$ as an oracle to solve the factoring problem.

$SolveFactoring(N, n)$:
input: $N$ which is the product of distinct primes $P$ and $Q$
        $n$ which is the product of distinct primes $p$ and $q$
        Also, $|n|$ must be even and $|p| = |q| = |N| = |n|/2$
output: *failure*, or a non-trivial factor of $N$ or $n$
1. compute $W = 2|N|$
2. for $k = 0$ to 3 do:

---

[10]Polynomial in $W/2$.

3.    do:
4.        choose $e_k$ randomly from $\mathbb{Z}_N^*$
5.        while $J(e_k/N) \neq (-1)^k$
6.  choose $ID$ to be a random $W/2$-bit string
7.  choose $i$ randomly from $\{1, 2, ..., \Theta\}$
8.  choose bit $b_0$ randomly
9.  if $b_0 = 0$ then
10.       compute $p = A(n, ID, i, N, e_0, e_1, e_2, e_3)$
11.       if $p < 2$ or $p \geq n$ then output $failure$ and halt
12.       if $n \bmod p = 0$ then output $p$ and halt /* factor found */
13.       output $failure$ and halt
14.  output $CaptureOracleArgument(ID, i, N, e_0, e_1, e_2, e_3)$ and halt


$CaptureOracleArgument(ID, i, N, e_0, e_1, e_2, e_3)$:
1.  compute $W = 2|N|$
2.  let $I$ be the $\Theta$-bit representation of $i$
3.  for $j = 0$ to $\infty$ do:    /* try to find an input that $A$ expects */
4.        choose $x$ randomly from $\{0, 1, 2, ..., N - 1\}$
5.        set $c_0 = x$
6.        if $gcd(x, N) = 1$ then
7.            choose bit $b_1$ randomly and choose $u_1$ randomly from $\mathbb{Z}_N^*$
8.            if $J(x/N) = +1$ then set $c_0 = e_0^{b_1} e_2^{1-b_1} u_1^2 \bmod N$
9.            if $J(x/N) = -1$ then set $c_0 = e_1^{b_1} e_3^{1-b_1} u_1^2 \bmod N$
10.       compute $(e, c_1) = PBRM(N, 2^{W/2}, c_0)$
11.       if $e = -1$ then continue
12.       if $u_1 > -u_1 \bmod N$ then set $u_1 = -u_1 \bmod N$
13.       let $T_0$ be the $W/2$-bit representation of $u_1$
14.       for $k = 0$ to $\infty$ do:
15.           compute $p = H(T_0||ID||I||j, \frac{kW}{2}, \frac{W}{2})$
16.           if $p \geq 2^{W/2-1} + 1$ and $p$ is prime then break
17.       if $p < 2^{W/2-1} + 1$ or if $p$ is not prime then continue
18.       $c_2 = RandomBitString1()$
19.       compute $n' = (c_1 \,||\, c_2)$
20.       solve for the quotient $q$ and the remainder $r$ in $n' = pq + r$
21.       if $q$ is not a $W/2$-bit integer or if $q < 2^{W/2-1} + 1$ then continue
22.       if $q$ is not prime then continue
23.       if $|pq| < W$ or if $p = q$ then continue
24.  simulate $A(pq, ID, i, N, e_0, e_1, e_2, e_3)$, watch calls to $R$, and
          store the $W/2$-most significant bits of each call in list $\omega$

25. remove all elements from $\omega$ that are not contained in $\mathbb{Z}_N^*$
26. let $L$ be the number of elements in $\omega$
27. if $L = 0$ then output *failure* and halt
28. choose $\alpha$ randomly from $\{0, 1, 2, ..., L-1\}$
29. let $\beta$ be the $\alpha^{\text{th}}$ element in $\omega$
30. if $\beta \equiv \pm u_1 \; mod \; N$ then output *failure* and halt
31. if $\beta^2 \; mod \; N \neq u_1^2 \; mod \; N$ then output *failure* and halt
32. compute $P = gcd(u_1 + \beta, N)$
33. if $N \; mod \; P = 0$ then output $P$ and halt
34. compute $P = gcd(u_1 - \beta, N)$
35. output $P$ and halt

Note that with non-negligible probability $A$ will not balk due to the choice of $ID$ and $i$. Also, with non-negligible probability $e_0$, $e_1$, $e_2$, and $e_3$ will conform to the requirements in the cryptotrojan attack. So, when $b_0 = 0$ these four arguments to $A$ will conform to what $A$ expects with non-negligible probability. Now consider the call to $A$ when $b_0 = 1$. Observe that the value $pq$ is chosen from the same set and probability distribution as in the cryptotrojan attack. So, when $b_0 = 1$ the arguments to $A$ will conform to what $A$ expects with non-negligible probability. It may be assumed that $A$ balks whenever $e_0$, $e_1$, $e_2$, and $e_3$ are not appropriately chosen without ruining the efficiency of $SolveFactoring$. So, for the remainder of the proof we will assume that these four values are as defined in the cryptotrojan attack.

Let $u_2$ be the square root of $u_1^2 \; mod \; n$ such that $u_2 \neq u_1$ and $u_2 < -u_2 \; mod \; n$. Also, let $T_1$ and $T_2$ be $u_1$ and $u_2$ padded with leading zeros as necessary such that $|T_1| = |T_2| = W/2$ bits, respectively. Denote by $E$ the event that in a given invocation algorithm $A$ calls the random oracle $R$ at least once with either $T_1$ or $T_2$ as the $W/2$ most significant bits. Clearly only one of the two following possibilities hold:

1. Event $E$ occurs with negligible probability.

2. Event $E$ occurs with non-negligible probability.

Consider case (1). Algorithm $A$ can detect that $n$ was not generated by the cryptotrojan by appropriately supplying $T_1$ or $T_2$ to the random oracle. Once verified, $A$ can balk and not output a factor of $n$. But in case (1) this can only occur at most a negligible fraction of the time since changing even a single bit in the value supplied to the oracle elicits an independently random response. By assumption, $A$ returns a non-trivial factor of $n$ a non-negligible fraction of the time. Since the difference between a non-negligible number and negligible number is a non-negligible number it follows that $A$ factors $n$ without relying on the random oracle. So, in case (1) the call to $A$ in which $b_0 = 0$ will lead to a non-trivial factor of $n$ with non-negligible probability.

Now consider case (2). Since $E$ occurs with non-negligible probability it follows that $A$ may in fact be computing non-trivial factors of composites $n$ by making oracle calls and constructing the factors in a straightforward fashion. However, whether or not this is the case is immaterial. Since $A$ makes at most a polynomial number of calls[11] to $R$ the value for $L$ cannot be too large. Since with non-negligible probability $A$ passes either $T_1$ or $T_2$ as the $W/2$ most significant bits to $R$ and since $L$ cannot be too large it follows that $\beta$ and $u_1$ will be ambivalent roots with non-negligible probability. Algorithm $A$ has no way of knowing which of the two smallest ambivalent roots $SolveFactoring$ chose in constructing the upper order bits of $pq$. Algorithm $A$, which may be quite uncooperative, can do no better than guess at which one it was, and it could in fact have been either. Hence, $SolveFactoring$ returns a non-trivial factor of $N$ with non-negligible probability in this case.

It has been shown that in either case, the existence of $A$ contradicts the factoring assumption. So, the original assumption that adversary $A$ exists is wrong. This proves that the cryptotrojan satisfies Property 4 of a SETUP attack.

Immediately following the test for $p = q$ in $C$ and in $C'$ it is possible to check that $gcd(e, (p-1)(q-1)) = 1$ and restart the entire algorithm if this does not hold. This handles the generation of RSA primes by taking into account the public RSA exponent $e$. This preserves the indistinguishability of the output of $C'$ with respect to $C$.

## 11.7   Detecting the Attack in Code Reviews

Since the attack is indistinguishable in black-box implementations, *the only way to detect its presence is to analyze what is in the black box.*[12] This, of course, implies that the black box can be breached and the assumption

---

[11]Polynomial in $W$.

[12]Care must be taken to buffer the computations and power consumption, and so on, in order to guard against side channel analysis.

broken. However, it is naive to think that the attack can be detected by analyzing the code for $GenPrivatePrimes1()$ alone. The reason for this is that the attack can be carried out at a lower level, for example, in a random number generation routine.

For concreteness, consider a dishonest version of $RandomBitString1$ called $RandomBitString2$. Rather than choosing strings perfectly at random, it utilizes $GenPrivatePrimes3$ to arrive at output values. This may be accomplished as follows. $GenPrivatePrimes3$ is invoked to obtain the compromised values $p$ and $q$. It then generates a series of perfectly random $W/2$-bit strings that it will utilize in the next set of outputs. The length of this series is determined as follows. The series terminates when exactly two values that satisfy the requirements for $p$ and $q$ in $GenPrivatePrimes1$ are found. Hence, the last value is the prime $q$. These two primes are then thrown away and replaced by the primes that were output by $GenPrivatePrimes3$ to obtain the actual series. Each time that $RandomBitString1$ is invoked it outputs the next value in the series. When the series is exhausted it mounts the attack again.

So why will this attack work? Observe that when $GenPrivatePrimes1$ invokes $RandomBitString2$ over and over, it will be going through the carefully chosen series of $W/2$-bit strings. As a result it will arrive at the compromised values for $p$ and $q$ since they are the first two satisfactory primes. The reason why the series was chosen as such was to prevent arousing any suspicion in $GenPrivatePrimes1$. Observe that the compromised primes $p$ and $q$ occur with the exact same frequency that one would expect from an honest random number generator $RandomBitString1$.

There is a terribly important message here for security practitioners that perform code reviews. A SETUP attack can be implemented at any level prior to the private key $p$ and $q$ being output by the key generation device. The attack could even occur within the casing that houses the source of physical randomness. Detecting a SETUP attack is an extremely involved process in practice and requires a generous amount of time as well as full and complete disclosure of all algorithms and schematic diagrams to truly rule out the possible existence of backdoors.[13]

This issue is of particular importance when company A hires company B to do a code review. Very often company A will have some form of flagship product or service that performs random number generation or key generation. They have a vested interest in their product or service being

---

[13]Even then the devices that are manufactured might not actually correspond to the circuit designs that are provided to the examiner.

viewed in a positive light by the general public. It is not uncommon for such companies to (1) hire company B that is well known for performing high-quality software reliability and security reviews, (2) assign their own developers as points of contact for company B, and (3) expect to derive a press release that states how amazing their product or service is. This is a recipe for disaster. The points of contact are in a precarious position. Giving the code to real software experts often make them very nervous, and justifiably so. Any bug, error, or fault that is found will imply a mistake on their part. Simply put, they don't want company B to find anything and will often take measures to prevent them from finding anything. *As a result they will often try to deliver as little code as possible for the review.* A SETUP attack cannot be detected *at all* unless all code and schematic diagrams are provided to company B by company A.[14]

Corporations charged with deploying smart cards as well as foreign information ministries need to pay particular attention to these backdoor attacks. When a tiger team is handed a smart card and its PIN and is asked to detect whether or not a backdoor exists, *they will not be able to do so.* A properly implemented SETUP attack cannot be detected under any circumstances. Such a SETUP attack would have to take into account timing analysis, differential power analysis, and so on, and be implemented accordingly.

Totalitarian governments are in an ideal position to force their populace to utilize smart cards. The rationale behind outfitting the people as such is manyfold. For one, in some countries women are not permitted to leave the country without the permission of their husbands or fathers. One can envision a situation in which a married woman cannot leave the country without a digitally signed form from her husband. In the event that a monarchy contracts the implementation work to a foreign corporation, the corporation or the vendor they choose would be in an ideal position to mount SETUP attacks in the smart cards that are sent.

To make matters worse, the cryptotrojans could be placed in only half the delivered devices, thereby confounding the detectability even under reverse engineering. These backdoors could allow foreign agents to masquerade as any given citizen. It behooves foreign information ministries and ordinary citizens alike to learn exactly what cryptographic algorithms they are using in black-box devices, since the migration to cryptographic

---

[14]We have seen this occur too many times during commercial consulting engagements and it has provided impetus for writing this book.

machinery can actually weaken authentication checks in certain circumstances.

## 11.8   Countering the SETUP Attack

To avoid this attack, the following heuristic can be used to generate composite keys. It is based on the SETUP attack itself with some obvious modifications.

*GenPrivatePrimes4*():
input: none
output: $W/2$-bit primes $p$ and $q$ such that $p \neq q$ and $|pq| = W$
1. for $j = 0$ to $\infty$ do:
2.     generate $s_1, s_2, c_2$ to be random $W/2$-bit strings
3.     compute $c_1 = H(s_1, 0, W/2)$
4.     for $k = 0$ to $\infty$ do:
5.         $p = H(s_1 || s_2, \frac{kW}{2}, W/2)$
6.         if $p \geq 2^{W/2-1} + 1$ and $p$ is prime then break
7.     compute $n' = (c_1 \ || \ c_2)$
8.     solve for the quotient $q$ and the remainder $r$ in $n' = pq + r$
9.     if $q$ is not a $W/2$-bit integer or if $q < 2^{W/2-1} + 1$ then continue
10.    if $q$ is not prime then continue
11.    if $|pq| < W$ or if $p = q$ then continue
12.    set $S = (p, q, s_1, s_2, k)$ and break
13. output $S$, zeroize all values in memory, and halt

The general public can verify that the SETUP attack has not been performed on a given modulus. This can be done by checking that either $H(s_1, 0, W/2)$ or $H(s_1, 0, W/2) + 1$ equals the $W/2$ uppermost bits of $n$. Here the $+1$ accounts for a potential borrow bit having been taken from $c_1$. The problem with publishing $s_1$ is that it can constitute a subliminal channel by itself. So, ideally the private key owner and possibly a certification authority should perform this check. The private key owner should always keep $(p, q, s_2, k)$ secret.

The seed $s_2$ is for the benefit of the owner of $p$ and $q$. A heuristic way to check that $p$ was generated using $H$ is to verify that the prime $p$ is equal to $H(s_1 || s_2, \frac{kW}{2}, W/2)$ and that a smaller value for $k$ does not make $H(s_1 || s_2, \frac{kW}{2}, W/2)$ a prime that is greater than or equal to $2^{W/2-1} + 1$. The goal is to force devices that implement this algorithm to first commit to $s_1$ in the upper order bits of $n$ and then commit to $s_2$ in the prime $p$. This method is not perfect since about $O(log(log(n)))$ bits can still be leaked in $n$ using brute force key generation.

It should be noted that this defense only protects against the particular SETUP attack described above. In general, it is not clear that the aforementioned attack that uses a pseudorandom tape $t_p$ for key generation can be avoided at all without resorting to an interactive form of key generation. It is well known that many subliminal channels can be foiled by relying on protocols in which a trusted party influences every random value that is derived. For RSA key generation in particular, a protocol has been given that allows for verifiable randomness [147]. In this protocol, the user and the CA (a trusted third party) generate a key pair for the user and the CA does not learn the private key. At the end of the protocol the CA is convinced that the key pair has the correct form, that it is randomly chosen, and that its randomness was influenced by the CA's coin tosses. It is mentioned that this protocol can be conducted using two independently designed implementations that communicate with each other to foil kleptographic attacks. For example, one peripheral device can act as the "user" and another peripheral can act as the trusted third party in the protocol. This is a promising direction for guarding against kleptographic attacks.

For non-interactive key generation, one can *try* to separate the source of randomness from the key generation algorithm, and users can verify the operation of the deterministic portion of the whole key generation process at most only polynomially many times. However, the deterministic key generation device may in fact have a secret on-board random number generator that it uses in a given invocation with inverse-polynomial probability. Hence, the resulting deterministic key generator may in fact be a probabilistic poly-time Turing machine that mounts randomized SETUP attacks infrequently. It then becomes a game for the manufacturer to see how many invocations he or she can compromise without being detected. It is a game because detecting the attack amounts to choosing a large enough polynomial to represent the number of output values that are analyzed. The manufacturer can always choose a larger polynomial for its inverse-polynomial attack probability.

A more general heuristic can be applied to any scenario involving a randomized algorithm. The device can choose a seed $s_1$ randomly, and use the oracle output $R(s_1)$ as the random tape in the probabilistic Turing machine. The device outputs its normal computation along with $s_1$. Given

$s_1$, a verifier can check the output against the advertised algorithm that the device is said to implement. This applies to cryptographic algorithms and in fact all randomized algorithms. For example, when Quicksort is implemented in hardware this approach can be used to help verify its operation. However, this approach still suffers from the possibility that the device will operate in a Byzantine fashion some of the time.

## 11.9  Thinking Outside the Box

Side channel analysis is another approach that can be used to attempt to steal private keys and other private information from smart card implementations. Side channels are *outside the box* attacks that seek to derive sensitive information from a cryptosystem based on the operating characteristics of the device. Devices are real machines and they use power, give off heat, and take a certain amount of time to run based on the particular parameters used in the cryptosystem.

Kocher presented timing attacks against public key cryptographic algorithms [159]. Kocher's result was in fact presented in the same session in Crypto '96 as the original SETUP attack on RSA. Timing attacks apply to both software as well as hardware cryptographic implementations. They exploit the fact that different private keys cause measurably different running times in many cryptographic algorithms whenever they are implemented in a straightforward fashion. It was shown that cryptographic operations need to be buffered to make them have indistinguishable running times irrespective of which particular private keys are used.

Power analysis is another form of side-channel analysis that seeks to derive secret key information from hardware based cryptosystems. It has been shown that for certain algorithms, by measuring the power consumption of devices during their operation it may be possible for the attacker to deduce private key information from the device [26, 160].

These side channels show that it is not sufficient in practice to rely entirely on abstract models of computation such as probabilistic Turing machines to develop secure cryptographic devices. To put it another way, formal proofs of security are necessary but not sufficient in achieving real-world security. *Side channel attacks are very important to consider when developing real-world cryptographic machinery* and are currently receiving a lot of attention by the research community.

## 11.10  The Isaac Newton Institute Lecture

The idea of a SETUP attack grew out of our research on cryptovirus attacks. The discovery resulted from the following question that we asked ourselves: what if the file that is asymmetrically encrypted by the virus resides inside a cryptosystem? The notion of *hiding data* in relation to a *cryptosystem* immediately suggested that subliminal channels should be considered. At the time, I was well aware of the notion of a subliminal channel. However, Adam had never heard of this notion and ended up rediscovering the concept by chancing upon the subliminal channel in RSA composites. I referred Adam to Simmons' work and Yvo Desmedt's work on abuses in cryptography [89] and he learned that both the notion of a subliminal channel as well as the particular channel in composites was far from new. However, leaking asymmetrically encrypted data through these channels *was* new, and together we articulated the result in Crypto '96, taking care to appropriately relate the discovery to previous work on information hiding.

Upon investigating the SETUP attack on RSA key generation it became clear that by combining public key cryptography with subliminal channels, very powerful backdoors could be implemented in cryptosystems. The idea is to take a cryptosystem that exhibits a subliminal channel, and plant a cryptotrojan inside it. The payload of the cryptotrojan leaks asymmetric ciphertexts through the subliminal channel in the cryptosystem. To prevent the subliminal attack from being found, two things became readily apparent. It is necessary that the cryptosystem be a black-box to hide the presence of the Trojan, and it is necessary that users not be able to detect when the subliminal channel is being used. This latter consideration suggested that it wasn't enough to rely on the fact that outputs look normal. The notion of polynomial indistinguishability was well known to us. So, the most obvious threat model to use was that of a probabilistic poly-time adversary that tries to distinguish honest cryptosystem outputs from those that result from the cryptotrojan.

The discovery showed that in addition to cryptovirus extortion attacks, public key cryptography proved to be an invaluable tool for stealing private keys secretly. It showed that even more cryptographic notions and techniques could be applied to subvert computer systems.

In particular, the notion of polynomial indistinguishability became critical for *formally proving the security of the backdoor*. It was the combination of data theft and strong cryptographic techniques that led to the term *kleptography*, which I coined.

In 1996 the Isaac Newton Institute for Mathematical Sciences at the University of Cambridge held a year-long program on *Computer Security, Cryptography, and Coding Theory*. I was invited to attend and stayed there from January to February. Adam and I agreed that this was a good time to present our findings on SETUP attacks to the greater research community.

As it turns out, Gus Simmons was present at the Isaac Newton Institute when I arrived. I met with him and mentioned that I had some results that might be of interest to him since they were closely related to his work on subliminal channels. One afternoon I went to his office and conveyed the ideas to him, and he absorbed them in their entirety. I later gave a talk that covered the attack on RSA key generation, and found myself having to explain a number of times at the board the specifics behind how the private key is encoded within the bit representation of the corresponding public key itself.

I remember a few reactions that I hope I will not misrepresent, since this all happened some time ago. Whitfield Diffie was in the audience and was carefully listening to every word I said. He explained that for years he had been telling people that the only way that cryptosystems can be trusted is by implementing them in hardware that is thoroughly tested. One of the key rationales behind this is that when the code is in read-only memory, it cannot be tampered with. He remarked that in light of the SETUP attack, this wisdom is flawed. Diffie added that the attack shows that the trust of the user must be placed in the manufacturer instead of the device. If I remember correctly I nodded my head and found that he truly understood the implications of this threat.

In response to the lecture, Peter Landrock (who was then at the University of Aarhus but has since joined Cryptomatics) commented, "You guys have really vicious minds."

Whereas in other scientific forums this sort of statement might have been insulting, I interpreted it as the highest form of compliment.

He then added, "You take the mathematical notion of public key crypto and apply it to do such nasty things."

"Yes," I responded, "that is exactly right."

I later e-mailed Adam a short note of encouragement and mentioned that the overall gist of our work was both clearly understood and well received by several distinguished cryptographers. At no time during my stay did I mention the fact that the idea was derived from a cryptovirus extortion attack. It seemed prudent to let the research community digest these attacks one at a time so that the software industry would have a chance to build defenses, and so that I would not develop a reputation as a renegade cryptographer. Adam and I deferred explaining these attacks in a comprehensive fashion until now.

# Chapter 12

# SETUP Attacks on Discrete-Log Cryptosystems

Existing cryptosystems based on the discrete logarithm problem are in no way immune to the threat of kleptographic attacks. This chapter expands upon the previous chapter by showing how to mount SETUP attacks on such cryptosystems. The notion of a discrete-log kleptogram is introduced that allows the attacker to obtain secret information covertly from fielded cryptosystems. What is novel about this approach is that it implements SETUP attacks without using explicit subliminal channels. Rather than employing information leaking channels, the implementation uses internal cryptographic tools to *generate* opportunities to leak information. As before, the approach avoids trivial attacks on the pseudorandomness of the device and similar simple attacks that would enable a successful reverse engineer to learn future states of the device.

The approach employs the discrete logarithm as a one-way function thereby assuring *forward secrecy*. The discrete-log kleptogram primitive is then used to attack the Diffie-Hellman key exchange [92]. The attack gives the attacker access to the shared secret key that is generated in the exchange. The primitive is then applied to discrete-log based public key encryption algorithms. It is shown how this gives the attacker access to plaintext. Finally, it is shown how to apply the primitive to discrete-log based signature algorithms to enable the attacker to gain access to signing private keys.

Some of the attacks presented in this chapter on discrete-log based signature algorithms are new and build on previous work [336, 339]. The proof of security for the Diffie-Hellman key exchange SETUP attack is sketched out and the approach is based on [341]. The attack is secure in

265

the random oracle model. Attacks are given for other discrete-log based cryptosystems as well, but no formal proof of security is given for them.

## 12.1    The Discrete-Log SETUP Primitive

A *kleptogram* is a publicly displayed value such as a ciphertext, signature, public key, and so on, that also serves as a backdoor. In the SETUP attack on the Diffie-Hellman key exchange, the device computes a kleptogram, displays it in one key exchange, and then uses the concealed value to securely compromise the next key exchange. This concealed value is used to derive the randomness in the subsequent key exchange.

Let $p$ denote a large prime and let $g$ be an element in $\mathbb{Z}_p^*$ with order $w$. Let $G$ denote the subgroup of $\mathbb{Z}_p^*$ generated by $g$. It is assumed that solving Diffie-Hellman in $G$ is difficult. So, $w$ must contain a large prime in its factorization to defend against the use of the Pohlig-Hellman algorithm [224].

In the kleptographic attack, the honest device outputs exponents for $g$ that are chosen honestly. The dishonest device contains an analogous subroutine that outputs exponents for $g$ that are securely compromised by the attacker.[1] These may be used as private exponents in a cryptosystem defined over $G$ to provide the attacker with a backdoor. The following is the exponent generation algorithm used by the honest device.

GenPrivateExponent1(K):
input: a value $K$ that is the empty string or a value contained in $\mathbb{Z}_w^*$
output: an element $k$ contained in $\mathbb{Z}_w^*$
1. choose $k$ to be random element in $\mathbb{Z}_w^*$
2. output $k$ and halt

Observe that *GenPrivateExponent1* patently ignores the input $K$. Let $|w|$ denote the number of bits used in representing $w$ in binary. Assuming that *GenPrivateExponent1* has access to a true random bit generator, it can be implemented as follows. Exactly $|w|$ bits are generated randomly. If the value is not contained in $\mathbb{Z}_w^*$ then these bits are thrown out and a new set of $|w|$ bits are generated. If this value is not contained in $\mathbb{Z}_w^*$, then it is thrown out and $|w|$ more bits are generated, and so on. This process guarantees that $k$ is chosen from the correct probability

---

[1] The attacker can be a hacker, a malicious manufacturer, or an insider.

distribution. It is possible to set $x = k$, use $x$ as a private key, and set $y = g^x \bmod p$. The public key is then $(y, g, p)$.

Let $X$ be a value contained in $\mathbb{Z}_w^*$ and let $Y = g^X \bmod p$. The value $X$ is the private key of the attacker. The public key of the attacker is $(Y, g, p)$. The algorithm $GenPrivateExponent2$ is used by a dishonest device that contains a $|p|$-bit identifier $ID$. The $ID$s for the devices are chosen randomly, subject to the constraint that they all be unique. It is anticipated that a device may eventually get reverse engineered, in which case $Y$ will become known to the reverse engineer in addition to the randomly chosen $ID$ in it. The device may or may not be destroyed during reverse engineering.

It is assumed that each device has a readable and writable memory capability. This non-volatile memory is used by the attacker to maintain a count $i$ of how many times the attack has been carried out. The value for $i$ is initially set to 0. Let $F_1$ be a random function with range $\mathbb{Z}_w^*$ (see Appendix B.4). The function $F_1$ can be implemented in practice using a suitable cryptographic hash function.

GenPrivateExponent2(K):
input: a value $K$ that is the empty string or a value contained in $\mathbb{Z}_w^*$
output: an element $k$ contained in $\mathbb{Z}_w^*$
1. if $i > \Theta$ then output $GenPrivateExponent1(K)$ and halt
2. update $i$ in non-volatile memory to be $i = i + 1$
3. compute $t = Y^K \bmod p$
4. let $T_0$ be the $|p|$-bit representation of $t$
5. compute $k = F_1(T_0 || ID || i)$
6. output $k$, zeroize everything in memory except $i$, and halt

The constant $\Theta$ is polynomial in $|p|$ and is used to eventually cease the attack. The reason this is done is to simplify the proof of security. The primitive is applied as follows. The device is supplied with a value $T = g^K \bmod p$. As will become clear in the specific attacks that are presented, $T$ will correspond to a Diffie-Hellman key exchange value, a public key, a portion of a digital signature, and so on. When the device is invoked the value $k = GenPrivateExponent2(K)$ is computed. In the attacks that are presented, $k$ will correspond to a Diffie-Hellman exponent, a nonce in a digital signature algorithm, and so on. The device outputs $g^k \bmod p$ in one form or another and possibly other information as well. The goal of the reverse engineer is to obtain $k$ from a given device based on what was learned from previous reverse engineering efforts and all other available information.

When the primitive is deployed, that attacker has a unique advantage. If the attacker obtains $T$, the attacker can compute $t = T^X \equiv Y^K \bmod p$ and then pad $t$ to obtain $T_0$. Since the attacker was the one that selected all of the $ID$s, the attacker is in a position to compute $k = F_1(T_0||ID||i)$ since $i \leq \Theta$ can be readily guessed. It is this unique advantage that forms the basis for the optimal-bandwidth attacks. In essence, a key exchange is being performed between the attacker and the device each time that the device is invoked. The shared secret is used to secretly convey a random nonce $k$ to the attacker. The use of the oracle and $ID$ guarantees that the user cannot distinguish the view of the honest device from the view of the attacked device, even if $Y$, $ID$, $i$, and so on are obtained through reverse engineering.

## 12.2    Diffie-Hellman SETUP Attack

The Diffie-Hellman key exchange (see Appendix C.1.2) exhibits a discrete log kleptogram that can be exploited to give an insider (e.g., the manufacturer) an advantage. Consider the event that Alice and Bob perform two separate key exchanges. In the first round Alice sends Bob $A_1 = g^{a_1} \bmod p$ and Bob sends Alice $B_1 = g^{b_1} \bmod p$. In the second round Alice sends Bob $A_2 = g^{a_2} \bmod p$ and Bob sends Alice $B_2 = g^{b_2} \bmod p$. The two shared secrets are $g^{a_1 b_1} \bmod p$ and $g^{a_2 b_2} \bmod p$, respectively.

In this attack, Alice's device is dishonest and mounts the SETUP attack.[2] So it is the one using $GenPrivateExponent2$. Bob's device $C$ is honest and uses $GenPrivateExponent1$. The attacker can utilize the backdoor provided that one or both of the devices mount the SETUP attack. To be conservative, it is assumed that Alice's device outputs $(a_i, g^{a_i} \bmod p)$ to Alice. This allows her to verify its computations by checking that $g$ raised to the first value equals the second. Of course, she must keep all of the values for $a_i$ secret. In the $i^{\text{th}}$ key exchange, the device will store $a_i$ and await $B_i$. When the device is given $B_i$ it outputs $B_i^{a_i} \bmod p$. The goal of the attacker is to learn the Diffie-Hellman value $g^{a_2 b_2} \bmod p$.

Alice's device chooses $a_1$ randomly from $\mathbb{Z}_w^*$ and outputs the pair of values $(a_1, g^{a_1} \bmod p)$ to Alice. It stores $a_1$ in non-volatile memory. Alice

---

[2]For example, the manufacturer could be a malicious entity.

supplies the device with $B_1$. The device then computes $B_1^{a_1} \bmod p$ and outputs this value to Alice. At this point an honest device would erase $a_1$, but Alice's device does not. Instead, it stores $a_1$ in non-volatile memory until the subsequent key exchange. When the next exchange is initiated, Alice's device does not choose $a_2$ randomly using a random bit generator. Instead, it computes $a_2 = GenPrivateExponent2(a_1)$. The device outputs $(a_2, g^{a_2} \bmod p)$ to Alice. The value $B_2$ is then supplied to the device by Alice, at which point it outputs $B_2^{a_2} \bmod p$ to Alice. Observe that Alice is essentially letting the device choose all the randomness for her. If she were suspicious, she could take the outputs of the device and compute the Diffie-Hellman secrets herself.[3]

Alice is in big trouble. She is in trouble because the attacker who is carrying out the attack on Alice, namely, the insider who created her device (or altered it), is passively eavesdropping on the network. The attacker obtains $(A_1, B_1, A_2, B_2)$ from the network. Let $T = A_1$. The attacker then uses the private key $X$ to compute,

$$t = T^X \equiv A_1^X \equiv Y^{a_1} \equiv Y^K \bmod p \qquad (12.1)$$

By padding $t$ with leading zeros the value $T_0$ is constructed. The attacker knows all of the $IDs$, and can guess $i$. So, the attacker can compute $k = a_2 = F_1(T_0 || ID || i)$. Since the attacker also obtains $A_2 = g^k = g^{a_2} \bmod p$ from the net the attacker is in a position to compute $B_2^{a_2} \bmod p$. To see this, note that the attacker can guess $ID$ and $i$ and compute a guess for $a_2$. To verify, the attacker raises $g$ to this guess and compares the result to $A_2$. If they match, then $a_2$ has been found without a shadow of a doubt. The attacker can therefore compute the second Diffie-Hellman secret $g^{a_2 b_2} \bmod p$ and listen in on Alice and Bob's second conversation.

The attack can be extended to encompass several key exchanges. This can be accomplished by having the dishonest device compute the values $a_3 = GenPrivateExponent2(a_2)$, $a_4 = GenPrivateExponent2(a_3)$, and so forth. Every so often a new $a_i$ should be chosen randomly to commence a new attack. This is necessary to guarantee forward secrecy, that is, to guard against the device being reverse engineered, studied, repaired, redeployed, and then subsequently compromised.

---

[3]But even then she'd be victimized.

## 12.3  Security of the Diffie-Hellman SETUP Attack

The entire proof that this attack constitutes a secretly embedded trapdoor with universal protection will not be given. However, the two non-trivial aspects of this proof will be sketched out. It is stressed that these are proofs in the random oracle model and that when the attack is implemented it is subject to the weaknesses of the primitive used to instantiate the oracle. The proof that the attack satisfies Property 2 will be outlined. It is shown that in the random oracle model, the exponents that are output by the cryptotrojan are computationally indistinguishable from the exponents that are output by the honest exponent generation algorithm. The proof that the outputs are confidential, even against a successful reverse engineer is then outlined. This is Property 4 of a SETUP attack and it holds using a reduction argument.

### 12.3.1  Indistinguishability of Outputs

It is assumed that the distinguishing adversary knows the cryptotrojan algorithm. This could be from prior reverse engineering endeavors. Hence, the attacker's public key $(Y, g, p)$ is known to the adversary. Since the adversary has not reverse engineered the particular device in question the adversary does not know the value $ID$ right off the bat.

There is nothing to distinguish when $i > \Theta$, so we will consider the case that $i < \Theta$. The first observation is that indistinguishability does not hold against an adversary that has unbounded computational resources. Such an adversary can solve Diffie-Hellman and hence knows $T_0$. This means that the adversary is capable of predicting the subsequent private exponents perfectly. The attacker can guess a value for $ID$ and then invoke the exponent generation device, say four times. The adversary then collects the four exponents that the device outputs. This data set is used to help test if the guess for $ID$ was correct or not. The adversary knows that the values for $i$ will be $i$, $i + 1$, $i + 2$, and $i + 3$. Since $i \leq \Theta$ can be guessed, the adversary will be able to verify correctly with overwhelming probability whether or not the guess for $ID$ was correct. The adversary can probe the integrity of the device's output values by performing the same computations that the device would do if it were dishonest and comparing the results with the data set. If the values do not match the data set, $ID$ may be guessed again. In time, the computationally unbounded adversary will be able to try all $IDs$ and hence distinguish an honest device from a dishonest one. The attack is, however, indistinguishable to all adversaries that are polynomially bounded in computational power.[4]

Let $C$ denote the honest device that uses $GenPrivateExponent1()$ and let $C'$ denote the dishonest device that uses $GenPrivateExponent2()$. A key observation is that the exponents that are output by the dishonest device are chosen from the same set and same probability distribution as the exponents that are output by the honest device. The honest device will always choose its outputs uniformly at random from $\mathbb{Z}_w^*$. Note that every device contains a unique string $ID$, and every device increments $i$ between calls to the oracle. When considering all devices it follows that the portion of the input string corresponding to $(ID||i)$ will never be supplied to the oracle more than once. Since the output of a random oracle is a randomly chosen string that is independent of every other query it follows that the exponents that are output by the dishonest device are drawn from the same set and probability distribution as the outputs of the honest device.

This implies that the only way to distinguish is to guess the oracle input $ID$ correctly. Since $ID$ is not guessable[5] and since it is kept secret from all adversaries in the black-box cryptosystem $C'$, it follows that the outputs of $C$ and $C'$ are indistinguishable to all computationally bounded adversaries.

## 12.3.2    Confidentiality of Outputs

Recall that Property 4 of a SETUP attack (see Section 11.4) is confidentiality against a reverse engineering adversary. In this section a reduction argument is given to prove that Property 4 holds. The claim is that there exists an algorithm that can break the confidentiality of the cryptotrojan attack if and only if there exists an algorithm that can compute Diffie-Hellman secrets efficiently. Clearly if Diffie-Hellman can be broken then there exists an efficient algorithm to break the confidentiality of the cryptotrojan. It remains to show the converse, namely, that if there exists an efficient algorithm that can break the cryptotrojan then solving Diffie-Hellman is easy.

In a nutshell this is proven by showing that if an efficient algorithm exists that violates the confidentiality property then Diffie-Hellman can

---

[4]Polynomial in $|W/2|$.

[5]It is exponential in the security parameter $|p|$.

be solved efficiently. This reduction is a randomized reduction and is therefore very strong.[6]

With regard to confidentiality, it is assumed that the computationally bounded adversary has reverse engineered the device in question and hence knows the value for $ID$ that it contains. It is assumed that the device has been reconstituted and redeployed. It is also assumed that the adversary knows the current value for $i$ that exists in the non-volatile memory store of the device. These are *very* generous assumptions about what the adversary knows.

To prove confidentiality of the dishonest device it is necessary to show that the adversary cannot compute $g^{a_2 b_2} \bmod p$ when the adversary has the following view,

$$view_{C'} = (ID, i, Y, g, p, A_1, B_1, A_2, B_2) \qquad (12.2)$$

The values $A_1$ and $A_2$ in this view are the outputs of $C'$. The adversary also knows the cryptotrojan algorithm. What the adversary does not have access to is the coin flips that the cryptotrojan will generate once it has been redeployed.

The proof of confidentiality is by contradiction. Suppose for the sake of contradiction that a computationally bounded algorithm $A$ exists. For a randomly chosen input, algorithm $A$ solves Diffie-Hellman on $(A_2, B_2)$ with non-negligible probability. The adversary could thus use algorithm $A$ to break the confidentiality of the system. Algorithm $A$ solves Diffie-Hellman on $(A_2, B_2)$ when it "feels" so inclined, but must do so a non-negligible portion of the time.

It is important to first set the stage for the proof. The adversary is trying to break the key exchange $(A_2, B_2)$ that was computed in part by the cryptotrojan. Hence, this Diffie-Hellman secret was created using a call to the random oracle $R$. It is conceivable that an algorithm $A$ that breaks the confidentiality will make oracle calls as well to break $(A_2, B_2)$. Perhaps $A$ will even make some of the *same* oracle calls as the cryptotrojan. However, in the proof we cannot assume this. All that can be assumed is that $A$ makes at most a polynomial[7] number of calls to the oracle and we are free to trap each one of these calls and take the arguments.

---

[6]Randomized reductions are very strong since when they hold for a fixed fraction of the inputs there typically exists a reduction that holds with overwhelming probability for all inputs.

[7]Polynomial in $|p|$.

Consider the following algorithm $SolveDiffieHellman$ that uses $A$ as an oracle to solve the Diffie-Hellman problem.

$SolveDiffieHellman(g, p, U, V)$:
input: prime $p$, generator $g$ of $G$, $U = g^u \bmod p$, and $V = g^v \bmod p$
output: an element $\psi$ contained in $G$
1. choose $r_1, r_2, r_3, r_4, r_5$, and $r_6$ randomly from $\mathbb{Z}_w^*$
2. choose $ID$ to be a random $|p|$-bit string
3. choose $i$ randomly from $\{1, 2, ..., \Theta\}$
4. simulate $k = A(ID, i, U^{r_2 r_1}, g^{r_2}, p, V^{r_2 r_3}, g^{r_2 r_4}, U^{r_2 r_5}, V^{r_2 r_6})$,
     watch calls to $R$, and store the $|p|$ most significant
     bits of each call in list $\omega$
5. compute $k_0 = k^{(r_2 r_5 r_6)^{-1}} \bmod p$
6. remove all elements from $\omega$ that are not contained in $G$
7. let $L$ be the number of elements in $\omega$
8. if $L = 0$ then
9.     set $\beta$ to be a random element in $G$
10. else
11.     choose $\alpha$ randomly from $\{0, 1, 2, ..., L-1\}$
12.     let $\beta$ be the $\alpha^{\text{th}}$ element in $\omega$
13. compute $k_1 = \beta^{(r_2 r_1 r_3)^{-1}} \bmod p$
14. generate bit $b$ randomly
15. output $\psi = k_b$ and halt

Note that with non-negligible probability $A$ will not balk due to the choice of $ID$ and $i$. Denote by $T_{uv}$ the $|p|$ bit binary string that corresponds to the value $g^{r_2 u r_1 v r_3} \bmod p$ when padded appropriately. Denote by $E$ the event that in a given invocation of $A$, algorithm $A$ calls the random oracle $R$ on $(T_{uv}||ID||i)$ at least once. Clearly only one of the two following possibilities hold:

1. Event $E$ occurs with negligible probability.

2. Event $E$ occurs with non-negligible probability.

Consider case (1). Algorithm $A$ can detect that $U^{r_2 r_5} \bmod p$ was not generated by the cryptotrojan by appropriately supplying $(T_{uv}||ID||i)$ to the random oracle. Once verified, $A$ can balk and not output the base $g^{r_2} \bmod p$ Diffie-Hellman secret corresponding to $(U^{r_2 r_5}, V^{r_2 r_6})$. But in case (1) this can only occur at most a negligible fraction of the time since changing even a single bit in the value supplied to the oracle elicits an inde-pendently random response. By assumption, $A$ returns the base $g^{r_2} \bmod p$ Diffie-Hellman secret corresponding to $(U^{r_2 r_5}, V^{r_2 r_6})$ a non-negligible frac-tion of the time. Since the difference between a non-negligible number and negligible number is a non-negligible number it follows that $A$ solves the base $g^{r_2} \bmod p$ Diffie-Hellman problem on $(U^{r_2 r_5}, V^{r_2 r_6})$ without re-lying on the random oracle. So, in case (1) it follows that with non-negligible probability $b$ will be 0 and $SolveDiffieHellman$ will output $\psi = k_0 = g^{uv} \bmod p$.

Now consider case (2). After making an oracle call with $T_{uv}$ algorithm $A$ will be able to detect that the value $U^{r_2 r_5} \bmod p$ was generated incor-rectly. Being adversarial in nature, algorithm $A$ may not wish to lend a helping hand and may in fact immediately balk. But, it is too late. Since $A$ makes at most a polynomial number of calls[8] to $R$ the value for $L$ cannot be too large. Since $A$ invokes the oracle with the string $(T_{uv}||ID||i)$ with non-negligible probability and since $L$ cannot be too large it follows that $T_{uv}$ will be equal to $T_c$ with non-negligible probability. So, with non-negligible probability $SolveDiffieHellman$ captures the needed Diffie-Hellman se-cret that was passed to the oracle and raises it to the $(r_2 r_1 r_3)^{-1}$ power. Recall that $U^{r_2 r_1} \bmod p$ was submitted to $A$ in place of $Y$ and $V^{r_2 r_3} \bmod p$ was submited to $A$ in place of $A_1$. So, despite any subsequent misbehavior by $A$, $SolveDiffieHellman$ computes $k_1 = g^{uv} \bmod p$ with non-negligible probability. It follows that with non-negligible probability $b$ will be 1 and $SolveDiffieHellman$ will output $\psi = k_1 = g^{uv} \bmod p$.

It has been shown that in either case, the existence of $A$ contradicts the Diffie-Hellman assumption. So, the original assumption that adversary $A$ exists is wrong. This proves that the cryptotrojan satisfies Property 4 of a SETUP attack.

This attack is the very essence of kleptography. It uses cryptography directly to attack cryptography itself. The Diffie-Hellman key exchange is used to securely and subliminally compromise a key exchange between two unwary users, namely, Alice and Bob. The notion of a reduction ar-gument is used to prove the confidentiality of the attack in the random oracle model. Assuming the existence of a random oracle, the attack on Diffie-Hellman is as secure as Diffie-Hellman itself. The notion of compu-tational indistinguishability of probability distributions is used to prove that the attack cannot be detected in black-box environments. It is a

---

[8]Polynomial in $|p|$.

demonstration that modern cryptographic paradigms and tools can be used to subvert computer systems in a forward-engineering fashion.

## 12.4   Intuition Behind the Attack

Having seen the application of this attack to Diffie-Hellman, it is now possible to shed more light on the intuition behind the attack. On the surface the attack is nothing more than a random number generator that takes an auxiliary input and outputs a value drawn uniformly at random from $\mathbb{Z}_w^*$. However, just below the surface something utterly insidious is occurring. When the auxiliary input is an exponent of $g$, the device performs a key exchange with the attacker's public key and submits the resulting shared secret to a random oracle. Provided that a modular exponentiation that uses the auxiliary value is made available to the attacker, the whole cryptosystem that uses the random number generator can be securely and subliminally compromised. As will become clear in the following sections, this modular exponentiation is a *discrete-log kleptogram.*

How and why is this attack possible? It is based on two very powerful notions: the ability to conduct key exchanges over untrusted networks and the notion of a cryptographic one-way function with certain randomness properties. The notion of a random oracle is more of a tool than a practical reality. It is a point in fact that no such efficient oracle can even be synthesized. Yet it nonetheless constitutes a very useful tool for proving the security of cryptographic algorithms. Random oracle proofs essentially show that if any weakness exists in a fielded cryptosystem that is based on a *correct* random oracle proof, then the weakness must reside in the choice of the primitive that was used to instantiate the oracle.

It might not be immediately clear what the advantages of this attack are over using a pseudorandom number generator with a fixed secret seed. First, note that if the device containing $C'$ is reverse engineered and subsequently repaired or replaced with an identical-looking device, the reverse engineer will still not be able to exploit the presence of $C'$. The attacker will continue to gain access to private keys and so forth, but the reverse engineer will not. Also, when the pseudorandom number generator approach is used, the device could be reverse engineered, the seed learned, the device reinstated, and the reverse engineer, along with the attacker, would know all of the future secrets. The attacker would be none the wiser. In covert applications, gathering data may not be acceptable if the act of doing so runs the risk of having it fall into enemy hands.

With some simple modifications, the attack is also favorable for deployment in software. The *ID* string could be replaced by the IP address of the current machine, or perhaps something else that is public and unique. This would ensure that the device chooses random values in each invocation. This way, the software containing *GenPrivateExponent2* could be duplicated as is. The public key $Y$ would act as a secret (until it is perhaps discovered and disclosed). Although far from tamper-resistant, this approach retains many of the properties of the approach that is taken here that assumes tamper-resistance.

## 12.5   Kleptogram Attack Methodology

The discrete-log SETUP primitive can be applied across a great many discrete-log based cryptosystems. There is an underlying methodology on how to synthesize a SETUP attack against a discrete-log based cryptosystem. This methodology is given below.

1. Identification of a kleptogram: To apply the discrete-log SETUP attack, it is necessary to find a modular exponentiation that the device outputs.

2. Availability of the kleptogram to the attacker: This modular exponentiation must eventually become available to the attacker (for example, the manufacturer). It can be encoded into a public key, a digital signature, a ciphertext, and so on. Sometimes a modular exponentiation can be reconstructed based on the outputs of a cryptosystem (for example, $g^k \bmod p$ can be reconstructed from a DSA signature).

3. Availability of the exponent to the SETUP mechanism: The exponent of this modular exponentiation must be available within the device at the time that the modular exponentiation is computed. This is necessary for the SETUP attack to function. Such a modular exponentiation constitutes a discrete-log kleptogram.

4. Exploitation of the kleptogram: The exponent of the kleptogram is fed as input to *GenPrivateExponent2*. As a result, this primitive will output a securely compromised random number.

5. Using the compromised nonce: The random number that is output by *GenPrivateExponent2* must be used as a secret nonce in

the underlying cryptosystem. Provided that the exposure of this nonce to the attacker will compromise the cryptosystem that uses *GenPrivateExponent*2, the attack (should) constitute a SETUP attack.

It is stressed that the above steps are a heuristic approach to identifying kleptographic attacks in discrete-log based cryptosystems. There is no guarantee that this approach will always work. Yet it is nonetheless a good way to think kleptographically.

## 12.6    PKCS SETUP Attacks

The two most basic types of asymmetric algorithms are encryption algorithms and digital signature algorithms. SETUP attacks exist against discrete-log based algorithms that fall into both of these categories. In this section SETUP attacks are presented against discrete-log based asymmetric encryption algorithms.

The SETUP mechanism is nefariously placed in encryption algorithms, not decryption algorithms, since it is anticipated that ciphertexts may become readily available to the attacker over a public network. These attacks may all be construed as cryptotrojan attacks against programs that perform public key encryption. The payload of the cryptotrojan securely and subliminally leaks plaintexts to the insider.

### 12.6.1    ElGamal PKCS SETUP Attack

Consider the ElGamal encryption algorithm (see Appendix C.2.1). Consider two different ElGamal encryptions $(a_1, b_1)$ and $(a_2, b_2)$. Let $a_1 = g^{k_1} \ mod \ p$ and let $a_2 = g^{k_2} \ mod \ p$. Also, let $b_1 = y^{k_1} m_1 \ mod \ p$ and let $b_2 = y^{k_2} m_2 \ mod \ p$.

The first objective is to identify a kleptogram. Observe that $a_1$ is a modular exponentiation and hence it satisfies step (1). Since the ciphertext $(a_1, b_1)$ may be sent across a public network, the value $a_1$ may eventually be obtained by the attacker. So the value $a_1$ satisfies step (2). The exponent $k_1$ is generated by the ElGamal encryption algorithm and so is readily available to the encryption algorithm.[9] So, $a_1$ satisfies property (3) as well. Suppose that $k_1$ is fed as input to *GenPrivateExponent*2. This

---

[9]The exponent $k_1$ can be thought of as a resource that can be exploited by a carefully designed cryptotrojan.

will satisfy step (4). Finally, by setting $k_2 = GenPrivateExponent2(k_1)$ instead of generating $k_2$ randomly, the output will constitute a random nonce in the second encryption. So, this approach satisfies step (5).

The question remains as to whether or not this is a SETUP attack. The attacker can obtain $a_1 = g^{k_1} \bmod p$ from the public network. By computing $t = a_1^X \bmod p$ and padding with zeros as necessary, the value $T_0$ can be obtained by the attacker. As a result, the attacker is in a position to compute $k_2 = F_1(T_0||ID||i)$ by guessing $ID$ and $i$. As in the attack on Diffie-Hellman, all guesses can be verified for correctness. Since the attacker can compute $k_2$, the attacker can compute $b_2 y^{-k_2} \bmod p$. This value is $m_2$.

Observe that this attack utilizes fresh randomness in the form of $k_1$. This assures confidentiality of future outputs against a cryptanalyzing adversary[10] that learns $ID$ and $g^X \bmod p$. The attack can be chained in the same way as the attack on the Diffie-Hellman key exchange. The proof that this is a secure SETUP is very much the same as the proof for the attack on Diffie-Hellman. This should come as no surprise due to the relationship between Diffie-Hellman and the ElGamal encryption scheme (see the reduction in Appendix C.2.2).

Typically, when public key cryptography is needed to encrypt bulk data, hybrid cryptosystems are used. Thus, in this mode of usage, the SETUP can leak keys. It can leak the randomly generated symmetric keys used to encrypt the data. An optimal bandwidth attack can be implemented in an ElGamal based hybrid system as follows. In a nutshell, the value $F_1(T_0||ID||i)$ can be used directly or indirectly to derive the bits in the symmetric key for the hybrid encryption. The legitimate message recipient decrypts $(a, b)$ to obtain the needed symmetric key. So does the attacker, in effect.

Another attack exists against cryptographic *providers* such as smart cards that are given access to private decryption keys and that are used to both encrypt and decrypt messages. Let Alice be the user of the provider that contains the cryptotrojan and let Bob be a user with public key $(y_b, g, p)$. Alice's public key is $(y_a, g, p)$. In this attack, the cryptotrojan in Alice's provider only mounts the attack when it obtains Alice's private key $x_a$ in $y_a = g^{x_a} \bmod p$. The provider must obtain access to it when she decrypts the first message that she receives.

Once the value $x_a$ is obtained by the provider, the attack commences.

---

[10]For example, a hacker that obtains an old snapshot of the signing algorithm at run-time.

In the attack, the nonce $k_i$ that is used to encrypt a message to Bob is not chosen randomly. Instead, it is chosen based on the shared Diffie-Hellman secret $g^{x_a X} \bmod p$. More specifically, when the ciphertext to Bob is the $i^{\text{th}}$ encryption that the provider computes after that attack commences, Alice's provider computes the nonce to be $k_i = F_1(T_0 || ID || i)$ where $T_0$ is Alice and the attacker's shared Diffie-Hellman secret, padded accordingly. Once again this demonstrates the use of cryptography to attack cryptography itself. The cryptotrojan uses the shared Diffie-Hellman secret of Alice and the attacker to compute $k_i$. The nonce $k_i$ is used to compute $y_b^{k_i} \bmod p$, a shared Diffie-Hellman secret between Alice's cryptographic provider and Bob. Recall that in ElGamal, this quantity is computed during data encryption.

The indistinguishability of this attack hinges on the secrecy of the value $ID$. To see this, note that Alice may be inquisitive and may try to determine if her device carries out this attack. She may have reverse engineered a similar device[11] and hence obtained $g^X \bmod p$. She thus knows the shared secret $T_0$ since she knows her own private key. However, since a random oracle is used and since $ID$ is unknown to Alice, indistinguishability still holds. This is a bandwidth-optimal attack on ElGamal encryption since the attacker need only obtain Alice's public key $(y_a, g, p)$ and the ElGamal encryption to perform decryption.

Now consider confidentiality against a cryptanalyzing adversary. Such an adversary may be assumed to have access to the value $ID$ in Alice's device, and also $g^X \bmod p$ via reverse engineering. It must, however, be the case that $x_a$ is not known to such an adversary. This happens when, for instance, the device is given only *temporary* access to $x_a$. Confidentiality holds based on the fact that neither $x_a$ nor $X$ is known to the adversary. Hence, the Diffie-Hellman secret $T_0$ that the attacker shares with Alice's device is not known to the cryptanalyzing adversary.

## 12.6.2    Cramer-Shoup PKCS SETUP Attack

The Cramer-Shoup cryptosystem is described in Appendix C.2.3. The public key in Cramer-Shoup is $(g_1, g_2, c, d, h)$ and the ciphertext is the tuple $(u_1, u_2, e, v)$.

---

[11]For instance, the process of reverse engineering may destroy the device in question. So, she may be able to reverse engineer other devices but not her own without destroying it.

$$u_1 = g_1^r, \ u_2 = g_2^r, \ e = h^r m, \ \alpha = H(u_1, u_2, e), \ v = c^r d^{r\alpha} \qquad (12.3)$$

For simplicity it will be assumed that $G$ is a cyclic subgroup of $\mathbb{Z}_p^*$ where $p$ is prime. Consider two separate encryptions in Cramer-Shoup. Let $(u_1, u_2, e, v)$ be an encryption of $m$ that uses $r$ as the nonce and let $(u_1', u_2', e', v')$ be an encryption of $m'$ that uses $r'$ as the nonce.

The first objective is to identify a kleptogram. Observe that $u_1$ is a modular exponentiation and hence it satisfies step (1). Since the ciphertext may be sent across a public network, the value $u_1$ may eventually be obtained by the attacker. So the value $u_1$ satisfies step (2). The exponent $r$ is generated by the Cramer-Shoup encryption algorithm and so is readily available to the encryption algorithm. So, $u_1$ satisfies property (3) as well. Suppose that $r$ is fed as input to $GenPrivateExponent2$. This will satisfy step (4). Finally, by computing $r' = GenPrivateExponent2(r)$ instead of choosing $r'$ randomly, the output will constitute a random nonce in the second encryption. So, this approach satisfies step (5).

The question remains as to whether or not this is a SETUP attack. The attacker can obtain $u_1 = g^r \bmod p$ from the public network. By computing $t = u_1^X \bmod p$ and padding with zeros as necessary, the value $T_0$ can be obtained by the attacker. As a result, the attacker is in a position to compute $r' = F_1(T_0||ID||i)$ by guessing $ID$ and $i$. As in the attack on Diffie-Hellman, all guesses can be verified for correctness. Since the attacker can compute $r'$, the attacker can compute the message $m' = e'h^{-r'} \bmod p$. The attack can be chained in the same way as the attack on the Diffie-Hellman key exchange.

## 12.7  SETUP Attacks on Digital Signature Algorithms

SETUP attacks against discrete-log based signature schemes constitute a direct extension of the work of Gus Simmons on the Prisoner's Problem. In this section SETUP attacks against discrete-log based signature schemes are given. The SETUP mechanism is placed in the algorithm that computes digital signatures, not the signature verification algorithm, since it is anticipated that digital signatures may eventually become available to the attacker. These attacks may be construed as cryptotrojan attacks against programs that compute and output digital signatures. The payload of the cryptotrojan securely and subliminally leaks signing private keys to the insider.

These attacks assume that the devices are implemented with a priori knowledge of the values for $g$, $p$, $q$, and so on that the users will use. The primes $p$ and $q$ can still be chosen using a one-way hash function so as to dismiss any suspicions that they are *trapdoor primes*. This will not hinder the effectiveness of the attacks. These parameters are often fixed for all users. In these SETUP attacks, trapdoor primes are not needed;[12] any primes will do.

A related, but different, attack on signature algorithms that uses weak pseudorandomness has been shown [17]. The main difference between this attack and SETUP attacks is that SETUP attacks use randomness as well as carefully computed pseudorandomness in concert with the attacker's public key that is included in the black-box device.

## 12.7.1 SETUP in the ElGamal Signature Algorithm

A SETUP attack on the ElGamal signature algorithm was proposed that is based on the notion of a subliminal channel [333]. However, the attack is a rather weak form of SETUP. The attack was later strengthened [336]. Both of these attacks required that the attacker obtain two digital signatures in order to recover the signing private key.

In this subsection the attack is improved substantially by making a simple observation. The observation is as follows. The attacker can include the public key $Y$ in the device to mount the attack. The unwary user has a public key $y$ and a corresponding signing private key $x$ that is supplied to the signature algorithm. This immediately implies that the user and the attacker have a shared Diffie-Hellman secret. The secret is $Y^x = y^X = g^{Xx} \bmod p$. This fact can be utilized to securely and subliminally leak the signing private key $x$ at a higher bandwidth than previous approaches.

The ElGamal digital signature algorithm is described in Appendix C.2.4. The user's public key is $(y, g, p)$ and the signature on $m$ is $(r, s)$. The value $r$ equals $g^k \bmod p$ where $k$ is the randomly chosen nonce for the signature.

The first objective is to identify a kleptogram. Observe that $y$ is a modular exponentiation and hence it satisfies step (1). Since the public

---

[12]Trapdoor primes were originally suspected in DSA.

key $(y, g, p)$ may be obtained by the attacker, the value $y$ satisfies step (2). The exponent $x$ is given to the ElGamal signing algorithm by the user and so is readily available within the signing algorithm. So, $y$ satisfies property (3) as well. Suppose that $x$ is fed as input to $GenPrivateExponent2$. This will satisfy step (4). Finally, by computing $k = GenPrivateExponent2(x)$ instead of choosing $k$ randomly, the output will constitute a random nonce in the signature $(r, s)$. So, this approach satisfies step (5).

The question remains as to whether or not this is a SETUP attack. Suppose that the attacker can obtain $y = g^x \bmod p$ from a public network. By computing $t = y^X \bmod p$ and padding with zeros as necessary, the value $T_0$ can be obtained by the attacker. As a result, the attacker is in a position to compute $k = F_1(T_0||ID||i)$ by guessing $ID$ and $i$. As in the attack on Diffie-Hellman, all guesses can be verified for correctness. In this attack the argument $T_0$ that is passed to the oracle will always be the same. It is the binary string corresponding to the secret that the unwary user and the attacker share. However, since $i$ is incremented in each device, random values for $k$ will always be used.

Suppose that $r$ has a multiplicative inverse modulo $p - 1$. If $r$ is even, then it clearly does not have such an inverse. The inverse will exist whenever $gcd(r, p - 1) = 1$. If the inverse exists, then the attacker can compute $x = r^{-1}(H(m) - sk) \bmod p - 1$ since the attacker can compute $k$. The possibility that $r$ does not have an inverse is becoming less of an issue year after year, since cryptosystems are typically defined over prime order subgroups for security reasons. It is not hard to see that this attack against classical ElGamal nonetheless leaks $x$ at a high bandwidth.

Consider the case that the user who knows $x$ is curious and wants to know if his or her black-box device is carrying out the attack. If this user reverse engineers a similar device then it may be assumed that $g^X \bmod p$ is obtained. Therefore, the user knows $T_0$. However, the particular value for $ID$ in the user's device is secret. It follows that under the random oracle assumption $k$ will be random. This assures indistinguishability. Confidentiality holds under a random oracle argument based on the Diffie-Hellman assumption.

## 12.7.2    SETUP in the Pointcheval-Stern Algorithm

The Pointcheval-Stern digital signature algorithm is described in Appendix C.2.5. The first objective is to identify a kleptogram. Observe that $y$ is a modular exponentiation and hence it satisfies step (1). Since the public key $(y, g, p)$ may be obtained by the attacker, the value $y$ satisfies step (2). The exponent $x$ is given to the Pointcheval-Stern signing algorithm by the user and so is readily available within the signing algorithm. So, $y$ satisfies property (3) as well. Suppose that $x$ is fed as input to $GenPrivateExponent2$. This will satisfy step (4). Finally, by computing $k = GenPrivateExponent2(x)$ instead of choosing $k$ randomly, the output will constitute a random nonce in the signature $(r, s)$. So, this approach satisfies step (5).

The question remains as to whether or not this is a SETUP attack. Suppose the attacker can obtain $y = g^x \ mod \ p$ from a public network. By computing $t = y^X \ mod \ p$ and padding with zeros as necessary, the value $T_0$ can be obtained by the attacker. As a result, the attacker is in a position to compute $k = F_1(T_0||ID||i)$ by guessing $ID$ and $i$. As in the attack on Diffie-Hellman, all guesses can be verified for correctness. In this attack the argument $T_0$ that is passed to the random oracle will always be the same. However, since $i$ is incremented in each device, random values for $k$ will always be used.

Suppose that $r$ has a multiplicative inverse modulo $p - 1$. In this case the attacker can compute $x = r^{-1}(H(r||m) - sk) \ mod \ p - 1$ since the attacker can compute $k$. Despite the potential non-existence of an inverse of $r$, this attack nonetheless leaks $x$ at a high bandwidth over the signatures that are output.

## 12.7.3 SETUP in DSA

The Digital Signature Algorithm is described in Appendix C.2.7. The order of $g$ in DSA is $q$ so $g$ generates a prime order subgroup of $\mathbb{Z}_p^*$ in DSA. The user's public key is $(y, g, p)$. The private key of the user is $x < q$. The signature on a message $m$ is $(r, s)$ where $r = (g^k \ mod \ p) \ mod \ q$.

The first objective is to identify a kleptogram. Observe that $y$ is a modular exponentiation and hence it satisfies step (1). Since the public key $(y, g, p)$ may be obtained by the attacker, the value $y$ satisfies step (2). The exponent $x$ is given to the DSA signing algorithm by the user and so is readily available within the signing algorithm. So, $y$ satisfies property (3) as well. Suppose that $x$ is fed as input to $GenPrivateExponent2$. This will satisfy step (4). Finally, by computing $k = GenPrivateExponent2(x)$ instead of choosing $k$ randomly, the output will constitute a random nonce in the signature $(r, s)$. So, this approach satisfies step (5).

The question remains as to whether or not this is a SETUP attack.

Suppose the attacker can obtain $y = g^x \bmod p$ from a public network. By computing $t = y^X \bmod p$ and padding with zeros as necessary, the value $T_0$ can be obtained by the attacker. As a result, the attacker is in a position to compute $k = F_1(T_0||ID||i)$ by guessing $ID$ and $i$. As in the attack on Diffie-Hellman, all guesses can be verified for correctness. In this attack the argument $T_0$ that is passed to the random oracle will always be the same. In essence, it is the Diffie-Hellman secret $Y^x = y^X = g^{Xx} \bmod p$ that is shared between the unwary user and the attacker. Since $i$ is incremented in each device, random values for $k$ will always be used. Since $r < q$ it follows that $r$ will have a unique multiplicative inverse modulo $q$. So, the attacker can compute $x = r^{-1}(sk - H(m)) \bmod q$ since the attacker can compute $k$.

This attack can applied to the Prisoner's Problem of Gus Simmons. Using this attack, Alice can securely and subliminally leak her signing private key $x$ to Bob under the observance of a warden *in a single digital signature*. As a result, it effectively increases the bandwidth of the Legendre channel from 14 bits to 160 bits, the size of the entire signing private key. Also, this attack has the novel feature that it can be accomplished without requiring that Alice give her private key to Bob before going to prison.

## 12.7.4   SETUP in the Schnorr Signature Algorithm

The Schnorr digital signature algorithm is described in Appendix C.2.6. The order of $g$ in Schnorr is $q$ so $g$ generates a prime order subgroup of $\mathbb{Z}_p^*$ in Schnorr. The user's public key is $(y, g, p)$ where $y = g^{-x} \bmod p$. The signature on a message $m$ is $(e, s)$ where $e = H(m||r)$ and $r = g^k \bmod p$.

The first objective is to identify a kleptogram. Observe that $y$ is a modular exponentiation and hence it satisfies step (1). Since the public key $(y, g, p)$ may be obtained by the attacker, the value $y$ satisfies step (2). The exponent $x$ is given to the Schnorr signing algorithm by the user and so is readily available within the signing algorithm. So, $y$ satisfies property (3) as well. Suppose that $x$ is fed as input to $GenPrivateExponent2$. This will satisfy step (4). Finally, by computing $k = GenPrivateExponent2(x)$ instead of choosing $k$ randomly, the output will constitute a random nonce in the signature $(e, s)$. So, this approach satisfies step (5).

The question remains as to whether or not this is a SETUP attack. Suppose the attacker can obtain $y = g^{-x} \bmod p$ from a public network. By computing $t = y^X \bmod p$ and padding with zeros as necessary, the value $T_0$ can be obtained by the attacker. As a result, the attacker is in a position to compute $k = F_1(T_0||ID||i)$ by guessing $ID$ and $i$. As in the attack on Diffie-Hellman, all guesses can be verified for correctness. Since $e < q$ it follows that $e$ will have a unique multiplicative inverse modulo $q$. So, the attacker can compute $x = e^{-1}(s - k) \ mod \ q$ since the attacker can compute $k$.

## 12.8   Rogue Use of DSA for Encryption

One of the criticisms of DSA was that it does not provide for secret key distribution, as RSA does. Smid and Branstad indicated that DSA is inherently different from RSA in this respect when they stated that "The DSA does not provide for secret key distribution because DSA is not intended for secret key distribution" [284]. This perceived feature of DSA over RSA is in fact non-existent. DSA can be exploited to securely communicate messages between two colluding users.

Nyberg and Rueppel showed a way to abuse DSA. They showed how to securely integrate DSA with key distribution by computing the signature $(r, s)$ with $H(m) = 1$ [209]. However, setting $H(m) = 1$ makes the abuse of DSA blatantly obvious.

Borrowing ideas from kleptography, it was shown how to abuse DSA without setting $H(m) = 1$ in the signature [336]. It is based on the observation that the value $g^k \ mod \ p$ can be recovered from $(r, s)$. This can be done as follows,

$$g^k = g^{s^{-1}H(m)}y^{s^{-1}r} \ mod \ p \tag{12.4}$$

So, Alice can send a DSA signed message to Bob that is effectively asymmetrically encrypted as follows. Alice chooses $k$ randomly and raises Bob's DSA public key $y$ to this $k$, thereby yielding a secret Diffie-Hellman key $z = y^k \ mod \ p$. Alice then encrypts this message using $z$ as the symmetric key in classical cipher. Alice signs the resulting ciphertext using her DSA private key, using $k$ as the nonce in her DSA signature. Bob can recover $g^k \ mod \ p$ using the signature $(r, s)$. He can then compute $z$ by raising $g^k \ mod \ p$ to his private key. With $z$ he can decrypt the signed message that was symmetrically encrypted. The only information that is sent is the encrypted file, which is the message that is signed, and $(r, s)$.

## 12.9    Other Work in Kleptography

There are numerous other results in kleptography and related areas that are not presented in this book. In this section some of these results are mentioned. In particular the topic of embedding a backdoor into a symmetric cipher is addressed. Also, heuristics are given for designers of symmetric ciphers for showing the absence of backdoors in the ciphers they create. These are only heuristics and are by no means foolproof. This list of results may not be exhaustive, so we apologize in advance if any results are omitted.

It has been shown how to use public key encryption to turn the Newton channel, which is a broadcast channel, into a private subliminal channel [339]. This is a form of kleptographic attack that utilizes the Newton channel directly. The attack can be used to leak the ElGamal signing private key in each ElGamal signature that is output by the signing device. The attack requires 160 bits of smoothness in $p-1$, where $p$ is the modulus in the ElGamal public key.

A challenging problem is to implement a secure backdoor in a symmetric cipher. This is challenging since typical symmetric ciphers are deterministic and therefore make it difficult to exploit randomness in computations. Symmetric ciphers have been proposed in the past that have secret specifications. Despite this security by obscurity approach, the U.S. government proposed Skipjack [41, 200] as a secret cipher and planned on deploying it in the Clipper chip. Efforts have been made to research the possibility of building backdoors into secret ciphers, as well as building backdoors into public ciphers. Such results are merely plausibility results, geared towards casting doubt on questionable COMSEC practices that are based in part on secrecy.

The construction of symmetric ciphers with backdoors was addressed by Blaze, Feigenbaum, and Leighton [29]. They showed that a symmetric cipher with such a backdoor is equivalent to a public key cryptosystem. To see this, note that if Alice chooses a symmetric key randomly and then encrypts a message with it using a backdoor symmetric cipher, she and the insider can access the plaintext. No one else can. Alice can thus send asymmetrically encrypted data to Bob by encrypting it with a randomly chosen symmetric key and then sending the resulting ciphertext to him. Bob need not know the symmetric key she used per se, as long as the backdoor gives him access to the plaintext. In this scenario the public keys are in fact the specification of the backdoor symmetric cipher themselves.

Rijmen and Preneel proposed a trapdoor cipher that has a public specification and that still provides the designer with an exclusive advantage [240]. The recovery ability in their algorithm is based on a very specific trapdoor that allows the designer to break the encryption using linear cryptanalysis. This cipher was subsequently cryptanalyzed [323]. Patarin and Goubin also proposed a symmetric cipher with a backdoor in it [220]. This method was also cryptanalyzed [24, 93].

Monkey is an example of a backdoor attack that requires that its design be kept secret [338]. It is a black-box symmetric cryptosystem with a public I/O specification, an 80-bit key, and a 64-bit block size. In order for Monkey to leak symmetric key information it is required that the designer obtain a sufficient amount of ciphertexts under a given key $k$ such that each contains a particular known-plaintext bit. This allows the designer to recover $k$. Monkey reveals one plaintext bit in each ciphertext to a successful reverse engineer.

A successor to Monkey, called Black-Rugose, was recently proposed [340]. This design eliminates the need for known plaintext entirely to leak symmetric key information to the insider. Monkey leaks a bound on the message entropy to the reverse engineer. It requires that the designer obtain a sufficient number of ciphertexts that encrypt messages with a requisite level of redundancy. The information leakage method that is used employs data compression as a basic tool to generate a subliminal channel.

The potential of inserting backdoors into symmetric ciphers suggests that all internal constants proposed in an algorithm have to be justified in order to argue that a design-level attack is not being carried out. There are two basic approaches to this. The first is to pass a seed through a one-way function and let the cipher constants be the output of the one-way function. The seed is used to help prove that the constants were not maliciously chosen. The MARS symmetric cipher utilized SHA-1 applied to seeding information to derive S-Box values [45]. MARS was chosen as a finalist in the AES selection process. Another approach is to utilize universal constants such as $\pi$ and $e$. The Blowfish cipher utilizes the digits of $\pi$ in hexadecimal as S-Box values [258]. In practice, candidate S-Box values must be tested against the threat of linear cryptanalysis [180], differential cryptanalysis [25, 72], and so on before they are used.

Weis and Lucks showed attacks on black-box ciphers that exploit the randomness used in the choice of initialization vectors and other avenues that might be readily available to a design-level attacker [316]. The attacks are geared exclusively towards deterministic devices that perform secret key encryption. It was shown how to kleptographically compromise stream ciphers.

Kleptographic attacks can be thought of as design-level abuses of cryptographic algorithms. The attacks that were shown affect key generation algorithms, public key encryption algorithms, and digital signing algorithms. Yet there are other primitives used in modern cryptography that may be undermined as well. Ways have been investigated on how to subjugate threshold cryptosystems based on the fact that no single user possesses the entire private key [324]. A source of potential abuses is the fact that third parties do not know whether or how a secret key is shared due to the transparent nature of secret sharing. This was dubbed the dark side of threshold cryptography.

## 12.10   Should You Trust Your Smart Card?

When implemented properly,[13] SETUP attacks give the manufacturer your private keys in such a way that you cannot detect the transgression without reverse engineering the card. In the case of RSA, for example, by virtue of publishing your public key you are giving your corresponding private key to the manufacturer when the manufacturer implements the malicious key generation algorithm described in Section 11.5. Given the current state of industry standards there is little reason to trust any smart card whatsoever unless you trust the manufacturer *entirely*. As PKI takes root, the potential payoff for a company that carries out a SETUP attack will only increase.

Countering the threat of a SETUP attack is a subtle business. Consider the attack on the Diffie-Hellman key exchange. The device can behave in a completely unpredictable, Byzantine fashion. It could flip a $2^{24}$ sided coin, and mount the attack if and only if the result of the toss is 1. The device would therefore *be* honest most of the time. This demonstrates the peril in trusting black-boxes. If Alice tests $2^{10}$ outputs to check for a SETUP, the device can flip a $2^{25}$ sided coin. If Alice tests $2^{15}$ outputs, the device could flip a $2^{35}$ sided coin, and so on.

---

[13]For example, taking into account timing attacks, differential power analysis, and so on.

In general there is no need for a Diffie-Hellman key exchange device to output the exponent it generates randomly in each key exchange to the user. The device need only output the modular exponentiation and the shared secret to be of use. The reason that the device in the Diffie-Hellman SETUP attack outputs exponents was to show that the attack works even in this worst-case scenario. However, the following countermeasure can be used to *help* show that the key exchanges are honest (that is, that no SETUP attack is being performed). Rather than choosing the exponent randomly, the device chooses a seed $s$ randomly and passes it through a public one-way hash function[14] to obtain $H(s)$. The value $H(s)$ is then used as the Diffie-Hellman key exchange exponent. In addition to the normal Diffie-Hellman key exchange value, the device outputs the seed $s$ to the user. So, Alice's device outputs $(s, g^{H(s)} \bmod p)$. If she is suspicious she can hash the seed and verify the output of the device.

This is a very general defense mechanism against the threat of discrete-log SETUP attacks. The oracle $H(\cdot)$ is in fact choosing the randomness that is used as the exponent. This countermeasure is by no means perfect. In fact, there is a weakness in it. The device can make numerous calls to the oracle $H(\cdot)$. For instance, the device can continually make calls until the 14 least significant bits of $g^{H(s)} \bmod p$ are as desired. This channel has a similar bandwidth as the Legendre channel of Gus Simmons. However, if Alice always verifies that her device is operating correctly, she will exert more computational effort than the device. This defeats the purpose of using the device altogether. She may as well do the exchanges herself since she is already computing just as many modular exponentiations as her device.

The approach of using $H(\cdot)$ and having the device output the tuple $(s, g^{H(s)} \bmod p)$ is nonetheless a very good one. On numerous consulting engagements[15] Adam has been asked to "try to get the private key off the smart card." This directive was administered with the wholehearted belief that it was possible to verify that no one would ever have access to the private key.[16] It was a joke, really. Yet a mechanism that permits

---

[14]The outputs must look random.

[15]Fortune 500 companies included.

[16]Mentioning the existence of kleptographic attacks was ineffectual. The argument was summarily dismissed as being *theory*. To translate, the Fortune 500 company was basically saying, "We don't care. We are paying our security consultants a lot of money. We are exercising due diligence and hence will not lose our jobs."

the verification of the devices' choice of randomness would help to say something meaningful about the integrity of the implementation.

A similar approach is to eliminate all randomness from the device. In this approach the requirement is made that the device be a deterministic algorithm. A separate device supplies the randomness and the device in question uses the randomness to perform public key operations. This approach is hazardous due to the coin-flipping problem. VLSI chips have a variety of ways of generating randomness themselves and it could still mount the SETUP attack once in a blue moon.

To summarize, the following two reasons form fundamental difficulties in dealing with insider threats in probabilistic cryptographic algorithms:

1. The device can always "cheat" when you're not looking. Even when you believe it to be deterministic and supply it with randomness yourself for verification purposes, it can with a very small probability ignore your randomness on a given occasion and substitute its own on the sly.

2. If you are always looking, then you are doing even more work than the device. This defeats the purpose of using the cryptographic device altogether.

Another option to mitigate the insider threat is to utilize multiple key pairs that are generated and stored on devices made by different manufacturers. In this approach an encryption is computed by encrypting the message multiple times using each different public key. This is often referred to as *cascading encryptions*. A given document is signed multiple times using each different private key. This way, if one smart card is compromised and another is not, the overall solution will inherit the security of the honest device. The ciphertext layer computed by the honest device will never be breached and the signatures from the honest device will never be forged. This is probably the best approach until industry standards start addressing this problem. (This may be overly optimistic.)

We recommend that users who must rely on smart cards exercise due diligence in investigating all of the manufacturers involved in the complete solution. The manufacturers should be at least as trustworthy as the certificate authority, if not more. We recommend that users be wary of snake oil. If a manufacturer claims they have a whiz-bang cryptographic algorithm or random number generator but will not disclose it in its entirety, then we recommend that their products *not be used*. Security by obscurity is an unacceptable practice, even when proprietary algorithms are concerned. Published (and preferably standardized) algorithms should always be used by vendors. If a manufacturer claims that there are no backdoors, we recommend that users get a third-party assessment of this and that users verify that the third party had unobstructed access to any and all source code, schematic diagrams, test data, requirements documents, and design documents. This includes any and all such documentation from the chip manufacturer(s). *Anything short of this fails to suggest that a backdoor is not present in the design.*

A naive response to this issue is the following. "My smart card is a NIST approved FIPS level 140-2 device and I have the certificate to prove it." Well, this is all fine and good. It could be that the certification lab actually took the time to look for flaws, weaknesses, and backdoors in the code. Even so, where is the guarantee that the specification they analyzed is the one that actually got manufactured? Who's to say that one in every hundred devices doesn't have a SETUP mechanism in it? *A commercial FIPS-140 certificate does not provide any assurance that the specification that was certified by NIST is the same one that was implemented in your particular smart card.* The payoff for such illicit behavior on behalf of a vendor may not be high now. But as PKI takes root, the potential payoff for a small-fry smart card company to actually carry out a SETUP attack may become staggering. The NIST smart card certification process is both honorable and helpful, yet this does not change the fact that a FIPS-140 certificate is likely to give many people who do not fully understand cryptography and the FIPS certification process a false sense of security against insider threats.

Personally, *we* would never completely trust a third-party smart card, no matter who made it. It is simply too easy to leak information securely and subliminally in cryptographic parameters or otherwise. If multiple cryptosystems cannot be simultaneously employed from multiple manufacturers *then our best advice is to simply assume that* **someone** *knows your private key.*

However, the following is a fail-safe way to generate a public key and certify it without worrying about backdoors. You will need a coin, pencil, paper, flashlight, and hard hat. It is of course necessary that you be a spelunker and that you leave all electronic devices behind, save for the flashlight.

1. Climb down into the deepest crevice in the earth's crust.

2. Make sure no one followed you down there.

3. Flip the coin and perform Neumann unbiasing on the results to generate unbiased coin tosses.[17]

4. Use the pencil to write down the resulting private key.

5. Compute the corresponding public key on the paper.

6. Memorize the key pair.

7. Burn the paper, pencil, and flashlight.

8. Climb back to the surface and submit the public key to a certificate authority.

This may be justly called the *Caveman key generation algorithm*. Provided that no one invades your brain using extrasensory powers and provided that you use your private key securely, your private key will be known only by you.[18]

---

[17]If it is weighted unfairly, then it is possible that the mint manufactured the coin with a deliberate statistical backdoor.

[18]This is a joke, of course.

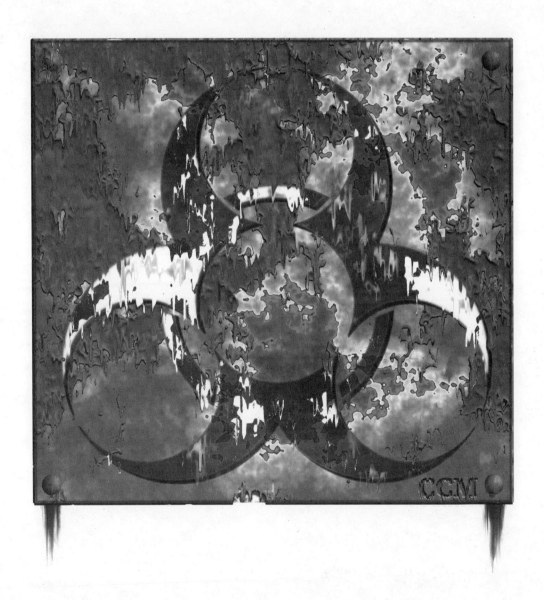

# Appendix A

# Computer Virus Basics

This appendix is intended to give a quick overview of malicious software for those who are not already familiar with the subject. The origins of malicious software are described, followed by a discussion of competing definitions for a virus and a worm. The structure of a simple IBM PC virus is then provided. The appendix concludes by dispelling a common misconception about how viruses and Trojans gain control from their hosts. It is shown that viruses and Trojans can utilize string matching to randomize the location of the jump instruction in the host that sends control to the malware.

## A.1  Origins of Malicious Software

The origin of the modern computer virus can be traced back to 1949, when John von Neumann presented lectures that encompassed the theory and organization of complicated automata [310]. Neumann postulated that a computer program could reproduce itself. Bell Laboratories employees eventually gave life to Neumann's theory in the 1950s in a game dubbed *Core Wars*. In this game, two programmers would unleash software organisms and watch as the programs attempted to lay claim to the address space in which they fought. The Core Wars were described in a May 1984 issue of *Scientific American* [91]. Ken Thompson, winner of the prestigious ACM Turing Award, mentioned in his Turing Award lecture that he had experimented with self-replicating code as an undergraduate [300]. At that time he had challenged himself to write the smallest self-replicating program possible in the usual vehicle, the FORTRAN programming language.

The notion of a backdoor in software, as we know it today, can be traced back to the late 1960s. The concept of multiuser operating systems grew out of the need to make efficient use of expensive computing machinery. Prior to this, physical controls could be used to maintain security of batch processing machines, yet the effectiveness of such controls began to wane as soon as programs from different users began sharing memory on a single computer.

It was when the military began utilizing multiuser and networked operating systems that security issues surrounding these systems came to a head. The discussion of computer subversion was addressed in an article by Petersen and Turn in the 1967 AFIPS Conference [223]. The question of security control in resource sharing systems was the focus of a series of events in 1967. The Advanced Research Projects Agency was asked to form a task force to study and recommend hardware and software safeguards to protect classified information in multiaccess resource sharing computer systems. The task force contained a technical panel that included, among others, James P. Anderson and Daniel J. Edwards. The report of the task force was printed in 1970 and published by the Rand Corporation under ARPA sponsorship [321]. The RAND report identifies a class of active infiltration that utilize "trap-door" entry points into the system to bypass the security facilities and permit direct access to data.

The notion of a Trojan horse was identified by Daniel J. Edwards[1] and was described as a "Trojan horse" in the Anderson report in 1972 [6]. One of the earliest Trojans was a segment of binary code that was inserted into Multics binary code and was distributed to all sites. Paul Karger and Roger Schell described this Trojan in 1974 [151].

In 1982, J. F. Shoch and J. A. Hupp published their work on computer worms [271]. While at the Xerox Palo Alto Research Center (PARC) they investigated the use of worms for the purposes of performing distributed computation over a network. They called their program a *worm* in honor of the computer tapeworm described in the science fiction novel *The Shockware Rider* [43], a cyberpunk novel that predates the term *cyberpunk*. These worms adhered to a prespecified protocol that enabled them to move from machine to machine without user intervention. They were programmed to look for idle machines in order to exploit free CPU power and were designed to control their numbers.

Scattered reports indicate that a computer virus spread on Apple computers as early as 1981. Also, numerous sources indicate that a virus called

---

[1]From the NSA.

the *Elk Cloner* was written in 1983 [129]. This virus became well known in the Apple community and spread on Apple Computer's DOS 3.3 operating system. Fred Cohen did a considerable amount of the initial research on computer viruses in the early and mid 1980s [66, 67, 69]. His doctoral dissertation covered virus theory and his faculty advisor, Professor Leonard Adleman (co-inventor of the RSA algorithm), also worked on the problem.

## A.2    Trojans, Viruses, and Worms: What Is the Difference?

Researchers have proposed competing definitions for what a worm is and what a virus is. For example, McAfee and Haynes refer to the infamous self-replicating program that Robert T. Morris, Jr. wrote as a virus.[2] Morris was a graduate student at Cornell University at the time, and his creation spread like wildfire across the Internet/Arpanet in November of 1988. McAfee and Haynes define a virus to be a computer program that is created to infect other programs with copies of itself and that has the ability to clone itself. They define a worm to be a program that can burrow its way into systems to manipulate, destroy, or alter data, and that does not contain instructions to replicate. In fact, they even state that worms cannot replicate.[3]

In contrast, Peter J. Denning referred to the Morris program as the Internet Worm [88]. Denning stated that some media reports mistakenly called the invading program a virus rather than a worm. He defined a virus to be a code segment that embeds itself inside a legitimate program, that is activated when the program is activated, and that then embeds another copy of itself in another legitimate but uninfected program.

To shed light on this apparent dichotomy, the exact nature of the Morris program must be considered. The Morris program had three different infection vectors [88]. Whenever an infection vector succeeded it established a connection with a remote shell and fed the shell a 99-line bootstrap program together with the commands that were needed to compile and execute it. If everything worked, the rest of the worm was sent to the new machine. The parent worm then issued commands to construct a new worm from the delivered pieces. The McAfee-Haynes definition of a worm is more in line with the beneficial worms that Shoch and Hupp

---

[2]See page 80 of [185].
[3]See page 29 of [185].

researched. Under this definition, a worm does not contain explicit instructions to replicate and hence adheres to the McAfee-Haynes notion of a worm.

It is perhaps safest to say that there is no single correct definition of a worm. The research at XEROX showed that worms could be quite useful for performing distribute computations when they are carefully controlled. News agencies like to go hog wild whenever a rapidly spreading program hits the Internet, and so this has cast worms with malicious propagation vectors in a negative light.

Rather than making the distinction between a virus and a worm contingent upon the insertion of a program's own code into a host program, we prefer to make the distinction contingent upon whether or not user intervention is required for replication. We prefer the following definition of worm.

**Definition 5** *A computer worm is a program that causes possibly altered copies of itself to be created without any user intervention.*

We use the *possibly altered* language to account for the fact that programs can change their own code (such as polymorphic viruses). We prefer the following definition of a virus.

**Definition 6** *A computer virus is a program that when triggered by an action of the user, causes possibly altered copies of itself to be created.*

The beneficial XEROX programs and the Morris program of '88 are worms under these definitions. Also, many e-mail "worms" are viruses under these definitions. This holds whenever the user has to open his or her inbox or open a specific e-mail for the virus to propagate.

The biological analogs of computer viruses and worms form a possible justification for our definitions. A worm will crawl beneath the earth of its own volition. In order for the common cold virus to spread, a host has to place him or herself within the proximity of another potential host and then cough, sneeze, and so forth. This is analogous to a virus that will only spread if the user types in the name of the infected program and then hits the carriage return or if the user double-clicks on the icon of the infected program, and so on. We are not arguing that our definitions are any better or worse than any other definitions. They just seem to make a good deal of sense.

An important aspect to our definition is that it says nothing about computer networks. If a program can spread on its own from program to program on a single machine while the user is asleep, then the program may be justifiably referred to as a worm.

Fortunately, no one would argue about the definition of a Trojan horse program. A Trojan horse program does not replicate. If it replicated, then it would be a virus or a worm.

**Definition 7** *A Trojan horse is a program that does not replicate and that performs something that the user does not intend the infected program to do.*

As shown in Chapter 9, a Trojan horse can be as simple as an exploitable bug that is deliberately placed in a program. Some exploitable bugs such as buffer overruns or improperly handled race conditions can appear to be honest programming errors.

## A.3 A Simple DOS COM Infector

An example will go a long way to show how a virus spreads on a typical disk operating system. Although admittedly outdated, a good example is a virus that infects MSDOS COM files. A COM file is an executable MSDOS program that has the .com extension at the end of the executable's file name. The reason why these programs are so simple to infect is that COM files are direct memory images of programs. The format of a COM file is as follows. It must be less than 64 kilobytes and the first instruction begins at offset 100h (256 bytes). The first 256 bytes can be all zeros, for instance.

When a COM file is executed, DOS loads what is called the program segment prefix (PSP) at the first available segment in memory. This is a data structure that is 256 bytes long and contains bookkeeping information for DOS. This bookkeeping information may overwrite the bytes that were there when the COM file was initially copied from the disk into random access memory. Immediately following the program segment prefix the code for the COM file begins, so MSDOS sends control to offset of 100h to execute the COM program. COM files must be small enough to fit within one segment, thereby limiting their maximum length to be just short of 64 kilobytes. When the COM file is finished running, it can send control back to MSDOS by executing the *int 20h* interrupt instruction, or it can execute the *ret* instruction that employs a return address on the stack.

The simplest form of virus that does not destroy data in its host is an appending virus. An appending COM virus stores virtually all of its code immediately following the last byte in the COM file. This code is called the virus body. Simply putting this code there will not allow the virus to gain control when the host COM file is executed by the operating system. So, the virus overwrites the first few executable bytes of the COM file with an unconditional jump that sends control to the beginning of the appended virus. The overwritten bytes are not destroyed, however. Instead, they are carefully saved within the virus. When the virus is finished executing, the executable bytes in memory that were overwritten are restored *in memory*. Control is then sent to the first executable instruction in the COM file. The COM file is then in its original form, save for the virus hanging out just beyond the last byte of the COM file. This is illustrated in Figure A.1. A COM infector must make certain that its operation does not modify the program segment prefix before sending control to the host. Otherwise, the host program might not operate correctly.

The simplest way to prevent a virus form infecting a host multiple times is to design it to detect itself. This can be accomplished by choosing a 20-byte value *IDENTIFIER* uniformly at random and then including it in the virus as a data constant. The virus can then detect itself by performing string matching using these 20 bytes. Since the identifier is 160 bits long, mismatches should occur with negligible probability. The downside is that this gives antiviral programs an excellent way to identify the virus as well.

Many viruses use tiny identification strings to let the virus detect itself. Sometimes it is a small string at a fixed offset that is used for identification. At the very least this could lead to false virus identifications. At the worst it could lead to programming errors. As the virus is developed its offsets will inevitably change. This could cause the virus to go out of control and escape the author's machine unexpectedly. This problem does not occur with a large randomly chosen identifier.

It is easy to embed a constant within assembly code. This can be accomplished by placing an unconditional jump instruction just before the constant that sends control immediately following the constant. To utilize the constant, a label can be placed just before it. This approach may be used in this example virus. The data that it jumps over is the value *IDENTIFIER* and the value *HOSTINSTR*. The value *HOSTINSTR*

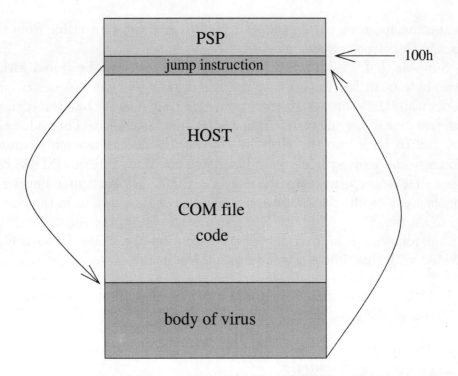

**Figure A.1** Simple appending COM virus

is the bytes that were overwritten at the beginning of the host COM file. They are stored as a constant so that the virus can repair the host at runtime prior to sending control to it. An example Intel assembly language implementation of this method is given below.

```
    nop
    jmp      AfterData
IDENTIFIER:
    db       1Eh,40h,1Ah,41h,5Eh,01h,1Eh,A2h,3Eh,90h
    db       02h,99h,02h,67h,10h,76h,4Fh,5Dh,1Eh,CFh
HOSTINSTR:
    dd       0    ;allocate 4 bytes
AfterData:
    nop
```

One thing that a virus typically needs to do is get a pointer to itself at run-time so that it can copy itself. A common approach is to call a subroutine and then obtain the return address of the subroutine from the stack.[4] This is not always necessary.

Suppose that it is known that the size of the virus can be stored within a two-byte quantity. In this case the size of the virus can be guessed and used within the source with the knowledge that it is probably incorrect. The true size of a virus can be found after it is assembled. This value can then be fed back into the virus by copying it into the assembly source. This way the virus source knows how large the virus is. An MSDOS call exists that lets a virus learn the size of a COM file. An appending virus can then get its offset by subtracting the size of the virus from the size of the COM file.

The following is an overview of the execution of a COM file $P_1$ that is infected with this simple appending COM virus.

1. $P_1$ begins executing. The jump instruction at offset 100h sends control to the virus at the end of $P_1$.

2. The virus chooses a COM file $P_2$ uniformly at random from all COM files on the computer.

3. The virus opens $P_2$ for reading and writing. If this fails, control is sent to step 10.

4. If $P_2$ contains the string $IDENTIFIER$, control is sent to step 10.

5. If $P_2$ does not have enough room for the virus, control is sent to step 10.

6. The virus copies itself to the end of the last byte of $P_2$ in RAM.

7. The virus stores the first three or four bytes starting at offset 100h in $P_2$ within the new copy of the virus.

8. The virus overwrites the first three or four bytes in $P_2$ that start at offset 100h with a jump instruction that sends control to the new virus.

9. The virus writes the changes to $P_2$ to the disk and closes $P_2$.

10. The virus repairs the first 3 or 4 bytes of code in $P_1$ that start at offset 100h in RAM using the stored values.

---

[4]This is so common that it is used as a virus detection heuristic.

11. The virus sends control to offset 100h in $P_1$.

The operations of opening files, closing files, reading files, writing files, and so on, are standard in any disk operating system. In older versions of MS-DOS these functions are called by invoking interrupt 21h. This interrupt is reserved for DOS function calls. The standard way to invoke a DOS call is to load the Intel CPU register $AH$ with a function value and then invoke the *int 21h* instruction. Table A.1 shows the function values needed to implement this simple COM infector.

For example, the following assembly code closes a file.

```
mov         ah,3e       ;close file
int 21
```

It loads the 8-bit Intel CPU register $AH$ with the 8-bit quantity 3Eh and then invokes interrupt 21h. The DOS interrupt reads the value in $AH$ and determines that the program wishes to perform the close file operation.

## A.4 Viruses Don't Have to Gain Control Before the Host

It is surprising how many people assume that viruses have to get control before their hosts. This is clearly the easiest way to implement a virus, but it is by no means the only way. A virus can search the host for a small set of code with known functionality and then replace it with a jump to the virus. An experimental Macintosh virus dubbed the SysBeep virus did exactly this.[5] SysBeep is a Macintosh OS call that takes a single argument, an integer indicating the duration of the system beep as measured in ticks. The SysBeep call can be implemented using the "move" instruction followed by the trap for SysBeep. The move instruction pushes an integer onto the stack. Address register $A7$ is the stack pointer. The trap instruction is two bytes and has the hexadecimal value $A9C8$. Only

---

[5]Experimentally demonstrated at Yale in the early 1990s by the first author and Matt Hastings.

| Hexadecimal value in AH | DOS operation |
|:---:|:---:|
| 23 | get file size |
| 3B | change current directory |
| 3C | create file/handle |
| 3D | open file/handle |
| 3E | close file/handle |
| 3D | open file/handle |
| 3F | read from file/device |
| 40 | write to file/device |
| 41 | delete file |
| 47 | get current directory |
| 4E | find match file |
| 56 | move file (rename it) |

**Table A.1** Old MSDOS calls

these two instructions are needed to invoke a system beep and as it turns out these two instructions were extremely common for making the call.

The following is an example of a call to SysBeep. It pushes the 16 bits of data stored in data register $D0$ onto the stack in the MOVE.W instruction. The mnemonic _SysBeep is a call to the Macintosh OS SysBeep call. This is a debugging listing that demonstrates the size of the instructions. The semicolon is used to indicate a comment that extends to the end of the line that it is on.

```
+0022 000026 MOVE.W     D0,-(A7)
+0024 000028 _SysBeep                   ; A9C8
+0026 00002A MOVEQ      #$03,D0
```

Below is a different debugging listing that shows the actual bytes of the instructions, that being $3F2E0008A9C8$.

```
0000000A: 3F2E 0008 MOVE.W      beepSize(A6),-(A7)
0000000E: A9C8         _SysBeep
```

The machine he was using was a Macintosh SE/30 that used the Motorola 68030 microprocessor. It is a complex instruction set computer (CISC), and so the instructions varied in size. The move instruction in the first listing above is 2 bytes long. The move instruction in the second listing is 4 bytes long.

A search algorithm was implemented that looked for a move word instruction followed by *A9C8*. The search algorithm took into account the fact that the move word instruction may vary in size. When found, the virus safely stored these two instructions within the body of the virus. It then replaced these two instructions with an unconditional jump to the body of the virus, adding padding bytes if necessary. Just before sending control back to the host, the virus repaired the two instructions using the two saved instructions. It then sent control to the first of the two instructions. The virus was written entirely in ANSI C.

The more general lesson is that a virus can search for any small set of instructions and overwrite them with an unconditional jump to the virus. This can be accomplished by choosing an offset into the code uniformly at random, searching the code for the small set of instructions from there on, and the wrapping around to the beginning of the code if one is not found when the end is reached. The search terminates when either the small set of instructions is reached, or the search leads back to the randomly chosen offset. This way, the small set of instructions that are replaced are chosen randomly from all possible sets of instructions that can be replaced.

Great care must be taken, for suppose that an "if" statement that occurs before the overwritten code sends control into the middle of the overwritten code. In this case, the virus might not have a chance to repair the code before the host sends control to it. This will more than likely cause a crash or bus error. The problem is that of atomicity. A virus can heuristically check that no jump instructions send control to the middle of the overwritten code.

This approach is a countermeasure to generic decryption. Recall that in generic decryption, the first several thousand instructions of a program are emulated to try to get a polymorph to decrypt itself if present. If a polymorphic virus gains control before the host and decrypts itself, then generic decryption should succeed as well as subsequent string-matching algorithms that are performed. By randomizing the location of the instruction that jumps to the virus, there is a good chance that the virus will slip by the generic decryption engine.

# Appendix B

# Notation and Other Background Information

This appendix describes most of the material that is needed to follow the ideas presented in this book without covering ideas from cryptography. First, standard notations are described that are used throughout the text as well as well-known definitions from number theory. Some basic facts and algorithms from number theory are also given. The appendix then focuses on a set of computational problems in the field of computational number theory. Most of these computational problems are believed to be intractable and many have only been identified recently. The appendix concludes with a description of the random oracle model.

## B.1   Notation Used Throughout the Book

In this section notation as well as some basic definitions are given that are used throughout the book. String notation is given followed by logic operations and logic statements. Standard notation from number theory is then given along with basic definitions. This is followed by set theory notation and notation from probability theory. The section concludes with asymptotic notation.

When $a$ is a bit string, $|a|$ denotes the length of $a$ in bits. For example, $|01001| = 5$. The operator $||$ denotes string concatenation. So, if $a$ and $b$ are bit strings then $a||b$ denotes the bit string that results from concatenating $a$ with $b$. For example, $010||11 = 01011$. When $x$ is a positive integer it is understood that $|x|$ denotes the length of $x$ in bits when $x$ is represented in base 2. The set of strings that are each $m$-bits in length is denoted by $\{0, 1\}^m$. The set of all bit strings that are each countably infinite in length is denoted by $\{0, 1\}^\infty$.

The operator $\oplus$ denotes the bitwise exclusive-or operation, also denoted by XOR. So, $a \oplus b$ denotes the bitwise XOR of bit string $a$ with bit string $b$. The bit strings $a$ and $b$ in $a \oplus b$ must be the same length in bits. For example, $0011 \oplus 0101 = 0110$. The notation $\Leftrightarrow$ denotes "if and only if." This is used for logic statements in which $A$ is true if and only if $B$ is true, written as A $\Leftrightarrow$ B. The notation $\overset{?}{=}$ is typically used in descriptions of digital signature algorithms and other cryptographic algorithms that require equality testing. It is a Boolean operator that takes two integers $a$ and $b$ as input. The value $a \overset{?}{=} b$ returns true if $a$ equals $b$ and false otherwise.

The function $gcd$ denotes the greatest common divisor function. Thus, $gcd(a, b)$ returns the greatest common divisor of integers $a$ and $b$. For example, $gcd(10, 15) = 5$.

If $a$ and $b$ are integers, then $a$ is said to be congruent to $b$ modulo $n$ if $n$ divides $a - b$ evenly. This is written as,

$$a \equiv b \bmod n \tag{B.1}$$

We say that "$a$ is *congruent* to $b$ modulo $n$." The integer $n$ is referred to as the modulus of the congruence. For example, $5 \equiv 19 \bmod 7$, $0 \equiv 8 \bmod 4$, and $-1 \equiv 9 \bmod 5$.

$\mathbb{Z}_n$ denotes the set of integers modulo $n$. So, $\mathbb{Z}_n = \{0, 1, 2, 3, ..., n-1\}$. The multiplicative group of $\mathbb{Z}_n$ is denoted by $\mathbb{Z}_n^*$. It is common practice to be sloppy and let $\mathbb{Z}_n^*$ also refer to the set that the group is defined over. So, $\mathbb{Z}_n^*$ consists of all elements $a \in \mathbb{Z}_n$ such that $gcd(a, n) = 1$. If $n$ is prime then the set $\mathbb{Z}_n^*$ consists of all integers $a$ such that $1 \le a < n$. When $A$ and $B$ are sets then $A - B$ denotes set subtraction. For example, $S = A - B$ may be found by setting $S = A$ and then removing from $S$ each element $e$ that is in both $A$ and $B$. For example, $\{1, 2, 3, 4, 5\} - \{2, 4\} = \{1, 3, 5\}$. The notation $\in$ is used to denote "contained in." When $S$ is a set of elements and an element $a$ is contained in $S$ we write $a \in S$. For example, $2 \in \mathbb{Z}_5$. But, it is incorrect to say $5 \in \mathbb{Z}_5$.

The notation $Pr[A]$ is used to indicate the probability that event $A$ occurs. For example,

$$Pr[tossing\ coin\ 1\ results\ in\ heads] = \frac{1}{2} \tag{B.2}$$

indicates that coin 1 is a fair coin since heads comes up with probability 50 percent. The notation $Pr[A|B]$ denotes the conditional probability that event $A$ will occur given that event $B$ occurs. Recall that,

$$Pr[A|B] = \frac{Pr[A \cap B]}{Pr[B]} \tag{B.3}$$

where $A$ and $B$ are events.

The notation $f(\cdot)$ is used to denote a function $f$ that takes one argument as input. The dot is used as a placeholder for the argument. For example, $f(x) = 2x^3 + x - 1$. Similarly, $f(\cdot, \cdot)$ denotes a function that takes two arguments as input. For example, $f(x, y) = 3x^2 - 2xy + 4y + 1$.

Big-$O$ notation is used in this book. Informally, $f(n) = O(g(n))$ means that $f$ does not grow faster asymptotically than $g(n)$ within a constant multiple. Formally speaking, this holds when there exists a constant $c > 0$ and an integer $n_0 > 0$ such that $0 \leq f(n) \leq cg(n)$ for all $n \geq n_0$. A polynomial time algorithm is an algorithm that has a worst-case running time of $O(n^k)$ where $k$ is a constant and $n$ is the size of the input to the algorithm. Generally speaking, poly-time algorithms are algorithms that can be expected to yield answers within a reasonable length of time.

## B.2 Basic Facts from Number Theory and Algorithmics

Number theory is a branch of mathematics that is central to modern cryptography and hence computer security. It is characterized by an enumerable number of problems whose elegance and simplicity are matched only by their difficulty in solving. There are a number of great introductory books on the subject [96, 128, 164, 247]. Many public key cryptosystems are rooted in unsolved problems in computational number theory and as such a basic understanding of this branch of mathematics is critical in understanding public key cryptography. This section is by no means a comprehensive introduction to the subject. The goal here is to convey some of the basic ideas so that the reader will know where to look for more information.

The Prime Number Theorem[1] [164] can be used to estimate the probability that a randomly chosen number is prime.

$$\pi(x) \sim \frac{x}{ln\ x} \tag{B.4}$$

The function $\pi(x)$ is defined as the number of prime numbers less than or equal to $x$. Generally speaking, a randomly chosen $k$-bit number is prime with probability about $1/k$.

The greatest common divisor of two integers can be computed using the *Euclidean algorithm*. Hence, this algorithm is used to compute $d = gcd(a, b)$ for two integers $a$ and $b$. This may well be one of the oldest non-trivial algorithms in the history of algorithmics. A more general computational problem is to compute the two integers $x$ and $y$ in $ax + by = d$ where $a$ and $b$ are non-negative integers with $a \geq b$. The *extended Euclidean algorithm* solves this computational problem efficiently. It is often used to compute multiplicative inverses. For example, it is used to compute the RSA private key $d$ given $e$, $p$, and $q$ (see Appendix C.1.7).

To describe various public key cryptosystems it is necessary to cover Euler's totient function $\phi(\cdot)$. It takes a single integer as an argument and has various properties. If $p$ is prime and $k \geq 1$ then $\phi(p^k) = (p-1)p^{k-1}$. The function is *multiplicative*. In other words, if $gcd(a, b) = 1$ then $\phi(ab) = \phi(a) * \phi(b)$. Finally, if

$$n = p_1^{e_1} p_2^{e_2} \cdots p_m^{e_m} \tag{B.5}$$

where the $p_i$'s are distinct primes and $e_i \geq 1$ for $1 \leq i \leq m$, then

$$\phi(n) = n(1 - 1/p_1)(1 - 1/p_2) \cdots (1 - 1/p_m) \tag{B.6}$$

The symbol $\lambda$ is used to denote Carmichael's lambda function. This function is defined as follows. The value $\lambda(2) = 1$, $\lambda(4) = 2$, and $\lambda(2^t) = 2^{t-2}$ if $t \geq 3$. Also, if $n$ is a positive integer with prime-power factorization $2^{t_0} p_1^{t_1} p_2^{t_2} \cdots p_m^{t_m}$ then $\lambda(n)$ is the least common multiple of

---

[1]This theorem was proven independently by Hadamard and De La Valleé Poussin in 1898.

$\lambda(2^{t_0}), \phi(p_1^{t_1}), ..., \phi(p_m^{t_m})$. The value $\lambda(n)$ is also commonly referred to as the minimal universal exponent [247].

A generator $g$ of $\mathbb{Z}_n^*$ is an element that is capable of generating all elements in the set $\mathbb{Z}_n^*$ by exponentiating $g$ modulo $n$. More formally, if $g$ is a generator of $\mathbb{Z}_n^*$ then $\mathbb{Z}_n^*$ consists of the elements $g^i \bmod n$ for $0 \le i \le \phi(n) - 1$. So, using modular exponentiation $g$ is capable of *generating* this set. If $\mathbb{Z}_n^*$ has a generator then $\mathbb{Z}_n$ is said to be *cyclic*.

The value $g$ is a generator of $\mathbb{Z}_n^*$ if and only if,

$$g^{\phi(n)/p} \ne 1 \bmod n \qquad (B.7)$$

for every prime divisor $p$ of $\phi(n)$. This immediately suggests a way to find a generator for a given value $n$. Provided that the factorization of $\phi(n)$ is known, the inequality B.7 is verified for each prime divisor of $\phi(n)$. If there exists a prime divisor $p$ for which it does not hold, then $g$ is not a generator. If $\mathbb{Z}_n^*$ is cyclic then the number of generators is $\phi(\phi(n))$. So, it is often possible to find a generator by choosing $g$ uniformly at random from $\mathbb{Z}_n^*$ and performing this test.

An algorithm is needed to compute $y = g^x \bmod p$ when $g$, $x$ and $p$ are large (for example, 1024-bit quantities). To see this, note that a 1024-bit number $g$ raised to a 1024-bit number is a quantity so large that it will never fit within the memory of a computer system. The value $y$ can be computed using the *square-and-multiply* algorithm. This algorithm works by repeatedly squaring the value $g$ and reducing modulo $p$ after each squaring. The end result is 1024 values each of which are about 1024 bits in length. The quantities are $g$, $g^2 \bmod p$, $g^4 \bmod p$, $g^8 \bmod p$, and so on. Depending on where binary ones appear in the exponent $x$, these values can be multiplied to compute $y$, all the while reducing modulo $p$.

There are even faster approaches. For example, *vector addition chains* may be used in concert with *Karatsuba multiplication* and *Montgomery reduction*. Also, when the base $g$ is fixed, it is possible to speed things up by precomputing the powers of $g$ as previously mentioned.

The value $a \in \mathbb{Z}_n^*$ is a *quadratic residue* modulo $n$ if there exists an $x \in \mathbb{Z}_N^*$ such that $a \equiv x^2 \bmod n$. If no such $x$ exists then $a$ is a quadratic non-residue modulo $n$. Euler's criterion is a method that may be used to test if a given integer $a$ is a quadratic residue modulo a prime $p$ or not. The value $a$ is a quadratic residue modulo $p$ if and only if $a^{\frac{p-1}{2}} \bmod p = 1$.

Quadratic residuosity is so pervasive in number theory that it has its own symbolic representation. The Legendre symbol is a tool for noting

whether or not $a$ is a quadratic residue modulo the prime $p$. The Legendre
of $a$ with respect to $p$ is written as $L(a/p)$ and is only defined for odd
primes $p$ and integers $a$. Note that this does not indicate that $a$ is divided
by $p$. It is notation for a symbol that has one of three values: 0, 1, or
$-1$. The value $L(a/p)$ is 0 if $p$ divides $a$ evenly. It is 1 if $a$ is a quadratic
residue modulo $p$, and it is $-1$ if $a$ is a quadratic non-residue modulo $p$.
Euler's criterion may be used to evaluate the Legendre of $a$ with respect
to $p$.

The Jacobi symbol $J(a/n)$ is a generalization of the Legendre symbol.
The Legendre symbol only applies to odd primes $p$ whereas the Jacobi
symbol applies to all odd numbers $n \geq 3$. Let $n$ be as defined in equation
B.5. The Jacobi of $a$ with respect to $n$ is defined as follows,

$$J(a/n) = L(a/p_1)^{e_1} L(a/p_2)^{e_2} \cdots L(a/p_m)^{e_m} \qquad (B.8)$$

Note that if $n$ is prime then the Jacobi symbol equals the Legendre symbol.[2]

The notation $\mathbb{Z}_n^*(+1)$ is used to represent the set of values $a \in \mathbb{Z}_n^*$ such
that $J(a/n) = 1$. A *pseudosquare* modulo $n = pq$ where $p$ and $q$ are prime
is a quadratic non-residue $y$ such that $J(y/n) = 1$.

Note that when $n$ is the product of two distinct primes $p$ and $q$, the pair
$(L(a/p), L(a/q))$ can have any of four possible values. These four possible
values are $(1, 1)$, $(-1, -1)$, $(-1, 1)$, and $(1, -1)$. The value $a$ is a quadratic
residue only in the case of $(1, 1)$. The value $a$ is a pseudosquare only in
the case of $(-1, -1)$. Furthermore, the number of quadratic residues in
$\mathbb{Z}_n^*(+1)$ equals the number of pseudosquares in $\mathbb{Z}_n^*(+1)$.

The following definition is relevant to the Paillier cryptosystem. Consider the integers modulo $n^2$. A number $a$ is said to be an $n^{\text{th}}$ residue
modulo $n^2$ if there exists a number $y \in \mathbb{Z}_{n^2}^*$ such that $a = y^n \bmod n^2$.
Furthermore, the set of $n^{\text{th}}$ residues is a multiplicative subgroup of $\mathbb{Z}_{n^2}^*$ of
order $\phi(n)$. Every $n^{\text{th}}$ residue $a$ has exactly $n$ roots, each of degree $n$.

# B.3   Intractability: Malware's Biggest Ally

Modern cryptography is made possible by the failures in modern algorithmics. Cryptosystems such as RSA and the Diffie-Hellman key exchange

---

[2]This is the basis for the Solovay-Strassen probabilistic primality test [286].

are regarded as secure since they are based on computational problems that are presumed to be intractable. It is well known that if you can factor, then you can break RSA, and so it is these very problems that keep unwanted intruders at bay.

Yet this entire book is dedicated to showing how these same cryptographic primitives can be used to mount novel attacks on host cryptosystems. The simplest such attack is a denial-of-service attack in which a virus public key encrypts critical host data. When backups aren't available, only the virus author can restore the information since only the virus author has the needed private decryption key. Intractability is therefore a powerful ally in the hands of malicious software programs.

In this section several computational problems in number theory are described. They form the basis of security for several public key cryptosystems. Some of these problems related to others in known ways. Most of the problems described in this section are assumed to be intractable in the proofs of security for various cryptosystems. However, the Phi-Sampling assumption is a necessary assumption for a given scheme to work properly.[3] Many of the known relationships between these problems are described.

## B.3.1    The Factoring Problem

The Rabin cryptosystem is based on the assumed intractability of solving the factoring problem (see Appendix C.1.5). This is often referred to as the *factoring assumption*. In the case of Rabin and other cryptosystems we are interested in whether or not the factoring problem is solvable for the product of two distinct primes $p$ and $q$. The more general integer factorization problem is the following. Given an integer $n$ find its factorization. That is, find $p_1, p_2, ..., p_m$, and $e_1, e_2, ..., e_m$ as in equation B.5.

The integer factorization problem is contained in the complexity class known as FNP. FNP is a class of function problems that have the following form: given an input $x$ and a polynomial time predicate $F(x, y)$, if there exists a $y$ satisfying $F(x, y)$ then output any such $y$, otherwise output "no." This is not to be confused with NP, the set of decision problems that are solvable by polynomial time Turing machines that answer "yes" if at least one computation path accepts and "no" otherwise.

There exist a number of algorithms for solving the factoring problem. Examples include the quadratic sieve method [82, 228] and the number

---

[3]Formally, speaking it is a requirement for *completeness* of the underlying cryptographic protocol.

field sieve [44, 171]. Yet there is no known algorithm to date that can efficiently factor RSA moduli $n$ that are 768 bits or larger.

## B.3.2   The $e^{\text{th}}$ Roots Problem

The RSA cryptosystem is based on the assumed intractability of solving the $e^{\text{th}}$ roots problem (see Appendix C.1.7) where $e \geq 3$. This is often referred to as the $e^{\text{th}}$ *roots assumption* or the *RSA assumption*. The $e^{\text{th}}$ roots problem is as follows. Given a composite number $n$, an integer $e \geq 3$ such that $gcd(e, \phi(n)) = 1$, and an integer $c \in \mathbb{Z}_n^*$, find an integer $m$ such that $m^e \equiv c \bmod n$. The RSA problem is to solve the $e^{\text{th}}$ roots problem when $n$ is the product of two distinct primes $p$ and $q$.

   The RSA problem is trivially solvable if factoring is solvable. To see this, note that if the factors $p$ and $q$ can be computed from $n$, then $d$ can be computed such that $ed = 1 \bmod (p-1)(q-1)$ using the extended Euclidean algorithm. The value $d$ is the private exponent corresponding to the RSA public key $(e, n)$. So once $d$ has been found the RSA problem can be solved using RSA decryption.

   When $e = 2$ the problem is to compute square roots modulo $n$. This problem has been proven to be equivalent to the factoring problem [237]. The non-trivial implication is proven using a randomized reduction argument that shows how to factor $n$ given an oracle that returns a square root.

## B.3.3   The Composite Residuosity Problem

The Paillier public key cryptosystem constitutes a one-way trapdoor under the assumed intractability of solving the computational composite residuosity problem (see Subsection 5.2.4). Let $n$ be the product of two large primes $p$ and $q$. Let $g$ be an element of $\mathbb{Z}_{n^2}^*$ having an order that is a non-zero multiple of $n$. The computational composite residuosity problem is as follows. Given $n$, $g$, and $w \in \mathbb{Z}_{n^2}^*$, compute the unique value $x \in \mathbb{Z}_n$ for which there exists a $y \in \mathbb{Z}_n^*$ such that $g^x y^n \equiv w \bmod n^2$. The computational composite residuosity assumption is that no probabilistic poly-time algorithm exists that solves this problem. The problem of inverting the Paillier cryptosystem is by definition the problem of solving the computational composite residuosity problem. It has been shown that this problem is solvable if the RSA problem is solvable when the public RSA exponent $e$ equals $n$ [216].

### B.3.4    The Decision Composite Residuosity Problem

The Paillier public key cryptosystem is semantically secure against plain-text attacks based on the assumed intractability of solving the decision composite residuosity problem. Let $n$ be the product of two large primes $p$ and $q$. Let $g$ be an element of $\mathbb{Z}_{n^2}^*$ having an order that is a non-zero multiple of $n$. The decision composite residuosity problem is as follows. Given $n$, $g$, $w \in \mathbb{Z}_{n^2}^*$, and a value $x \in \mathbb{Z}_n$, decide whether or not there exists a $y \in \mathbb{Z}_n^*$ such that $g^x y^n \equiv w \bmod n^2$. The decision composite residuosity assumption is that no probabilistic poly-time algorithm exists that solves this problem. There exist other cryptosystems that are predicated on the difficulty of deciding higher order residuosity [23, 196]. It has been shown that the ability to solve the computational composite residuosity problem implies the ability to solve the decision composite residuosity problem [216].

### B.3.5    The Quadratic Residuosity Problem

The Goldwasser-Micali public key cryptosystem is based on the assumed intractability of solving the quadratic residuosity problem (see Appendix C.1.9). Let $n$ be an odd composite integer. The quadratic residuosity problem is as follows. Given $n$ and a randomly chosen element $a$ from $\mathbb{Z}_n^*(+1)$ decide whether or not $a$ is a quadratic residue modulo $n$. The quadratic residuosity assumption is that no probabilistic poly-time algorithm exists that solves this problem.

The Goldwasser-Micali cryptosystem is concerned with the particular case that $n$ is the product of two distinct large primes. This problem is easily solvable if factoring is solvable. If factoring is solvable then $p$ and $q$ can be computed efficiently given $n$. The value $a$ is a quadratic residue modulo $n$ if and only if $L(a/p) = 1$ and $L(a/q) = 1$. So, using Euler's criterion, these two Legendre symbols can be computed using $p$ and $q$.

### B.3.6    The Phi-Hiding Problem

The Phi-Hiding private information retrieval scheme is based on the assumed intractability of solving the Phi-Hiding problem (see Subsection 6.2.1). The formal definition of the Phi-Hiding assumption was given by Cachin et al in Eurocrypt '99 [48]. It is a relatively new intractability assumption and as such many readers may not be familiar with it. For this reason both an informal and formal definition of it is given.

Let $m$ be the product of two large primes $p$ and $q$. Let $p_0$ and $p_1$ be $b$-bit primes such that only one of them divides $\phi(m)$ evenly. Recall that $\phi$ is the Greek letter phi. Informally, the Phi-Hiding problem is as follows. Given $m$, $p_0$, and $p_1$ decide with non-negligible probability whether $p_0$ divides $\phi(m)$ evenly or whether $p_1$ divides $\phi(m)$ evenly. Informally, the Phi-Hiding assumption is that no efficient algorithm exists that solves this problem. We say that a composite integer $m$ $\phi$-hides a prime $p_1$ if $p_1$ divides $\phi(m)$ evenly.

The formal definition of the Phi-Hiding assumption will now be given. Rather than utilizing the notion of a probabilistic Turing machine, the definition utilizes a different computational model. It is based on the notion of a circuit. A $k$-gate circuit is a finite function that is computable by acyclic circuitry that consists of $k$ gates in which a gate implements the NOT logical operation or the AND logical operation. The definition also utilizes a number of number theoretic sets. These are given in Table B.1.

It follows from Table B.1 that $\overline{H}^b(m)$ is the set of $b$-bit primes that are not $\phi$-hidden by $m$. Recall that a poly-time Turing machine $M$ is a machine that on input $x \in \{0,1\}^*$ halts in at most $p(|x|)$ steps where $p(t)$ is a polynomial in $t$.

**Phi-Hiding Assumption:** There exist constants $e, f, g, h > 0$ such that for all $k > h$ and for all $2^{ek}$-gate circuits $C$, after the ordered execution of the following steps:

1. choose a composite $m$ randomly from $H_{kf}^k$,

2. choose $p_0$ randomly from $H^k(m)$,

3. choose $p_1$ randomly from $\overline{H}^k(m)$,

| Set | What the set contains |
|---|---|
| $PRIMES_b$ | set of all $b$-bit primes |
| $H_a$ | set of composites $pq$ where $|p| = |q| = a$ |
| $H^b(m)$ | set of $b$-bit primes that are $\phi$-hidden by $m$ |
| $\overline{H}^b(m)$ | $PRIMES_b - H^b(m)$ |
| $H_a^b$ | set of composites $m \in H_a$ that $\phi$-hide a $b$-bit prime |

**Table B.1** Sets relating to the $\Phi$-hiding assumption

4. choose a bit $b$ randomly,

the probability that $C(m, p_b) = b$ is less than $\frac{1}{2} + \frac{1}{2^{gk}}$. $\diamond$

The Phi-Hiding problem is to find a circuit $C$ that violates this assumption.

Revealing a large prime $p_1$ that divides $\phi(m)$ evenly may expose the factorization of $m$. Coppersmith gave an efficient algorithm that factors $m$ on input $m$ and $p_1$ if $p_1 > m^{1/4}$ and $p_1$ divides $\phi(m)$ evenly [73, 74]. Therefore, it is easy to decide if $p_1$ divides $n$ when $p_1 > m^{1/4}$. Also, this assumption does not hold when $p_1 = 3$ and $m \equiv 2 \bmod 3$ where $m = pq$. To see this, note that one of $p$ or $q$ is congruent to 1 mod 3 and the other is congruent to 2 mod 3. Suppose that $p = 3k_1 + 1$ and $q = 3k_2 + 2$ for some integers $k_1$ and $k_2$. Clearly, 3 divides $(p-1)(q-1)$ in this case.

The Phi-Hiding assumption is a conservative assumption regarding the security of $\phi(m)$ even though the prime $p_1$ that divides $\phi(m)$ is available to the distinguisher $D$. To see this, note that the prime $p_1$ is not assumed to be a constant fraction shorter than $m$, but polynomially shorter. This follows from the assumed existence of $f$ to constitute the $k^f$-bit composite $m$.

## B.3.7   The Phi-Sampling Problem

The completeness[4] of the Phi-Hiding PIR scheme is based on the assumed tractability of performing $\phi$-sampling (see Subsection 6.2.1). Let $p_1$ be a given prime number. Informally, the Phi-Sampling problem is to efficiently find a random composite[5] $m$ such that $p_1$ divides $\phi(m)$ evenly. The Phi-Sampling assumption is that the Phi-Sampling problem is tractable. The formal definition of the Phi-Sampling problem will now be given. The definition utilizes the set $H_{k^f}^k$ as defined in Table B.1.

**Phi-Sampling Assumption:** There exists a constant $h > 0$ such that for all $k > h$, there exists a probabilistic poly-time Turing machine $S$ such that for all $k$-bit primes $p_1$, $S(p_1)$ outputs the factorization of a random $k^f$-bit number $m \in H_{k^f}^k$ where $p_1$ divides $\phi(m)$ evenly.

---

[4]That is, the ability for a user to construct queries and perform the private information retrieval.

[5]Generally speaking, a randomly chosen composite will be difficult to factor if it is large enough.

## B.3.8    The Discrete Logarithm Problem

The Pointcheval-Stern digital signature algorithm is based on the assumed intractability of the discrete logarithm problem (see Appendix C.2.5). Let $p$ be a prime such that $p-1$ has a large prime divisor. Let $g$ be a generator of $\mathbb{Z}_p^*$. Informally, the discrete logarithm problem is to compute $a$ given $(g, p, g^a \bmod p)$ for randomly chosen $a < p - 1$. The discrete logarithm assumption is that no probabilistic poly-time algorithm exists that solves this problem. This problem is efficiently solvable using the Pohlig-Hellman algorithm when all prime divisors of $p - 1$ are small [224]. When this is the case $p - 1$ is said to be a *smooth integer*.

## B.3.9    The Computational Diffie-Hellman Problem

The Diffie-Hellman key exchange is based on the assumed intractability of solving the Diffie-Hellman problem (see Subsection C.1.2). Let $p$ be a prime such that $p - 1$ has a large prime divisor. Let $g$ be a generator of $\mathbb{Z}_p^*$. Informally, the computational Diffie-Hellman problem is to compute $g^{ab} \bmod p$ given $(g, p, g^a \bmod p, g^b \bmod p)$ for randomly chosen exponents $a$ and $b$. The computational Diffie-Hellman assumption is that no probabilistic poly-time algorithm exists that solves this problem. The set of values $(g^a \bmod p, g^b \bmod p, g^{ab} \bmod p)$ is called a Diffie-Hellman triple.

If the discrete logarithm problem can be efficiently solved then so can the Diffie-Hellman problem. This can be shown via a randomized reduction argument. It has yet to be shown whether or not the ability to solve Diffie-Hellman implies the ability to solve the discrete logarithm problem in the general case. These two problems have been shown to be equivalent in certain cases [84, 181, 182, 183]. There have been some results on the hardness of computing individual bits in a Diffie-Hellman shared secret [34].

## B.3.10    The Decision Diffie-Hellman Problem

The Cramer-Shoup cryptosystem is based on the assumed intractability of solving the Decision Diffie-Hellman (DDH) problem (see Appendix C.2.3). Let $p$ be a prime. Let $g$ be an element that generates a large subgroup of $\mathbb{Z}_p^*$. Also, let the order of $g$ have no small prime divisors. Informally, the DDH problem is to distinguish with non-negligible probability the triple $(g^a \bmod p, g^b \bmod p, g^{ab} \bmod p)$ from the triple $(g^a \bmod p, g^b \bmod p, g^c \bmod p)$ where $a$, $b$, and $c$ are chosen randomly modulo the order of $g$. The Decision Diffie-Hellman assumption is that no probabilistic poly-time distinguisher exists that solves this problem.

If the order of $g$ is divisible by a small prime $r \geq 2$, then it is possible to distinguish randomly chosen Diffie-Hellman triples from randomly chosen triples. This follows from the fact that the $r^{\text{th}}$ residuosity of each of the values,

$$g^a \bmod p, g^b \bmod p, g^{ab} \bmod p, g^c \bmod p \qquad (\text{B}.9)$$

can be determined. For example, if the prime 2 divides the order of $g$ evenly, then testing for quadratic residuosity can help indicate the presence of Diffie-Hellman triples. To see this, note that when $g^a \bmod p$ is a quadratic residue and $g^b \bmod p$ is a quadratic residue it will always be the case that $g^{ab} \bmod p$ is a quadratic residue. Hence, a suitable setting for DDH is one in which breaking Diffie-Hellman is difficult and one in which the order of $g$ is not divisible by any small primes. A survey on the Decision Diffie-Hellman problem was written by Dan Boneh [35].

# B.4  Random Oracles and Functions

Random oracles are a theoretical tool used for proving the security of cryptosystems. It is a complete idealization of the functionality that some hash functions "seem" to provide on the surface. Informally, a random oracle $R$ is a function that takes as input a single bit string $s$ and that returns a countably infinite stream of randomly chosen bits. So, $R(s)$ is an infinitely long bit string. For example, $R(01001) = 010011010...$, $R(01000) = 101101110....$ An important aspect of $R$ is that all of its outputs are predetermined. That is, if $R$ is given $s$ as a query twice, $R$ will respond with the same infinitely long bit string. Below is the formal definition of a random oracle.

**Definition 8** *A **random oracle** $R$ is a function from $\{0,1\}^*$ to $\{0,1\}^\infty$ such that for a given query $s$ to $R$, each and every output bit of $R(s)$ is chosen uniformly at random and independent of every bit in $s$.*

A random oracle cannot be implemented in practice. Yet, they are useful tools for arguing the security of a cryptosystem when the cryptosystem relies on a cryptographic hash function. The idea is to replace the hash function with a random oracle and then try to prove that the resulting algorithm is secure. It is then reasoned that any weaknesses that exist in the actual implementation must result from a weakness in the hash function that was used to instantiate the oracle, and not the cryptographic design [18].

In this book the term *random function* is used. A random function is the same as a random oracle except that the range is defined to be a finite set. It is possible to define a random function $F$ from $\{0,1\}^*$ to $\mathbb{Z}_N^*$ using a random oracle $R$ as follows. Suppose that $N$ is $k$-bits long. A given element $e \in \{0,1\}^*$ maps to an element in $\mathbb{Z}_N^*$ as follows. Let $m$ be the first $k$ bits of the infinitely long string $R(e)$. If $m \in \mathbb{Z}_N^*$ then $F(e) = m$. Otherwise, consider the next $k$ bits in $R(e)$. If this quantity is contained in $\mathbb{Z}_N^*$ then this quantity is $F(e)$, and so on. It is easy to see that $F(e)$ maps to an element drawn uniformly at random from $\mathbb{Z}_N^*$.

# Appendix C

# Public Key Cryptography in a Nutshell

This appendix is not intended to be a comprehensive overview of public key cryptography.[1] There are a number of great books covering cryptography for practitioners as well as researchers [115, 156, 190, 257, 293]. The purpose of this appendix is to introduce the reader to some of the basic concepts of public key cryptography and hopefully provide enough information to enable readers who are new to cryptography to gain a better understanding of this book without having to go elsewhere. Public key cryptography is a technology that is *central* to the design of advanced malicious software.

## C.1 Overview of Cryptography

Cryptology is the study of the hidden word. It is broken down into two subfields called cryptography and cryptanalysis. Cryptography is the science of developing cryptosystems that encipher and decipher data, among other things. Cryptanalysis is the study of breaking cryptosystems. A *cryptanalyst* is one who seeks to break or find weaknesses in the ciphers that are developed by a *cryptographer*. One who dabbles in both subfields may be justly referred to as a *cryptologist*.

Classical cryptography dates back thousands of years and has been employed for such things as concealing command and control information

---

[1]Indeed, it is arguably an injustice to the field to try to sum it up in a single albeit lengthy appendix on the subject. But, we have done so for the sake of those readers who might not look elsewhere.

during times of war. Command and control information must be secured, even against the messengers that carry it, so that it does not fall into enemy hands while in transit. In this respect the most basic use of cryptography can be regarded as malicious in nature. It is *malicious* from the perspective of allied forces whenever it is used by the enemy to hide enemy command and control information from allied forces. This book is the study of malicious cryptography in a more literal sense, since it describes how to use cryptography to craft advanced malicious software agents that traverse hostile networks and execute cryptographic payloads.

A classical cryptosystem consists of an encryption algorithm and a corresponding decryption algorithm. To encrypt data, the encryption algorithm requires the user to supply it with a cryptographic *key*. When prompted for a key, a user will typically enter a word or phrase that will be easy to remember. This text is then transformed into a binary string that in turn serves as an encryption key. The encryption algorithm then uses the key to algorithmically transform the input message into a cryptogram, or *ciphertext*. No information is lost in this process and provided that the key is available, the ciphertext can be converted back into the original message using the decryption algorithm.

## C.1.1   Classical Cryptography

More formally, a classical cryptosystem consists of an encryption algorithm $E$, a decryption algorithm $D$, a message space $\mathcal{M}$, a ciphertext space $\mathcal{C}$, and a key space $\mathcal{K}$. The key space is a large set of numbers from which a key is chosen in order to encipher data. For example, in AES-128 the key space consists of all bit strings of length 128 bits [204]. The key space therefore contains $2^{128}$ unique encryption keys. To encrypt a message $m$ chosen from the message space, a key $k$ is chosen randomly from $\mathcal{K}$ and the ciphertext $c$ is computed. This may be represented as,

$$c = E(m, k) \tag{C.1}$$

The encryption algorithm $E$ takes $m$ and $k$ as input and computes the ciphertext $c$ of the message $m$. The message $m$ is often referred to as the plaintext, or cleartext of $c$. Although there typically exist various cryptanalytic methods for making an educated guess at $k$ given a set of plaintext/ciphertext pairs computed using $k$, a straightforward guess at the value of $k$ in AES-128 would be correct with probably one in $2^{128}$. In general, the ciphertexts will differ whenever a different key is used to encrypt the message.[2] The ciphertext $c$ is decrypted using algorithm $D$ and the same key $k$.

$$m = D(c, k) \qquad\qquad (C.2)$$

This type of cryptosystem is called a *symmetric cipher* since decryption requires the same key that was used in encryption. Many symmetric ciphers have been proposed over the years. Examples include DES, Blowfish, Twofish, AES, and so on [204, 210, 258, 259, 261].

In the past it has been the case that various organizations and companies have kept algorithms $E$ and $D$ secret in the implementations that they endorse. For example, the U.S. government proposed a classified block cipher called Skipjack [41, 200] as part of the Clipper Initiative. This algorithm was later declassified and made readily available. Another example is the RC4 cipher which was initially a trade secret of RSA Data Security Inc. [241]. RC4 has since become public. Cryptographers often criticize the practice deploying secret symmetric ciphers. Ciphers are typically regarded as secure because they resist known cryptanalytic methods and because the general public has scrutinized them. Secret ciphers are not subject to public scrutiny, and hence tend to foster little trust within the open research community. Such ciphers can harbor backdoors or at the very least suffer from vulnerabilities or design errors. Kerckhoffs' principle states that the strength of a cryptosystem should reside entirely in the difficulty of determining the key $k$ from specific attacks (e.g., chosen plaintext) not from the secrecy or obscurity of the algorithm. The insistence that both $E$ and $D$ be private is an instance of *security by obscurity*.

Classical cryptography solves the problem of concealing message traffic over public networks, but it assumes that the sender and receiver have previously agreed upon a randomly chosen key $k$. In a system consisting of thousands of users, this initial exchange can be at best cumbersome to arrange. Consider a network of $n$ users in which each user fears that the other users will try to read their messages. To guarantee the privacy of communications, each possible pair of users needs a randomly chosen key $k$. The total number of keys needed to solve this problem is therefore $\binom{n}{2} = n(n-1)/2$. This corresponds to the number of edges in the complete

---

[2]In other words, if $k_1 \neq k_2$ then chances are that $c_1 = E(m, k_1) \neq c_2 = E(m, k_2)$.

graph on $n$ vertices, denoted by $K_n$. For example, when $n = 6$ a total of 15 keys is necessary (see Figure C.1). The number of keys is therefore quadratic in the number of users.

## C.1.2    The Diffie-Hellman Key Exchange

When two users need to establish a shared secret key $k$ and they have a secure channel at their disposal, then they can do so by communicating over the channel. Once $k$ is agreed upon, messages can be privately sent from one user to the other over a public network such as the Internet. A protocol that allows two users to establish a key over a public network is enormously beneficial since it eliminates the need to establish keys out-of-band. The first solution to this problem was proposed by Whitfield Diffie and Martin Hellman in their seminal 1976 paper covering the Diffie-Hellman key exchange [92]. The algorithm utilizes a large prime $p$ and a generator $g$ of $\mathbb{Z}_p^*$. The values $p$ and $g$ must provide a suitable setting for the discrete-logarithm problem.

The values $p$ and $g$ are publicly known. Let Alice and Bob be two users who want to establish a shared secret key over a public network. To perform the exchange, Alice chooses an integer $a$ uniformly at random such that $1 \leq a < p - 1$. Alice sends Bob the value $A = g^a \ mod \ p$. At the same time Bob chooses an integer $b$ uniformly at random such that $1 \leq b < p - 1$ and sends Alice the value $B = g^b \ mod \ p$. Alice computes $k_a = B^a \ mod \ p$ and Bob computes $k_b = A^b \ mod \ p$. Observe that $k_a = k_b$ since,

$$k_a \equiv A^b \equiv (g^a)^b \equiv (g^b)^a \equiv B^a = k_b \ mod \ p \qquad (C.3)$$

Both Alice and Bob have therefore agreed upon the symmetric key $k = k_a = k_b$. The key exchange is based on the Diffie-Hellman assumption (see Appendix B.3.9).

The Diffie-Hellman key exchange solved the problem of negotiating secret keys over an untrusted network wherein there exist passive eavesdroppers.[3] However, it does not minimize the total number of keys that are needed to allow each user to communicate privately with each other user. The Diffie-Hellman key exchange is used to establish a symmetric

---

[3]In practice it is necessary to utilize a more advanced key agreement method. This is due to the existence of threats such as man-in-the-middle attacks (explained later).

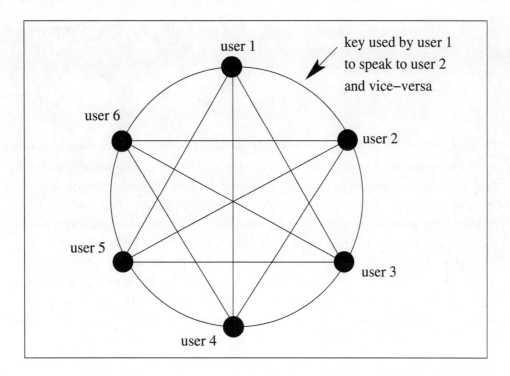

user 1

key used by user 1
to speak to user 2
and vice-versa

user 6

user 2

user 5

user 3

user 4

**Figure C.1** Symmetric keys needed for six users

key, so the number of symmetric keys that are needed is still quadratic in the number of users. This provided the motivation for the concept of a public key cryptosystem. In a public key cryptosystem, the number of required keys is only linear in the number of users. W. Diffie and M. Hellman proposed this concept in the original Diffie-Hellman key exchange paper.

## C.1.3    Public Key Cryptography

A public key cryptosystem consists of an encryption algorithm $E$, a decryption algorithm $D$, a message space $\mathcal{M}$, a ciphertext space $\mathcal{C}$, a private key space $\mathcal{K}$, and a public key space $\mathcal{P}$. The public key space typically differs from the private key space. A user chooses a private key $x$ randomly from $\mathcal{K}$. This value is then used to compute the public key $y$. To encrypt a message $m$ contained in $\mathcal{M}$, the user obtains the public key $y$ of the recipient and computes,

$$c = E(m, y) \qquad\qquad (C.4)$$

The ciphertext $c$ is then transmitted to the recipient. Using the private key $x$, the user recovers $m$ as follows,

$$m = D(c, x) \qquad\qquad (C.5)$$

Only the recipient can recover $m$ from $c$ since only the recipient knows $x$. This type of cryptosystem is also referred to as an *asymmetric cryptosystem* since the decryption key is different from the encryption key.

The security of a public key cryptosystem rests on the presumed intractability of one or more computational problems. Under the intractability assumption it is intractable to compute the private key $x$ given the corresponding public key $y$ and other available information. Private communications are conducted as follows. The public keys of the users are displayed in a public database. To send a message to a recipient, the public key $y$ of the recipient is obtained in a secure fashion from the trusted database. The sender computes the encryption of $m$ to be $c = E(m, y)$ and sends $c$ to the recipient. The recipient obtains the secret message by computing $m = D(c, x)$.

## C.1.4   Attacks on Cryptosystems

If a cryptanalyst is able to learn the plaintext in every ciphertext then the cryptanalyst has completely broken the encryption scheme. This is accomplished by deducing the secret key, or by other means. The following are attacks that can be mounted on an encryption algorithm. They all assume that both the encryption algorithm and decryption algorithm are publicly known. The attacks are ordered from the weakest threat model to the strongest threat model.[4]

1.  **Ciphertext-only attack:** The threat model for this attack is one in which the cryptanalyst is only given access to ciphertexts above and beyond that which is publicly known. The goal of the cryptanalyst is to try to determine one or more plaintexts correctly. Any scheme that succumbs to this type of attack is insecure.

2.  **Known-plaintext attack:** The threat model for this attack is one in which the cryptanalyst is given access to several ciphertexts and

---

[4]A cryptosystem that is secure within a strong threat model is significant indeed, since it is secure against a very powerful adversary.

corresponding plaintexts. Furthermore, it may be assumed that all ciphertexts were produced using the same key and that the cryptanalyst is aware of this. The goal of the cryptanalyst is to try to determine one or more plaintexts correctly for one or more ciphertexts that the cryptanalyst has not yet seen.

3. **Chosen-plaintext attack:** The threat model for this attack is one in which the cryptanalyst is allowed to choose one or more plaintexts to be encrypted and is permitted to submit them to an encryption oracle all at once. The oracle then gives the corresponding ciphertexts to the cryptanalyst. It may be assumed that all ciphertexts are produced using the same key and that the cryptanalyst is aware of this. The goal of the cryptanalyst is to try to determine one or more plaintexts correctly for one or more ciphertexts that the cryptanalyst has not yet seen.

4. **Adaptive chosen-plaintext attack:** The threat model for this attack is one in which the cryptanalyst is allowed to choose one or more plaintexts to be encrypted and is permitted to submit them to an encryption oracle. The cryptanalyst is permitted to submit a plaintext, receive the corresponding ciphertext, and then formulate another plaintext to submit. Hence, the cryptanalyst can adaptively choose the plaintexts to be encrypted based on previously received ciphertexts. It may be assumed that all ciphertexts are produced using the same key and that the cryptanalyst is aware of this. The goal of the cryptanalyst is to try to determine one or more plaintexts correctly for one or more ciphertexts that the cryptanalyst has not yet seen.

5. **Chosen-ciphertext attack:** The threat model for this attack is one in which the cryptanalyst is allowed to choose one or more ciphertexts to be decrypted and is permitted to submit them to a decryption oracle all at once. The oracle then gives the corresponding plaintexts to the cryptanalyst. The decryption oracle is a device that the cryptanalyst is given temporary access to, but that is still able to conceal the secret key from the cryptanalyst. The goal of the cryptanalyst is to try to determine one or more plaintexts correctly without access to the device for one or more ciphertexts that the cryptanalyst has not yet submitted to the oracle.

6. **Adaptive chosen-ciphertext attack:** The threat model for this attack is one in which the cryptanalyst is allowed to choose one or more ciphertexts to be decrypted and is permitted to submit them to a decryption oracle. The cryptanalyst is permitted to submit a ciphertext, receive the corresponding plaintext, and then reformulate another ciphertext to submit. Hence, the cryptanalyst can adaptively choose the ciphertexts to be decrypted based on previously received plaintexts. The decryption oracle is a device that the cryptanalyst is given temporary access to, but that is still able to conceal the secret key from the cryptanalyst. The goal of the cryptanalyst is to try to determine one or more plaintexts correctly without access to the device for one or more ciphertexts that the cryptanalyst has not yet submitted to the oracle.

There is an extensive body of research surrounding security against malleability, chosen-ciphertext attacks, and adaptive chosen ciphertext attacks [32, 78, 95, 199, 238, 342]. To maintain rigorous security, the goal has been to devise an asymmetric cryptosystem that is based on well-accepted (and if possible, very weak) intractability assumptions. Of secondary importance is to make the ciphertexts that are output by the cryptosystem as small as possible.

Similar types of attacks exist against digital signature algorithms. A signature algorithm succumbs to an *existential forgery* if a cryptanalyst is able to compute a signature for one or more messages. The cryptanalyst need not have any control over which message or messages are signed for an existential forgery attack to be regarded as a success. The mere fact that a valid signature on a message was produced by the cryptanalyst without the involvement of the legitimate signer implies that the scheme is vulnerable to an existential forgery. A signature algorithm succumbs to a *selective forgery* attack if a cryptanalyst is able to compute digital signatures on a particular class of messages. It must be possible for the signatures to be produced without the involvement of the legitimate signer for the attack to be regarded as a success. A *complete break* for a signature algorithm occurs when a cryptanalyst is able to forge the signature on any chosen message. For instance, the cryptanalyst could either deduce the private signing key or devise an efficient algorithm that is capable of forging signatures.

As in the case of encryption schemes, signature algorithms can be broken down into various attacks that adhere to different threat models. The following are attacks that can be mounted on a signature algorithm.

They all assume that both the signing and verification algorithms are publicly known. The attacks are ordered from the weakest threat model to the strongest threat model.

1. **Key-only attack:** The threat model for this attack is one in which the cryptanalyst is only given access to the public signature verification key above and beyond that which is publicly known. The goal of the cryptanalyst is to produce a valid signature on any message.

2. **Known-message attack:** The threat model for this attack is one in which the cryptanalyst is given access to several messages and corresponding signatures. Furthermore, it may be assumed that all signatures were produced using the same signing private key. The goal of the cryptanalyst is to produce a valid signature on a different message.

3. **Chosen-message attack:** The threat model for this attack is one in which the cryptanalyst is allowed to choose one or more messages to be signed and is permitted to submit them to a signing oracle all at once. The oracle then gives the corresponding signatures to the cryptanalyst. It may be assumed that the oracle always uses the same private signing key. The goal of the cryptanalyst is to produce a valid signature on a different message.

4. **Adaptive chosen-message attack:** The threat model for this attack is one in which the cryptanalyst is allowed to choose one or more messages to be signed and is permitted to submit them to a signing oracle. The cryptanalyst is permitted to submit a message, receive the corresponding signature, and then formulate another message to submit. Hence, the cryptanalyst can adaptively choose the messages to be signed based on previously received signatures. It may be assumed that the oracle always uses the same private signing key. The goal of the cryptanalyst is to produce a valid signature on a different message.

There is an extensive amount of literature regarding secure signature schemes [125, 126, 131, 191, 198, 213]. Some of these approaches attempt to utilize the weakest possibility intractability assumptions, whereas others try to keep the size of each digital signature at a bare minimum.

## C.1.5   The Rabin Encryption Algorithm

The Rabin cryptosystem is based on the computational intractability of factoring [237]. The private key in Rabin is two large primes $p$ and $q$ that are roughly equal in size. The corresponding public key is $n = pq$. In this rendition of Rabin it will be assumed that $p \equiv 3 \ mod \ 4$ and that $q \equiv 3 \ mod \ 4$ since this gives rise to a very simple decryption algorithm.[5] The message space for Rabin is $\mathbb{Z}_n$. The integers $a$ and $b$ are needed for decryption and are found by solving the following diophantine equation.

$$ap + bq = 1 \qquad (C.6)$$

The extended Euclidean algorithm can be used to find these two values. They can then be stored along with the private key $(p, q)$.

To encrypt a message $m$ in Rabin the ciphertext $c$ is computed as follows.

$$c = m^2 \ mod \ n \qquad (C.7)$$

Given the special form of $p$ and $q$ the following algorithm can be used to decrypt $c$.

1. compute $r = c^{\frac{p+1}{4}} \ mod \ p$

2. compute $s = c^{\frac{q+1}{4}} \ mod \ p$

3. compute $t = aps + bqr \ mod \ n$

4. compute $u = aps - bqr \ mod \ n$

The plaintext $m$ is either $t$, $-t \ mod \ n$, $u$, or $-u \ mod \ n$. These are the four square roots of $c$ modulo $n$. It is possible that $gcd(m, n) \neq 1$ in which case there may be only one or two square roots of $c$.

It is possible to use a redundancy function (e.g., a checksum) to help disambiguate $m$ from the other square roots. For example, this can be done using a hash function. The idea is to shrink the message space and

---
[5]When $n$ is as such, $n$ is contained in the set of *Blum integers*.

make some of the most significant bits of $m$ the hash of the lower order bits.

This cryptosystem is provably secure against chosen-plaintext attacks. However, it completely succumbs to a chosen-ciphertext attack. To see this, note that the attacker can choose a value $r$ randomly from $\mathbb{Z}_n^*$ and compute the ciphertext $c = m^2 \bmod n$. If the attacker has access to the decryption device, the attacker can use the device to obtain a square root $m'$. With probability $1/2$, $m'$ will not be congruent to $\pm m \bmod n$ in which case $gcd(m - m', n)$ is a non-trivial divisor of $n$.

Rabin also works when $p$ and $q$ are not of this special form. In this case $c$ is reduced modulo $p$ and then its two square roots modulo $p$ are found using a probabilistic poly-time root finding algorithm [12]. The two roots of $c \bmod q$ are also found. Using the Chinese Remainder Theorem these four values can be used to compute the four square roots of $c$ modulo $n$.

Scott Lindhurst wrote a comprehensive treatise on computing square roots modulo a prime [173]. Also, Kumanduri and Romero provide a nice description of a Las Vegas algorithm for computing a square root of quadratic residue modulo a prime [164]. The Las Vegas version can easily be converted into a Monte Carlo algorithm with fixed polynomial running time and negligible failure probability. The way to do so is as follows. One of the steps in the algorithm finds a randomly chosen quadratic non-residue. By bounding the number of attempts to find such a non-residue in this step, the algorithm can be made Monte Carlo. If a non-residue is not found by the time the bound is reached, then the algorithm halts with *failure*. Hence, the entire algorithm is Monte Carlo.

## C.1.6 The Rabin Signature Algorithm

The Rabin digital signature algorithm is based on the computational intractability of factoring [234]. The public and private keys are the same as those in the Rabin encryption algorithm. To sign a message it is necessary that the message be a quadratic residue modulo $n$. It is also necessary that the message contain some redundancy to guard against existential forgeries. Let $R(\cdot)$ be a redundancy function that hashes its input message to an appropriate size, adds redundancy, and guarantees that the final output value of $R(\cdot)$ is a square modulo $n$.

1. compute $m' = R(m)$

2. compute a square root $r = \sqrt{m'} \bmod n$ using $p$ and $q$

The signature on $m$ is $r$. There are four unique square roots of $m'$ modulo $n$. To verify the signature the verifier computes $m' = R(m)$ and makes sure that the following equation holds.

$$m' \stackrel{?}{=} r^2 \; mod \; n \tag{C.8}$$

If the public key is not current or if Equation C.8 does not hold, then the signature is rejected.

## C.1.7    The RSA Encryption Algorithm

The Rivest-Shamir-Adleman (RSA) public key cryptosystem [245] was the first public key cryptosystem to implement the concept of a public key cryptosystem [92]. It is perhaps the most widely used public key cryptosystem today. The RSA primitive may be used for public key encryption and decryption and also for digitally signing and verifying messages. In this appendix the classic RSA algorithm will be described and it will be shown how to use it to encrypt and decrypt messages.

The space of private keys in RSA consists of pairs of randomly chosen large prime numbers. So, to generate an RSA private key the user chooses two large prime numbers $p$ and $q$ randomly. Currently, 384-bit primes or larger are deemed sufficient to use RSA securely. A standard way to generate an RSA prime is to generate a large number randomly and then test it for primality. This process is repeated if the number is found to be composite. The Rabin-Miller probabilistic primality test is often used for this purpose [194, 235], although an efficient method for testing primality was recently discovered that is deterministic [5].

The values $p$ and $q$ must satisfy another requirement in addition to being prime. RSA utilizes a public exponent $e$ that is typically shared by all of the users in the system. The primes $p$ and $q$ must also satisfy the property that $e$ and $(p-1)(q-1)$ be relatively prime. In other words, the greatest common divisor of $e$ and $(p-1)(q-1)$ must be 1.

$$gcd(e, (p-1)(q-1)) = 1 \tag{C.9}$$

The prime number $e = 2^{16} + 1$ is often used in modern RSA implementations. Once $p$ and $q$ are found, the private key $d$ is computed using the extended Euclidean algorithm. The value $d$ is chosen by solving the following diophantine equation for $d$ and $w$.

$$ed + w(p-1)(q-1) = 1 \qquad \text{(C.10)}$$

The value $w$ is discarded. Finally, the composite number $n$ is computed to be the product of $p$ and $q$. In RSA, the public key is the pair of values $(e, n)$ and the private key is $d$. The values $e$ and $d$ are multiplicative inverses of each other modulo $(p-1)(q-1)$.

The message space for RSA consists of all messages $m$ such that $1 < m < n$ and such that $gcd(m, n) = 1$. The ciphertext space is the same as the message space. The following is how to encrypt a message $m$ using RSA,

$$c = m^e \bmod n \qquad \text{(C.11)}$$

The private key $d$ is required to decrypt the public key ciphertext $c$. The message is recovered as follows,

$$m = c^d \bmod n \qquad \text{(C.12)}$$

It may not be immediately clear why decryption should yield $m$ every time. Euler's generalization to Fermat's Little Theorem may be utilized to show that this is indeed the case:

*For all $u$ relatively prime to $n$, $u^{\phi(n)} \equiv 1 \bmod n$.*

Here $\phi$ is Euler's totient function. When $n = pq$, $\phi(n) = (p-1)(q-1)$. The proof that RSA decryption is correct is as follows. Let $m$ be any valid RSA message. Observe that $c^d = m^{ed} = m^{1-w(p-1)(q-1)} = m^1 * m^{\phi(n)(-w)} \bmod n$. Since $m$ is relatively prime to $n$, it follows from Euler's generalization that $m^{\phi(n)} = 1 \bmod n$, so $c^d = m * (1)^{-w} = m \bmod n$.

It is important to dispel one of the popular misconceptions about RSA. It is not uncommon for industry practitioners to say something along the lines of "breaking RSA is equivalent to factoring." Whereas this might in fact be true, it is not known as of this writing. RSA as originally defined is based on the computational difficulty of computing $e^{\text{th}}$ roots (see Appendix B.3.2).

## C.1.8   The RSA Signature Algorithm

The concept of a digital signature is based on the concept of a digital identity. In its most basic form, the idea is to assign to a user, who for the sake of argument will be called Alice, a large randomly chosen number.[6] The number must be large enough so that with overwhelming probability Alice's number is unique. Anyone in possession of this number can masquerade as Alice, so she must make sure to keep it secret. This schema would be of little use if Alice were unable to use her number in any meaningful way, so there should be some mechanism for her to use it. One of the most basic usages of such numbers is in a *digital signature algorithm*. The concept of a digital signature was introduced by Diffie and Hellman [92], but no realization of the primitive appeared until later [236, 245].

In a digital signature algorithm, a private key serves as this secret number and is chosen randomly from the set of all possible private keys. A digital signature algorithm is much like a public key cryptosystem except that it involves algorithms for signing messages and verifying signed messages as opposed to algorithms for encrypting messages and then decrypting them. In a digital signature algorithm, a message $m$ is signed using a private key $x$ to produce a digital signature $s$. The pair of values $(m, s)$ constitutes a signed message. To verify $(m, s)$ as being a valid signed message, the public key $y$ in addition to $(m, s)$ is supplied as input to the signature verification algorithm. This algorithm returns true if and only if $s$ is a valid digital signature on $m$. One of the most widespread digital signature algorithms in use today is RSA that utilizes the same keys as the RSA encryption algorithm. RSA is therefore often used to refer to both the RSA public key cryptosystem and the RSA digital signature algorithm.

The original RSA signature algorithm is as follows. To sign a message $m$ contained in $\mathbb{Z}_n^*$, the signer Alice computes,

$$s = m^d \ mod \ n \qquad\qquad (C.13)$$

using her private key $d$. The message $m$ is accompanied by the digital signature $s$. In typical e-mail applications, a signed e-mail is transmitted with $s$ as well as the digital certificate needed to verify the signature $s$ on $m$.

---

[6]Or numbers, like the two primes in RSA.

Anyone in possession of $(m, s, (e, n))$ can verify the digital signature $s$. The signature is regarded as valid if and only if the following equation holds.

$$m \stackrel{?}{=} s^e \ mod \ n \tag{C.14}$$

However, this approach is subject to *existential forgery* attacks. To see this, observe that anyone can choose a signature $s$ randomly from $\mathbb{Z}_n^*$ and compute $m = s^e \ mod \ n$. When this is performed, $s$ is a valid signature on $m$. A well-known heuristic to remedy this problem is to compute the signature $s$ using a cryptographic one-way hash function $H$ as such,

$$s = H(m)^d \ mod \ n \tag{C.15}$$

The signature is verified by hashing the message that was signed to obtain $H(m)$ and then verifying that the following equality holds.

$$H(m) \stackrel{?}{=} s^e \ mod \ n \tag{C.16}$$

## C.1.9   The Goldwasser-Micali Algorithm

One of the drawbacks to the RSA encryption algorithm as originally defined is that it leaks a single plaintext bit in every ciphertext. This bit is the Jacobi symbol of the plaintext, and is either "1" or "−1." Since $e$ is odd it is straightforward to see that $J(m/n) = J(m^e/n)$ for all valid RSA plaintexts $m$.

This observation pointed to a problem in public key cryptography in general. It should not be possible for an adversary to so much as even distinguish one encryption from another. This problem can be formulated as an experiment. Let an adversary choose any two different plaintexts $m_1$ and $m_2$, let the encryption algorithm choose one of the messages randomly, encrypt it, give the resulting ciphertext to the adversary, and then let the adversary guess which message was encrypted. In a truly secure public key cryptosystem the adversary should be able to guess with probability significantly greater than 1/2 which message was encrypted. In RSA, the adversary can choose a message $m_1$ such that $J(m_1/n) = 1$ and another message $m_2$ such that $J(m_2/n) = -1$ and then distinguish correctly every time.

The GM cryptosystem was the first cryptosystem to provably solve this problem. It was presented by Goldwasser and Micali along with a rigorous definition of security known as *semantic security* and a proof that the GM cryptosystem is semantically secure against plaintext attacks [117].

The private key in GM is a pair of large primes $p$ and $q$ that are roughly equal in size. This cryptosystem makes use of *pseudosquares* modulo $n$. The public key in GM is $n$ and a pseudosquare $y$ modulo $n$. It is not hard to show that $-1$ is a pseudosquare modulo $n$ when $p \equiv 3 \ mod \ 4$ and $q \equiv 3 \ mod \ 4$. For other primes a pseudosquare $y$ can be found as follows. Find a quadratic non-residue $a$ modulo $p$ and a quadratic residue $b$ modulo $q$. By applying the Chinese Remainder Theorem to $a$ and $b$, the value that results is a pseudosquare modulo $n$.

A message $m = m_1 m_2 \cdots m_t$ in GM is represented as a bit string of length $t$. Each bit $m_i$ for $1 \le i \le t$ in $m$ is encrypted by choosing $r_i$ at random from $\mathbb{Z}_n^*$ and computing $c_i$ as follows.

$$c_i = y^{m_i} r_i^2 \ mod \ n \qquad (C.17)$$

The ciphertext on $m$ is $c = c_1 c_2 \cdots c_t$. The value $c_i$ is a quadratic residue if and only if $m_i = 0$. The value $c_i$ is a pseudosquare otherwise. The ciphertext is decrypted as follows. For $i$ ranging from 1 to $t$ the following is computed.

$$\ell_i = L(c_i/p) \qquad (C.18)$$

$m_i$ is set to 0 if $\ell_i = 1$ and $m_i$ is set to 1 if $\ell_i = -1$.

The GM cryptosystem solves the problem in RSA in which Jacobi symbols are revealed by making message distinguishability hold based on the quadratic residuosity assumption (see Appendix B.3.5).

## C.1.10   Public Key Infrastructures

When two users decide to use a public key cryptosystem to communicate privately over a public network, there is a danger in having the sender transmit his or her public key to the receiver. If an active adversary is present, the adversary could potentially intercept the public key $y$ and substitute it with another public key $y'$. The person who wants to send the plaintext message $m$ would then receive $y'$ thinking that it is the public key of the recipient of $m$, when in fact it is the public key of the adversary. This same adversary could then intercept the ciphertext $c$ encrypted using $y'$ and then decrypt $c$ using $x'$ which only the adversary knows. The plaintext message could then be encrypted using $y$ and the resulting ciphertext could be forwarded on to the intended recipient. This active attack is called a man-in-the-middle attack since the adversary carries out the attack in between the sender and the receiver.

The problem with using a public key cryptosystem by itself is that there is no way to *authenticate* the public keys of users. The standard way to foil a man-in-the-middle attack is to have a trusted entity securely distribute the public keys of the users. This trusted entity is called a *certification authority* (CA). The CA has its own key pair and everyone is assumed to have the correct public key of the CA. The CA issues a digital certificate to each user in the public key system. A digital certificate consists of the user's name, public key, and other identifying information, along with the CA's digital signature on this information. This way, when a user obtains a digital certificate, the user can verify the signature on it to be certain that the public key it contains came from the CA. This is a public key infrastructure (PKI) in its most basic form [161].

In addition to establishing secure channels over public networks, public key cryptosystems reduce the complexity of symmetric ciphers since they reduce the total number of keys that are needed by the $n$ users. In a system of $n$ users, only $n$ keys need to be exchanged and only $2n$ keys are needed in total. These $2n$ keys consist of the $n$ private keys and $n$ corresponding public keys. The advantages of public key cryptography are therefore twofold: it enables private communication channels to be established over open networks and it minimizes the required number of cryptographic keys.

## C.2   Discrete-Log Based Cryptosystems

The discrete-log cryptosystems in this section are all closely related to the Diffie-Hellman key exchange as well as the Decision Diffie-Hellman assumption. They form the basis for many advanced cryptographic protocols such as electronic voting and e-cash.

## C.2.1   The ElGamal Encryption Algorithm

The ElGamal public key cryptosystem is an elegant cryptosystem that gets its security from the Diffie-Hellman key exchange [110]. This cryptosystem employs the same parameters $(p, g)$ used in Appendix C.1.2. The private key is an integer $x$ chosen uniformly at random such that $1 \leq x < p - 1$. The corresponding public key is $y = g^x \bmod p$. The public key of a user is represented by the three values $(y, g, p)$. The value $y$ will vary from user to user in a public key infrastructure while $g$ and $p$ can be shared by all. The message space in ElGamal is $\mathbb{Z}_p$. To encrypt a message $m$, an integer $k$ is chosen uniformly at random such that $1 \leq k < p - 1$. The ciphertext of $m$ is the pair $(a, b) = (g^k \bmod p, y^k m \bmod p)$. The pair $(a, b)$ is decrypted by computing $m = ba^{-x} \bmod p$. The following equation demonstrates that decryption will always succeed for properly formed ciphertexts.

$$ba^{-x} \equiv y^k m (g^k)^{-x} \equiv g^{xk} m g^{-kx} \equiv m \bmod p \qquad \text{(C.19)}$$

The inverse of $a$ is denoted by $a^{-1} \bmod p$. This inverse exists, is unique, and can be computed using the extended Euclidean algorithm.

## C.2.2   Security of ElGamal

It can be shown via a reduction argument that the Diffie-Hellman key exchange is no more or less secure than ElGamal. Suppose that an oracle $O_{DH}$ exists that solves the Diffie-Hellman problem. That is, for a random choice of $t$ and $u$, $O_{DH}(g, p, g^t \bmod p, g^u \bmod p)$ returns $g^{tu} \bmod p$ with non-negligible probability.[7] It will now be shown how to use $O_{DH}$ to break the ElGamal ciphertext $(a, b)$. Choose the integers $r_1, r_2, r_3$ uniformly at random such that $1 \leq r_1, r_2, r_3 < p - 1$. Then compute,

$$y_1 = y^{r_1 r_3} \bmod p \qquad \text{(C.20)}$$

and,

$$y_2 = a^{r_2 r_3} \bmod p \qquad \text{(C.21)}$$

---

[7]For simplicity this statement is not quantified over a random choice of $p$, although this is often the case in formal results relating to Diffie-Hellman.

The oracle is then invoked and the value $w = O_{DH}(g^{r_3} \bmod p, p, y_1, y_2)$ is found. With non-negligible probability $w$ will be equal to $g^{r_3 x k r_1 r_2} \bmod p$. To see this, note that with non-negligible probability the oracle returns the Diffie-Hellman secret corresponding to $y_1 = g^{r_3 x r_1} \bmod p$ and $y_2 = g^{r_3 k r_2} \bmod p$. Assuming that $w$ is indeed as such, $t$ is as follows,

$$t = w^{(r_1 r_2 r_3)^{-1}} \bmod p = g^{xk} \bmod p \qquad (C.22)$$

It is easy to see that $bt^{-1} \equiv m \bmod p$.

The reason that the random values $r_1$, $r_2$, and $r_3$ were used was to demonstrate a *randomized reduction*. A randomized reduction is a strong form of reduction since it allows the oracle to refuse to give correct answers most of the time but can *still* be used to break ElGamal with high probability. If the oracle fails to decrypt $(a, b)$, then new random values can be chosen and the oracle can be queried again.

It remains to show that given an oracle $O_{ElG}$ that breaks ElGamal with non-negligible probability the Diffie-Hellman key exchange can be broken. Let the Diffie-Hellman key exchange problem instance be $T = g^t \bmod p$ and $U = g^u \bmod p$. The key exchange value is $g^{ut} \bmod p$. Suppose that with non-negligible probability $O_{ElG}(g, p, y, a, b) = m$. Again, values for $r_1$, $r_2$, and $r_3$ are chosen randomly. An integer $b$ is chosen randomly from $G_q$. Then compute,

$$y_1 = T^{r_1 r_3} \bmod p \qquad (C.23)$$

and,

$$y_2 = U^{r_2 r_3} \bmod p \qquad (C.24)$$

The oracle is then invoked to obtain the value,

$$m = O_{ElG}(g^{r_3} \bmod p, p, y_1, y_2, b) \qquad (C.25)$$

With non-negligible probability the value $bm^{-1} \bmod p$ will be equal to the Diffie-Hellman secret corresponding to $y_1$ and $y_2$ using the generator $g^{r_3} \bmod p$. Assuming that $m$ is as such, it follows that $bm^{-1} =$

$(g^{r_3})^{tr_1ur_2}$ *mod p*.   Therefore, it follows that $(bm^{-1})^{(r_1r_2r_3)^{-1}}$ *mod p* = $g^{tu}$ *mod p*.  It has been shown that Diffie-Hellman is breakable if and only if ElGamal is breakable.

To implement ElGamal in a way that is semantically secure against plaintext attacks the original ElGamal cryptosystem needs to be redefined a little [304]. It is sufficient that the order of $g$ be devoid of small prime factors and that the message space consists only of elements that have the same order as $g$. In general it is a good practice to choose $g$ so that its order is a large prime and to define the message space to be the prime order subgroup generated by $g$. For instance, prime numbers of the form $p = 2q + 1$ can be used where $q$ is prime. Such a prime $p$ is said to be a *safe prime*. ElGamal is semantically secure against plaintext attacks when $p$ is a safe prime, $g$ has order $q$, and the message space is the set of quadratic residues modulo $p$. However, this approach is still not secure against adaptive chosen-ciphertext attacks [238].

### C.2.3   The Cramer-Shoup Encryption Algorithm

The Cramer-Shoup public key cryptosystem is secure against adaptive chosen ciphertext attacks [76]. It is based on the Decision Diffie-Hellman problem (see Appendix B.3.10) and the existence of a collision intractable hash function. The scheme involves only a few exponentiations over a group, making it a rather efficient scheme from a computational standpoint.

Cramer-Shoup utilizes a group $G$ of prime order $q$ where $q$ is large. It also uses a collision intractable hash function $H$ that hashes long strings to values contained in $\mathbb{Z}_q$. The private key in Cramer-Shoup is the six values $(x_1, x_2, y_1, y_2, z_1, z_2)$, all of which are chosen randomly from $\mathbb{Z}_q$. The public key includes the values $g_1$ and $g_2$ that are chosen randomly from $G$. The public key also includes the following three values.

$$c = g_1^{x_1} g_2^{x_2}, \ d = g_1^{y_1} g_2^{y_2}, \ h = g_1^{z_1} g_2^{z_2} \qquad (C.26)$$

It is assumed that the values are computed within the group $G$ (for example, by performing modular reductions using the prime modulus $p$). So, the public key is $(g_1, g_2, c, d, h)$.

The message space for Cramer-Shoup is $G$. To encrypt a message $m$, a value $r$ is chosen randomly from $\mathbb{Z}_q$ and the following values are computed,

$$u_1 = g_1^r, \; u_2 = g_2^r, \; e = h^r m, \; \alpha = H(u_1, u_2, e), \; v = c^r d^{r\alpha} \qquad \text{(C.27)}$$

The ciphertext on $m$ is $(u_1, u_2, e, v)$.

The nice thing about chosen-ciphertext secure cryptosystems is that they allow the receiver to verify that the sender knows the plaintext. In other words, it is not possible to send a message to someone using their public key without knowing what the plaintext is. Such a cryptosystem is said to be *plaintext-aware*. The first thing that the receiver should do upon obtaining ciphertext computed using Cramer-Shoup is verify its integrity. This is performed by computing $\alpha = H(u_1, u_2, e)$ and then verifying that the following equality holds.

$$v \overset{?}{=} u_1^{x_1} u_2^{x_2} (u_1^{y_1} u_2^{y_2})^{\alpha} \qquad \text{(C.28)}$$

If it does not hold then the decryption algorithm outputs "reject." This prevents the recipient from going ahead and interpreting the plaintext as if it were valid. It also guarantees that despite any subsequent publication of the plaintext, the sender only *learns* that which he or she already knows.[8] If this equality holds then the ciphertext is decrypted as follows.

$$m = e u_1^{-z_1} u_2^{-z_2} \qquad \text{(C.29)}$$

It will now be shown that a properly constructed ciphertext will always cause the correct plaintext to be output by the decryption algorithm. First, the decryption algorithm will never output "reject" in this case. To see this, note that since $u_1 = g_1^r$ and $u_2 = g^r$ it follows that,

$$u_1^{x_1} u_2^{x_2} = g_1^{r x_1} g_2^{r x_2} = c^r \qquad \text{(C.30)}$$

So, $u_1^{x_1} u_2^{x_2}$ in Equation C.28 is equal to $c^r$. Likewise, since $u_1^{y_1} u_2^{y_2} = d^r$ it follows that the term in the parenthesis in C.28 equals $d^r$. But then this equality must hold due to the rightmost equality in (C.27).

---

[8]In fact, this prevents the sender from being able to use the receiver as a decryption oracle.

Since $u_1^{-z_1} u_2^{-z_2} = g_1^{-rz_1} g_2^{-rz_2} = h^{-r}$ it follows that,

$$eu_1^{-z_1} u_2^{-z_2} = h^r m h^{-r} = m \qquad (C.31)$$

The elegant proof of security of Cramer-Shoup can be found in the original paper.

## C.2.4  The ElGamal Signature Algorithm

The ElGamal digital signature algorithm utilizes the same parameters as the ElGamal public key cryptosystem. There are numerous variants of this digital signature algorithm [208, 209].

To sign a message $m$ an integer $k$ is chosen uniformly at random such that $1 \leq k < p - 1$ and such that $gcd(k, p - 1) = 1$. The fact that $gcd(k, p - 1) = 1$ guarantees the existence of a unique inverse of $k$. The signature on $m$ is the pair $(r, s) = (g^k \bmod p, k^{-1}(H(m) - xr) \bmod p - 1)$. $H$ is a cryptographic one-way function that may, for instance, be the *secure hash algorithm* (SHA-1) [202] or MD5 [243]. The digital signature on the message $m$ is the pair of values $(r, s)$.

Anyone who is in possession of $(m, (r, s), (y, g, p))$ can verify the signature $(r, s)$ on $m$. The signature is regarded as valid if and only if $1 \leq a < p$ and the following equality holds:

$$y^r r^s \bmod p \stackrel{?}{=} g^{H(m)} \bmod p \qquad (C.32)$$

In the case that $(y, g, p)$ was obtained from a digital certificate it is also necessary to verify the validity of the digital certificate. This is typically done by verifying the CA signature in the certificate, checking certification revocation lists, and so on.

It will now be shown that signature verification will always succeed for properly computed signatures. Suppose that $(r, s)$ is constructed according to the algorithm. Consider the equation for the signature value $s$. By multiplying both sides of the equation by $k$ it follows that,

$$ks = H(m) - xr \bmod p - 1 \qquad (C.33)$$

Adding $xr$ modulo $p-1$ to both sides of Equation C.33 yields the following equation.

$$xr + ks = H(m) \; mod \; p - 1 \tag{C.34}$$

Then, by raising $g$ to the value on each side of this equation the following equation is obtained,

$$g^{xr}g^{ks} = y^r r^s = g^{H(m)} \; mod \; p \tag{C.35}$$

This is the equality that is tested during signature verification. So, signature verification will always succeed for properly constructed signatures.

The use of $H$ is necessary to avoid existential forgery attacks. To see this, suppose that $H$ is not used. Hence, let $m$ be used in place of $H(m)$. The following is a one-parameter forgery attack on ElGamal. Choose a value $e$ uniformly at random such that $1 \le e < p - 1$ and compute $r = g^e y \; mod \; p$. Then compute $s = -r \; mod \; p - 1$ and $m = es \; mod \; p - 1$. The pair $(r, s)$ is a valid signature on $m$ as illustrated by the following equation.

$$y^r r^s = g^{xr}r^s = g^{-xs}(g^e g^x)^s = g^{es} = g^m \; mod \; p \tag{C.36}$$

## C.2.5 The Pointcheval-Stern Signature Algorithm

David Pointcheval and Jacques Stern [225] (see also [226]) showed that by altering ElGamal slightly, it can be proven to be secure against adaptive chosen-message attacks. In this model they showed that forgeries are possible if and only if the discrete-logarithm problem is solvable. This proof was shown in the *random oracle model*.

To sign a message $m$ an integer $k$ is chosen uniformly at random such that $1 \le k < p - 1$ and such that $gcd(k, p-1) = 1$. The fact that $gcd(k, p-1) = 1$ guarantees the existence of a unique inverse of $k$. First, the signature value $r$ is computed.

$$r = g^k \; mod \; p \tag{C.37}$$

Once $r$ is computed, the value $s$ is found as follows.

$$s = k^{-1}(H(m\|r) - xr) \ mod \ p - 1 \qquad \text{(C.38)}$$

The digital signature on the message $m$ is the pair of values $(r, s)$. Anyone who is in possession of $(m, (r, s), (y, g, p))$ can verify the signature $(r, s)$ on $m$. The signature is regarded as valid if and only if $1 \leq a < p$ and the following equality holds.

$$y^r r^s \ mod \ p \overset{?}{=} g^{H(m\|r)} \ mod \ p \qquad \text{(C.39)}$$

Pointcheval and Stern introduced the notion of a *forking lemma* and used it to construct their random oracle based proof. The forking lemma technique has since been utilized to show the security of other random oracle based cryptographic algorithms.

## C.2.6    The Schnorr Signature Algorithm

The Schnorr algorithm [262, 263] has the nice feature that its signatures are very small. It makes use of a cryptographic one-way hash function $H$ that outputs values in $\mathbb{Z}_q$. Let $p$ and $q$ be large primes such that $q$ divides $p - 1$. Let $g$ be an element of $\mathbb{Z}_p^*$ with order $q$. The signing private key in Schnorr is a value $x$ chosen uniformly at random from $\mathbb{Z}_q$. The corresponding public key is $y = g^{-x} \ mod \ p$. To sign a message $m$ the value $k$ is chosen randomly from $\mathbb{Z}_q$. A Schnorr digital signature is the pair $(e, s)$ that is computed as follows.

$$r = g^k \ mod \ p \qquad \text{(C.40)}$$

$$e = H(m\|r) \qquad \text{(C.41)}$$

$$s = k + xe \ mod \ q \qquad \text{(C.42)}$$

A signature is regarded as valid if and only if the following equation holds.

$$e \stackrel{?}{=} H(m \parallel (g^s y^e \bmod p)) \tag{C.43}$$

## C.2.7   The Digital Signature Algorithm (DSA)

The Digital Signature Algorithm is similar to ElGamal except that it is defined using a value $g < p$ that generates a prime order subgroup $G$ of $\mathbb{Z}_p^*$. Let the prime $q$ denote the order of $g$. It is part of a U.S. government standard called the Digital Signature Standard (DSS) [203]. Let $H$ denote a cryptographic one-way hash function such as SHA-1 and let $q$ be a 160-bit prime number. To sign a message $m$, an integer $k$ is chosen uniformly at random from $\mathbb{Z}_q^*$. The signature on $m$ is the pair $(r,s) = ((g^k \bmod p) \bmod q, k^{-1}(H(m) + xr) \bmod q)$. Anyone who is in possession of $(m, (r,s), (y,g,p))$ can verify the validity of the digital signature $(r,s)$ on the message $m$. Observe that signatures are quite small. The pair $(r,s)$ occupies a mere 320 bits.

The digital signature $(r,s)$ on the message $m$ is regarded as valid if and only if $0 < r, s < q$ and the following equality holds.

$$r \stackrel{?}{=} (g^{s^{-1}H(m)} y^{rs^{-1}} \bmod p) \bmod q \tag{C.44}$$

It will now be shown that signature verification will always succeed for properly computed signatures. Suppose that $(r,s)$ is constructed according to the algorithm. Consider the equation for the signature value $s$. Multiplying both sides of this equation by $ks^{-1} \bmod q$ yields,

$$k = s^{-1}(H(m) + xr) \bmod q \tag{C.45}$$

Raising $g$ to each side of this equation modulo $p$ yields $g^k \bmod p$ on the left side and,

$$g^{H(m)s^{-1}}(g^x)^{rs^{-1}} \bmod p = g^{H(m)s^{-1}} y^{rs^{-1}} \bmod p \tag{C.46}$$

on the right side. But this implies that $r = (g^k \bmod p) \bmod q$ will always equal $(g^{H(m)s^{-1}} y^{rs^{-1}} \bmod p) \bmod q$ and so signature verification will always succeed for properly computed signatures.

An obvious advantage of DSA is that it produces short signatures. A DSA signature consists of two positive integers, both less than $q$, whereas an ElGamal signature consists of a value less than $p$ and a value less than $p - 1$. It is not uncommon for $q$ to be 160 bits and $p$ to be 768 bits or more in size.

# Glossary

**ACL** Access Control List.

**anonymous remailer** An e-mail system that allows a sender to send a message anonymously to a receiver over an insecure network.

**ANSI** American National Standards Institute.

**ANSI C** Version of the C programming language that was standardized by ANSI.

**API** Application Programming Interface.

**ARDA** Advanced Research and Development Activity. ARDA is an Intelligence Community (IC) center for conducting advanced research and development related to information technology.

**ASCII** American Standard Code for Information Interchange.

**BIOS** Basic Input Output System.

**bus error** A bus error occurs in a computer when an invalid address is issued from the processor to the memory bus.

**call-back function** A function that has its address passed as an argument to another function. The receiving function will invoke the call-back function under prespecified conditions. Typically, the address of a call-back function is passed to an operating system routine.

**cascaded encryption** An encryption is cascaded if the plaintext was encrypted using two or more different keys, thereby consisting of multiple ciphertext layers.

**CERT** Computer Emergency Response Team. Founded by DARPA in 1988.

**cleartext** Data that has not been enciphered in any way.

**composite quadratic residuosity problem** A computational decision problem that is believed to be intractable. The problem is to distinguish quadratic residues from pseudosquares modulo $n$ where $n$ is a large composite number. (They both have a Jacobi symbol of unity.)

**COMSEC** Communications Security. COMSEC products are capable of encrypting data, digitally signing data, and so on.

**CRL** Certificate Revocation List. Used by a certification authority to publicly disclose key pairs that have been revoked. It lists revoked key pairs and is digitally signed by the certification authority. A CRL is typically updated on a regular basis (for example, every day or two).

**Cyberpunk** A term used to describe a futuristic sci-fi genre involving greedy multinational corporations and rebellious computer hackers.

**DARPA** Defense Advanced Research Projects Agency.

**DCR** Decision Composite Residuosity assumption. This is a decision problem that is believed to be intractable when defined over a suitable set of parameters.

**DDH** Decision Diffie-Hellman assumption. This is a decision problem that is believed to be intractable when defined over a suitable set of parameters.

**Denial-of-Service (DoS)** An attack that denies a victim or group of victims access to some service. Examples include deleting data, clogging up computer networks with data packets, hogging up CPU time, and so on.

**DES** Data Encryption Standard. The Data Encryption Standard defines a symmetric encryption algorithm with a 56-bit key space and a 64-bit block size. The standard also covers the corresponding decryption algorithm.

**Diffie-Hellman secret** This term is often used to refer to the key that results from conducting a Diffie-Hellman key exchange.

**directed graph** A graph in which each edge is an arrow from one vertex to another. Sometimes referred to as a digraph.

**DLL** Dynamic Linked Library.

**double-spending** An attempt to spend a given e-money note more than once.

**DOS** Disk Operating System.

**EEPROM** Electrically Erasable Programmable Read Only Memory. A type of ROM chip that can actually be written to by performing a specialized operation. Such chips often support at most 100,000 or so writes.

**efficiently computable** A problem is efficiently computable if it is solvable by a probabilistic poly-time Turing machine. A decision problem is efficiently computable if it is contained in BPP.

**entropy extractor** An entropy extractor is an algorithm that takes data from an entropy source as input and that extracts entropy from this data. The extractor outputs values that are uniformly distributed provided that the input data adheres to the underlying assumptions associated with the extractor.

**forward secrecy** A cryptosystem or protocol has the *forward secrecy* property if the disclosure of confidential secrets does not compromise *previous* communications between Alice and Bob.

**ftp** File Transfer Protocol.

**GNU** **G**nu's **N**ot **U**nix. GNU is the name of a complete Unix-compatible software system that is freely available in binary and source code form, but that may not be used for commercial purposes.

**GNU MP** The GNU project's multiprecision library.

**Gnutella** A decentralized Internet protocol developed in 1999 for sharing files indiscriminately.

**graph** A graph $G$ is a pair $(V, E)$ where $V$ is a set of vertices and $E$ is a set of edges defined over the vertices.

**GUI** Graphical User Interface.

**Halting Problem** The problem of constructing a Turing machine that can decide whether or not an arbitrary Turing machine halts on all inputs. Alan Turing proved that this problem is not computable using a Cantor diagonalization argument.

**hash function** A computationally efficient function that maps arbitrary length binary strings to binary strings that are fixed in length called *hashes* or *hash values*. In practice hash functions are often assumed to exhibit various properties, such as mapping their inputs to pseudorandom output values. When the domain of a hash function is larger than its range *collisions* result (at least two inputs map to the same output).

**hexadecimal** Base-16 number system. The hexadecimal numbering system consists of the digits $0,1,2,...,9,A,B,C,D,E,F$.

**honest but curious** A model for multiparty computation in which the honest but curious party does not hinder with the computations, but wants to know the values involved in the computation.

**hybrid encryption** A method of encryption that employs both symmetric and asymmetric cryptography. Used to encrypt bulk data efficiently.

**IDE** Integrated Drive Electronics.

**inter-mix detour** A method that reroutes a mix net message by sending it on a short series of randomly chosen mix net nodes.

**intractable problem** A problem is intractable if in general it cannot be solved efficiently. A problem cannot be solved efficiently if there does not exist a probabilistic poly-time Turing machine that solves it.

**ITAR** International Traffic in Arms Regulations. U.S. federal regulations that govern the traffic of articles that are considered to be munitions. This includes various enciphering/deciphering machines.

**Jacobi symbol** The Jacobi symbol of $a \geq 0$ with respect to $n$ is defined whenever $n$ is an odd positive integer. It is defined in terms of the Legendre symbol. The Jacobi symbol of a number with respect to $n$ is 0, 1, or $-1$.

**Las Vegas algorithm** A Las Vegas algorithm is an algorithm that may never halt, but if it does, it halts with the correct answer.

**logic bomb** Code surreptitiously inserted into a program that causes it to perform some destructive or security-compromising activity whenever a specified condition is met.

**malleable ciphertexts** A ciphertext is malleable if its corresponding plaintext can be modified in a known way by modifying the ciphertext such that decryption yields the modified plaintext. The notion of non-malleable cryptography was put forth by Dolev et al [95].

**malware** Malicious Software. Examples of malicious software include computer viruses, worms, and Trojan horses.

**MITM** Man-In-The-Middle. An active attack that is carried out when two users exchange their public key over the network. The man in the middle is able to read and potentially even modify messages that are later sent between the two users.

**mix network** A tool for sending information anonymously. A mix net is an interconnected network consisting of several nodes that takes as input encrypted messages, mixes them by bouncing them from node to node, and eventually sends them to their final destinations.

**model of computation** A general method for computing those problems that are computable. Examples include Grammars, $\mu$-recursive functions, and Turing machines. It has been proven that Turing machines can be imitated by Grammars, that can be imitated by $\mu$-recursive functions, that can be imitated by Turning machines. Hence, these models are all equivalent.

**Monte Carlo algorithm** A Monte Carlo algorithm is an algorithm with a bounded running time, but that may halt with an incorrect answer.

**MOTD** Message-of-the-Day.

**MP3** MPEG-1 Layer 3. MP3 is an audio file format for compressing sound (usually a song) into a small file with hardly any noticeable loss in quality.

**MSCAPI** Microsoft Cryptographic API.

**Multics** Multiplexed Information and Computing Service is a timesharing mainframe operating system that began in 1965. It was originally a research project and influenced the design of operating systems. Multics became a commercial product sold by Honeywell.

**multipartite virus** A virus that resides in two or more distinct forms. For example, the virus may propagate from an executable, to the boot sector, to a patched operating system interrupt routine in memory, and then back again.

**multiprecision library** A set of functions that perform elementary operations on multiprecision numbers. For example, it may implement addition, subtraction, multiplication, division, modular exponentiation, logic operations, and so forth.

**multiprecision number** A number whose word length exceeds that of the underlying computer's native word length. For example, on a 32-bit machine a multiprecision number may be 512 bits in length, consisting of sixteen 32-bit words.

**nonce** A word often used in the descriptions of cryptographic algorithms to denote a randomly chosen value or parameter.

**NSA** National Security Agency. The branch of the U.S. government responsible for establishing information superiority through cryptologic prowess, among other disciplines.

**OAEP** Optimal Asymmetric Encryption Padding. A PKCS based on RSA that is secure in the random oracle model.

**onion routing** A method used to implement mix networks. Each message is encrypted multiple times and each encryption layer is removed by performing decryption as the message travels through the mix network to its final destination.

**PDP** Programmed Data Processor. A series of computers manufactured by Digital Equipment Corporation.

**PIR** Private Information Retrieval. A method of retrieving information from a database without revealing to the database administrator which entry has been queried. Schemes exist to solve this problem that are *information theoretically* secure and other schemes exist that are only *computationally secure.*

**PKCS** Public Key Cryptosystem

**PKI** Public Key Infrastructure

**polymorphic virus** A virus that is designed to change its outward appearance to avoid being detected by antiviral programs.

**poly-time** Polynomial time. A polynomial time algorithm $M$ (i.e., a poly-time Turing machine M) is an algorithm for which there exists a polynomial $p(\cdot)$ such that the running time of $M$ on any given input $x$ is at most $p(|x|)$, where $|x|$ denotes the length of $x$.

**PRNG** Pseudorandom Number Generator.

**probabilistic poly-time Turing machine** A Turing machine in which zero or more state transitions are random choices among a finite number of alternatives. The running time of the machine is bounded by a polynomial.

**pseudocode** Source code, usually in an imperative programming language, which may not conform to a specific language but is readily understood.

**public key infrastructure** An infrastructure that is designed to distribute the public keys of users securely, thereby avoiding man-in-the-middle attacks.

**random oracle** A function $f$ that when given any string $\delta \in \{0,1\}^*$ responds with a string $\Omega_\delta$ chosen uniformly at random from $\{0,1\}^\infty$. Furthermore, $f$ always responds with $\Omega_\delta$ when given $\delta$.

**random oracle model** A computational model that assumes the existence and availability of a random oracle. It is a hypothetical model used to argue the security of cryptographic algorithms.

**relatively prime** Two integers $\alpha$ and $\beta$ are *relatively prime* if their greatest common divisor is 1.

**RNG** Random Number Generator. An algorithm or device that generates truly random numbers. Often used to generate seed values for pseudorandom number generators.

**root** A user in a UNIX system that has all possible privileges on the machine. System administrators often log in as root to make critical changes to the system.

**rootkit** A rootkit is a set of tools used after infiltrating a computer system that hides logins, processes, and logs and also often sniff terminals, connections, and the keystrokes. It is called a rootkit after the fact that originally it referred to allowing the attacker to maintain root access to a machine.

**security by obscurity** The often perilous rationale that a system is secure due to the fact that its inner workings are not publicly known.

**semantic security** A formal notion of security for public key cryptosystems. A PKCS is semantically secure (against a particular type of attack) if for all probability distributions over the message space, anything that a passive adversary can compute efficiently about the plaintext given the ciphertext can also be efficiently computed without the ciphertext.

**smooth integer** An integer $n$ is *smooth* if it consists of no large prime factors. An integer $n$ is *p-smooth* if it is not divisible by any primes larger than $p$.

**snake oil** A liquid sold as medicine (for example, in a traveling medicine show) that is medically worthless. In cryptography it refers to a security product, typically with a proprietary (i.e., secret) design, with questionable or otherwise unachievable security properties.

**subliminal channel** A communications channel, usually within cryptosystems, that when utilized allows information to be transferred in secret without hindering the normal operation of the cryptosystem.

**tractable problem** A problem is tractable if in general it can be solved efficiently. A problem is efficiently solvable if there exists a probabilistic poly-time Turing machine that solves it.

**trapdoor** A trapdoor is a single value or a tuple that can be used as a public key in a public key encryption algorithm.

**trapdoor primes** It was originally suspected that the primes chosen for the Digital Signature Algorithm might give the U.S. government an advantage in forging signatures, and so on. These primes were referred to as trapdoor primes.

**triple-DES** An algorithm based on DES that typically utilizes two different keys $k_1$ and $k_2$. The data is DES encrypted using $k_1$, then the result is DES decrypted using $k_2$, and then that result is DES encrypted using $k_1$.

**Trojan horse** A code segment that is appended, designed, or integrated into another program that does something that the user does not expect.

**TSR program** A terminate-and-stay resident (TSR) program. This usually refers to DOS programs that remain active in memory while the user runs other programs.

**Turing machine** A computing device consisting of a finite control, an unbounded sequential tape, and a head that can be used for reading and writing symbols on the tape. It is a conceptual model of computation used for proving computability and complexity results.

**Turing undecidable** A language (i.e., a finite or countably infinite set of strings) is Turing undecidable if there does not exist a Turing machine that can decide membership for that language.

**VLSI** Very Large Scale Integration. A term describing semiconductor circuits composed of hundreds of thousands of logic elements.

# References

[1] Martin Abadi, Joan Feigenbaum, and Joe Kilian. On hiding information from an oracle. In *Proceedings of the 19th ACM Symposium on Theory of Computing*, pages 195–203. ACM, 1987.

[2] Martin Abadi, Joan Feigenbaum, and Joe Kilian. On hiding information from an oracle. *Journal of Computer and Systems Science*, 39(1):21–50, 1989.

[3] L. M. Adleman. An abstract theory of computer viruses. In S. Goldwasser, editor, *Advances in Cryptology—Crypto '88*, pages 354–374. Springer-Verlag, 1988. Lecture Notes in Computer Science No. 403.

[4] L. M. Adleman, K. Manders, and G. Miller. On taking roots in finite fields. In *Proceedings of the 18th IEEE Symposium on Foundations of Computer Science*, pages 175–177, 1977.

[5] Manindra Agarwal, Nitin Saxena, and Neeraj Kayal. PRIMES is in P. Preprint, August 6, 2002.

[6] James P. Anderson. Computer security technology planning study. Technical Report ESD–TR–73–51, USAF Electronic Systems Division, Hanscom AFB, October 1972.

[7] R. Anderson, S. Vaudenay, B. Preneel, and K. Nyberg. The Newton Channel. In *Workshop on Information Hiding*, pages 151–156, 1996.

[8] Ross Anderson and Markus Kuhn. Tamper resistance—a cautionary note. In *Proceedings of the 2nd USENIX Workshop on Electronic Commerce*, pages 1–11, November 1996.

[9] Ross Anderson, Harry Manifavas, and Chris Sutherland. A practical electronic cash system, 1995. Available from author: Ross.Anderson@cl.cam.ac.uk.

[10] Ross J. Anderson and Markus Kuhn. Low cost attacks on tamper resistant devices. In *Security Protocols—Proceedings of the 5th International Workshop*, pages 125–136. Springer-Verlag, April 7–9, 1997. Lecture Notes in Computer Science No. 1361.

[11] N. Asokan, Victor Shoup, and Michael Waidner. Optimistic fair exchange of digital signatures. *IEEE Journal on Selected Areas in Communications*, 18(4):593–610, April 2000.

[12] Eric Bach and Jeffrey Shallit. *Algorithmic Number Theory—Volume I: Efficient Algorithms, Chapter 7—Solving Equations over Finite Fields*. MIT Press, 1996.

[13] P. Baran. On distributed communications: IX. security, secrecy, and tamper-free considerations. Technical Report RM-3765-PR, The Rand Corp., 1964.

[14] Donald Beaver. Multiparty protocols tolerating half faulty processors. In G. Brassard, editor, *Advances in Cryptology—Crypto '89*, pages 560–572. Springer-Verlag, 1990. Lecture Notes in Computer Science No. 435.

[15] Donald Beaver. Efficient multiparty protocols using circuit randomization. In J. Feigenbaum, editor, *Advances in Cryptology—Crypto '91*, pages 420–432. Springer, 1992. Lecture Notes in Computer Science No. 576.

[16] Donald Beaver and Shafi Goldwasser. Multiparty computation with faulty majority. In G. Brassard, editor, *Advances in Cryptology— Crypto '89*, pages 589–590. Springer-Verlag, 1990. Lecture Notes in Computer Science No. 435.

[17] Mihir Bellare, Shafi Goldwasser, and D. Micciancio. Pseudo-random number generation within cryptographic algorithms: the DSS case. In *Advances in Cryptology—Crypto '97*, pages 277–291. Springer-Verlag, 1997.

[18] Mihir Bellare and Phillip Rogaway. Random oracles are practical: A paradigm for designing efficient protocols. In *First ACM Conference on Computer and Communications Security*, pages 62–73, 1993.

[19] Mihir Bellare and Phillip Rogaway. Optimal asymmetric encryption. In Alfredo De Santis, editor, *Advances in Cryptology—Eurocrypt '94*, pages 92–111. Springer, 1995. Lecture Notes in Computer Science No. 950.

[20] Michael Ben-Or, Shafi Goldwasser, Joe Kilian, and Avi Wigderson. Multi-prover interactive proofs: How to remove intractability assumptions. In *Proceedings of the 20th ACM Symposium on Theory of Computing*, pages 113–132. ACM, 1988.

[21] J. Benaloh. Secret sharing homomorphisms: Keeping shares of A secret sharing. In A. M. Odlyzko, editor, *Advances in Cryptology— Crypto '86*. Springer, 1987. Lecture Notes in Computer Science No. 263.

[22] J. Benaloh and J. Leichter. Generalized secret sharing and monotone functions. In S. Goldwasser, editor, *Advances in Cryptology—Crypto '88*, pages 27–36. Springer-Verlag, 1988. Lecture Notes in Computer Science No. 403.

[23] Josh C. Benaloh. *Verifiable Secret-Ballot Elections*. PhD thesis, Yale University, 1988.

[24] E. Biham. Cryptanalysis of Patarin's 2-round public key system S-Boxes (2R). In *Advances in Cryptology—Eurocrypt '00*, pages 408–416. Springer-Verlag, 2000.

[25] E. Biham and A. Shamir. *A Differential Cryptanalysis of the Data Encryption Standard*. Springer-Verlag, 1993.

[26] E. Biham and A. Shamir. Power analysis of the key scheduling of the AES candidates. In *Second AES conference*, pages 115–121, 1999.

[27] Loyd Blankenship. Gurps Cyberpunk—high-tech low-life roleplaying sourcebook. Steve Jackson Games, 1990.

[28] Matt Blaze. Protocol failure in the escrowed encryption standard. In *Proceedings of the 2nd ACM Conference on Computer and Communications Security*, pages 59–67. ACM, 1994.

[29] Matt Blaze, Joan Feigenbaum, and F. T. Leighton. Master-key cryptosystems. Technical Report DIMACS: TR 96-02, Center for Discrete Mathematics and Theoretical Computer Science, 1996.

[30] L. Blum, M. Blum, and M. Shub. A simple unpredictable pseudo-random number generator. *SIAM Journal on Computing*, 15(2):364–383, May 1986.

[31] M. Blum. Coin flipping by telephone: A protocol for solving impossible problems. In *Proceedings of the 24th IEEE Computer Conference (CompCon)*, pages 133–137. IEEE, 1982.

[32] M. Blum, P. Feldman, and S. Micali. Proving security against chosen cyphertext attacks. In S. Goldwasser, editor, *Advances in Cryptology—Crypto '88*, pages 256–268. Springer-Verlag, 1988. Lecture Notes in Computer Science No. 403.

[33] Manuel Blum. Coin flipping by telephone. In Allen Gersho, editor, *Advances in Cryptology: A Report on Crypto '81*, pages 11–15. U.C. Santa Barbara Dept. of Elec. and Computer Eng., 1982. Tech Report 82-04.

[34] D. Boneh and R. Venkatesan. Hardness of computing the most significant bits of secret keys in Diffie-Hellman and related schemes. In *Advances in Cryptology—Crypto '96*, pages 129–142. Springer-Verlag, 1996.

[35] Dan Boneh. The decision Diffie-Hellman problem. In *Third Algorithmic Number Theory Symposium*, pages 48–63, 1998. Lecture Notes in Computer Science No. 1423.

[36] Dan Boneh and Matt Franklin. Identity-based encryption from the Weil pairing. In *Advances in Cryptology—Crypto '01*, pages 213–229. Springer-Verlag, 2001. Lecture Notes in Computer Science No. 2139.

[37] Stefan Brands. Untraceable off-line cash in wallets with observers. In Douglas R. Stinson, editor, *Advances in Cryptology—Crypto '93*, pages 302–318. Springer, 1994. Lecture Notes in Computer Science No. 773.

[38] G. Brassard, C. Crépeau, and Jean-Marc Robert. Information theoretic reductions among disclosure problems. In *Proceedings of the 27th IEEE Symposium on Foundations of Computer Science*, pages 168–173. IEEE, 1986.

[39] G. Brassard, C. Crépeau, and Jean-Marc Robert. All-or-nothing disclosure of secrets. In A. M. Odlyzko, editor, *Advances in Cryptology—Crypto '86*, pages 234–238. Springer-Verlag, 1987. Lecture Notes in Computer Science No. 263.

[40] E. F. Brickell. Some ideal secret sharing schemes. *Journal of Computer and Systems Science*, 37:156–189, 1988.

[41] E. F. Brickell, D. E. Denning, S. T. Kent, D. P. Maher, and W. Tuchman. *Skipjack Review, Interim Report: The Skipjack Algorithm*, July 28, 1993.

[42] Ernest F. Brickell and Daniel M. Davenport. On the classification of idea secret sharing schemes. In G. Brassard, editor, *Advances in Cryptology—Crypto '89*, pages 278–285. Springer-Verlag, 1990. Lecture Notes in Computer Science No. 435.

[43] John Brunner. *The Shockwave Rider*. Del Rey, 1975.

[44] J. P. Buhler, H. W. Lenstra, and Carl Pomerance. *The development of the number field sieve*, volume 1554 of *Lecture Notes in Mathematics*. Springer-Verlag, 1994.

[45] C. Burwick, D. Coppersmith, E. D'Avignon, R. Gennaro, S. Halevi, C. Jutla, S. Matyas, L. O'Connor, M. Peyravian, D. Safford, and N. Zunic. MARS—A candidate cipher for AES. NIST AES Proposal, June 1998.

[46] Samuel Butler. *Erewhon*. Indypublish.com, 1872.

[47] Christian Cachin, Jan Camenisch, Joe Kilian, and Joy Muller. One-round secure computation and secure autonomous mobile agents. In U. Montanari, J. P. Rolim, and E. Welzl, editors, *Proceedings of the 27th International Colloquium on Automata, Languages, and Programming (ICALP)*, pages 512–523. Springer, 2000. Lecture Notes in Computer Science No. 1853.

[48] Christian Cachin, Silvio Micali, and Markus Stadler. Computationally private information retrieval with polylogarithmic communication. In J. Stern, editor, *Advances in Cryptology—Eurocrypt '99*, pages 402–414. Springer-Verlag, 1999. Lecture Notes in Computer Science No. 1592.

[49] J. Camenisch and I. B. Damgård. Verifiable encryption, group encryption, and their applications to separable group signatures and signature sharing schemes. In *Advances in Cryptology—Asiacrypt '00*, Lecture Notes in Computer Science No. 1976, pages 331–345. Springer-Verlag, 2000.

[50] Jan Camenisch, Ueli Maurer, and Markus Stadler. Digital payment systems with passive anonymity-revoking trustees. In *European Symposium on Research in Computer Security (ESORICS)*, pages 33–43, 1996.

[51] James Cameron. *The Terminator*, January 1984. Screenplay: Harlan Ellison, James Cameron, Gale Anne Hurd, William Wisher.

[52] R. Canetti, C. Dwork, M. Naor, and R. Ostrovsky. Deniable encryption. In *Advances in Cryptology—Crypto '97*, pages 90–104. Springer-Verlag, 1997. Lecture Notes in Computer Science No. 1294.

[53] D. Chaum, A. Fiat, and M. Naor. Untraceable electronic cash. In S. Goldwasser, editor, *Advances in Cryptology—Crypto '88*, pages 319–327. Springer-Verlag, 1988. Lecture Notes in Computer Science No. 403.

[54] David Chaum. Untraceable electronic mail, return addresses, and digital pseudonyms. *Communications of the ACM*, 24:84–88, February 1981.

[55] David Chaum. The dining cryptographers problem: Unconditional sender and recipient untraceability. *Journal of Cryptology*, 1:65–75, 1988.

[56] David Chaum. The spymasters double-agent problem: Multiparty computations secure unconditionally from minorities and cryptographically from majorities. In G. Brassard, editor, *Advances in Cryptology—Crypto '89*, pages 591–603. Springer-Verlag, 1990. Lecture Notes in Computer Science No. 435.

[57] David Chaum, Claude Crépeau, and Ivan Damgård. Multiparty unconditionally secure protocols. In Carl Pomerance, editor, *Advances in Cryptology—Crypto '87*, pages 462–462. Springer-Verlag, 1988. Lecture Notes in Computer Science No. 293.

[58] David Chaum, Ivan B. Damgård, and Jeroen van de Graaf. Multiparty computations ensuring privacy of each party's input and correctness of the result. In Carl Pomerance, editor, *Advances in Cryptology—Crypto '87*, pages 87–119. Springer-Verlag, 1988. Lecture Notes in Computer Science No. 293.

[59] B. Chor, S. Goldwasser, S. Micali, and B. Awerbuch. Verifiable secret sharing and achieving simultaneity in the presence of faults. In *Proceedings of the 26th IEEE Symposium on Foundations of Computer Science*, pages 383–395. IEEE, 1985.

[60] Benny Chor and Niv Gilboa. Computationally private information retrieval. In *Proceedings of the 29th ACM Symposium on Theory of Computing*, pages 304–313. ACM, 1997.

[61] Benny Chor, Oded Goldreich, Eyal Kushilevitz, and Madhu Sudan. Private information retrieval. In *Proceedings of the 36th IEEE Symposium on Foundations of Computer Science*, pages 304–313. IEEE, 1995.

[62] Cristina Cifuentes and Mike Van Emmerik. Recovery of jump table case statements from binary code. *Science of Computer Programming*, 40:171–188, 2001.

[63] Cristina Cifuentes and Antoine Fraboulet. Intraprocedural static slicing of binary executables. In *Proceedings of the IEEE International Conference on Software Maintenance*. IEEE, 1997.

[64] Cristina Cifuentes and Doug Simon. Procedure abstraction recovery from binary code. In *Proceedings of the Conference on Software Maintenance and Reengineering*, pages 55–64, 2000.

[65] Cristina Cifuentes, Doug Simon, and Antoine Fraboulet. Assembly to high-level language translation. In *Proceedings of the IEEE International Conference on Software Maintenance*, pages 228–237. IEEE, 1998.

[66] Fred Cohen. Computer viruses: theory and experiments. In *Proceedings of the 7th DoD/NBS Computer Security Conference*, pages 240–263, September 1984.

[67] Fred Cohen. Computer viruses—theory and experiments. In *IFIP-TC11 Computers and Security*, volume 6, pages 22–35, 1987.

[68] Fred Cohen. A cryptographic checksum for integrity protection in untrusted computer systems. In *IFIP-TC11 Computers and Security*, volume 6, 1987.

[69] Fred Cohen. *Computer Viruses*. PhD thesis, University of Southern California, 1988.

[70] Fred Cohen. Implications of computer viruses and current methods of defense. In Peter J. Denning, editor, *Computers Under Attack: Intruders, Worms, and Viruses*. Addison-Wesley, 1990.

[71] David A. Cooper and Kenneth P. Birman. Preserving privacy in a network of mobile computers. In *Proceedings of the 16th IEEE Symposium on Security and Privacy*, pages 26–38. IEEE, 1995.

[72] Don Coppersmith. The data encryption standard (DES) and its strength against attacks. Technical Report RC 18613(81421), IBM T.J. Watson Research Center, December 1992.

[73] Don Coppersmith. Finding a small root of a bivariate integer equation; factoring with high bits known. In Ueli Maurer, editor, *Advances in Cryptology—Eurocrypt '96*, pages 178–189. Springer, 1996. Lecture Notes in Computer Science No. 1233.

[74] Don Coppersmith. Finding a small root of a univariate modular equation. In Ueli Maurer, editor, *Advances in Cryptology— Eurocrypt '96*, pages 155–165. Springer, 1996. Lecture Notes in Computer Science No. 1233.

[75] Lance Cottrell. Mixmaster & remailer attacks. Available at http://www.obscura.com/~loki/remailer/remailer-essay.html.

[76] Ronald Cramer and Victor Shoup. A practical public key cryptosystem provably secure against adaptive chosen ciphertext attack. In Hugo Krawczyk, editor, *Advances in Cryptology—Crypto '98*, pages 13–25. Springer-Verlag, 1998. Lecture Notes in Computer Science No. 1462.

[77] Claude Crépeau and Alain Slakmon. Simple backdoors for RSA key generation. In Marc Joye, editor, *Topics in Cryptology CT-RSA, The Cryptographers' Track at the RSA Conference*, pages 403–416. Springer, 2003. Lecture Notes in Computer Science No. 2612.

[78] I. Damgård. Towards practical public key systems secure against chosen ciphertext attacks. In J. Feigenbaum, editor, *Advances in Cryptology—Crypto '91*, pages 445–456. Springer, 1992. Lecture Notes in Computer Science No. 576.

[79] Ivan Damgård and Mads Jurik. A generalisation, a simplification and some applications of Paillier's probabilistic public-key system. In Kwangjo Kim, editor, *Proceedings of the 4th Workshop on Practice and Theory in Public Key Cryptography (PKC)*, pages 119–136. Springer, February 2001.

[80] DARPA. Workshop on foundations for secure mobile code, March 1997. http://www.cs.nps.navy.mil/research/languages/wkshp.html.

[81] Don Davis, Ross Ihaka, and Philip Fenstermacher. Cryptographic randomness from air turbulence in disk drives. In Yvo G. Desmedt, editor, *Advances in Cryptology—Crypto '94*, pages 114–120. Springer, 1994. Lecture Notes in Computer Science No. 839.

[82] J. A. Davis and D. B. Holdridge. Factorization using the quadratic sieve algorithm. In D. Chaum, editor, *Advances in Cryptology—Crypto '83*, pages 103–113. Plenum Press, 1984.

[83] R. DeMillo and M. Merrit. Protocols for data security. *IEEE Computer*, 16(2):39–50, 1983.

[84] B. denBoer. Diffie-Hillman is as strong as discrete log for certain primes. In S. Goldwasser, editor, *Advances in Cryptology—Crypto '88*, pages 530–539. Springer-Verlag, 1988. Lecture Notes in Computer Science No. 403.

[85] Dorothy E. Denning. *Cryptography and Data Security*, pages 232, 318, Addison-Wesley, 1983.

[86] Dorothy E. Denning. *Information Warfare and Security*, page 270, Addison-Wesley, 1999.

[87] Peter J. Denning. The science of computing: Computer viruses. *American Scientist*, 76:236–238, May–June 1988.

[88] Peter J. Denning. The internet worm. In Peter J. Denning, editor, *Computers Under Attack: Intruders, Worms, and Viruses*. Addison-Wesley, 1989. Reprinted from *American Scientist*, March-April 1989, pages 126-128.

[89] Y. Desmedt. Abuses in cryptography and how to fight them. In S. Goldwasser, editor, *Advances in Cryptology—Crypto '88*, pages 375–389. Springer-Verlag, 1988. Lecture Notes in Computer Science No. 403.

[90] Yvo Desmedt. Simmons' protocol is not free of subliminal channels. In *Proceedings of the Computer Security Foundations Workshop*, pages 170–175. IEEE Computer Society Press, 1996.

[91] A. K. Dewdney. Computer recreations: In the game called Core War hostile programs engage in a battle of bits. *Scientific American*, 250(5):14–22, May 1984.

[92] W. Diffie and M. E. Hellman. New directions in cryptography. *IEEE Transactions on Information Theory*, IT-22:644–654, November 1976.

[93] Y. Ding-Feng, L. Kwok-Yan, and D. Zong-Duo. Cryptanalysis of the "2R" schemes. In *Advances in Cryptology—Crypto '99*, pages 315–325. Springer-Verlag, 1999.

[94] H. Dobbertin. Alf Swindles Ann, *CryptoBytes* (3) 1, Autumn, 1995.

[95] D. Dolev, C. Dwork, and M. Naor. Non-malleable cryptography. In *Proceedings of the 23rd ACM Symposium on Theory of Computing*, pages 542–552. ACM, 1991.

[96] Underwood Dudley. *Elementary Number Theory, 2nd edition*. W. H. Freeman and Co., September 1978.

[97] D. Eastlake, S. Crocker, and J. Schiller. Randomness recommendations for security, December 1994. RFC 1750.

[98] Shimon Even. *Algorithmic Combinatorics*. Macmillan, New York, 1973.

[99] Joan Feigenbaum. Encrypting problem instances, or, Can you take advantage of someone without having to trust him? In H. C. Williams, editor, *Advances in Cryptology—Crypto '85*, pages 477–488. Springer-Verlag, 1986. Lecture Notes in Computer Science No. 218.

[100] Joan Feigenbaum and Michael Merritt. Open questions, talk abstracts, and summary of discussions. In *DIMACS Series in Discrete Mathematics and Theoretical Computer Science*, volume 2, pages 1–45. AMS, 1991.

[101] P. Feldman. A practical scheme for non-interactive verifiable secret sharing. In *Proceedings of the 28th IEEE Symposium on Foundations of Computer Science*, pages 427–438. IEEE, 1987.

[102] W. Feller. *An Introduction to Probability Theory and its Applications*. John Wiley & Sons, Inc., 1957.

[103] Pierre-Alain Fouque, Jacques Stern, and Geert-Jan Wackers. Cryptocomputing with rationals. In *Proceedings of the Sixth International Financial Cryptography Conference*. Springer-Verlag, March 11–14 2003.

[104] Yair Frankel and Moti Yung. Escrow encryption systems visited: Attacks, analysis and design. In Don Coppersmith, editor, *Advances in Cryptology—Crypto '95*, pages 222–235. Springer, 1995. Lecture Notes in Computer Science No. 963.

[105] Matthew Franklin. *Complexity and Security of Distributed Protocols*. PhD thesis, Department of Computer Science, Columbia University, 1994.

[106] Matthew Franklin and Stuart Haber. Joint encryption and message-efficient secure computation. In Douglas R. Stinson, editor, *Advances in Cryptology—Crypto '93*, pages 266–277. Springer, 1994. Lecture Notes in Computer Science No. 773.

[107] Matthew K. Franklin and Moti Yung. Communication complexity of secure computation (extended abstract). In *Proceedings of the 24th ACM Symposium on Theory of Computing*, pages 699–710. ACM, 1992.

[108] E. Fujisaki and T. Okamoto. A practical and provably secure scheme for publicly verifiable secret sharing and its applications. In Kaisa Nyberg, editor, *Advances in Cryptology—Eurocrypt '98*, pages 32–46. Springer-Verlag, 1998. Lecture Notes in Computer Science No. 1403.

[109] E. Fujisaki, T. Okamoto, D. Pointcheval, and J. Stern. RSA-OAEP is secure under the RSA assumption. In J. Kilian, editor, *Advances in Cryptology—Crypto '01*, volume 2139 of *Lecture Notes in Computer Science*, pages 260–274. Springer-Verlag, 2001.

[110] T. El Gamal. A public key cryptosystem and a signature scheme based on discrete logarithms. *IEEE Transactions on Information Theory*, 31:469–472, 1985.

[111] Michael Gilleland. Working with fractions in java—harmonic numbers. Table of the first 100 harmonic numbers. Downloaded from http://www.merriampark.com/fractions.htm.

[112] Ceki Gülcü and Gene Tsudik. Mixing e-mail with Babel. In *Symposium on Network and Distributed System Security*, pages 2–16. Internet Society, February 1996.

[113] O. Goldreich, S. Goldwasser, and S. Micali. How to construct random functions. In *Proceedings of the 25th IEEE Symposium on Foundations of Computer Science*, pages 464–479. IEEE, 1984.

[114] O. Goldreich, S. Goldwasser, and S. Micali. How to construct random functions. *Journal of the ACM*, 33(4):792–807, October 1986.

[115] Oded Goldreich. *The Foundations of Cryptography*, volume 1. Cambridge University Press, June 2001.

[116] Oded Goldreich, Silvio Micali, and Avi Wigderson. How to play any mental game or a completeness theorem for protocols with honest majority. In *Proceedings of the 19th ACM Symposium on Theory of Computing*, pages 218–229. ACM, 1987.

[117] S. Goldwasser and S. Micali. Probabilistic encryption. *Journal of Computer and System Sciences*, 28(2):270–299, April 1984.

[118] S. Goldwasser, S. Micali, and C. Rackoff. The knowledge complexity of interactive proof-systems. In *Proceedings of the 17th ACM Symposium on Theory of Computing*, pages 291–304. ACM, 1985.

[119] P. Golle and D. Boneh. Almost entirely correct mixing with applications to voting. In *Proceedings of the 9th ACM conference on Computer and Communications Security*, pages 59–68. ACM, 2002.

[120] Philippe Golle, Markus Jakobsson, Ari Juels, and Paul Syverson. Universal Re-encryption for Mixnets. RSA Conference—Cryptographer's Track, 2003.

[121] G. S. Graham and P. J. Denning. Protection—principles and practice. *AFIPS Spring Joint Computer Conference*, 40:417–429, 1972.

[122] Ronald Graham, Oren Patashnik, and Donald Ervin Knuth. *Concrete Mathematics: A Foundation for Computer Science* (2nd edition), page 29, Addison-Wesley, 1994.

[123] Roger A. Grimes. *Malicious Mobile Code*. O'Reilly & Associates, Inc., 2001.

[124] M. Gude. Concept for a high-performance random number generator based on physical random phenomena. *Frequenz*, 39:187–190, 1985.

[125] L. C. Guillou and J.-J. Quisquater. A "paradoxical" indentity-based signature scheme resulting from zero-knowledge. In S. Goldwasser, editor, *Advances in Cryptology—Crypto '88*, pages 216–231. Springer-Verlag, 1988. Lecture Notes in Computer Science No. 403.

[126] Louis Guillou and Jean-Jacques Quisquater. Efficient digital public-key signature with shadow. In Carl Pomerance, editor, *Advances in Cryptology—Crypto '87*, pages 223–223. Springer-Verlag, 1988. Lecture Notes in Computer Science No. 293.

[127] Katie Hafner and John Markoff. *Cyberpunk: Outlaws and Hackers on the Computer Frontier*. Simon & Schuster, 1991.

[128] G. H. Hardy and E. M. Wright. *An Introduction to the Theory of Numbers, 4th edition*. Oxford Clarendon Press, 1975.

[129] David Harley, Robert Slade, and Urs E. Gattiker. *Viruses Revealed*. Osborne/McGraw-Hill, 2001.

[130] B. Hayes. Anonymous one-time signatures and flexible untraceable electronic cash. In J. Seberry and J. Pieprzyk, editors, *Advances in Cryptology—Auscrypt '90*, volume 453 of *Lecture Notes in Computer Science*, pages 294–305. Springer-Verlag, 1990.

[131] A. Herzberg, M. Jakobsson, S. Jarecki, H. Krawczyk, and M. Yung. Proactive public key and signature schemes. In *Proceedings of the Fourth Annual Conference on Computer and Communications Security*, pages 100–110. ACM, 1997.

[132] Greg Hoglund and Gary McGraw. *Exploiting Software*, Chapter 8: Rootkits, Addison-Wesley, 2004.

[133] Patrick Horster, Markus Michels, and Holger Petersen. Subliminal channels in discrete logarithm based signature schemes and how to avoid them. Technical Report TR-94-13-D, University of Technology Chemnitz-Zwickau, September 1994.

[134] D. A. Huffman. A method for the construction of minimum-redundancy codes. *Proceedings of the Institute of Radio Engineers (IRE)*, 40(9):1098–1101, September 1952.

[135] American National Standards Institute. ANSI X9.17: Financial institution key management (wholesale), 1985. ASC X9 Secretariat— American Bankers Association.

[136] M. Jakobsson and A. Juels. Proofs of work and bread pudding protocols. In *Proceedings of the IFIP TC6 and TC11 Joint Working Conference on Communications and Multimedia Security (CMS '99)*. Kluwer, 1999.

[137] Markus Jakobsson. A practical mix. In Kaisa Nyberg, editor, *Advances in Cryptology—Eurocrypt '98*, pages 448–461. Springer-Verlag, 1998. Lecture Notes in Computer Science No. 1403.

[138] Markus Jakobsson and D. M'Raihi. Mix-based electronic payments. In Stafford E. Tavares and Kenk Meijer, editors, *Selected Areas in Cryptography '98, Canada, August 17-18*, pages 157–173. Springer, 1999. Lecture Notes in Computer Science No. 1556.

[139] Markus Jakobsson, Elizabeth A. M. Shriver, Bruce Hillyer, and Ari Juels. A practical secure physical random bit generator. In *ACM Conference on Computer and Communications Security*, pages 103–111. ACM, 1999.

[140] Markus Jakobsson and Moti M. Yung. Revokable and versatile e-money. In *Proceedings of the Third Annual ACM Conference on Computer and Communications Security*, pages 76–87. ACM, 1996.

[141] N. Johnson, Z. Duric, and S. Jajodia. *Information Hiding: Steganography and Watermarking—Attacks and Countermeasures*. Kluwer Academic Publishers, 2000.

[142] S. M. Johnson. Generation of permutations by adjacent transpositions. *Mathematics of Computation*, 17:282–285, 1963.

[143] D. F. Jones. *Colossus*. Berkeley Pub Group, 1966. Reissue March, 1985.

[144] Antoine Joux. The Weil and Tate pairings as building blocks for public key cryptosystems. In Claus Fieker and David R. Kohel, editors, *Proceedings of the Fifth Algorithmic Number Theory Symposium (ANTS)*, pages 20–32. Springer, 2002. Lecture Notes in Computer Science No. 2369.

[145] M. Joye, P. Paillier, and S. Vaudenay. Generating RSA moduli with predetermined portion. In Ç. K. Koç and Christof Paar, editors, *Proceedings of the 2nd Workshop on Cryptographic Hardware and Embedded Systems (CHES)*, pages 340–354. Springer-Verlag, 2000. Lecture Notes in Computer Science No. 1965.

[146] A. Juels and J. Brainard. Client puzzles: A cryptographic defense against connection depletion attacks. In S. Kent, editor, *Proceedings of Networks and Distributed Security Systems*, pages 151–165. Internet Society, 1999.

[147] A. Juels and J. Guajardo. RSA key generation with verifiable randomness. In D. Naccache and P. Paillier, editors, *Proceedings of the 5th Workshop on Practice and Theory in Public Key Cryptography (PKC)*, pages 357–374. Springer-Verlag, 2002.

[148] A. Juels, M. Jakobsson, E. Shriver, and B. Hillyer. How to turn loaded dice into fair coins. *IEEE Transactions on Information Theory*, IT-46(3):911–921, 2000.

[149] Benjamin Jun and Paul Kocher. The Intel random number generator, April 22, 1999. White Paper—Downloaded from http://download.intel.com/design/security/rng/CRIwp.pdf (prepared for Intel Corporation).

[150] A. A. Karatsuba and Yu. P. Ofman. Multiplication of multidigit numbers by automata. *Physics Doklady*, 7:595–596, 1963. Translated from *Doklady Akad. Nauk*, vol. 145, no. 2, pages 293–294, 1962.

[151] Paul A. Karger and Roger R. Schell. Multics security evaluation: Vulnerability analysis. Technical Report ESD-TR-74-193 volume II, HQ Electronic Systems Division, Hanscom AFB, MA 01731, June 1974.

[152] Jonathan Katz, Steven Myers, and Rafail Ostrovsky. Cryptographic counters and applications to electronic voting. In Birgit Pfitzmann, editor, *Advances in Cryptology—Eurocrypt '01*, pages 78–92. Springer-Verlag, 2001. Lecture Notes in Computer Science No. 2045.

[153] John Kelsey, Bruce Schneier, and David Wagner. Related-key cryptanalysis of 3-WAY, Biham-DES, CAST, DES-X, NewDES, RC2, and TEA. In *International Conference on Information and Communications Security*, pages 233–246, 1997.

[154] Brian W. Kernighan and Dennis M. Ritchie. *The C Programming Language, 2nd edition*. Prentice Hall Software Series. Prentice Hall, March 1989.

[155] J. Kilian and F. T. Leighton. Fair cryptosystems revisited. In *Advances in Cryptology—Crypto '95*, pages 208–221. Springer-Verlag, 1995.

[156] N. Koblitz. *A Course in Number Theory and Cryptography*. Springer-Verlag, New York, 1987.

[157] N. Koblitz. Elliptic curve cryptosytems. *Mathematics of Computation*, 48(177):203–209, 1987.

[158] N. Koblitz. Constructing elliptic curve cryptosystems in characteristic 2. In A. J. Menezes and S. A. Vanstone, editors, *Advances in Cryptology—Crypto '90*, pages 156–168. Springer-Verlag, 1991. Lecture Notes in Computer Science No. 537.

[159] Paul C. Kocher. Timing attacks on implementations of Diffie-Hellman, RSA, DSS, and other systems. In Neal Koblitz, editor, *Advances in Cryptology—Crypto '96*, pages 104–113. Springer-Verlag, 1996. Lecture Notes in Computer Science No. 1109.

[160] Paul C. Kocher, Joshua Jaffe, and Benjamin Jun. Differential power analysis. In M. Wiener, editor, *Advances in Cryptology—Crypto '99*, pages 388–397. Springer-Verlag, 1999. Lecture Notes in Computer Science No. 1666.

[161] Loren M. Kohnfelder. Towards a practical public-key cryptosystem. B.S. Thesis, supervised by L. Adleman, May 1978.

[162] K. Koyama, U. M. Maurer, T. Okamoto, and S. A. Vanstone. New public-key schemes based on elliptic curves over the ring $Z_n$. In J. Feigenbaum, editor, *Advances in Cryptology—Crypto '91*, pages

252–266. Springer, 1992. Lecture Notes in Computer Science No. 576.

[163] D. L. Kreher and D. R. Stinson. *Combinatorial Algorithms— Generation, Enumeration, and Search.* Encyclopedia of Mathematics and its Applications. CRC Press, 1998.

[164] R. Kumanduri and C. Romero. *Number Theory with Computer Applications, Algorithm 9.2.9.* Prentice Hall, 1998.

[165] Eyal Kushilevitz and Rafail Ostrovsky. Replication is not needed: Single database, computationally-private information retrieval. In *Proceedings of the 38th IEEE Symposium on Foundations of Computer Science*, pages 364–373. IEEE, 1997.

[166] J. B. Lacy, D. P. Mitchell, and W. M. Schell. Cryptolib: Cryptography in software. In *Proceedings of the 4th USENIX Security Symposium*, pages 1–17, 1993.

[167] Butler W. Lampson. A note on the confinement problem. *Communications of the ACM*, 16(10):613–615, 1973.

[168] Laurie Law, Susan Sabett, and Jerry Solinas. How to make a mint: the cryptography of anonymous electronic cash. National Security Agency, Office of Information Security Research and Technology, Cryptology Division, June 1996.

[169] Sammuel J. Leffler, Marshall Krik McKusick, Michael J. Karels, and John S. Quarterman, editors. *The Design and Implementation of the 4.3BSD UNIX Operating System.* Addison-Wesley, 1989.

[170] Birgitta Lemmel. The Nobel Medals and the Medal for the Memorial Prize in Economic Sciences. Nobel e-Museum. See http://www.nobel.se/nobel/medals/index.html.

[171] A. K. Lenstra, H. W. Lenstra, Jr., M. S. Manasse, and J. M. Pollard. The number field sieve. In *Proceedings of the 22nd ACM Symposium on Theory of Computing*, pages 564–572. ACM, 1990.

[172] Arjen K. Lenstra. Generating RSA moduli with a predetermined portion. In Kazuo Ohta and Dingyi Pei, editors, *Advances in Cryptology—Asiacrypt '98*, pages 1–10. Springer-Verlag, 1998. Lecture Notes in Computer Science No. 1514.

[173] Scott Lindhurst. An analysis of shanks algorithm for computing square roots in finite fields. In Rajiv Gupta and Kenneth S. Williams, editors, *Proceedings of the 5th Conference of the Canadian Number Theory Association (1996)*, volume 19 of *CRM Proceedings and Lecture Notes*. American Mathematical Society, August 1999.

[174] Scott Charles Lindhurst. *Computing roots in finite fields and groups, with a jaunt through sums of digits—Chapter 3: Extensions of Shanks Algorithm.* PhD thesis, University of Wisconsin at Madison, 1997.

[175] R. Lipton. How to cheat at mental poker. In *In Proceedings of AMS Short Course on Cryptography*, 1981.

[176] Richard Lipton and Tomas Sander. An additively homomorphic encryption scheme or how to introduce a partial trapdoor in the discrete log (submitted for publication), November 1997.

[177] Michael Luby. *Pseudorandomness and Cryptographic Applications.* Princeton University Press, 1996.

[178] R. Duncan Luce and Howard Raiffa. *Games and Decisions—Introduction and Critical Survey.* Dover Books, 1985.

[179] Kirk Makin. Article written for the *Globe and Mail*, November 3, 1987.

[180] M. Matsui. Linear cryptanalysis method for DES cipher. In T. Helleseth, editor, *Advances in Cryptology—Eurocrypt '93*, volume 765 of *Lecture Notes in Computer Science*, pages 386–397. Springer-Verlag, 1994.

[181] Ueli Maurer and Stefan Wolf. Diffie-Hellman oracles. In *Advances in Cryptology—Crypto '96*, pages 268–282. Springer-Verlag, 1996.

[182] Ueli Maurer and Stefan Wolf. The relationship between breaking the Diffie-Hellman protocol and computing discrete logarithms. *SIAM Journal on Computing*, 28(5):1689–1721, 1999.

[183] Ueli M. Maurer. Towards the equivalence of breaking the Diffie-Hellman protocol and computing discrete algorithms. In Yvo G. Desmedt, editor, *Advances in Cryptology—Crypto '94*, pages 271–281. Springer, 1994. Lecture Notes in Computer Science No. 839.

[184] T. C. May. Section 3.8: Blacknet. In *High Noon on the Electronic Frontier*, MIT Press, 1996.

[185] John McAfee and Colin Haynes. *Computer Viruses, Worms, Data Diddlers, Killer Programs, and Other Threats to Your System.* St. Martin's Press, 1989.

[186] Declan McCullagh. Crypto-convict won't recant. In *Wired News*. Wired Digital Inc., April 14, 2000. Jim Bell's quote appears on http://jya.com/ap.htm.

[187] A. Menezes and S. A. Vanstone. The implementation of elliptic curve cryptosystems. In J. Seberry and J. Pieprzyk, editors, *Advances in Cryptology—Auscrypt '90*, volume 453 of *Lecture Notes in Computer Science*, pages 2–13. Springer-Verlag, 1990.

[188] A. J. Menezes, editor. *Elliptic Curve Public Key Cryptosystems*. Kluwer Academic Publishers, 1993.

[189] A. J. Menezes and S. A. Vanstone. Elliptic curve cryptosystems and their implementation. *Journal of Cryptology*, 6:209–224, 1993.

[190] Alfred J. Menezes, Paul C. van Oorschot, and Scott A. Vanstone. *Handbook of Applied Cryptography*. CRC Press, 1997.

[191] S. Micali and A. Shamir. An improvement of the Fiat-Shamir identification and signature scheme. In S. Goldwasser, editor, *Advances in Cryptology—Crypto '88*, pages 244–248. Springer-Verlag, 1988. Lecture Notes in Computer Science No. 403.

[192] Silvio Micali. Fair public-key cryptosystems. In Ernest F. Brickell, editor, *Advances in Cryptology—Crypto '92*, pages 113–138. Springer-Verlag, 1992. Lecture Notes in Computer Science No. 740.

[193] Silvio Micali. Guaranteed partial key escrow. Technical Report MIT/LCS/TM-537, MIT Laboratory for Computer Science, September 1995.

[194] Gary L. Miller. Riemann's hypothesis and tests for primality. *Journal of Computer and System Sciences*, 13(3):300–317, 1976.

[195] Dukjae Moon, Kyungdeok Hwang, Wonil Lee, Sangjin Lee, and Jongin Lim. Impossible differential cryptanalysis of reduced round XTEA and TEA. In *Proceedings of the Fast Software Encryption Workshop*, pages 49–60, 2002.

[196] David Naccache and Jacques Stern. A new public-key cryptosystem based on higher residues. In *ACM Conference on Computer and Communications Security*, pages 59–66. ACM, 1998.

[197] Carey Nachenberg. Computer virus-antivirus coevolution. *Communications of the ACM*, 40(1):46–51, January 1997.

[198] M. Naor and M. Yung. Universal one-way hash functions and their cryptographic applications. In *Proceedings of the 21st ACM Symposium on Theory of Computing*, pages 33–43. ACM, 1989.

[199] Moni Naor and Moti M. Yung. Public-key cryptosystems provably secure against chosen ciphertext attack. In *Proceedings of the 22nd ACM Symposium on Theory of Computing*, pages 427–437. ACM, 1990.

[200] National Institute of Standards and Technology (NIS). SKIPJACK and KEA algorithm specifications, May 1998. http://csrc.nist.gov/encryption/skipjack-1.pdf, skipjack-2.pdf.

[201] National Institute of Standards and Technology (NIST). Proposed federal information processing standard for secure hash standard. *Federal Register*, 57(21):3747–3749, January 31, 1992.

[202] National Institute of Standards and Technology (NIST). FIPS Publication 180-1: Secure Hash Standard. *Federal Register*, April 17, 1995.

[203] National Institute of Standards and Technology (NIST). FIPS Publication 186-2: Digital Signature Standard. *Federal Register*, January 27, 2000.

[204] National Institute of Standards and Technology (NIST). FIPS Publication 197: Advanced Encryption Standard (AES). *Federal Register*, November 26, 2001.

[205] Peter G. Neumann. Logic bombs and other system attacks—in Canada. *The Risks Digest*, 5(63), November 23, 1987.

[206] Peter G. Neumann. IEEE Symposium on Security and Privacy. *The Risks Digest*, 17(69), February 7, 1996. Reprint of Security & Privacy program by Dale M. Johnson.

[207] Noam Nisan and Amnon Ta-Shma. Extracting randomness: A survey and new constructions. *Journal of Computer and System Sciences*, 58(1):148–173, 1999.

[208] K. Nyber and R. Rueppel. Message recovery for signature schemes based on the discrete logarithm problem. In *Journal of Cryptology*, volume 8, pages 27–37, 1995.

[209] K. Nyberg and R. Rueppel. Message recovery for signature schemes based on the discrete logarithm problem. In *Advances in Cryptology—Eurocrypt '94*, pages 182–193. Springer-Verlag, 1994.

[210] National Bureau of Standards. FIPS Publication 46: Announcing the data encryption standard, January 1977.

[211] National Bureau of Standards. Secure hash standard. Technical Report FIPS Publication 180, National Bureau of Standards, 1993.

[212] T. Okamoto and K. Ohta. Universal electronic cash. In J. Feigenbaum, editor, *Advances in Cryptology—Crypto '91*, pages 324–337. Springer, 1992. Lecture Notes in Computer Science No. 576.

[213] Tatsuaki Okamoto. Provably secure and practical identification schemes and corresponding signature schemes. In Ernest F. Brickell, editor, *Advances in Cryptology—Crypto '92*, pages 31–53. Springer-Verlag, 1992. Lecture Notes in Computer Science No. 740.

[214] Tatsuaki Okamoto and Kazuo Ohta. Disposable zero-knowledge authentications and their applications to untraceable electronic cash. In G. Brassard, editor, *Advances in Cryptology—Crypto '89*, pages 481–497. Springer-Verlag, 1990. Lecture Notes in Computer Science No. 435.

[215] Rafail Ostrovsky and Moti Yung. How to withstand mobile virus attacks. In *Proceedings of the 10th ACM Symposium on Principles of Distributed Computing*, pages 51–59. ACM, 1991.

[216] Pascal Paillier. Public-key cryptosystems based on composite degree residue classes. In Jacques Stern, editor, *Advances in Cryptology—Eurocrypt '99*, pages 223–238. Springer-Verlag, 1999. Lecture Notes in Computer Science No. 1592.

[217] Pascal Paillier and Moti Yung. Self-escrowed public-key infrastructures. In *Information Security and Cryptology (ICISC)*, pages 257–268. Springer, 1999. Lecture Notes in Computer Science No. 1787.

[218] The Symantec Enterprise Papers. Understanding and managing polymorphic viruses, XXX, July 1999. (whitepaper downloaded from http://www.symantec.com/avcenter/whitepapers.html).

[219] Donn B. Parker. *Crime by Computer*. Charles Scribner's Sons, 1976.

[220] J. Patarin and L. Goubin. Asymmetric cryptography with S-Boxes. In *Proceedings of ICICS '97*, pages 369–380. Springer, 1997. Lecture Notes in Computer Science No. 1334.

[221] David A. Patterson and John L. Hennessy. *Computer Organization & Design—The Hardware/Software Interface*. Morgan Kaufmann Publishers Inc., 1994.

[222] Y. Peres. Iterating von Neumann's procedure. *The Annals of Statistics*, 20(1):590–597, 1992.

[223] H. E. Petersen and R. Turn. System implications of information privacy. *Proceedings of the AFIPS Spring Joint Computer Conference*, 30:291–300, 1967.

[224] S. C. Pohlig and M. E. Hellman. An improved algorithm for computing logarithms over $GF(p)$ and its cryptographic significance. *IEEE Transactions on Information Theory*, IT-24(1):106–110, January 1978.

[225] David Pointcheval and Jacques Stern. Security proofs for signature schemes. In U. Maurer, editor, *Advances in Cryptology—Eurocrypt '96*, pages 387–398. Springer-Verlag, 1996. Lecture Notes in Computer Science No. 1070.

[226] David Pointcheval and Jacques Stern. Security arguments for digital signatures and blind signatures. *Journal of Cryptology*, 13(3):361–396, 2000.

[227] J. M. Pollard. Monte Carlo methods for index computation (mod $p$). *Mathematics of Computation*, 32(143):918–924, 1978.

[228] Carl Pomerance. The quadratic sieve factoring algorithm. In T. Beth, N. Cot, and I. Ingemarsson, editors, *Advances in Cryptology—Eurocrypt '84*, pages 169–182. Springer-Verlag, 1985. Lecture Notes in Computer Science No. 209.

[229] M. Pondsmith, E. Bolme, S. Shirley, A. Swenson, C. Fisk, W. Moss, J. Smith, M. MacDonald, and L. Pondsmith. Night City, 1991. ISBN: 0-937279-11-0, total number of pages: 184.

[230] G. J. Popek and D. A. Farber. A model for verification of data security in operating systems. *Communications of the ACM*, 21(9):737–749, September 1978.

[231] J. Posegga and G. Karjoth. Mobile agents and telcos' nightmares. *Annales des Telecommunications, special issue on communications security*, 55:29–41, 2000.

[232] G. Poupard and J. Stern. Fair encryption of RSA keys. In Bart Preneel, editor, *Advances in Cryptology—Eurocrypt '00*, pages 172–189. Springer, 2000. Lecture Notes in Computer Science No. 1807.

[233] OpenSSL Project. Current version—openssl 0.9.7b, April 10, 2003. Open source toolkit that implements SSL, Transport Layer Security (TLS), and a full featured cryptographic library. OpenSSL is available at http://www.openssl.org.

[234] M. Rabin. Digitalized signatures as intractable as factorization. Technical Report MIT/LCS/TR-212, MIT Laboratory for Computer Science, January 1979.

[235] M. Rabin. Probabilistic algorithms for testing primality. *Journal of Number Theory*, 12:128–138, 1980.

[236] M. O. Rabin. Digitalized signatures. In Richard A. DeMillo, David P. Dobkin, Anita K. Jones, and Richard J. Lipton, editors, *Foundations of Secure Computation*, pages 155–168. Academic Press, 1978.

[237] Michael Rabin. Digitalized signatures and public-key functions as intractable as factorization. Technical Report MIT/LCS/TR-212, Laboratory for Computer Science, Massachusetts Institute of Technology, January 1979.

[238] C. Rackoff and D. R. Simon. Non-interactive zero-knowledge proof of knowledge and chosen ciphertext attack. In J. Feigenbaum, editor, *Advances in Cryptology—Crypto '91*, pages 433–444. Springer, 1992. Lecture Notes in Computer Science No. 576.

[239] *Virus Bulletin*. Virus Bulletin Ltd., Richard Ford, editor, page 4, March, 1993.

[240] V. Rijmen and B. Preneel. A family of trapdoor ciphers. In E. Biham, editor, *Proceedings of the Fast Software Encryption Workshop*, pages 139–148. Springer, 1997.

[241] R. L. Rivest. *The RC4 Encryption Algorithm (Proprietary)*. RSA Data Security, Inc., March 12, 1992.

[242] Ronald L. Rivest. The MD4 message digest algorithm. Technical Report MIT/LCS/TM-434, MIT Laboratory for Computer Science, October 1990.

[243] Ronald L. Rivest. The MD5 message-digest algorithm. Internet Request for Comments, April 1992. RFC 1321.

[244] Ronald L. Rivest, Leonard Adleman, and Michael L. Dertouzos. On data banks and privacy homomorphisms. In R. DeMillo, D. Dobkin, A. Jones, and R. Lipton, editors, *Foundations of Secure Computation*, pages 169–180. Academic Press, 1978.

[245] Ronald L. Rivest, Adi Shamir, and Leonard M. Adleman. A method for obtaining digital signatures and public-key cryptosystems. *Communications of the ACM*, 21(2):120–126, 1978.

[246] M. J. B. Robshaw. Recent proposals to implement Fair Cryptography. Technical Report TR-301, RSA Laboratories, October 1993.

[247] Kenneth H. Rosen. *Elementary Number Theory and its Applications, 4th Edition*. Addison-Wesley, 2000.

[248] RSA Data Security, Inc. SecurPC for Windows 95 Users Manual, 1997.

[249] RSA Data Security, Inc. *PKCS #1: RSA Cryptography Standard, Version 2.1*, June 2002.

[250] Tomas Sander and Christian F. Tschudin. Towards mobile cryptography. In *Proceedings of the 19th IEEE Symposium on Security and Privacy*, pages 215–224. IEEE, May 1998.

[251] Tomas Sander and Christian F. Tschudin. Towards mobile cryptography. Technical Report TR-97-049, ICSI Technical Report, November 22, 19997.

[252] Tomas Sander, Adam L. Young, and Moti M. Yung. Non-interactive cryptocomputing for $NC^1$. In *Proceedings of the 40th IEEE Symposium on Foundations of Computer Science*, pages 554–567. IEEE, October 17–19, 1999.

[253] M. Santha and U. V. Vazirani. Generating quasi-random sequences from slightly-random sources. In *Proceedings of the 25th IEEE Symposium on Foundations of Computer Science*, pages 434–440. IEEE, 1984.

[254] Joseph Sargent. *Colossus: The Forbin Project*, 1969. Screenplay: James Bridges.

[255] Stuart Schechter and Michael Smith. How much security is enough to stop a thief? In *Proceedings of the Seventh International Financial Cryptography Conference*. Springer-Verlag, January 27–30, 2003.

[256] W. L. Schiller. Design of a security kernel for the PDP-11/45. Technical Report ESD–TR–73–294, The MITRE Corporation, December 1973.

[257] Bruce Schneier. *Applied Cryptography: Protocols, Algorithms, and Source Code in C*. John Wiley & Sons, New York, 1993.

[258] Bruce Schneier. Description of a new variable-length key, 64-bit block cipher (Blowfish). In Ross Anderson, editor, *Proceedings of the Fast Software Encryption Workshop*, pages 191–204. Springer-Verlag, December 1993. Lecture Notes in Computer Science No. 809.

[259] Bruce Schneier. The Blowfish encryption algorithm. *Dr. Dobb's Journal*, pages 38–40, April 1994.

[260] Bruce Schneier and Niels Ferguson. *Practical Cryptography*. Wiley, 2003.

[261] Bruce Schneier, John Kelsey, Doug Whiting, David Wagner, Chris Hall, and Niels Ferguson. *The Twofish encryption algorithm, a 128-bit block cipher*. Wiley, 1999.

[262] C. P. Schnorr. Efficient identification and signatures for smart cards. In G. Brassard, editor, *Advances in Cryptology—Crypto '89*, pages 239–252. Springer, 1990. Lecture Notes in Computer Science No. 435.

[263] C. P. Schnorr. Efficient signature generation by smart cards. *Journal of Cryptology*, 4:161–174, 1991.

[264] Berry Schoenmakers. A simple publicly verifiable secret sharing scheme and its application to electronic voting. In M. Wiener, editor, *Advances in Cryptology—Crypto '99*, pages 148–164. Springer, 1999. Lecture Notes in Computer Science No. 1666.

[265] Ridley Scott. *Alien*, May 25, 1979. Screenplay: Dan O'Bannon and Ronald Shusett, Creature Design: H. R. Giger.

[266] Ronen Shaltiel. Recent developments in explicit constructions of extractors. *Bulletin of the European Association for Theoretical Computer Science (EATCS)*, 77:67–95, 2002.

[267] Ronen Shaltiel and Christopher Umans. Simple extractors for all min-entropies and a new pseudo-random generator. In *Proceedings of the 42nd IEEE Symposium on Foundations of Computer Science*, pages 648–657. IEEE, 2001.

[268] A. Shamir and N. van Someren. Playing hide and seek with stored keys. In *Financial Cryptography*, pages 118–124. Springer-Verlag, 1999. Lecture Notes in Computer Science No. 1648.

[269] Adi Shamir. Identity-based cryptosystems and signature schemes. In G. R. Blakley and D. C. Chaum, editors, *Advances in Cryptology—Crypto '84*, pages 47–53. Springer, 1985. Lecture Notes in Computer Science No. 196.

[270] C. E. Shannon. Communication theory of secrecy systems. *Bell System Technical Journal*, 28:657–715, 1949.

[271] John F. Shoch and Jon A. Hupp. The worm programs: Early experience with a distributed computation. *Communications of the ACM*, 25(3):172–180, 1982.

[272] V. Shoup. OAEP reconsidered. In J. Kilian, editor, *Advances in Cryptology—Crypto '01*, pages 239–259. Springer-Verlag, 2001.

[273] V. Shoup and J. Camenisch. Practical verifiable encryption and decryption of discrete logarithms. In *Advances in Cryptology—Crypto '03*. Springer-Verlag, 2003.

[274] Gustavus J. Simmons. The prisoners' problem and the subliminal channel. In D. Chaum, editor, *Advances in Cryptology—Crypto '83*, pages 51–67. Plenum Press, 1984.

[275] Gustavus J. Simmons. The subliminal channel and digital signatures. In T. Beth, N. Cot, and I. Ingemarsson, editors, *Advances in Cryptology—Eurocrypt '84*, pages 364–378. Springer-Verlag, 1985. Lecture Notes in Computer Science No. 209.

[276] Gustavus J. Simmons. An introduction to the mathematics of trust in security protocols. In *Proceedings of the Computer Security Foundations Workshop*, pages 121–127. IEEE Computer Society Press, 1993.

[277] Gustavus J. Simmons. The subliminal channels of the U.S. Digital Signature Algorithm (DSA). In *Proceedings of the Third Symposium on State and Progress of Research in Cryptography*, pages 35–54, 1993.

[278] Gustavus J. Simmons. Subliminal communication is easy using the dsa. In T. Helleseth, editor, *Advances in Cryptology—Eurocrypt '93*, pages 218–232. Springer-Verlag, 1993. Lecture Notes in Computer Science No. 0765.

[279] Gustavus J. Simmons. Cryptanalysis and protocol failures. *Communications of the ACM*, 37(11):56–65, November 1994.

[280] Gustavus J. Simmons. Subliminal channels: Past and Present. *IEEE European Transactions on Telecommunication*, 5(4):459–473, 1994.

[281] Gustavus J. Simmons. The history of subliminal channels. *IEEE Journal on Selected Areas in Communication*, 16(4):452–462, May 1998.

[282] Rune Skardhamar. *Virus Detection and Elimination*. Academic Press, 1996.

[283] Robert Slade. *Robert Slade's Guide to Computer Viruses*, pages 45, 60, 89, 102, 106-110, 454, Springer-Verlag, 1994.

[284] Miles E. Smid and Dennis K. Branstad. Response to comments of the NIST proposed digital signature standard. In Ernest F. Brickell, editor, *Advances in Cryptology—Crypto '92*, pages 76–88. Springer-Verlag, 1992. Lecture Notes in Computer Science No. 740.

[285] IEEE Computer Society. CIPHER. Newsletter of the IEEE Computer Society's TC on Security and Privacy, Ed. Carl Landwehr, Assoc. Ed. Hilarie Orman, Issue 10, November 1, 1995.

[286] R. Solovay and V. Strassen. A fast Monte-Carlo test for primality. *SIAM Journal on Computing*, 6:84–85, 1977.

[287] Eugene H. Spafford. The internet worm program: An analysis. Technical Report CSD-TR-823, Purdue University Department of Computer Science, 1988.

[288] Eugene H. Spafford. The internet worm: Crisis and aftermath. *Communications of the ACM*, 32(6):678–687, 1989.

[289] Eugene H. Spafford, Kathleen A. Heaphy, and David J. Ferbrache. A computer virus primer. In Peter J. Denning, editor, *Computers Under Attack: Intruders, Worms, and Viruses*. Addison-Wesley, 1990.

[290] Michale J. Spier, Thomas N. Hastings, and David N. Cutler. An experimental implementation of the kernel/domain architecture. In *Proceedings of the Fourth ACM Symposium on Operating System Principles*, pages 8–21. ACM, January 1973.

[291] Markus Stadler. Publicly verifiable secret sharing. In Ueli M. Maurer, editor, *Advances in Cryptology—Eurocrypt '96*, pages 190–199. Springer, 1996. Lecture Notes in Computer Science No. 1070.

[292] Bruce Sterling. *Islands in the Net*. Ace Books, March 1989.

[293] Douglas R. Stinson. *Cryptography: Theory and Practice, First Edition*. CRC Press, 1995.

[294] Cliff Stoll. *The Cuckoo's Egg: Tracing a Spy Through the Maze of Computer Espionage*. Doubleday, 1989.

[295] P. F. Syverson, D. M. Goldschlag, and M. G. Reed. Anonymous connections and onion routing. In *Proceedings of the 18th IEEE Symposium on Security and Privacy*, pages 44–54. IEEE, May 1997.

[296] Amnon Ta-Shma. On extracting randomness from weak random sources (extended abstract). In *Proceedings of the 28th ACM Symposium on Theory of Computing*, pages 276–285. ACM, 1996.

[297] Amnon Ta-Shma, Christopher Umans, and David Zuckerman. Lossless condensers, unbalanced expanders, and extractors. In *Proceedings of the 33rd ACM Symposium on Theory of Computing*, pages 143–152. ACM, 2001.

[298] Amnon Ta-Shma, David Zuckerman, and Shmuel Safra. Extractors from reed-muller codes. In *Proceedings of the 42nd IEEE Symposium on Foundations of Computer Science*, pages 638–647. IEEE, 2001.

[299] Amnon Ta-Shma, David Zuckerman, and Shmuel Safra. Extractors from reed-muller codes. *Electronic Colloquium on Computational Complexity (ECCC)*, 8(36), 2001.

[300] Ken Thompson. Reflections on Trusting Trust. *Communications of the ACM*, 27(8), 1984.

[301] H. F. Trotter. ACM Algorithm 115: Perm. *Communications of the ACM*, 5(8):434–435, August 1962.

[302] Yiannis Tsiounis. Personal Communication, February 2003.

[303] Yiannis Tsiounis. *Efficient Electronic Cash: New Notions and Techniques.* PhD thesis, Northeastern University, 1997.

[304] Yiannis Tsiounis and Moti M. Yung. On the security of ElGamal-based encryption. In Hideki Imai and Yuliang Zheng, editors, *Proceedings of the 1st Workshop on Practice and Theory in Public Key Cryptography (PKC)*, pages 117–134. Springer, February 1998. Lecture Notes in Computer Science No. 1431.

[305] Albert W. Tucker. On Jargon: The Prisoner's Dilemma, *UMAP Journal* 1, 101, 1980.

[306] Alan Turing. On computable numbers, with an application to the entscheidungsproblem. *Proceedings of the London Mathematical Society*, pages 230–265, 1936.

[307] U. V. Vazirani and V. V. Vazirani. Efficient and secure pseudo-random number generation. In *Proceedings of the 25th IEEE Symposium on Foundations of Computer Science*, pages 458–463. IEEE, 1984.

[308] G. S. Vernam. Cipher printing telegraph systems for secret wire and radio telegraphic communications. *Journal of the American Institute for Electrical Engineers*, 45:109–115, 1926.

[309] John von Neumann. Various techniques for use in connection with random digits. In *von Neumann's Collected Works*, volume 5, pages 768–770. Pergamon, 1963.

[310] John von Neumann. (Part One) Transcripts of lectures given at the University of Illinois, Dec. 1949. In A. W. Burks, editor, *Theory and Organization of Complicated Automata*, pages 29–87. University of Illinois Press, 1966.

[311] Sebastiaan von Solms and David Naccache. On blind signatures and perfect crimes. *Computers and Security*, 11(6):581–583, October 1992.

[312] B. J. Walker, R. A. Kemmerer, and G. J. Popek. Specification and verification of the UCLA UNIX security kernel. *Communications of the ACM*, 23(2):118–131, 1980.

[313] Peter Wayner. *Digital Cash: Commerce on the Net*. Academic Press, 1996.

[314] Michael Weber, Matthew Schmid, David Geyer, and Michael Shatz. A toolkit for detecting and analyzing malicious software. In *18th Annual Computer Security Applications Conference*, pages 423–431, December 9–13, 2002.

[315] Ingo Wegener. *The Complexity of Boolean Functions*. John Wiley and Sons Ltd., 1987.

[316] Rüdiger Weis and Stefan Lucks. All your key bit are belong to us—the true story of black box cryptography. In *Proceedings of the 3rd International system administration and networking Conference (SANE)*, May 27-31, 2002.

[317] David J. Wheeler and Roger M. Needham. TEA, a Tiny Encryption Algorithm. *Proceedings of the Fast Software Encryption Workshop*, pages 363–366, 1994. Lecture Notes in Computer Science No. 1008.

[318] David J. Wheeler and Roger M. Needham. TEA extensions. Draft technical report, University of Cambridge, downloaded from http://www.cl.cam.ac.uk/ftp/users/djw3/xtea.ps, 1997.

[319] David J. Wheeler and Roger M. Needham. Correction to XTEA. Draft technical report, University of Cambridge, downloaded from http://www.cl.cam.ac.uk/ftp/users/djw3/xxtea.ps, October 1998.

[320] Steve R. White. Covert distributed processing with computer viruses. In G. Brassard, editor, *Advances in Cryptology—Crypto '89*, pages 616–619. Springer-Verlag, 1990. Lecture Notes in Computer Science No. 435.

[321] Security Controls for Computer Systems. Technical Report R-609, Willis H. Ware, editor, Rand Corp., February 1970. Declassified Oct. 10, 1975 by DARPA.

[322] Sydney Fowler Wright. *Automata*. DNA Publications (currently), September 1929.

[323] H. Wu, F. Bao, R. Deng, and Q. Ye. Cryptanalysis of Rijmen-Preneel trapdoor ciphers. In *Advances in Cryptology—Asiacrypt '98*, pages 126–132. Springer, 1998.

[324] Shouhuai Xu and Moti Yung. The dark side of threshold cryptography. In Matt Blaze, editor, *Proceedings of the Sixth International Financial Cryptography Conference*. Springer, 2002.

[325] A. C. Yao. Protocols for secure computations. In *Proceedings of the 23rd IEEE Symposium on Foundations of Computer Science*, pages 160–164. IEEE, 1982.

[326] A. C. Yao. How to generate and exchange secrets. In *Proceedings of the 27th IEEE Symposium on Foundations of Computer Science*, pages 162–167. IEEE, 1986.

[327] S. Yau and R. Cheung. Design of self checking software. In *IEEE Conference on Reliable Software*, pages 450–457, 1975.

[328] Adam Young and Moti Yung. Auto-escrowable and auto-recoverable cryptosystems, 1997. U.S. Patent 6,202,150, issued March 13, 2001, filed May 28, 1997.

[329] Adam L. Young. Found bug in Rabin-Miller probabilistic primality test in OpenSSL. It was fixed in distributions 0.9.6a and later. OpenSSL is available at http://www.openssl.org, 2002.

[330] Adam L. Young. cryptoviruses. Message posted to the sci.crypt newsgroup, ayoung@news.cs.columbia.edu, 1996/05/21.

[331] Adam L. Young. Non-zero sum games and survivable malware. In *Proceedings of the 4th Annual IEEE Information Assurance Workshop*, June 18–20, 2003. United States Military Academy, West Point, New York.

[332] Adam L. Young and Moti M. Yung. Cryptovirology: Extortion-based security threats and countermeasures. In *Proceedings of the 17th IEEE Symposium on Security and Privacy*, pages 129–141. IEEE, May 1996.

[333] Adam L. Young and Moti M. Yung. The dark side of black-box cryptography, or: Should we trust capstone? In Neal Koblitz, editor, *Advances in Cryptology—Crypto '96*, pages 89–103. Springer-Verlag, 1996. Lecture Notes in Computer Science No. 1109.

[334] Adam L. Young and Moti M. Yung. Deniable password snatching: On the possibility of evasive electronic espionage. In *Proceedings of the 18th IEEE Symposium on Security and Privacy*, pages 224–235. IEEE, May 1997.

[335] Adam L. Young and Moti M. Yung. Kleptography: Using cryptography against cryptography. In Walter Fumy, editor, *Advances in Cryptology—Eurocrypt '97*, pages 62–74. Springer-Verlag, 1997. Lecture Notes in Computer Science No. 1233.

[336] Adam L. Young and Moti M. Yung. The prevalence of klepto-graphic attacks on discrete-log based cryptosystems. In Burton S. Kaliski, editor, *Advances in Cryptology—Crypto '97*, pages 264–276. Springer-Verlag, 1997. Lecture Notes in Computer Science No. 1294.

[337] Adam L. Young and Moti M. Yung. Auto-recoverable auto-certifiable cryptosystems. In Kaisa Nyberg, editor, *Advances in Cryptology—Eurocrypt '98*, pages 17–31. Springer-Verlag, 1998. Lecture Notes in Computer Science No. 1403.

[338] Adam L. Young and Moti M. Yung. Monkey: Black-box symmetric ciphers designed for monopolizing keys. In *Proceedings of the Fast Software Encryption Workshop*, pages 122–133. Springer, 1998.

[339] Adam L. Young and Moti M. Yung. Bandwidth-optimal klepto-graphic attacks. In Ç. K. Koç, D. Naccache, and C. Paar, editors, *Proceedings of the 3rd Workshop on Cryptographic Hardware and Embedded Systems (CHES)*, pages 235–250. Springer, 2001. Lecture Notes in Computer Science No. 2162.

[340] Adam L. Young and Moti M. Yung. Backdoor attacks on black-box ciphers exploiting low-entropy plaintexts. In *Eighth Australasian Conference on Information Security and Privacy (ACISP)*, pages 297–311. Springer-Verlag, 2003. Lecture Notes in Computer Science.

[341] Adam Lucas Young. *Kleptography: Using Cryptography Against Cryptography*. PhD thesis, Columbia University Graduate School of Arts & Sciences, 2002. Thesis Advisor: Zvi Galil (and Moti M. Yung).

[342] Yuliang Zheng and Jennifer Seberry. Practical approaches to at-taining security against adaptively chosen ciphertext attacks. In Ernest F. Brickell, editor, *Advances in Cryptology—Crypto '92*, pages 292–304. Springer-Verlag, 1992. Lecture Notes in Computer Science No. 740.

[343] Philip R. Zimmermann. *The Official PGP User's Guide*. MIT Press, June 1995.

# Index

$NC^1$, *see* Nick's Class
$\phi(\cdot)$, 310
$\pi(\cdot)$, 310
$e^{\text{th}}$ roots assumption, 314
$gcd(\cdot, \cdot)$, 310
1963 virus, 175
3DES, *see* symmetric cipher, 3DES

activity monitor, 186
adaptive attacks
    chosen-ciphertext, 53, 80, 328, 340
    chosen-message, 329, 343
    chosen-plaintext, 327
AES, *see* symmetric cipher, AES
algorithmic combinatorics, 53
all-or-nothing disclosure, 137
ambivalent root, 166, 248, 256
Anderson Report, 190, 202
anonymous remailer, 45, 90
ANSI C, 232
ARDA, 77
assassination politics, 92, 93, 97
asymmetric cryptography, 39
asymmetric cryptosystem, 326
AT&T, 34
authentication systems, 35

battleprogs, 17
bias matching, heuristic, 60
biased coin, 52, 57
Big-$O$ notation, 309
Binomial Theorem, 110
black-box cryptosystem, 231
Blowfish, *see* symmetric cipher, Blowfish
Blum integer, 330
busy-waiting, 53

call graph, 193

call-back function, 34
Capstone, 230
card shuffling, 71
Carmichael lambda function, 310
cascading encryptions, 290
CERT, 21, 348
certificate of recoverability, 227
certificate revocation list, *see* CRL
certification authority, 225, 227, 259, 292, 337
CFB, *see* cipher feed-back
chaotic air-turbulence, 54
checksum, 18, 30, 46, 135, 330
Chernoff bounds, 232
Chinese Remainder Theorem, 111, 331, 336
chosen-ciphertext attack, 327, 331
chosen-message attack, 329
chosen-plaintext attack, 327, 331
cipher feed-back, 46
ciphertext-only attack, 326
circularly linked list, 21, 100, 133
Clipper chip, 230, 286
Columbia University, 36
complete break, 328
composite key generation
    honest, 231
    SETUP attack on, 246
    weak attacks on, 232
Computational Composite Residuosity assumption, 314, 315
conditional probability, 309
Confinement Problem, 214
congruence, 308
constant sum game, 150, 160
cookie-monster virus, 191
Core Wars, 295
correctness property, 120

Coupon Collector's Problem, 219
covert channel, 214
CRL, 200, 342, 348
cross-certified, 152, 153
cryptanalysis
    definition of, 321
    differential, 287
    linear, 287
cryptanalyst, 321
cryptanalyzing adversary, 242
cryptocomputing, 114, 136, 142
cryptocounter, 103, 104, 111
    based on additive group $\mathbb{Z}_2$, 111
    ElGamal based, 105
    Paillier based, 108, 111
cryptographer, 321
cryptography
    definition of, 321
cryptolib, 34
cryptologist, 321
cryptology
    definition of, 321
cryptotrojan, 77, 191, 238, 271, 281
cryptovirus, 43, 44, 48, 51, 78, 115, 191
cyberpunk, 6, 25

DARPA, 77, 144
database algorithm, 117, 119, 123, 127
database replication, 116
DCR, 108, 315, 348
DDH, 112, 318, 319, 337, 348
decision problem, 171
Den Zuk virus, 103
deniable encryption, 139
deniable password-snatching, 97, 132
denial-of-service, 40, 313, 348
DES, see symmetric cipher, DES
differential power analysis, 261, 288
Diffie-Hellman assumption, 318, 324
Diffie-Hellman key exchange, 213, 265,
        266, 268, 271, 274, 278, 288,
        289, 313, 318, 324, 337, 338
Diffie-Hellman triple, 318
digital certificate, 199, 227, 233, 334,
        337, 342
digital signature algorithm, 280, 334
        DSA, 217, 218, 222, 283, 345

ElGamal, 216, 223, 342
    Pointcheval-Stern, 282, 318
    Rabin, 331
    RSA, 334
    Schnorr, 284, 344
Digital Signature Standard, 345
discrete logarithm, 106, 143, 217, 235,
        265, 280, 318, 324, 337, 343
discrete logarithm assumption, 318
disk-locking program, 30
distinguishing adversary, 242, 249
double-spending, 91
DSA, see digital signature algorithm,
        DSA

e-money, 91–94
EDE mode, 47, 48, 67
electronic voting, 96
ElGamal cryptosystem, see public key
        cryptosystem, ElGamal
Elk Cloner virus, 297
elliptic curve cryptosystems, 252
entropy extractor, 46, 52, 55
entropy sources
    CPU crystal, 34, 53
    free-running oscillators, 62
    hard disk air-turbulence, 54
    keyboard presses, 53
    mouse timings, 53
    radioactive emissions, 53
    system time, 56
    thermal noise, 62
Euclidean algorithm, see greatest com-
        mon divisor
Euler's criterion, 217, 220, 311, 312, 315
Euler's totient function, 310, 333
existential forgery, 55, 328, 331, 335,
        343
extended Euclidean, 310, 314, 330, 333,
        338
Extended Riemann Hypothesis, 119
Extended Tiny Encryption Algorithm,
        see symmetric cipher, XTEA

factoring assumption, 313, 330
fair cryptosystem, 227
fault-tolerance, 167
Feistel cipher, 36

Fermat's Little Theorem
    generalized form, 333
Fiat-Shamir heuristic, 125
FIPS, 66
FIPS-140, 76, 237, 291
FNP, 313
forward secrecy, 235–237, 265, 269, 349
friend-or-foe, 35

game theory, 149, 150
gcd, *see* greatest common divisor
generator, 311, 318, 324
    finding an, 311
generic decryption, 180, 305
GNUmp, 34, 46
gnutella protocol, 94
greatest common divisor, 231, 234, 256,
        282, 310, 314, 330–332, 342,
        343
    definition of, 308

halting problem, 27, 171, 350
Harmonic numbers, 72
hash function, 52, 54, 267, 319, 330, 340
    collision intractability, 55, 340
    extracting entropy with, 55
    MD4, 55
    MD5, 342
    non-invertability, 55
    SHA-1, 55, 122
hexadecimal, 350
homomorphism
    additive, 111, 142
    multiplicative, 142
honest-but-curious model, 104
honeypot, 10
hooks, *see* operating system, hooks
Huffman compression, 197
hybrid encryption, 45, 278

identity-based cryptosystem, 228
inoculation, 199
integrity checks, 17, 197
Intel hardware RNG, 62
inter-mix detour, 83
Internet Worm, 173, 297
interrupt addresses, 20
intractable, 313, 350

Israeli virus, 173
ITAR, 33, 350

Jacobi symbol, 39, 78, 213, 312, 335,
        336

Karatsuba multiplication, 34, 192, 311
Kerchhoff's principle, 323
key escrow, 226
key-only attack, 329
kleptogram, 266
kleptogram, discrete-log, 265, 268, 275–
        277, 280–283
kleptographic attack, 80, 205, 219, 230,
        277
known-message attack, 329
known-plaintext attack, 36, 326

Lagrange interpolation, 121
Las Vegas, 58, 76, 179, 246, 331, 351
Legendre symbol, 311, 315
logic bomb, 202, 351
Lucent Technologies, 54
lunch time attacks, 194

malleable ciphertext, 101, 104, 105, 351
MARS, *see* symmetric cipher, MARS
MD4, *see* hash function, MD4
memory-resident, 20
message indistinguishability, 79, 335
Millionaire problem, 144
minimal change algorithm, 73
minimal universal exponent, 311
MITM, 155, 159, 324, 337, 351, 353
mix network, 53, 80, 91, 94–96, 132,
        133, 153, 158, 168, 212, 230
    asynchronous, 81
    sandwich attack, 83
    synchronous, 81
mobile agent, 107, 122, 132, 142, 146
Monkey virus, 176
Monte Carlo, 67, 76, 239, 246, 331, 351
Montgomery reduction, 34, 311
MP3, 352
multipartite, 17
multiprecision library, 34, 75, 349, 352

Napster, 95

Neumann's unbiasing algorithm, 57, 71, 292
   iterated, 59
Newton channel, *see* subliminal channel, Newton channel
Nick's Class, 145
Night City, 6
NIZK proof, 125, 227
non-zero sum game, 147, 149, 150, 160, 168
nonce, 138, 267, 276, 278, 352
NP, 313
Nullsoft, 94
number field sieve, 314

OAEP, 79, 80, 98, 135, 158, 352
One-half virus, 38
One-time pad, 36, 64, 159, 221
one-way function, 9, 18, 265, 275, 287, 289, 335, 344, 345
onion routing, 81, 352
OpenSSL, 52, 70, 75
operating system
   hooks, 13
   interrupt handler patch, 20
   routines, 20

Paillier, *see* public key cryptosystem, Paillier
Pakistani Brain virus, 190
PAP, *see* pretty-awful-privacy
password-snatching, 2, 10, 31, 97, 115, 126, 135, 141, 203
patch, *see* operating system, interrupt handler patch
PBRM, *see* probabilistic bias removal method
PEAT toolkit, 183
perfect crime, 93, 94, 97
permutation generation, 71
personal information exchange, 233
PGP, *see* pretty-good-privacy
Phi-Hiding assumption, 117, 316
Phi-Sampling assumption, 119, 317
PIR, *see* private information retrieval
PKCS #12, *see* personal information exchange

PKI, 95, 152, 153, 158, 199, 225, 226, 288, 291, 336, 338
plaintext-aware, 341
Pohlig-Hellman, 224, 266, 318
Pollard's Rho, 224
polymorphic virus, 17, 36, 46, 175, 176, 184, 191, 298, 305
polynomially indistinguishable, 68, 139, 244, 250, 252, 271
Power Residue Hypothesis, 145
pretty-awful-privacy, 238, 245
pretty-good-privacy, 238
primality test, 191, 312, 332
   deterministic, 118, 123, 232, 332
Prime Number Theorem, 123, 232, 310
Prisoner's Dilemma, 149, 150
Prisoner's Problem, 215, 284
privacy property, 120
private information retrieval, 113, 115, 120, 131, 136, 141
   computationally secure, 116
   Phi-Hiding scheme, 117, 315, 317
   Trojan, 132
   unconditionally secure, 116
PRNG, *see* pseudorandom generator
probabilistic bias removal method, 239, 246
proof of work, 165
pseudonym, 96, 162
pseudorandom function, 234–236
pseudorandom generator, 52, 66–68, 76, 138, 236, 238, 275
   ANSI X9.17, 66, 78
   BBS, 64, 67, 236
pseudosquare, 136, 312, 336, 348
public key cryptosystem, 325
   Cramer-Shoup, 279, 318, 340
   ElGamal, 134, 277, 338
   Goldwasser-Micali, 229, 315, 335
   Paillier, 108, 312, 314, 315
   Rabin, 213, 229, 246, 248, 249, 313, 330
   RSA, 39, 78, 79, 136, 143, 224, 229, 244, 256, 312, 314, 332

quadratic residuosity assumption, 112, 136, 315, 336

quadratic sieve, 313
quasi-random, 52
query generator, 117, 118, 123, 126
questionable encryption, 102, 134, 138

Rabin-Miller algorithm, 52, 332
race condition, 181
random function, 125, 166, 267, 320
random oracle, 124, 221, 245, 255, 272,
         273, 275, 283, 284, 319
    assumption, 122, 282
    model, 79, 230, 249, 266, 270, 274,
         343
random self-reducible, 145
ranking algorithm, 73
reduction argument, 67, 249, 252, 270,
         272, 274, 314, 318, 338
reference monitor, 190
relative primality, 216, 250, 333, 353
repeated XOR encryption, 36
residues, 319
    higher order, 128, 145, 315
    quadratic, 67, 248, 311, 315, 319,
         331, 336, 340
response retriever, 117, 120, 124, 127
revocable anonymity, 93
Rivest-Shamir-Adleman cryptosystem,
         see public key cryptosystem,
         RSA
rootkit, 203, 354
rotational delay, 54
rotational latency, 54
RSA assumption, 314

safe prime, 195, 340
salami slicing attack, 202
Salt II treaty, 212, 213, 218
Santha-Vazirani algorithm, 62, 64
scanner, 174, 177
secret sharing, 159
secretly embedded trapdoor with uni-
         versal protection, see SETUP
secure multiparty computation, 144
SecurID, 100
security by obscurity, 98, 215, 291
security kernel, 190
security parameter, 118, 122, 252
selective forgery, 328

semantic security, 49, 79, 101, 315, 336,
         340
semaphore, 181
SETUP, 191, 229, 243, 249, 256–258,
         261, 263, 265, 268, 276, 283,
         288
    definition of, 243
SHA-1, see hash function, SHA-1
shadow public key, 225
side channel analysis, 80, 256, 261
Skipjack, see symmetric cipher, Skip-
         jack
smart card, 219
smooth integer, 144, 223, 286, 318, 354
snake oil, 290, 354
Solovay-Strassen algorithm, 312
sprawl, 6
square-and-multiply, 311
stealth virus, 175, 190
steganography, 96, 101, 133, 215
subliminal channel, 101, 133, 211, 214,
         216, 241, 243, 259, 262, 281,
         287
    card marking using residues, 222
    ElGamal signature, 216
    history of, 212
    impact on research, 226
    Legendre channel, 217, 284
    Newton channel, 223, 286
    Oracle channel, 220, 221
    product of primes, 224, 262
sum-of-products method, 130
symmetric cipher, 192, 323
    3DES, 30
    AES, 67, 322
    Black-Rugose, 287
    Blowfish, 287, 323
    DES, 66
    MARS, 287
    Monkey, 287
    RC4, 323
    Skipjack, 286
    TEA, 35, 46
    Twofish, 323
    XTEA, 36
SysBeep virus, 303

tamper-resistance, 219, 230, 276

TEA, *see* symmetric cipher, TEA

terminate-and-stay resident, 7, 203, 355

threat model, 80, 326

tick, 34

timing attacks, 261, 288

Tiny Encryption Algorithm, *see* symmetric cipher, TEA

tractable, 112, 248, 317, 354

Tremor virus, 176

Trotter-Johnson algorithm, 73, 179

truerand, 34, 46, 53

tunneling, 188

Twofish, *see* symmetric cipher, Twofish

unbiasing, 52, 208, 292

uniform sampling, 52, 68

universal gate, 143

universal re-encryption, 84, 153

unranking algorithm, 73, 179

vector addition chains, 34, 311

verifiable encryption, 227

Vernam cipher, 36, 64, 155, 221

worm, 52, 69, 71, 85, 142, 147, 173, 296–298

XEROX PARC, 85

XTEA, *see* symmetric cipher, XTEA

zero-sum game, 150, 160

ZKIP, 35, 100, 125